NATURAL
PRESCRIPTIONS

Also by Robert M. Giller, M.D., and Kathy Matthews

MEDICAL MAKEOVER

MAXIMUM METABOLISM

NATURAL PRESCRIPTIONS

Dr. Giller's
Natural Treatments &
Vitamin Therapies
for over 100
Common Ailments

ROBERT M. GILLER, M.D.
& KATHY MATTHEWS

Carol Southern Books
New York

This book is not intended to replace the services of a physician, nor is it meant to encourage diagnosis and treatment of illness, disease, or other medical problems by the layman. Any application of the recommendations set forth in the following pages is at the reader's discretion and sole risk. If you are under a physician's care for any condition, he or she can advise you whether the recommendations in this book are suitable for you.

Copyright © 1994 by Robert Giller and Kathy Matthews

Published by Carol Southern Books, an imprint of Crown Publishers, Inc., 201 East 50th Street, New York, New York 10022. Member of the Crown Publishing Group.

Random House, Inc. New York, Toronto, London, Sydney, Auckland

CAROL SOUTHERN BOOKS and colophon are trademarks of Crown Publishers, Inc.

Manufactured in the United States of America

Design by Paula Kelly

Library of Congress Cataloging-in-Publication Data
Giller, Robert M.
    Natural prescriptions: Dr. Robert Giller's natural treatments and vitamin therapies for over 100 common ailments / by Dr. Robert M. Giller and Kathy Matthews.—1st ed.
    Includes index.
    1. Alternative medicine—Popular works.   I. Matthews, Kathy.
II. Title.
    R733.G55   1994
    615.5'3—dc20   93-19681
                                                                                CIP

    ISBN 0-517-58689-4

10 9 8 7 6 5 4 3

First Edition

To my wife, Nancy, for her love and support in making this book possible

—*R.M.G.*

To my parents, Loretta and Jim Matthews, for their endless love and encouragement

—*K.M.*

ACKNOWLEDGMENTS

Many thanks to Carol Southern, our editor, for her unflagging enthusiasm for this project as well as for her patient and skillful editing. Also thanks to Al Lowman, our agent, for his early commitment to the book.

We'd also like to thank the crew at Carol Southern Books for their hard work, particularly Michelle Sidrane, Steve Magnuson, Jo Fagan, Phyllis Fleiss, Robin Strashun, Ken Sansone, Barbara Marks, Tina Zabriskie Constable, Jill Cohen, Laurie Stark, Mark McCauslin, Bill Peabody, Paula Kelly, and Eliza Scott.

CONTENTS

INTRODUCTION

NOT TOO LONG ago a patient, upon learning that the results of her Pap test were abnormal, asked whether she should be treated with drugs or surgery. She was surprised when I told her we had a very good chance of treating her condition naturally. We did try natural methods—vitamin supplementation in her case—and her subsequent Pap test was normal. But her question stayed with me because it reminded me of how far many of us have come regarding the treatment of disease. Her assumption that drug therapy or surgical intervention are the two automatic responses to disease seemed almost old-fashioned to me. I'm very happy to say that most of my patients are ready and willing to try a natural treatment before they resort to more drastic measures. In fact, here is a sampling of the kinds of questions I'm asked every day.

"All the older women in my family have osteoporosis. My doctor suggested that I take hormones but I really don't want to. Is there anything else I can do to prevent it?"

"I have macular degeneration. What can I do about it?"

"I have yeast infections constantly. A few weeks after one clears up, another develops. Isn't there a way I can get rid of them once and for all?"

"My husband has high blood pressure. If he exercises, can he stop taking his medication?"

"I have to travel a lot on business. How can I avoid jet lag?"

"My baby gets ear infections constantly and is on antibiotics all the time. Isn't there anything I can do to help her?"

My patients know that my goal is to treat the *cause* of symptoms rather than the symptoms themselves, and often the best way to do this is by natural means. I've always advocated a conservative and natural approach to healing. I first became interested in natural ways of treating disease while I was in medical school. I found it disturbing to see people treated as a collection of faulty organs, and I felt convinced that there must be a more effective way. In the army I was trained in preventive medicine and I realized that, for me, the traditional drug and surgery treatments that were the mainstay of traditional medicine were too crisis oriented. I wanted to be involved *before* the crisis in an effort to prevent it.

In 1971 I went to Hong Kong for a year to study acupuncture, and I became familiar with the philosophy of Chinese medicine. Upon my return to the United States, I began to teach nutrition and alternative medicine at the New School in New York. In my own practice I developed a method of treating patients that I hoped combined the best of both worlds: the solid tradition and technique of modern medicine combined with the philosophy of natural healing. What this comes down to in my practice is that I can make every effort to steer people to natural means of healing, but I also know when it's necessary for them to turn to drugs and/or surgery.

I've been aware for many years that more and more people are trying to follow a natural approach to healing, but I had no idea how great the public thirst for information had become until I broadcast my first radio call-in show, "In the Doctor's Office," in 1991. I wasn't quite sure what kind of calls to expect from listeners. Of course those who were familiar with my books knew that I specialize in nutrition and "lifestyle therapy." So I certainly expected to get calls from people with questions about diet and supplements and also perhaps about stress reduction, weight loss, and exercise. What surprised me was that most of the callers asked questions like the ones posed above; they wanted help with a particular ailment that had become a disturbing background to their life. Many of these people have followed traditional treatment recommendations without success or with troubling side effects, or they've decided that they didn't want to take the drugs recommended for their condition on a long-term basis. These people are desperate for more natural solutions than those offered by most conventional medical treatments.

Some of my callers are amazingly sophisticated about natural treatments; they only want to fine-tune a vitamin dosage. Others are new to natural treatments; they've been driven to investigate them by the failure or disappointment of conventional therapies. Sometimes my callers have tips for me. They tell me about highly touted treatments that did nothing for them or, better yet, an approach that worked, sometimes like a miracle.

All these people have sharpened my awareness of the need for a solid, *conservative,* well-informed source of information on natural treatments for common ailments. I hope that *Natural Prescriptions* will fill that need.

I've tried in this book to outline a simple natural treatment for each of over one hundred ailments and conditions. In some cases, the treatment involves simply vitamin/mineral therapy. More often it involves an over-all regime that includes exercise, diet, and stress control. Some people will be surprised to see entries that include everything from colds to congestive heart failure to multiple sclerosis. Keep in mind that some conditions you can prevent (like a cold), and some you can improve (like heartburn). With others you can ease symptoms and perhaps halt the progression (like arthritis). Many people with conditions or ailments I cover will be under the care of a physician who will be critical to their treatment.

I am not against conventional therapies for disease; I am, after all, a physician who studied for years to learn those therapies, and I'm well aware of how essential they can be in saving lives and promoting health. But I also know that sometimes there's another, more natural, way.

That's the approach I've taken in this book: the first step you take in trying to deal with an ailment should be simple and natural. Natural means are far more effective than most people realize. For example:

> The live culture in yogurt—*Lactobacillus acidophilus*—really does help cure vaginal yeast infections and may help them from recurring.

> The mineral boron is highly effective in fighting menopausal symptoms. Many patients have told me that it has worked remarkably well in eliminating hot flashes.

> There is a drug treatment for cold sores; there's also a natural therapy that not only helps relieve an outbreak but may also help prevent future ones.

> While aspirin may relieve the pain of arthritis, it will do nothing to prevent the progression of the disease. Natural remedies have helped many people find greater mobility and relief from pain.

> The proper nutrients can reverse the results of a Pap smear that indicate the first stages of abnormal tissue growth.

The fact is that natural treatments can be safe, simple, inexpensive, and effective. Moreover, they are beneficial to the whole body: the premise being that natural treatments help the body heal itself.

Natural treatments used to be considered suspect by practitioners of traditional medicine. I'm happy to say that is less the case today, especially since the National Institutes of Health have recently funded a department to study alternative therapies. As research has focused more on nutritional causes of disease and as the public has become more responsive to natural treatments, physicians have begun to adopt these techniques. Many of my patients tell me that their doctors have suggested one or more vitamins and/or minerals for their various conditions. For example, many ophthalmologists now routinely recommend zinc to prevent macular degeneration. Many neurologists recommend vitamins C and E for Parkinson's disease. Little by little these natural approaches are becoming mainstream.

But there is still a great deal of resistance to changing the way doctors treat disease. Despite overwhelming evidence that some ulcers can be cured—not just temporarily relieved—by antibiotic therapy, it is a rare doctor who recommends this therapy to ulcer patients. Why? It's difficult to change a lifetime of training, and unfortunately in some cases new treatments are less expensive for the patients, take more time for the doctor to administer, and are not paid for by insurance.

What does this mean for the interested patient? You must take charge of your health care and be open to new treatments and techniques that have been demonstrated to be safe. With perseverance, you will find doctors who are willing to discuss these new techniques and approaches with you.

Determining exactly what *is* safe and effective has been a stumbling block when dealing with natural treatments for disease. Day after day the newspapers announce yet another discovery that connects diet and/or supplements with disease treatment. But these news stories are confusing for the public. Frequently the results of these tests are disparaged; sometimes the researchers themselves take a wait-and-see approach. Many listeners call my radio show simply to ask whether a natural treatment they've heard about is actually okay. This book answers these particular questions and also addresses the more general apprehension many people have about natural treatments.

The information in this book comes from a number of sources. Once I realized the interest on the part of my radio audience for the latest information on natural therapies, I reviewed all the respected medical journals here and abroad, *The Journal of the American Medical Association, The Lancet,* and *The Journal of Clinical Nutrition,* among others, for research published within the past few years that validate particular natural approaches. In most cases there is a consensus on what works and what doesn't. These treatments have helped my patients. Obviously I can't recommend a treatment that I have not used successfully, even if a number of journals print studies that say it works.

Safety is a major concern in any treatment for disease. Nutritional supplements must be used with discretion. Some patients think that if 100 mg. of something is good, 500 mg. is better. This is almost never the case. There is no danger in any of the treatments recommended herein when directions are followed as to amounts and duration of treatment. The suggestions I've made in this book for supplementation are very conservative. Some conditions could require higher doses than those suggested here, but if that's the case I feel you should be under the care of a physician who will supervise your consumption. Of course, if you have a question about any treatment, you can always discuss it with your doctor.

I've tried to be very clear in this book about

when your symptoms indicate that you should consult a doctor,
when you can use natural therapies *in conjunction* with traditional methods,
when you can use natural methods on your own.

I've also tried to be very specific about amounts of nutrients to take and for what period of time. I've included recommendations concerning drug interactions where appropriate. I've also included notes at the end of some sections of the book under the heading In Addition, reporting new or important treatments that you should ask your doctor about or the latest information on natural treatments that I haven't tried myself with my patients but which I suggest you explore.

I have tried to make *Natural Prescriptions* as close as possible to an actual consultation with a doctor committed to a nondrug, noninvasive, natural approach to health care. I believe this book can help you to take charge of your own well-being and allow you not only to avoid illness but also to achieve optimum vigorous good health.

BLUEPRINT FOR HEALTH

MOST PEOPLE WILL pick up this book, look up an ailment that troubles them, and then follow the suggestions listed. But I want to make the point here that in order to achieve optimum health you need to follow an overall plan. You cannot achieve good health simply by taking supplements. It's absolutely crucial that you pay attention to diet, exercise, and stress control. Many of the diseases we develop in later life (or even at a relatively young age) are caused by neglecting simple basic habits that promote good health. I've outlined in great detail what I consider the best overall health plan in my book *Medical Makeover*. Here is a condensed version of that plan.

Before I go into the details, it's important to mention by way of encouragement that most people will find it impossible to change their lives overnight. The things that you do or don't do every day are habits. If you have ice cream every night while you watch TV or if you never exercise, these are habits: It takes more than a decision to change them.

I tell my patients that they should try to "exchange" habits: Don't just try to give up ice cream, try to substitute a healthy food. You might just start with yogurt or fruit. Make your focus the new food or treat, and don't agonize about the ice cream you're no longer eating. The same goes for exercise. Don't decide that you must join a health club or jog every morning. For many people these good intentions evaporate in the demands of everyday life. Instead, try to find something that you do nearly every day and see how you can add exercise to it. Maybe you can ride a stationary bike while you watch the news or walk a few blocks to get your newspaper instead of having it delivered. I'm always amazed at people who drive around a parking lot for ten minutes looking for a space near the health club! If they simply parked at the far end of the lot and walked briskly to their destination, they would get some good exercise.

As you read through this outline for good health, think about *small* changes you can make in your daily life. Remember, you don't have to do it all at once, and every little bit you do will help you toward a healthier future.

DIET

A good diet is crucial to good health: The diet that will help prevent chronic disease in the future is the same diet that will make you feel better today. Remember the notion of habit exchange: the focus should be on substituting good foods for unhealthy ones. Here are my suggestions for achieving the best possible diet.

- Eat regular meals at regular times. That means no skipped breakfasts, no late meals, no coffee and candy for lunch. No matter what your schedule, you should eat three meals daily. I've had patients who are airline pilots on erratic schedules, people who work night shifts, and entertainers who get at noon. No matter what your schedule is, shortly after you get up, whatever the time, you should have your first meal; four or five hours later, you should have a second meal; and usually five or six hours after that, have your final meal of the day.

  You need regular meals to supply your body with a steady supply of fuel throughout the day. Many of my patients who feel tired and irritable eat sporadically. When they've gone without food for six or seven hours, their blood sugar drops and they feel weak, irritable, and fatigued. Quick fixes like coffee, sweets, or even a cigarette will send their blood sugar soaring and they feel temporarily better. But of course they soon crash and need another fix. The toll these highs and lows take on the body is significant, both in terms of how they feel throughout the day and also in its effect on the development of disease in the future.

- Vary your diet. Too many people eat the same thing for breakfast and lunch day after day. I had one patient who had eaten nothing but cottage cheese and peaches for lunch for over a year! This practice can limit your intake of crucial nutrients. The more varied your diet, the better your chances of covering all your nutritional bases and satisfying your hunger. When you eat the same thing all the time, you tend not to notice what you've eaten or even that you've eaten at all! Finally, repeating meals on a regular basis can contribute to food sensitivities. I do a lot of work with patients who suffer from this condition: They have vague symptoms that they never connected with the foods they eat. These symptoms can be as obvious as hives but more likely are subtle disorders including fatigue, dizziness, blurred vision, headaches, frequent colds and sore throats, irritable-bowel syndrome, and excessive hunger. A varied diet will help prevent development of food sensitivities. My basic rule of thumb is try not to eat the same thing at the same meal two days in a row.

- Limit your fat intake. Fat is the most concentrated source of calories in your diet. A diet rich in fat puts you at risk for heart disease, our number one killer. A high-fat diet has also been linked to two cancers that are major killers among Americans—cancer of the colon and breast cancer.

  You can cut down on fat by eating less dairy food, less beef and pork, eliminating fried foods, and avoiding commercial baked items and commercial salad dressings. (One to two tablespoons of olive or canola oil a day can be included in a healthy diet.) If you eliminate the following fatty foods, you'll still get about 20 percent of your calories from the naturally occurring fat in fish, chicken, tuna, and turkey. Here are the major fatty foods to avoid:

avocado	fried foods	oils (except olive
butter	ice cream	or canola)
cheese	junk foods	peanut butter
chocolate	luncheon meats	red meat
coconut	margarine	seeds
cream sauces	mayonnaise	shortenings
eggs	nuts	whole milk

There are simple steps you can take to cut down on fat in your diet.

- For example, avoid commercial baked goods that are made with saturated fats, make your own salad dressing with low- or nonfat yogurt, spices, garlic, and herbs mixed in the blender.

- Eat more complex carbohydrates, which you'll find in starchy vegetables, whole grain bread, unrefined cereals, brown rice, beans, and whole-wheat pasta. These foods should comprise over half your total calories. Carbohydrates are not fattening. They are rich in fiber, which has been shown to help prevent a number of diseases. Carbohydrates are also helpful in stabilizing blood sugar, thereby helping to control your appetite.

- Increase your fiber intake. More fiber in your diet can help you prevent colon cancer, lower cholesterol, and possibly help prevent the development of heart disease. Fiber also helps stabilize blood sugar, preventing periods of tiredness, irritability, and moodiness. And fiber will help you fight constipation. Eat more whole grains, fresh fruits and vegetables, salads, and root vegetables. Think of foods like oatmeal and bran muffins (but not the commercial ones, which are loaded with fat and sugar) for breakfast. Beans are an excellent source of fiber and, as they're becoming more popular, it's easier to find bean soups and bean dishes on restaurant menus and recipes in cookbooks. Try always to have fresh fruit on hand and rely on it as your main snack food. Even though some fresh fruits can be expensive, especially in winter, they're really no more expensive than many other snacks that are loaded with sugar and saturated fats. Don't forget salads: Try to have one a day (and remember to make your own dressing using low-fat ingredients). In addition to these dietary shifts, I usually recommend that my patients take a teaspoon of miller's bran daily, or more if they have constipation.

- Shift the main source of your protein from meat to fish, poultry, and soy products, including tofu and soybeans. Most of us get over 70 percent of our protein from animal and dairy products and most of these foods are too high in fat. Meals based on beans and peas are filling and keep blood sugar on an even keel. Experiment with meatless meals such as a vegetable lasagna made with low-fat cheese or stir-fried vegetables with slices of tofu.

- Avoid chemical additives. Try whenever possible to eat whole, natural foods. Read labels. Cook for yourself when you can, instead of relying on prepared foods.

SUGAR

Cut down on your sugar consumption. Sugar not only interferes with your metabolism but also can promote various diseases including tooth decay and diabetes. It also contributes to fatigue, irritability, and inability to concentrate and it makes dieting more difficult. Limiting sugar consumption can make a big difference. Many of my patients find that when they give up or cut way down on their sugar intake they experience higher and more consistent energy levels.

There's sugar in more foods than you think. Learn to read labels and look for the following terms that identify different types of sugars:

corn syrup	glucose	molasses
sucrose	lactose	maple syrup
fructose	maltose	sorghum

If a label lists one or more of these, you know that there's sugar (and maybe lots of it!) in that food. If you eliminate sugar from your diet, you'll be surprised at how quickly you'll lose your sweet tooth.

CAFFEINE

Many people are addicted to caffeine. While studies attempting to prove that caffeine is implicated in everything from heart disease to high blood pressure have never been conclusive, I believe that the damage excessive caffeine consumption does can't be ignored. Caffeine wreaks havoc on your metabolism and creates a real stress that could precipitate symptoms including headaches, fatigue, irritability, inability to concentrate, depression, and nervousness.

Caffeine is a stimulant. After you ingest it your heart beats faster, your blood pressure rises, your stomach jumps, your bowels may react, and your blood vessels constrict. Your body begins to depend on this stimulation. (Indeed, most of my patients who drink coffee have mild to severe withdrawal symptoms when they cut down.) While this stimulation may seem benign, its effect on your body is as if you were constantly in overdrive. It creates a stress that eventually causes mild and major symptoms to develop. In addition, caffeine can interact with over-the-counter and prescription drugs in unwelcome ways. Birth control pills can slow the elimination of caffeine from the system. Asthma medications may cause excessive nervousness if taken with caffeine.

Caffeine is not found just in coffee and tea. Be sure to avoid medications that contain caffeine (read the label) as well as colas and other drinks that contain it. I suggest you drink no more than one caffeinated or decaffeinated beverage daily. Patients ask why they can't simply have a caffeinated cup of coffee followed by additional cups of decaf. The point is that you need to break the habit of drinking coffee; many people find that if they continue to drink decaf, they quickly slip back into drinking too much caffeinated coffee. Besides, even decaf contains caffeine in measurable amounts.

Here are some common foods and drinks that contain caffeine: coffee, tea, cocoa, chocolate milk, chocolate, many soft drinks, many prescription drugs including Fiorinal and Darvon, weight-control aids, alertness tablets, analgesics/pain relievers including Anacin, Excedrin, and Midol, diuretics, and cold/allergy remedies including Dristan and Triaminicin.

ALCOHOL

Cut down, or better yet, eliminate alcohol from your diet. It can cause major health problems as well as social ones. Some people find that a daily habit that began innocently enough as a glass of wine with dinner or a drink right after work soon escalates into a half bottle or more of wine a night or a series of drinks. It can be difficult to be "moderate" with alcohol; it's safer to abstain. I do have many patients who are able to drink one glass of wine with dinner and who argue that there are studies demonstrating that this limited amount is beneficial. If you can stick to a single glass every other day, I think it's an acceptable habit.

If you doubt the pervasive effects of alcohol, try abstaining completely for a few days. I promise that you'll notice a real difference in how you feel in the morning and all day long, even if you're a very light drinker. You'll wake up refreshed without a trace of that nagging morning headache that so many who drink learn to live with, you'll have more energy, and you'll simply feel healthier. And, of course, you'll be saving all the calories of alcohol and will probably begin to lose some weight.

EXERCISE

Exercise is absolutely crucial to optimum health. Its effect on disease is quite dramatic and there are very few diseases that exercise won't help. I suggest that at the very least you exercise for a half hour, three times a week. This can include a brisk walk, a bike ride, a swim, and so on. Aerobic exercise is best. It increases your heart rate and keeps it elevated for the duration of the exercise.

STRESS CONTROL

Stress control is like exercise; sometimes it's difficult to convince someone to do something when they can't *see* results. But it's been proven over and over again that stress control will help prevent and relieve disease. For more information, see Stress Control, page 314.

SMOKING

I've left this until last because I hope that most people who are willing to take charge of their health and use natural treatments don't smoke. If you do smoke, you *must* give it up. There's is no point in trying to solve medical problems with nutritional therapy if you are at the same time encouraging all the serious and fatal problems that are caused by smoking. It's like trying to heat a house with all the windows open. There are effective programs to help you stop smoking. For more information, contact the American Cancer Society.

VITAMIN/MINERAL SUPPLEMENTS

According to a health food industry report, 75 million Americans take a daily supplement, but other people still wonder why they should take vitamins. Can't I just eat a balanced diet? they ask. While I don't recommend megavitamins, I do believe that most everyone needs at least basic supplementation to ensure that their body is getting the necessary vitamins to allow daily metabolic processes to function efficiently and prevent the onset of chronic diseases.

Most people don't eat a diet that is rich or varied enough to supply them with adequate vitamins and minerals. One large study that involved 28,000 people showed that more than 60 percent of the people, regardless of income level, showed at least one symptom of malnutrition. Countless other studies have had similar results. And remember that the RDA (the recommended daily allowance, which some people argue is adequate for almost everyone) for vitamins and minerals is set at a level shown to prevent the development of serious disease. I think that our goal should go beyond preventing serious disease; I think that we should be moving toward optimum health and that we should be nourishing our bodies today in a way that will enable them to withstand the onslaughts of disease tomorrow.

Here are two recent telling reports.

In a ten-year study of 11,000 men and women at the University of California in Los Angeles, it was found that those who took 300 to 500 mg. of vitamin C daily had a 25 to 45 percent lower death rate from heart disease and a 10 to 42 percent lower mortality from all causes when compared with people who had a substantially lower intake of vitamin C.

In another study, 87,000 nurses were evaluated over an eight-year period. Those who consumed more than 15 to 20 mg. a day of beta-carotene had 40 percent fewer strokes and a 22 percent reduction of heart attacks when compared with those who took less than 6 mg. a day. Vitamin E in doses greater than 100 mg. daily was associated with a 36 percent lower risk of heart attack than when the amount taken was less than 30 mg. a day.

These are just a tiny sampling of the reports that flood my desk concerning the importance of vitamin and mineral supplementation.

The most exciting recent news about vitamins has concerned the antioxidants. The antioxidants include beta-carotene, vitamin E, vitamin C, and selenium. These chemicals fight the disease and aging processes by acting to absorb the free radicals—waste products of cell metabolism—that act to harm a cell's fragile genetic material. Antioxidants fight cancer, prevent cholesterol from becoming the sticky stuff that clogs arteries, protect against pollutants, and generally enhance our immune responses. Many studies are showing that people who consume relatively high amounts of the antioxidants experience much lower rates of various cancers, cardiovascular disease, and other degenerative diseases.

YOUR DAILY BASIC VITAMIN/MINERAL ANTIOXIDANT SUPPLEMENTS

I feel strongly that you should take a good quality multiple vitamin/mineral supplement and/or supplements daily. Many people are confused about buying vitamins and this is understandable: There are so many brands and formulations that choosing can be difficult. To simplify matters for you, here's the easiest way to recognize a good quality multivitamin/mineral supplement that should save you an afternoon devoted to reading the small print on the back of all those bottles. Your daily supplement should have approximately 50 mg. of the most important B vitamins—B_1, B_2, and B_6. In my experience, a multiple that contains at least this amount of the B's will be well balanced and will also contain a good range of other vitamins, minerals, and trace minerals.

Be sure to check the dosage instructions on the label of whatever brand supplement you buy. Some varieties must be taken two or three times daily. I had a patient who took a good quality vitamin/mineral for over a year without having read the label indicating three pills a day. She was getting only one third the potency she thought she was.

Most formulations of a vitamin/mineral supplement (even those that contain 50 or more mg. of the B's) do not contain enough of the antioxidant vitamins and minerals that I believe you need for optimum health. The amounts I feel are important are 1,000 mg. of vitamin C; 400 to 600 I.U. of vitamin E; 10,000 to 25,000 I.U. of beta-carotene; and 100 to 200 mcg. of selenium. If your formulation does not fall within these ranges, I recommend that in addition to your daily vitamin/mineral supplement, you take the following antioxidants:

500 mg. of vitamin C
200 I.U. of vitamin E
10,000 I.U. of beta-carotene
50 micrograms of selenium

You can buy these supplements separately or you can buy an "antioxidant" formula that should contain these nutrients. Remember that the "antioxidant formula supplements should be taken in addition to your daily vitamin/mineral supplement, not instead of it.

Of course, in addition to the supplements I've outlined above, you should take any supplements recommended in the text to treat any conditions that apply to you.

Many of my patients have questions about vitamins, and here are their most common concerns. Many wonder why there is such a great range in prices for vitamins. In general, except for the caveats noted below, you will get what you pay for with supplements. A brand that contains 50 mg. of the B's will probably cost more than one that has only 15 mg. In some cases, an expensive advertising budget may drive up the price of a vitamin, but an important defining factor in terms of price is the fact that some very expensive supplements are hypoallergenic. Hypoallergenic supplements are free of the extra ingredients that could cause reactions in sensitive people. If you have known allergies and/or if you notice a reaction that might include headaches, nausea, fatigue, palpitations, or loose bowel movements within two or three days of taking a new supplement, you may be reacting to an ingredient in that supplement. For example, most vitamin C is derived from corn; many patients are sensitive to corn products and thus will not be able to take this type of vitamin C. Additionally, many supplements are prepared in a yeast base; some people are sensitive to yeast. If you notice a reaction that could be connnected to a supplement, discontinue any supplements and reintroduce them one at a time at four-day intervals until a reaction signals the problem supplement. Hypoallergenic supplements are more expensive than others but are required for some people.

Another factor that affects the price of vitamins is that some are defined as "natural" and this usually means that they cost more. As to "synthetic" versus "natural" vitamins, there is really no difference in terms of the effect of the nutrients on your body. I don't think it's worth paying extra for supplements that are called "natural" as the processing they endure is virtually identical to the processing of the "synthetic" variety and, more important, they are chemically identical. Some argue that the "natural" supplements contain components that are not yet recognized but may be important or even essential to the absorption of that supplement. There's no evidence to back up this claim and, indeed, there is research to show that some "synthetic" supplements may be more readily absorbed.

What about time-released capsules? Many patients wonder if they are effective. I've never found any independent research that demonstrates that these time-release supplements really work as claimed. I think it's best to simply spread your supplement intake through the day. For example, take your basic supplement with meals (whether you take one or two or more daily), and take your additional antioxidants with different meals. This will help to provide continuing anitoxidant protection.

Patients have also asked me about chelated minerals. Chelation is a process that is supposed to enhance the absorbability of minerals by changing their electrical charge. Again, I have never found chelated minerals to be better absorbed.

As to storing vitamins, you should keep them in a cool, dark place. You shouldn't refrigerate them, as the moisture in a refrigerator could damage them. Supplements should be kept in the opaque containers that they come in as they are thus best protected from sunlight. You shouldn't buy huge quantities of vitamins as they will lose potency over a period of time. Some brands of supplements have expiration dates on them; others don't. If in doubt, I suggest you discard any supplements not used within six months of opening.

INFORMED PREVENTION

I have one final recommendation: In the course of my studies concerning natural therapies for disease, I have been impressed over and over again at how both genetics and nutrition play a role in whether or not we stay well. Family history is an important predictor in the development of disease. At the same time, adequate vitamin and mineral intake can play an important role in preventing or slowing the development of that same disease. With this in mind, I suggest that you take a look at any diseases that you know are common in your family. Whether it's macular degeneration, osteoporosis, gout, varicose veins, or glaucoma, make a list of all the diseases that your mother, father, or grandparents have suffered from and read about them in this book. Pay special attention to the Natural Prescription for these diseases and adopt some of the recommendations. You may never develop these diseases, but, on the other hand, you could be in the earliest stages of them right now. If you begin to "treat" the disease before it has actually manifested itself, you will be helping to slow or arrest its possible progression.

PLEASE NOTE

You will notice that in almost every entry in this book there is a notation in the Prescription section that suggests that the supplements are to be taken *in addition* to the basic daily vitamin/mineral you are already taking. If you are troubled by more than one ailment—say, arthritis, hay fever, and macular degeneration—do *not* duplicate any amount of supplements you take. In other words, if one entry recommends 400 I.U. of vitamin E in addition to your daily vitamin, and another entry recommends 400 I.U. of vitamin E in addition to your daily vitamin, *do not* take an additional 800 I.U. of vitamin E. Never take more of a supplement than recommended in The Blueprint for Health plus a single prescription without consulting your doctor.

NATURAL
PRESCRIPTIONS

ACNE

FOR MANY PEOPLE acne is less an ailment than a curse. It often occurs at a time—during adolescence—when self-consciousness is most acute and self-esteem most vulnerable. In addition, there's no simple remedy, even if you resort to the most extreme traditional cures. Fortunately, there is good news on the natural front. I've had great success with both adults and adolescents by going to the root of the problem.

Acne is a disease of the skin that causes the pores to clog and produce pimples known as whiteheads and blackheads, most often on the face, but sometimes spreading to the neck, upper back, chest, and shoulders. It usually starts in adolescence—by age seventeen over 84 percent of American teens have had acne—and disappears by early adulthood, but in a few instances may continue through life. We don't know exactly what causes acne, which is why it's been so difficult to treat. Heredity seems to play a distinct role; oily skin, while it does not cause acne, appears to aggravate the condition. Other aggravating factors include stress, seasonal changes, diet, and sun exposure. In people who develop acne in their twenties or thirties, allergies to cosmetics or food may be to blame. In my experience, detection and elimination of hidden food allergies is the most important approach in the successful treatment and prevention of acne.

While acne does not have any serious physical side effects, it's often deeply troubling to the four out of five teenagers who suffer from it. Their embarrassment is aggravated by the myths about acne, such as its being caused by too much or too little sex or unsanitary conditions. The myths are unfounded. Acne is activated by natural hormonal activity, and, in some women, it may flare up before a menstrual period.

Typically, acne starts at puberty along with an increase in androgens, the male sex hormone produced by the testes or ovaries and adrenal glands in both sexes. The increased androgens stimulate the oil glands to produce increased amounts of sebum, which comes up through the hair follicles to lubricate the skin. In acne, excess sebum combines with skin pigmentation to form blackheads on the surface of the skin, or it may block the pores beneath the surface of the skin, forming whiteheads. In either case, if the follicle ruptures due to irritation and pressure, bacteria may enter the area to produce additional inflammation and painful nodules and cysts that can cause scarring if improperly treated.

Severe acne is usually treated with antibiotics to prevent scarring. However, there are problems associated with long-term antibiotic therapy. Yeast infections, one of the most frequent side effects, clear when the antibiotic is discontinued, but the acne returns.

Many of my patients with acne first came to see me because they found themselves caught up in this cycle of antibiotics. I begin by checking their history for potential allergies. Is there a history of allergies in the family? Were they allergic as children? Did the start of their acne coincide with the use of a new cosmetic, moisturizer, or sunscreen? Or with the start of a new diet?

Since allergies to food or cosmetics play an important part in adult-onset acne, you should use only hypoallergenic skin products, and take hypoallergenic vitamins and minerals, because even the binders and fillers of over-the-counter vitamins and minerals may cause allergic reactions. You should, of course, avoid any food or drink to which you are allergic. For more information on this subject, refer to Food Allergy, page 146, and follow the suggestions.

It's important to evaluate what you eat because there seems to be correlation between acne and our Western diet, which tends to be too high in fat and too low in fiber. Some interesting observational studies have shown that people on low-fat, high-fiber diets have far less acne than their counterparts, perhaps because dietary fat is believed to promote sebum, the lubricant that causes pimples when trapped by clogged pores. I tell my patients to reduce their dietary fat to 20 percent of their caloric intake, and to supplement their fiber with 1 ounce of an all-bran cereal (see Blueprint for Health, page xvii).

There are natural treatments for acne, some of which can make a dramatic difference if used in conjunction with a healthy diet. Vitamin A has been shown to virtually eliminate acne in milder cases; it should be a staple supplement. An important antioxidant and immune-system-enhancing vitamin that helps to maintain a healthy skin, vitamin A and its derivatives have also been found to reduce the production of pore-clogging sebum. I prescribe vitamin A in doses ranging from 10,000 to 25,000 I.U. Since higher doses of vitamin A can cause side effects, it should be taken only under your doctor's supervision.

Vitamin E affects the biologic utilization of vitamin A: It promotes maximum vitamin A absorption. Therefore, I recommend that you take vitamin E along with vitamin A.

Zinc insufficiency is found in patients with aggravated acne, and several nutritional studies indicate that zinc supplements have cleared up the condition. A doctor in Sweden, who conducted several studies to gauge the effectiveness of zinc supplements, found that, taken over twelve weeks, they were as effective in clearing up acne as antibiotics or Accutane, and without the serious side effects!

Patients with severe, or postular acne, are often deficient in the trace mineral selenium, and selenium supplements have helped to clear up the condition. The recommended antioxidant multiple vitamin and mineral supplements will contain adequate selenium for this purpose.

Vitamin B_6 may also be helpful in controlling acne, particularly for women who experience flare-ups of acne before and during their menstrual period. Some experts recommend taking B_6 for the week before and the week after a period; my patients have found better results by taking it every day all month.

And then there are the essential fatty acids or "omegas," whose effectiveness against various inflammations is just beginning to be fully understood in the prevention and treatment of skin disease. For acne, I prescribe omega 6, which is found in evening primrose oil, black currant seed oil, or borage seed oil. These oils are composed of both linoleic and linolenic fatty acids, which have been shown to reduce, and sometimes eliminate, inflammatory skin conditions.

There is one more thing that my patients have found helpful. Topical tea-tree oil, an essential oil of the Australian native tree *Melaleuca alternifolia,* has an antimicrobial effect and when used on the skin affected by acne, can be of help in reducing outbreaks. It is usually compared to benzoyl peroxide, but it has fewer undesirable side effects. It does take longer to work, so you have to be patient. You apply it topically to the affected area daily.

The effects of a low-fat, high-fiber diet, supplemented with vitamins and minerals, should become evident within a period of three months. In the meantime, to minimize irritations and to prevent possible scarring, you must be sure to take proper care of your skin.

GUIDELINES FOR SKIN CARE

1. Wash your face gently. Use a mild soap, such as Dove or Neutrogena. The bacteria that cause acne are not on the surface of the skin, so scrubbing with harsh soaps will not help, and may make things worse by irritating the skin. You may also use a cleanser containing salicylic acid, which will loosen the debris so you can just rinse it away.

2. Whiteheads are clogged pores beneath the outermost layer of skin and should not be squeezed. They will go away on their own within three to four weeks. Squeezing can make them inflamed or infected and can cause scarring. The only time you should squeeze a pimple is when it's already infected, and has yellow pus. Take a warm bath or shower or apply a warm moist compress to the area for a few minutes to help open the pores. Then squeeze the pimple gently with a tissue until the pus pops out so that the remaining pimple can heal more quickly.

3. Remove blackheads carefully. Blackheads are plugs of oil that darken upon contact with the air. They are not dirt, and scrubbing will only make them worse. You can, however, remove blackheads with an extractor, which you can buy at any pharmacy, after taking a warm bath or shower to open the pores. Never use your hands or fingernails, as this may cause scarring of the skin.

4. Discourage new blemishes with medicated lotions. Lotions with benzoyl peroxide are very helpful in controlling acne. However, since these can dry and redden the skin, start with a 5 percent concentration, which can be as effective as the 10 percent. Apply the lotion to the affected area and about an inch of the surrounding skin. To minimize irritation, don't leave the lotion on for extended periods. You can apply it in the evening, leave it on for a couple of hours, and wash it off before going to bed. Alternatively, you can try tea-tree oil, the natural substitute for benzoyl peroxide, which I mentioned above.

5. Use moisturizer if your skin is dry, but be sure that it's hypoallergenic.

6. Use hypoallergenic makeup and suntan lotions.

NATURAL PRESCRIPTION FOR ACNE

- Modify your diet: Eat a low-fat (no more than 20 percent of calories from fat), high-fiber diet. Eat lots of fresh fruits and vegetables and whole grain breads and cereals.

- Investigate the possibility of food allergies. See Food Allergy, page 146, for more information. If you have no success dealing with this on your own, see a doctor who specializes in nutritional medicine. Once you've identified a food allergy, you must be scrupulous in eliminating it from your diet. You may find that you're allergic to several foods or a whole category, such as dairy foods.

- Take special daily care of your skin and follow the skin care guidelines given above.

IN ADDITION TO YOUR DAILY SUPPLEMENTS, PAGE xxiv, TAKE

- Vitamin A: 10,000 I.U. daily. (Note: See your doctor before taking a higher dosage or if taking vitamin A for extended periods.)

- Vitamin E (to be taken in conjunction with vitamin A): 400 I.U. daily.

- Zinc: 50 mg. daily.

- Vitamin B_6: 50 mg. daily. (Note: Vitamin B_6 is particularly helpful for women who experience premenstrual acne flare-ups, who should take it throughout the month.)

- Evening primrose oil: 500 mg. three times daily.

- Tea-tree oil: Apply topically to affected area once daily.

• • •

ALZHEIMER'S DISEASE

ALZHEIMER'S DISEASE IS a progressive, degenerative disease of the brain. We used to regard older people who were showing signs of memory loss as senile; today we know they may be suffering from Alzheimer's.

But Alzheimer's is far more than simple memory loss; it's the gradual, permanent tangling of the nerve fibers that surround the memory center of the brain. Alzheimer's begins with simple repeated memory loss, particularly for recent events, develops into obvious confusion, and ultimately causes troubling personality changes and a complete inability to communicate or survive independently.

A diagnosis of Alzheimer's is usually made by process of elimination —only an autopsy of the brain will reveal the definitive evidence—and it is important when suspecting Alzheimer's to eliminate other factors that can cause memory loss or behavior that mimics Alzheimer's. Here are some of the possibilities that should be investigated.

DRUG INTERACTION: Many people, particularly older people, take various medications—prescription and nonprescription—that could be having an effect on their memory, either alone or due to an interaction with another drug.

HIGH BLOOD PRESSURE: Uncontrolled high blood pressure, often caused by hardening of the arteries, can cause strokes that destroy brain tissue and result in memory loss.

INFECTIONS: Various kinds of infections, including syphilis, can cause symptoms that resemble Alzheimer's. Lyme disease has recently been recognized as a cause of symptoms that have been mistaken for Alzheimer's.

POOR THYROID FUNCTION: A thyroid that is not functioning properly can also cause Alzheimer's-like symptoms.

BRAIN TUMOR: The pressure from a brain tumor can disrupt the normal functioning of the brain and can cause symptoms that involve the memory.

It's important to eliminate all these possibilities before deciding that someone is suffering from Alzheimer's disease. A recent fascinating study has suggested a diagnostic tool by which simple forgetfulness can be distinguished from Alzheimer's. Patients were asked to draw the face of a clock with the time showing 2:45. People who were able to do so, despite other symptoms, were found to be normal; those with Alzheimer's disease could not draw the clock.

While no one has yet been able to pinpoint the precise cause of Alzheimer's disease, some very interesting recent research has shown that hardened buildups of a protein called beta-amyloid is instrumental. These buildups used to be recognized as a result of the disease, but now there's mounting evidence that they're part of the cause. Recent findings suggest that low levels of a chemical that carries messages between nerve cells—acetylcholine—contributes to the formation of these deposits that in effect clog brain tissue. It's encouraging to note that researchers have found that there's a natural hormone called substance P that's effective in disabling the beta-amyloid. Research on this front has just begun, but it bodes well for one day developing a real prevention and/or cure for Alzheimer's.

What can you do for someone who *does* have Alzheimer's disease? Unfortunately, there is no cure, either natural or otherwise, for Alzheimer's. The one drug approved by the government for treating Alzheimer's has recently been found to be ineffective. Hydergine (the eleventh most prescribed drug in the world) was found to "cause cognitive dysfunction, perhaps through a direct toxic effect or by accelerating the progression of Alzheimer's disease," according to a study published in the *New England Journal of Medicine*.

But there are many steps that can be taken to help Alzheimer's victims retard the progression of the disease, and, perhaps more important, to help people who are suffering from the very beginning stages of Alzheimer's delay the development of symptoms. All these steps relate to the various causes of Alzheimer's and are an effort to improve weakened functions or stave off the degeneration of other functions.

Many Alzheimer's victims have significantly low levels of vitamin B_{12}. Since typical blood tests often do not reveal this deficiency, there has been some skepticism about B_{12} supplementation for Alzheimer's sufferers. But the fact is, a deficiency need not be severe enough to reveal itself in a blood test in order to cause symptoms, and sometimes changes in the blood never occur even though there are severe deficiencies in other tissues. B_{12} deficiency is associated with depression, memory lapses, confusion, and neurologic degeneration—all symptoms shared by Alzheimer's victims.

Though the role of aluminum toxicity in promoting Alzheimer's disease has been debated, there is a great deal of evidence that there is a connection. Autopsies of the brains of people with Alzheimer's have revealed increased levels of aluminum as well as silicon. An extremely convincing argument for the role of aluminum in Alzheimer's is that patients who are undergoing kidney dialysis often develop "dialysis dementia" as a combined result of using antacids containing aluminum and elevated aluminum levels in the water used for dialysis.

Every one of us is consuming a great deal of aluminum: acid rain draws aluminum out of the soil and into drinking water; aluminum is a common food additive; everything from beer stored in aluminum cans to dandruff shampoos contain certain amounts of aluminum salts. While you can't completely eliminate aluminum from your diet, it's prudent for everyone to make an effort to avoid as many sources of aluminum as possible including:

- Aluminum cookware.

- Antacids: Many antacids contain aluminum hydroxide, which is an aluminum salt. Di-Gel, Gelusil, Maalox, Mylanta, Riopan, and Rolaids are among those that do contain aluminum. I recommend that you do not take antacids containing aluminum for calcium supplementation. Read the label when you buy antacids: There are at least twenty antacids that don't contain aluminum.

- Buffered aspirin can contain up to 88 mg. of aluminum per dose. Again, read the label before you buy.

- Douches can contain aluminum salts, and we don't really know how much of these salts the body absorbs.

- Medicines for diarrhea, including Kaopectate and Donnagel, can contain up to 600 mg. of aluminum salts. Check the label before you buy.

Free radicals are unstable chemical compounds that react with other, stable compounds, thus causing a chain reaction that impairs and ultimately damages cells and then tissues of the body. Damage from free radicals has been implicated in many diseases including Alzheimer's. Of course the body has a natural system to deactivate free radicals; if it didn't it would quickly become crippled and destroyed. Certain vitamins, minerals, and enzymes link with the free radicals and stabilize them so they are rendered safe. These vitamins, minerals, and enzymes comprise the body's antioxidant system. But many people may be deficient in certain vitamins and minerals, and it is believed that these deficiencies can ultimately allow free radicals to severely damage the body and result in diseases including atherosclerosis, rheumatoid arthritis, asthma, multiple sclerosis, cancer, premature aging, and Alzheimer's disease. More than one study has demonstrated that the brains of people with Alzheimer's are low in antioxidant vitamins, possibly exposing brain neurons to increased oxidative damage. Many researchers believe that supplements of antioxidants offer a measure of protection against Alzheimer's. The antioxidants that I recommend in connection with Alzheimer's include the antioxidant vitamin/mineral formula that contains 50 mg. of the B vitamins along with vitamin C, vitamin E, beta-carotene, and selenium.

Extract of *Ginkgo biloba,* a plant, has been shown to facilitate the rate at which the nerve cells can transmit information—a system that becomes impaired in the course of Alzheimer's disease. A number of studies have demonstrated that taking supplements of *Ginkgo biloba* can help patients with Alzheimer's reach near-normal levels of vigilance and performance. You can get ginkgo extract at health food stores.

There has also been promising research that's shown that choline, a nutrient essential for the formation of one of the crucial neurotransmitters in the brain, can be helpful in increasing memory.

Zinc, a mineral that plays a role in preventing the degeneration of the nerve system, can be useful in fighting Alzheimer's.

NATURAL PRESCRIPTION FOR ALZHEIMER'S DISEASE

- Investigate all possible causes of Alzheimer's-like symptoms as described to be sure that the problem is not being caused by drug interaction, high blood pressure, infections, poor thyroid function, or a brain tumor.

- Aluminum elimination: Avoid all potential sources of aluminum including any cookware, antacids, buffered aspirin, douches, or diarrhea medicines.

IN ADDITION TO YOUR DAILY SUPPLEMENTS, PAGE xxiv, TAKE

- Vitamin C: 1,000 mg. daily.

- Vitamin E: 400 I.U. daily.

- Beta-carotene: 10,000 I.U. daily.

- Selenium: 50 mcg. daily.

- **Vitamin B$_{12}$:** 1,000 mcg. daily dissolved under the tongue.

- *Ginkgo biloba:* 40 mg. three to four times daily.

- **Choline:** 650 mg. three times daily.

- **Zinc:** 50 mg. daily.

IN ADDITION: In one recent study, thirty patients with Alzheimer's took the following supplements daily: 6 g. of evening primrose oil, 90 mg. of zinc sulfate, and 2 mg. of selenium. These patients had significant improvements in performace tests.

Another study found that patients who received supplements of L-carnitine had less deterioration in attention span and performance of tasks. They received 2.5 g. of L-carnitine daily for three months followed by 3 g. daily for three months.

• • •

ANGINA

ANGINA IS A SYMPTOM, not a disease. It is the name for the pain that occurs when the muscle of the heart is temporarily deprived of oxygen. The pain is usually felt just to the left of the center of your chest, but it can spread to your throat, back, jaw, and arms, particularly your left arm. The pain of angina is commonly described as dull and constricting. You may also experience sweating, nausea, dizziness, and difficulty breathing. Angina can be precipitated by exertion or emotional upset or even eating too much. There are more than twenty drugs that can cause or aggravate angina in certain people. They include amphetamines, ergot preparations, cocaine, oral contraceptives, and certain anticancer drugs.

If you have experienced what you think is angina, you should definitely consult with a doctor. Angina can be the first symptom of an impending heart attack. Many people live for years with angina, but it is a warning signal that cannot be ignored. Whereas I have had great success in helping patients eliminate angina, these patients have always been treated by conventional, traditional means as well. Natural therapy is an effective adjunct to traditional treatment in helping to eliminate the pain of angina.

Sometimes there are causes for chest pain other than angina. The pain of hiatal hernia (see Heartburn, page 173, and Hiatal Hernia and Esophagitis, page 186) can also mimic a heart attack. Hiatal hernia—the bulging of a portion of the stomach above the diaphragm—can cause indigestion and a burning sensation that starts below the breastbone and travels upward toward the neck. Some experts estimate that at least 25 percent of patients seen in hospital emergency rooms for chest pains are suffering with symptoms of a hiatal hernia. Regardless, it is always safer to have an episode of chest pain completely evaluated to make sure it's not cardiac in origin. If you are told that your symptoms are from heartburn, see Heartburn, page 173, and Indigestion, page 212.

There have also been cases of people who believed they had angina and were treated as such but who ultimately turned out to have allergies (in one case a woman developed her symptoms after a new carpet was installed in her home) and also osteoarthritis of the upper spine, which produced symptoms that simulated angina.

What do you do about angina? Assuming you are under the care of a doctor, your goal is to control the frequency of the attacks or try to eliminate them altogether and to completely prevent a heart attack. Both of these goals are achievable.

Many of the angina patients who come to see me are already on medications that are used to control angina, but they are still bothered by symptoms. Nitroglycerin is extremely effective in that it dilates the blood vessels immediately and relieves the congestion. Beta blockers and calcium channel blockers are other drugs used to control angina.

Surgery is always an option for people with resistant angina. There are various surgical techniques that aim to increase the flow of blood to the heart. Bypass is perhaps the most common surgery, and it is performed about as frequently as appendectomies in the United States. But there is a mounting body of evidence that bypass surgery may be ultimately ineffective. It is my belief, and it's certainly been my experience, that angina can be helped using natural means and medications under supervision of a doctor. It is very important for angina patients to recognize that lifestyle changes and natural therapies can significantly prolong their lives and dramatically increase the quality of their lives; to depend solely on medications and surgery to "cure" angina is to ignore a ticking time bomb.

Coronary artery disease, particularly atherosclerosis, is almost always the cause of angina. Atherosclerosis, or the buildup of deposits on the walls of the arteries, impedes the flow of blood and causes pain. The main goal of someone suffering with angina is to reduce the effects of atherosclerosis, which research has shown, can be reversed with diet, exercise, and relaxation techniques. For a complete analysis of how best to achieve this, please see the chapter Atherosclerosis page 31, which deals primarily with reducing cholesterol and improving the blood supply to the heart. This chapter is geared to improving the function of the heart itself. The suggestions in both chapters should be adopted (along with the recommendations of a physician, of course) in order for the treatment for angina to be most successful.

The supplement that has given my angina patients the most significant help when used in the context of an overall treatment plan is coenzyme Q10 (CoQ10). This supplement, also known as ubiquinone, plays an important role in fat and energy metabolism. It has been shown to be of extreme benefit to people who suffer with angina. It helps to prevent the accumulation of fatty acids within the heart muscle. Some reports claim that CoQ10 is ineffective, but I know that my patients invariably find that the supplement reduces their angina pain and increases their ability to exert themselves without discomfort. I suggest 30 to 60 mg. of CoQ10 three times a day. You should see results in one to three weeks.

In addition to coenzyme Q10 there are other supplements that can help give relief to angina. Beta-carotene, a powerful antioxidant, has been shown to have a significant effect in reducing attacks of angina (as well as strokes, heart attacks, and sudden cardiac deaths) in addition to reducing the likelihood of requiring surgical procedures related to angina. The most impressive evidence comes from a long-term study involving more than 22,000 male doctors who have been taking beta-carotene for an average of six years. The best effect seems to come when the beta-carotene is in the form of food and I suggest that my angina patients make a serious effort to eat at least five half-cup servings of fruits and vegetables daily—primary sources of beta-carotene. This is not as difficult to achieve as you may think: A half cup is just an average serving of sliced carrots or a slice of cantaloupe. The best sources of beta-carotene are yellow/orange fruits and vegetables including carrots, sweet potatoes, apricots, peaches, and cantaloupes and dark green leafy vegetables such as broccoli, spinach, kale, and arugula. You can also take beta-carotene supplements.

Low levels of vitamin E have been implicated in the development of angina. One study conducted in Scotland revealed that men with low levels of vitamin E were twice as likely to suffer from angina as those with high levels. One explanation may be that platelet adhesion—the "stickiness" of blood cells that correlates to heart disease—decreased as vitamin E levels increased. A World Health Organization study found low levels of vitamin E to be a major risk factor for death from heart disease. I think that vitamin E supplements are important.

Low levels of vitamin C are also related to heart disease, and I suggest that angina patients take a daily supplement of C.

Selenium is a mineral that has been connected to an increased incidence of angina and heart-related problems, and I suggest that my patients take a selenium supplement.

Magnesium is another mineral that's important for proper heart functioning. In fact, magnesium deficiencies have been shown to stimulate spasms of the coronary arteries. Magnesium has been used to control irregular heartbeat and, in some compelling studies, men dying of heart attacks have significantly lower levels of magnesium than normal men.

There's another supplement, carnitine, that is very helpful for angina patients. It improves the burning of fatty acids and thereby improves the heart muscle's exercise tolerance. There have also been studies that reveal that in addition to helping strengthen the heart muscle and improving exercise tolerance, carnitine aids in lowering of total cholesterol and triglyceride levels and prevents irregular heartbeat. Carnitine is a substance natural to the body, so there's no risk in taking it. I tell my angina patients to take DL-carnitine (available in health food stores).

Aspirin, as you may have heard, can help keep blood flowing freely and is therefore useful in treating angina. I recommend that patients take one baby aspirin (60 mg.) daily unless they have some other condition that precludes taking aspirin, like bleeding or peptic ulcer, sensitivity to aspirin, or very high blood pressure.

There are two other dietary modifications that you may have heard about in connection with angina. We now have evidence that olive oil plays a protective role in heart disease. You don't need to take excessive amounts of olive oil, but it simply makes sense to use it in cooking when you have an option and to choose dishes made with olive oil when eating at restaurants.

Fish oil is another substance that's connected with improved heart function. While no one is precisely certain exactly what component of fish oil has the desired effect, many studies have shown that increasing the consumption of fatty fish can make a dramatic difference in preventing heart disease. Evidence points to the fact that fish oil seems to "thin" the blood and also reduces dangerous blood fats, in particular triglycerides. One or two capsules of MaxEPA fish oil seem to have the desired effect although you also should make efforts to eat fish regularly instead of relying entirely on the MaxEPA supplement.

The supplements are important in improving heart function if you have angina, but you can no more rely on vitamins and minerals alone to help you than you can rely on nitroglycerin. You have to make changes in the way you live.

If you have angina, exercise is very important, but it should be done in a supervised situation. Make sure you discuss this with your cardiologist and ask for concrete recommendations.

Caffeine is a problem for people with heart disease, as it heightens the blood pressure and puts stress on the circulatory system. I tell my patients with angina to limit themselves to no more than one caffeinated drink per day. Most people opt for a cup of coffee in the morning and cut out all additional coffee or caffeinated sodas or teas. I might mention here that some of the bottled iced teas and soft drinks (even "un-colas" like Mountain Dew) have a great deal of caffeine in them.

Smoking takes a great toll on the heart, and it's crucial that if you have angina you stop smoking.

Alcohol can have a damaging effect on your heart; I instruct anyone with angina to stop drinking alcohol.

Stress management is important in managing your overall health and in preventing a heart attack. It's very helpful to learn some stress management techniques such as progressive relaxation or guided imagery.

NATURAL PRESCRIPTION FOR ANGINA

- Natural remedies will not preclude the need for the care of a cardiologist. You should follow your doctor's recommendations concerning your care, and don't discontinue any medication without consulting your doctor. The following measures are geared to work in conjunction with a supervised medical program.

- Reduce the amount of fat in your diet (see page xvii).

- Stop smoking.

- Eliminate caffeine or reduce consumption to no more than one cup of coffee or tea daily.

- Eliminate alcohol from your diet.

- Adopt a program of supervised exercise. Discuss this with your cardiologist.

- Adopt a program of stress management, for example progressive relaxation (see Stress Control, page 314).

IN ADDITION TO YOUR DAILY SUPPLEMENTS, PAGE xxiv, TAKE

- Coenzyme Q10: 30 to 60 mg. three times a day.

- Beta-carotene: five one-half cup servings of fruits and vegetables rich in beta-carotene including carrots, sweet potatoes, apricots, peaches, and cantaloupes and dark green leafy vegetables such as broccoli, spinach, kale, and arugula. Alternatively, you can take supplements of beta-carotene in amounts of 10,000 I.U. daily.

- Vitamin E: 400 I.U. daily.

- Vitamin C: 1,000 mg. daily.

- Selenium: 50 mcg. daily.

- Magnesium: 250 mg. three times a day.

- DL-Carnitine: 250 mg. three times a day.

- MaxEPA: 1,000 mg. three times a day.

- One baby aspirin (60 mg.) daily unless you suffer from aspirin sensitivity, high blood pressure, or bleeding or peptic ulcer.

IN ADDITION: Though research is preliminary, there is some fascinating material that supports the effectiveness of the amino acid L-lysine, taken in conjunction with vitamin C, in relieving angina. I suggest you try taking up to 3,000 mg. a day of lysine for a few weeks to see if this gives you any relief.

•   •   •

ARTHRITIS

IF YOU ARE OVER fifty years of age, there's an 80 percent chance that you have some degree of osteoarthritis, commonly known as arthritis. Most people are generally familiar with arthritis symptoms due to years of exposure to aspirin ads; they know that it affects the hands, hips, back, feet, and other weight-bearing joints. And they know that aspirin, or some version of a pain killer, is the major remedy. They are right that arthritis affects the joints, but they are under a common and sometimes dangerous misconception regarding aspirin and other pain killers. If you have arthritis, you should know that aspirin and other antiinflammatory drugs treat only the symptoms of the disease, and, in fact, they may actually facilitate its progress.

As arthritis develops, the joints become inflamed and begin to cause pain and swelling. Often people who feel mild symptoms go to their doctors, complain of stiffness, and are x-rayed in an effort to diagnose arthritis. However, arthritis shows up on an x-ray only after the joint has been affected long enough for it to actually change in appearance. Thus, if you feel symptoms of arthritis, even without concrete x-ray evidence, it is wise to begin natural therapy right away to prevent the further development of the disease.

Osteoarthritis usually begins with morning stiffness in a joint—a hip, a hand, the neck, or a knee. As you limber up during the course of the day, the pain disappears, but if the joint is overused the pain worsens. The weight-bearing joints are most commonly affected as cartilage between the joints is destroyed and joints rub against one another. The remaining cartilage can then harden and the edges of the bones develop small growths called spurs that inhibit movement. A patient will sometimes develop arthritis at the site of a surgery or an injury.

Arthritis can be difficult to live with. While painful, it's common and often doesn't seem to elicit much sympathy. But for some people it can inhibit everyday activities so that just making a cup of coffee in the morning can become an act of the will. ·

Your goal should be to reduce pain while at the same time encouraging joint mobility. Traditionally, symptoms are treated with aspirin and aspirin-like NSAIDs (nonsteroidal antiinflammatory drugs) or ibuprofen like Nuprin or Advil or stronger prescription medications. Many people simply take as much of these drugs as they can tolerate to relieve pain while trying to avoid side effects. The drawback of this course is that these drugs have been shown to inhibit cartilage repair—the very goal that the arthritic patient should hold uppermost. In addition, by masking pain, they can encourage people to overuse joints.

There is a roster of natural treatments that has proven to be dramatically effective for many people afflicted with arthritis. I suggest that all my patients try the treatments outlined here and many of them have been thrilled with the results.

The first thing to keep in mind if you have arthritis and you're past the age of fifty, as most arthritis patients are, is that your body is no longer as efficient at absorbing nutrients as it once was. What this means is that you may have nutritional deficiencies that could be affecting your overall health. Therefore, it's especially important for you to be taking a good quality antioxidant vitamin/mineral supplement as described in Blueprint for Health, page xvii.

One of the first goals of a patient with arthritis is to maintain a normal body weight. Excess body weight obviously puts a stress on the skeletal system and weight-bearing joints. One of my patients found that just losing 8 pounds and keeping her weight at an optimum 130 made a huge difference in the knee pain that she had endured for years.

In general I recommend that all my arthritis patients follow a good basic diet as described in Blueprint for Health, page xvii. It should be rich in whole grains, fresh vegetables, and fruits. Try to eliminate as many refined foods as possible as well as refined sugars, margarine, and preserved meats, all of which can exacerbate arthritic symptoms. Avoid fatty foods, including fried foods, butter, cream sauces, red meat, cheese, and nuts. Remember that your goal is not only to eliminate substances that might cause symptoms to flare up but also to compensate nutritionally for any aspirin and antiinflammatory drugs that you may have been taking.

You're probably heard about arthritis and the nightshade family of foods. This connection was originally made by Childers, a horticulturist, who found that eliminating foods of the nightshade family cured his arthritis. While his theory—that long-term consumption of the alkaloids in potatoes, tomatoes, eggplant, peppers, paprika, cayenne, and tobacco inhibit collagen and cartilage repair—has never been proven, it is true that some patients find relief from their symptoms when they eliminate the named foods. Try it for a month to see if you find any symptomatic relief. If not, reintroduce the foods gradually to see if you notice any change in symptoms.

The artificial sweetener Aspartame should be avoided by people with arthritis. Aspartame does not cause arthritis but many people who consume moderate or large amounts of it complain of joint pain. If you have joint pain, whether you think it's arthritis or not, eliminate all foods and drinks that contain Aspartame to see if your symptoms are affected.

There are several nutritional supplements that I have found successful in treating patients with arthritis. One is the mineral boron. It seems that people who live in places where there is a minimal amount of boron in the soil have a much higher incidence of arthritis. I tell my patients to supplement their diet with boron daily.

The other substance that I've had success with is an amino acid, methionine, which contributes to the creation and repair of cartilage. In one study, it was shown to be even more effective than Motrin in treating the pain of arthritis.

There's a great deal of evidence that fish oils protect and "lubricate" the joints, aiding in relief from arthritis. The best natural sources are herring, salmon, bluefish, and tuna, which lead the list in milligrams of fish oil. In addition there's a supplement, MaxEPA, found in health food stores, that contains fish oils and can be beneficial in relieving the symptoms of arthritis.

Aside from the more unusual supplements, there are familiar vitamins and minerals that have helped relieve the symptoms of arthritis, and I use them routinely with my patients.

Pantothenic acid, part of the vitamin B complex, has been shown to help prevent and alleviate arthritis. The connection between this nutrient and arthritis was made nearly forty years ago, and researchers are still struggling to come up with a definitive study that shows precisely how it works. But we do know that many people find relief from their symptoms with pantothenic acid. I suggest a supplement of 3 g. daily; you'll have to wait one to two weeks before you see any result. If no results are seen in three weeks, discontinue the supplement. Some physicians recommend up to 12 g. of pantothenic acid a day, but this should be taken only under your doctor's supervision.

Vitamin E, because of its antioxidant properties and also because it has been found to inhibit the breakdown of cartilage, is useful in treating arthritis.

Vitamin C, which is important for the synthesis of collagen and the repair of connective tissue, is helpful.

Vitamin B_6 has been helpful for many people. Interestingly, many older people are deficient in B_6: The first symptoms of a deficiency include tingling, pain, and stiffness in the hands. I suggest that arthritis patients take a supplement of B_6 in addition to the B_6 that's in your recommended daily antioxidant vitamin/mineral supplement.

One study found an important relationship between doses of NSAIDs and vitamins B_1 and B_{12}. It seems that in patients with arthritis, administration of these two B vitamins enhanced the effectiveness of the pain-killing drugs, allowing for a lower dosage of the drugs. The effect was seen in as little as seven days. If you take drugs for pain relief, it would be worth taking vitamins B_1 and B_{12} to see if they help you reduce your dosage.

Finally, vitamin A and the minerals zinc and copper are crucial to the formation of collagen and connective tissues. Be sure that your daily multivitamin contains at least the minimum RDA of these.

Exercise is vital to your success in dealing with arthritis. Many people will do anything to avoid exercise, even if they're perfectly well. Once they have a problem like arthritis, they feel they've found the perfect excuse not to exercise at all. In fact, arthritis is almost a commandment to exercise; if you don't you will find that your pain increases as muscles weaken and joints stiffen. The "move it or lose it" dictum is particularly true for people with arthritis, but it's important that you keep your exercise mild: If you exercise too vigorously, you can aggravate your condition and cause pain. I recommend that all my arthritis patients adopt at least one form of exercise. Pool exercise is the best choice because it strengthens muscles and increases circulation to the joints without putting any stress on them. Walking is great exercise for people with arthritis. A simple program that gets you walking briskly for twenty minutes to a half hour daily is fine. And now that so many shopping malls are open early for walkers, you can't even blame the weather for not getting in your daily half hour. Yoga is also an excellent exercise for arthritics. You might also contact your local Y to see if they have any exercises geared for arthritics.

In addition to exercise, there are physical therapies such as moist heat and cold packs that can provide short-term relief. Sometimes taking a soak in a warm tub once a day can relax the body and soothe the joints. Some patients find an afternoon nap that completely rests the body is enormously helpful.

NATURAL PRESCRIPTION FOR ARTHRITIS

- Maintain optimum body weight.

- Follow a good basic diet by eliminating as many refined foods as possible and adding whole grains, fresh vegetables, and fruits. It's particularly important to avoid sugars, fried foods, preserved meats, red meats, cheeses, cream sauces, and nuts.

- Increase your consumption of fish, especially herring, salmon, and tuna, to add fish oils to your diet.

- Avoid foods from the nightshade family including tomatoes, potatoes, eggplant, peppers, paprika, cayenne, and tobacco for a month. If you do not experience relief, reintroduce these foods to see if they affect your symptoms.

- Avoid the artificial sweetener Aspartame.

- Exercise daily for at least twenty minutes. Swimming, walking, and yoga are good choices.

- Use a heating pad or moist heat such as a soak in a warm tub to give relief.

- Try a regular afternoon nap to relax the body.

IN ADDITION TO YOUR DAILY SUPPLEMENTS, PAGE xxiv, TAKE

- Boron: 2 mg. daily.

- Methionine: 500 mg. two times daily.

- MaxEPA: 1,000 mg. three times daily.

- Pantothenic acid: 3 g. daily for three weeks; if no lessening of symptoms, discontinue. Some doctors recommend up to 12 g. of pantothenic acid daily, but this should be attempted *only* under a doctor's supervision.

- Vitamin E: 400 I.U. daily.

- To enhance the effectiveness of NSAIDs: vitamin B$_1$: 100 mg. daily; vitamin B$_{12}$: 1,000 mcg. in tablets dissolved under the tongue daily.
- Vitamin B$_6$: 50 to 100 mg. daily in divided doses.

IN ADDITION: I'm a great advocate of acupuncture for arthritis, and many of my patients have found it gives them dramatic relief from their symptoms, particularly in afflicted hips, knees, feet, and hands.

I've read recent reports of patients with arthritis who have been able to eliminate NSAIDs after taking glucosamine sulfate (three to four capsules daily for at least six weeks) along with one or two teaspoons daily of spray-dried barley grass juice (available under various names in health food stores).

• • •

ASTHMA

MANY PEOPLE HAVE a preconception about asthma that is totally out-dated. They imagine an overprotected kid who's a bit of a hypochondriac, sitting by the sidelines as his classmates play a vigorous game of kickball. Almost everything is wrong with this picture. First of all, asthma is not a psychosomatic illness; it's a very real chronic condition in which the upper airways become obstructed, resulting in wheezing and difficulty in breathing. It can be life-threatening. And an asthmatic is not precluded from athletics. In fact, in the 1972 Summer Olympics, five gold medalists in swimming events were asthmatics.

In an intense asthma attack, each inhalation or exhalation is a struggle as air whistles or wheezes through narrowed passages. A number of things happen during an attack: The smooth muscles of the bronchial tree (made up of tubes that distribute air throughout the lungs) go into spasmodic contractions; there is a swelling of the membranes that line the bronchial tubes; and the secretion of an abnormally sticky mucus increases. Coughing does not expel the mucus and it collects, clogging the smaller air passages. An attack can be brief or it can last long enough to require emergency treatment and lifesaving measures.

Asthma is a frustrating ailment because we still have a lot to learn about its exact causes. In addition, there has been recent bad news about the disease: Over the past few decades, deaths from asthma have increased slightly, but since 1980 the rate has gone up by 30 percent. And, while deaths from asthma are still relatively rare, the number of people suffering from the disease, particularly children and teenagers, is increasing. Speculations as to this increase in asthma cases range from greater pollution of air, water, and food supplies to the medications themselves.

The intensity of asthma cases varies widely. Some people will have occasional attacks of wheezing precipitated by specific exposure to cold, cats, certain foods, infection, or exercise. These attacks are usually self-limited and may not require any treatment. Others may only experience attacks when under stress. Some children "outgrow" their asthma only to have it return when they are older and under stress. For some unfortunate others, asthma is a lifelong illness. Some asthmatics require no medication whereas others require a spectrum, including inhaled bronchodilators, oral bronchodilators, inhaled corticosteroids, oral corticosteroids, and other inhaled medications to prevent attacks. Although drugs like bronchodilators may be essential for many, they treat only the symptoms without affecting the inflammatory response that is present in all cases of asthma.

Natural methods will not cure asthma any more than drug therapy will, but natural methods can help prevent attacks and perhaps reduce or eliminate the drugs required to control symptoms. My goal with asthmatics is to help them live a life as unaffected by symptoms as possible, with the ability to engage in any activity, to sleep through the night by strengthening the immune system, and to avoid the triggers that stimulate an asthma attack.

Some people experience an asthma attack once or twice a year following a bad cold or during a spell of unusually damp weather. Other people live with the effects of asthma every day. As we learn more about asthma, we begin to appreciate that it is, at least in part, an allergic response. The allergic responses associated with asthma are similar to those involved in other respiratory diseases such as hay fever and perennial allergic rhinitis (runny, congested nose). Here are some of the common triggers:

- Food allergies.
- Foods containing sulfites like beer, wine, fruit juices, shellfish, snack foods, fresh and dried foods, salads, and potatoes. Also foods containing MSG and the food-coloring additive tartrazine.
- Viral respiratory-tract infections including colds and the flu.

- Atmospheric pollutants including cigarette and industrial smoke, ozone, sulfur dioxide, nitrogen dioxide, and formaldehyde.
- Cold or dry air.
- Stress or emotional upset.
- Allergens including feathers, animal danders, dust mites, molds, and pollens.
- Exercise.
- Perfumes.
- Sawdust, particularly from oak and western red cedar.
- Dust from coffee, flour, and tea.
- Drugs including aspirin and nonsteroidal antiinflammatory drugs (like ibuprofen, indomethacin, fenoprofen, mefenamic acid, naproxen, phenylbutazone), beta blockers (including those given as eyedrops), cholinergic drugs (used to promote bladder contraction and as eyedrops for glaucoma), some inhalantional bronchodilator solutions, and drugs that contain sulfites or dyes such as tartrazine.
- Alcoholic beverages.
- Enzymes, including those in laundry detergents.
- Chemicals, including toluene and other ingredients used in solvents, paints, rubbers, and plastics.

Obviously, this is an exhaustive list. But not every asthmatic will react to each item on the list. If you are asthmatic, you should familiarize yourself with this list of triggers so that you can begin to make connections between your attacks and what may be causing them.

The best course for you to take is to keep a careful food diary of everything eaten for a period of one or two weeks. Any asthmatic reactions should be listed in the diary. Usually a pattern will evolve showing which foods cause a reaction. For more information, see Food Allergy, page 146.

When I was in medical school, I read a book by a physician who had had good results in treating asthma in children by eliminating all milk and dairy products. When I discussed the book with my professors, they said it was nonsense. I guess there are still people around who discredit the idea, but I've found that eliminating milk and cheese from the diet can be helpful for both asthmatic adults and children. This is not because dairy products stimulate mucus production but because they're very common causes of allergy, upper-respiratory allergies, and asthma.

Asthmatics must be particularly careful about food additives. The three most troublesome ones are MSG, sulfites, and tartrazine. Most people are aware of MSG problems. Also known as "Chinese restaurant syndrome" because of the large amounts used in some Chinese cooking, MSG can cause symptoms that include asthmatic attacks. Sometimes it's difficult to get a restaurant to tell you if they're using MSG, but if you tell them that you're asthmatic and that you could require emergency treatment if you eat MSG, they should be cooperative. Tartrazine, another food additive, can be more difficult to track down. It is a yellow dye (FD&C Yellow Dye No. 5) and is found in yellow foods, but it's also sometimes mixed with blue to color a food green. Over 300 items contain tartrazine, including commonly prescribed drugs. The food list includes beverages (particularly orange and lime drinks), ice cream and sherbets, desserts (gelatins and puddings), salad dressings, cheese dishes, cakes mixes and icings, seasoned salt and confections (butter flavor, banana and pineapple extract), and many miscellaneous items such as candies and fruit chews. Some asthmatics have had reactions to toothpaste and gum, particularly peppermint and wintergreen flavors. The only certain way to avoid tartrazine is to check the label (a manufacturer must list tartrazine if it's in the product), and if you're unsure, call the manufacturer.

Sulfites can cause serious problems for asthmatics. The Center for Science in the Public Interest has estimated that one in eleven asthmatics is sensitive to sulfites. Sulfites are no longer sprinkled on salads and fresh fruits but you can still find them in beer, wine, shrimp, and dried fruits like apricots. The various types of sulfites include sulfur dioxide, sodium or potassium sulfite, bisulfite, and metabisulfite. Incredibly, sulfites can also be an ingredient in many drugs that are used to treat asthma.

Avoid aspirin and aspirin-containing drugs as well as ibuprofen. Many asthmatics are sensitive to aspirin and reactions can be severe. Even if you've never had a reaction before, you could suddenly develop one.

FOODS CONTAINING SALICYLATES

Almonds	Cherries	Nectarines	Raisins
Apples	Cucumbers	Oranges	Raspberries
Apricots	Currants	Peaches	Strawberries
Blackberries	Gooseberries	Plums	Tomatoes
Boysenberries	Grapes	Prunes	

DRINKS CONTAINING SALICYLATES

Beer

Birch beer

Cider

Cider vinegars

Diet drinks and supplements

Distilled beverages
  (except vodka)

Kool-Aid and other
  artificially flavored beverages

Soft drinks

Tea

Wine

Wine vinegars

One very common stimulant to an asthma attack is simply lying down. Nearly 90 percent of asthma sufferers will regularly or occasionally wake between three and five o'clock in the morning coughing, wheezing, and short of breath. Some people only have asthmatic symptoms at night. The latest theory holds that this is because acid from the stomach flows back into the esophagus, causing reflux. The acid stimulates the nerves to the chest and lungs, and this stimulation/irritation leads to constriction of the bronchi. The solution is to prevent the acid reflux from occurring by avoiding late meals, lifting the head of the bed, and using medication to reduce stomach acid.

One of the long-term effects of asthma is that the lungs become clogged with mucus and lose their ability to function. You can help remedy this by drinking plenty of fluids. Ideally, you should drink about a half cup of water or other liquid every waking hour. If you can't manage this, at least drink eight glasses of fluid daily. Water and other beverages are natural expectorants that will help to keep mucus thin. I've suggested to asthmatic patients that they take a bottle of seltzer or mineral water to work and try to drink the whole thing by the end of the day. It's best to drink it at room temperature.

Warm liquids, like herb teas, soups, and warm cider, can be particularly soothing to asthmatics. Not only do they keep mucus fluid, they also can act as natural bronchodilators, relaxing the airways and, in some cases, preventing an attack entirely. This can be especially useful for children with asthma. If the child begins to feel an attack coming on, a warm drink can be distracting and relaxing. Sometimes averting anxiety can avert an attack.

While I advise all my patients not to drink more than one cup of coffee daily, if you're asthmatic and you feel an attack coming on, you can sometimes stop it by drinking a cup of coffee (not decaffeinated). Caffeine is actually very similar in effect to a popular asthma medication and can be effective on an occasional basis. I recommend coffee only in an unusual situation, such as leaving your medication at home.

It is critical for asthmatics to avoid smoke of any kind. That means they should live in a smoke-free house (even secondhand smoke is dangerous for asthmatics), and they should avoid exposure to auto exhaust, fireplace smoke, and the like as much as possible. If you like to run or exercise outdoors, be sure to do so away from major traffic routes where the fumes could bring on an attack.

Cold can cause an asthma attack. Most people can't move to a warm environment, but they can protect themselves from blasts of frigid air. If the weather is very cold, try to stay indoors. If you must go out, be sure to wear a scarf over your nose and mouth or a facemask. Try to avoid drinking very cold liquids.

Learn to breathe deeply. Many asthmatics use shallow breathing in an unconscious effort to preserve their lungs, breathing at only 60 to 70 percent of capacity. Try this breathing exercise a few times a day to encourage deeper breathing: Breathe in deeply and slowly through the nose, placing your hand just above your navel, feeling the air fill your stomach. Now exhale slowly through your mouth, feeling your stomach flatten until you're empty before you take your next breath. Repeat this about a dozen times.

Keep your air as clean as possible. Many asthmatics are aware that pets, mold, dander, and pollen can cause attacks. You should make every effort to keep your home free of these triggers. Bedrooms are particularly important. It's best to avoid dust-catchers including drapes, venetian blinds, and knickknacks. Also avoid rugs, woolen blankets, bedspreads, feather or kapok-filled pillows or quilts, horsehair mattresses, upholstered furniture, and stuffed animals. The house, and bedroom in particular, should be cleaned regularly. Change bed linens frequently, wash them in hot water, and vacuum your mattress once a week. The vacuums available that don't circulate dust are particularly useful for asthmatics. In addition I recommend an air filter for the bedroom. The best models are the high-efficiency particulate-arresting (HEPA) filters, which can relieve asthma symptoms in ten to thirty minutes.

Because as colds and upper-respiratory infections can cause an asthmatic attack, it's important to do your best to avoid catching a cold. This means taking special precautions during cold and flu season: avoid people who are sick; wash your hands frequently and keep them away from your nose and mouth; be sure to get a flu shot each season. If you do feel a cold coming on, treat it immediately: Take extra vitamin C, get plenty of rest, and drink lots of fluids.

Despite what you may have heard, exercise is beneficial to asthmatics. I recommend mild aerobic exercise like walking and swimming. Activities like baseball or golf that involve brief spurts of action separated by rests are much less likely to trigger an attack than sports that demand continuous action, like basketball or long-distance running. You should discuss exercise with your doctor to be sure it is safe for you; once you adopt an exercise program, *never* exercise to exhaustion. It is helpful to take vitamin C before exercise to help prevent an attack. If you or your doctor has any doubts about exercise, you might read *Asthma and Exercise* by Nancy Hogshead and Gerald Couzens. Ms. Hogshead, who has asthma, is an Olympic athlete with four medals.

Relaxation therapy can be useful in preventing the onset of an attack as it loosens the tightened muscles around the airways and helps to restore free breathing. I tell my asthma patients to learn the relaxation technique in Stress Control, page 314, and use it whenever they feel an attack beginning.

There are supplements that have proven helpful for asthmatics. Vitamin B_6, or pyridoxine, can be particularly useful. One well-known study completed in 1975 divided asthmatic children into two groups. One group received two 100 mg. tablets of B_6 daily; the other group, a placebo. After five months the results were tabulated, and the children on the B_6 had experienced fewer asthma attacks, less wheezing, less coughing, tightness, and breathing difficulty than the other children. Since then, other studies have confirmed these results. It's important to remember that you must continue the B_6 for at least three months before you can expect to see results. In the study with the asthmatic children, the most dramatic results were seen between the second and fifth month.

Vitamin C, mentioned earlier in connection with exercise, has been shown to reduce the number and severity of attacks. One study in Nigeria found that 1,000 mg. of vitamin C daily reduced attacks by 75 percent in comparison with a group taking a placebo.

Studies have also shown that people suffering from asthma are deficient in both zinc and selenium; it is useful to supplement both of these minerals.

Finally, magnesium and vitamin B_{12} supplementation can also be helpful.

NATURAL PRESCRIPTION FOR ASTHMA

- Become familiar with the triggers to asthma listed on pages 24–25 and try to avoid them.

- If you suffer from nighttime or early-morning asthma, consider an allergy to dust.

- Drink plenty of fluids, ideally one half cup of liquid every hour.

- Drink warm liquids, including herbal teas and soups, to relax bronchial passages.

- If you feel an attack coming on and medication is not available, drink one or two cups of caffeinated coffee.

- Avoid all smoke from cigarettes, auto exhaust, wood fires, and industry. If you exercise outdoors, do so well away from busy roads.

- Avoid cold air. Try to stay indoors on extremely cold days. If you do go out in the cold, cover your mouth and nose with a mask or scarf.

- Learn to breathe deeply. Practice the exercise described to recondition your breathing habits.

- Clean air is important. Avoid dust, pollen, pets with fur or feathers. Consider buying a HEPA-type air cleaner and a vacuum cleaner that does not spew dust.

- Avoid food additives including MSG, sulfites, and tartrazine (FD&C Yellow Dye No. 5).

- Investigate food allergies and avoid all potential allergenic foods, particularly milk and cheese.

- Try to prevent colds from developing.

- Avoid aspirin and nonsteroidal antiinflammatory drugs (like ibuprofen, indomethacin, fenoprofen, mefenamic acid, naproxen, phenylbutazone).

- Avoid foods that contain salicylates.

- Exercise (after consultation with your doctor). Take 1,000 mg. of vitamin C before exercise.

- Learn relaxation techniques to subvert an attack. See Stress Control, page 314.

IN ADDITION TO YOUR DAILY SUPPLEMENTS, PAGE xxiv, TAKE

- B_6: 100 mg. two times daily.

- Vitamin C: 1,000 mg. daily and 1,000 mg. before exercise.

- Magnesium: 400 mg. daily.

- Vitamin B_{12}: 1,000 mg. tablet dissolved under the tongue three or four times daily.

- Zinc: 50 mg. daily.

- Selenium: 100 mcg. daily.

IN ADDITION: There is some evidence that onions have an antiasthmatic and antiinflammatory effect. It couldn't hurt to add an onion a day to your diet to see if it's beneficial for you.

• • •

ATHEROSCLEROSIS

ATHEROSCLEROSIS AND ITS complications are the major causes of illness and death in the United States. Atherosclerosis is the excessive accumulation of cholesterol along the inner lining of arteries. But cholesterol is *not* the only cause of atherosclerosis and heart disease; it is a contributing factor. Cholesterol can only attach to the inner lining of the artery if it is damaged. This is the crucial factor that we will look at in an effort to understand how to control and reduce the development of atherosclerosis. Once the lining of the artery is damaged, white blood cells rush to the site followed by cholesterol, calcium, and cellular debris. The muscle cells around the artery are altered and also accumulate cholesterol. The fatty streaks in the arteries continue to develop and bulge into the arteries, thus cutting down the blood and oxygen supply of the tissues that are fed by that blood vessel. In addition, the elasticity of the blood vessel is diminished, and the arteries' ability to control blood pressure is compromised. Ultimately, if the progress of the atherosclerosis is not halted, the artery can be completely closed off and/or blood clots and debris that formed the blockage can break off and block other arteries. If the closed artery feeds the heart, its blockage can cause a heart attack. If the closed artery feeds the brain, its blockage can lead to a stroke. All arteries that are compromised—more rigid and less elastic—contribute to hypertension.

Most people are unaware that they suffer from atherosclerosis until they have a heart attack. You can have up to 80 percent closure of your arteries without ever feeling a symptom. Most people begin to develop atherosclerosis as children, and it's the unusual adult in the United States who does not have some degree of atherosclerosis.

A simple way to determine if you have atherosclerosis may be to examine your ears. Many studies have shown that a slightly curved vertical crease on the lower, fleshy part of the earlobe correlates with the degree of atherosclerosis. Because the earlobe is so dense with blood vessels, it is believed that when the blood flow is compromised over a period of time and the vessels begin to collapse, the evidence becomes obvious in the earlobe crease. The earlobe crease (about one quarter inch from the face) is not age related, although it is more common as you age and, of course, so is atherosclerosis. A crease in your ear does not mean that you definitely have atherosclerosis but it is certainly a warning signal to be taken seriously.

A fascinating report from a physician in Tennessee tells of a patient who, at the age of forty, developed an earlobe crease. After following a general fitness program, including walking and a regime of nutritional therapy, his earlobe crease had disappeared by age forty-nine. It's interesting to note that this man did not modify his cholesterol consumption. This case helps to make the point: You can reduce your level of atherosclerosis and improve your chances of avoiding our number one killer by adopting changes in your lifestyle.

Most people who come to see me in connection with atherosclerosis do so because they're concerned about elevated cholesterol levels. It's easy to focus on cholesterol levels as the demon messenger of heart disease. Perhaps the hardest task I have as a physician is to convince people that their emphasis on cholesterol level is misplaced; cholesterol is not the only major determining factor of their chances of having a heart attack. Many people with low cholesterol levels have heart attacks and strokes. Dr. Michael DeBakey, a prominent heart surgeon, has been quoted as saying: "I operate on people with severe atherosclerosis. Only a third of them have high cholesterol."

Some people, upon learning that their cholesterol level is "high," are determined to simply take a drug to lower it. But it's alarming to recognize, as recent studies have shown, that many cholesterol-lowering drugs themselves cause a higher incidence of death from both heart disease and other causes including everything from gallbladder disease to kidney failure. Despite this, many people continue to take them. Unless you have severe hyperlipidemia (a genetic abnormality that affects the way the body responds to cholesterol), you should reconsider use of cholesterol-lowering medications and stick with natural remedies that provide a comprehensive approach to fighting atherosclerosis.

What factors, besides cholesterol, encourage development of atherosclerosis?

- There's evidence that the female sex hormone estradiol, which is present in the blood of men, plays a role in development of atherosclerosis: Some research has determined that the higher the level of estradiol, the greater the chance of heart disease. This hormone level is affected by a number of things including heredity and nutrition.

- There's evidence that high levels of insulin promote heart disease.

- Research points to a common virus, the cytomegalovirus, as the first step in the development of atherosclerosis.

- Additional research links low levels of vitamin B_6 to incidence of atherosclerosis and heart disease.

- There's compelling evidence that uncontrolled stress promotes heart disease.

- And there's overwhelming evidence that lack of exercise puts more people at risk for atherosclerosis and heart disease than high cholesterol levels!

What do all these findings mean to you? The important lesson is that you must make a multipronged approach to fighting atherosclerosis. You can't depend on working feverishly at lowering your cholesterol and nothing else. You can't ignore other factors if you already have low cholesterol. You can't simply exercise constantly and think that will take care of everything—you have to look at *all* the factors involved. The treatment for atherosclerosis is the same as the prevention. In addition, most of the changes you'll make to prevent atherosclerosis will promote overall good health.

In addition to adopting a low-fat diet to help reduce cholesterol, there are four lifestyle changes that are important factors: adopting an exercise program, cutting out smoking, eliminating alcohol, and controlling stress.

The first and perhaps most important is adopting an exercise program. Sedentary living is the major cause of fatal heart attacks. This is exciting news because it is the easiest thing to change. Sedentary people are almost twice as likely to die of heart attacks as people who are active. Regular exercise strengthens the heart muscle, reduces blood pressure, keeps blood sugar levels regulated, helps reduce stress, and lowers body weight. It also lowers blood levels of damaging LDL cholesterol while raising the HDL, or good cholesterol, levels. Almost all of my patients have been able to do this, even the ones who resisted most vehemently, by simply walking briskly for about a half hour several days a week. Many of my patients are veterans of gyms that they gave up on and exercise tapes and free-weights, and a variety of other failed efforts. Walking is the perfect answer for them—they don't need equipment, they can walk anywhere, and they're not dependent on a class or a schedule. And, of course, it's easy. There are many excellent books available on how to establish a program of exercise walking, and I suggest that you buy one and get started.

As you might guess, smoking promotes the developing of atherosclerosis. Tobacco smoke actually is more damaging to the heart than it is to the lungs. Smokers have a greater chance of having a heart attack—three times greater than nonsmokers—and a greater risk of dying of the attack —twenty-one times greater than nonsmokers. Tobacco smoke contains carbon monoxide, which is uniquely damaging to the heart. Not only does it reduce the amount of oxygen the heart is able to receive, but it also actually damages the cells of the heart, making them less able to produce energy and thereby weakening the heart. In addition to the dangers of carbon monoxide, there's the danger of nicotine. Nicotine interferes with the electrical impulses that cause the heart to beat. When the blood flow is compromised, the heart can beat in the fast, uncontrolled, irregular beats that actually cause a heart attack. If you smoke, reducing the risks of atherosclerosis is yet another reason to quit. Even if you've smoked for years, stopping now will immediately help combat the development of atherosclerosis.

You've probably read about the recent studies suggesting that red wine is helpful in preventing heart disease. This finding is not new, and it's been controversial for years. The bottom line is that the evidence on alcohol in terms of atherosclerosis is mixed. A modified amount *may* be helpful; more than a moderate amount is definitely harmful. I think that it's very difficult for people to interpret these findings, and the medical community wants to be conservative but not reactionary. The problem is that moderate for some people is a glass of wine with dinner while for others it's a half a bottle of Scotch over the course of an evening, every evening. While moderate amounts of alcohol may reduce your risk for heart disease, anything above "moderate" elevates your serum cholesterol triglycerides and your uric acid levels and also may increase your blood pressure, all of which promote the development of atherosclerosis. My advice is to eliminate alcohol completely.

Stress management is the dark horse of atherosclerosis control. Most people pay it lip service, but they're not sure exactly what it means or how it can even be accomplished. Dr. Dean Ornish, the guru of heart disease combat, made stress control and even "spirituality" an important factor in his program for heart disease. It seems that some people who were stringent about other factors but lax about stress control were still vulnerable to a heart attack. One recent study showed that office workers under enormous pressure to meet a deadline had much higher cholesterol and triglyceride levels than those same workers a few weeks later when the deadlines had been met.

Stress isn't only caused by an angry boss; you actually create your own stress in a sense when you get angry. A recent study in *The American Journal of Cardiology* found that when people with heart disease get angry, the pumping efficiency of their hearts drops by five percentage points. This study found that once you've gotten to the point where you have heart disease, getting angry has a direct negative effect on your heart. But anger can affect you before you develop actual heart damage; one study found that doctors with the highest levels of hostility while in medical school were seven times as likely to have died by the age of fifty as were those with low levels. In fact, hostility was a stronger predictor of death than other risk factors including smoking, high blood pressure, and high cholesterol. You can't completely avoid anger, but by being aware of it and by using stress control techniques, you can mitigate the danger of anger to your heart.

You must take stress reduction seriously if you want to combat atherosclerosis. Stress management techniques are simple and easy to learn. For more information on this subject see Stress Control, page 314.

If you make the life changes recommended above, you'll considerably lessen your development of atherosclerosis. But there is more you can do by modifying your diet and taking supplements.

As you might guess, one of the main goals of a heart-healthy diet is a reduction of serum cholesterol. (This is a concern only if your cholesterol level is over 200. If your cholesterol is below that number, you should still make the dietary recommendations, but you should not consider using any supplements to lower your cholesterol.)

You may know that both high-density lipoprotein (HDL) and low-density lipoprotein (LDL) cholesterol levels are important. While high readings for the total cholesterol and LDL cholesterol are considered the classic predictors of high risk, there's strong evidence that low HDL levels are just as good an indicator of risk for heart disease. Some research shows that in women low HDL levels may be even more indicative of potential problems—below 40 mg. (50 mg. for premenopausal women) could signal trouble even if total cholesterol is normal. On the other hand, high levels of HDL can shoot a total cholesterol score into the theoretical danger zone when, in fact, concern may be misplaced.

People with serum cholesterol levels of 256 mg./dl. or over have a five times greater risk of developing heart disease than those people whose levels are below 200. There's no escaping that connection. The serum levels of LDL cholesterol are directly related to your increased risk of heart disease: The higher the figure, the greater your risk. On the other hand the HDL cholesterol is actually protective against atherosclerosis.

If you are on medications to lower your cholesterol, despite the fact that, as I mentioned earlier, some of these medications do more harm than good, I don't recommend that you simply stop them. You should follow my recommendations after consulting with your doctor, and never stop taking medications *without* a consultation. Some of my patients have been able to reduce or eliminate their cholesterol-lowering drugs while others have not.

How do you lower your cholesterol? Remember that it's not just by eating foods with less cholesterol, though that's important. Exercising, limiting alcohol, reducing stress, and taking supplements, as well as reducing your intake of all fats, will help. It is too difficult for people to follow a diet that prescribes a percentage level of fat. It's much easier to work with the foods themselves. Cut way down on high-fat foods including red meat, cheese, eggs, cream sauces, nuts, chocolate, ice cream, butter, margarine, mayonnaise, and avocado. (Olive oil can be a part of a cholesterol-reducing diet.) It's best to completely avoid fried foods and it's important to cut down on sugar intake. Most people don't realize that sugar affects cholesterol and definitely affects triglycerides, another fat in the blood which is now recognized as a factor in heart disease. Sugar stimulates insulin production, which in turn increases triglycerides. Men, in particular, seem to be sensitive to this effect from sugar (see Blueprint for Health, page xvii, concerning fat and sugar in the diet).

Speaking of sugar, I should mention that the mineral chromium, which helps stabilize blood sugar, can also raise the level of the HDL or "good" cholesterol. If you're trying to improve your cholesterol reading, take 100 mcg. of chromium three times daily.

Another dietary factor that's connected with the development of atherosclerosis is caffeine. People who drink large amounts of caffeine—six cups a day or more—are far more prone to elevated cholesterol. This connection doesn't hold for tea drinkers. I tell my patients to limit themselves to one cup of coffee a day and eliminate caffeinated sodas entirely.

It's also important to increase the fresh fruits and vegetables you consume daily. Just a few simple additions to your diet can make a significant overall change. In one study, people who ate just two carrots daily had an 11 percent reduction in their cholesterol levels. And this was after just eleven days! Concentrate on increasing your consumption of fresh fruits and vegetables: You should eat four servings daily. You'll also be increasing your fiber intake, which is very useful in lowering cholesterol levels: It decreases LDL levels while increasing HDL levels. The best way to get adequate amounts of fiber is to eat oat bran cereal for breakfast.

There are certain foods that have been shown to be helpful in lowering cholesterol and preventing the development of atherosclerosis. They include onions and garlic, which have been shown to decrease the tendency for blood to clot after a fatty meal. In addition, onions and garlic have been shown to reduce hypertension and to lower cholesterol. You don't need to make a fetish of eating onions and garlic, but I do recommend that you use them freely in cooking.

Garlic also lowers cholesterol and triglycerides while it increases HDL levels. Garlic capsules can be bought at health food stores; I tell my patients to take three capsules a day.

If you are unable to lower your cholesterol with diet and exercise, then niacin supplements could be helpful to you. There is a "no flush" niacin that's been proven safe and helpful that I recommend to my patients.

In addition to the lifestyle and dietary changes outlined above, there are certain supplements that have been shown to help reduce and eliminate the progress of atherosclerosis.

As mentioned, the deposits on the artery walls that begin the process of atherosclerosis start with actual damage to the artery wall; cholesterol does not simply build up in the blood and then get stored along the walls of healthy arteries.

As one of the primary causes of atherosclerosis is a damaged site on an artery that allows fatty buildup, we have to look at how the artery walls become damaged in the first place. Much evidence points to free-radical damage as being one of the instigators of arterial wall damage. Free radicals are highly reactive substances that are found all around us —in polluted air, herbicides, tobacco smoke, radiation—and also within us as a by-product of normal metabolic processes. Free radicals attack and damage cells and thus subvert the normal course of cell activity. Most of us witness examples of the work of free radicals every day: They make metal rust, make fruit spoil, and make oil go rancid.

Our first line of defense against free radicals is the antioxidant supplements (see page xxiv), which include the vitamins C, E, beta-carotene, and selenium, the cornerstones of our body's pollution-control device that inactivates free radicals. Many studies have found a direct connection between intake of the antioxidant vitamins and the incidence of atherosclerosis. A recent eight-year study showed that taking daily doses of vitamin E appears to cut the risk of heart disease by one third to one half. Another fascinating study found that a high level of antioxidants in the blood can be more significant to your health than either your cholesterol level or your blood pressure. I suggest that all my patients take antioxidants; patients who are on a program geared to controlling and reducing atherosclerosis should take even greater amounts.

There are other nutrients that play a significant role in preventing atherosclerosis. Indeed, quite recently a cover story in *The New York Times* was titled "Support Grows for Vitamins as Roadblocks to Heart

Disease." It seems that every day there's new evidence supporting the protective ability of certain nutrients against the development of atherosclerosis, among other diseases.

One nutrient that has received a great deal of attention in this regard is vitamin B_6, or pyridoxine. According to one widely held theory, a deficiency of B_6 can lead to the accumulation of a substance that is damaging to the cells that line the circulatory system, thus setting in motion the first step in the development of atherosclerosis. Vitamin B_6 has other benefits in relation to the heart and circulatory system; for example, it inhibits the platelet aggregation or clotting that slows the flow of blood.

Another supplement that seems to be enormously helpful in fighting the development of atherosclerosis is coenzyme Q10, which is also known as ubiquinone. This supplement helps to prevent the accumulation of fatty acids within the heart muscle.

Magnesium is a mineral that's critical for proper heart functioning. In fact, magnesium deficiencies have been shown to stimulate spasms of the coronary arteries. Men dying of heart attacks have significantly lower levels of magnesium than healthy men. Moreover, magnesium increases HDL levels, decreases platelet aggregation, and lessens clotting potential. One interesting study revealed that the rate of heart disease is inversely correlated to the magnesium content of the water supply.

There's another nutritional supplement, carnitine, that's useful in fighting atherosclerosis. It improves the burning of fatty acids and thereby improves the heart muscle's exercise tolerance. It also increases HDL levels while decreasing triglyceride and cholesterol levels.

Fish oils or omega-3 oils have been recognized as helpful in preventing the development of atherosclerosis. Eskimos and the Japanese, who eat diets that are high in fish oils, have lower rates of cardiovascular disease. The best natural source of fish oils is fish, particularly fatty fish such as salmon. I also recommend that you take a MaxEPA supplement.

NATURAL PRESCRIPTION FOR ATHEROSCLEROSIS

- Reduce all fats in the diet, particularly cholesterol-rich foods including red meat, cheese, eggs, cream sauces, nuts, chocolate, ice cream, butter, margarine, mayonnaise, and avocado.

- Eliminate fried foods entirely.

- Reduce sugar intake.

- Eliminate caffeine consumption or cut down to one caffeinated drink daily.

- Eat at least four servings of fresh fruits and vegetables daily.

- Increase fiber intake. Oat bran cereal at breakfast is a good way to do this.

- Use onions liberally in cooking.

- Use garlic liberally in cooking and/or take garlic capsules: one capsule three times daily.

- Adopt a regular exercise program. Walking three times a week for a half hour is a good beginning.

- Stop smoking.

- Eliminate alcohol.

- Control stress and work particularly hard to control anger (see Stress Control, page 314).

- Increase consumption of fish, particularly salmon.

IN ADDITION TO YOUR DAILY SUPPLEMENTS, PAGE xxiv, TAKE

- Vitamin C: 1,000 mg. daily.

- Vitamin E: 400 I.U. daily.

- Beta-carotene: 10,000 mg. daily.

- Selenium: 50 mcg. daily.

- Vitamin B$_6$: 100 mg. daily.

- Coenzyme Q10: 30 to 60 mg. three times daily.

- Magnesium: 250 mg. three times daily.

- Carnitine: 250 mg. three times daily.

- MaxEPA: 1,000 mg. three times daily.

- Chromium: 100 mcg. three times daily.

IF YOUR CHOLESTEROL IS HIGH TAKE:

- Niacin: 500 mg. three times daily of the "no flush" variety.

• • •

ATHLETE'S FOOT

IN THE DAYS WHEN only athletes spent hours in sweaty socks and gyms, they were the primary victims of athlete's foot. But today, as more and more of us work out regularly, athlete's foot is more common. A combination bacterial/fungal infection, athlete's foot usually begins with redness between the toes that eventually cracks, peels, burns, and itches and sometimes blisters.

When you understand the actual cause and conditions that promote athlete's foot, you'll see that prevention is the best course. The fungal/bacterial infection that develops into athlete's foot requires dead skin and a moist, warm environment. The calluses and dead skin that surround toenails as well as the dead skin on the feet that usually doesn't get scrubbed away provide an ideal growth medium for athlete's foot. When the bacteria have been introduced to the foot and the foot is stuffed into a pair of sweaty socks and hot shoes, you create a perfect environment for a troublesome case of athlete's foot. Once athlete's foot develops, it is easily transmitted by a damp bath mat or a wet shower-room floor.

Here are some basic steps to take to prevent athlete's foot and to avoid recurrence.

- Keep your feet clean. Once any soreness or cracking has cleared up, scrub your feet and toes with a brush to remove dead skin when you shower. Pay special attention to your toenails, brushing beneath them as well as you can. If you bathe instead of shower, rinse your feet in fresh water after your bath.

- Keep your feet dry. Let them dry for five or ten minutes after a shower before putting on shoes. Use a hair dryer on your feet to thoroughly dry them, and dust them with antifungal powder before putting on your socks.

- Wear clean, dry cotton socks. Change them a couple of times a day if necessary to ensure dryness. Make sure you wash your socks in hot water to help kill fungus spores.

- Dust the insides of your shoes with antifungal powder.

- Let your shoes dry thoroughly between wearings: This usually means alternating shoes instead of wearing the same pair every day.

- Wear shower shoes to prevent infection at the gym or pool or any place where people go barefoot.

If you do develop a case of athlete's foot, there are some natural remedies that should help you.

Vitamin E can help the skin heal. Puncture a vitamin E capsule and squeeze it directly onto the irritation.

Take a teaspoon of acidophilus (available at health food stores) mixed in water on an empty stomach in the morning and at night. These bacteria—the ones used to make yogurt—help restore the normal, healthy balance of good bacteria that protect you from infection.

Finally there's an over-the-counter topical preparation that used to be available only by prescription that can really help. It's a 1 percent clotrimazole cream and, if you use it for two or three nights in a row according to the package directions, you will get the infection under control.

NATURAL PRESCRIPTION FOR ATHLETE'S FOOT

- If you do develop athlete's foot, you should immediately adopt all the steps recommended above for avoiding and preventing it, except for brushing the feet while showering (until the worst irritation clears up).

- Puncture a capsule of vitamin E and squeeze it directly onto the irritation.

- Take one teaspoon of acidophilus mixed in water on an empty stomach in the morning and at night.

- Use an over-the-counter preparation containing 1 percent clotrimazole (brand name: Lotrimin), according to package directions.

. . .

BACK PAIN

BACK PAIN IS almost as common as the common cold in keeping people from work, keeping them from activities they enjoy, and keeping them generally uncomfortable and sometimes in serious pain. The tragedy of most back pain is that it's avoidable. Of course, there are different varieties of back pain. Some people suffer an occasional backache after they do too much yardwork; some women get a backache every month with their period; some people get a backache after an all-day car ride. These backaches have obvious causes. Usually a bit of rest, an aspirin or a simple pain reliever, and a heating pad solve the problem. But the people who often complain to me are those who have chronic "bad backs." That is, they feel fine most of the time, but then, seemingly out of the blue their lower back will begin to ache. They may be under particular stress, or perhaps they just moved in an odd way when they got into the car. Sometimes they can point to a particular event that participated the pain, but often they can't. Occasionally the pain is so bad that they have to go to bed. Sometimes the pain lasts for a day; sometimes for a few weeks; sometimes for a month or two.

Before I say any more about backs, I should tell you that if you have severe pain, pain that lasts for more than several days, or weakness or tingling in your legs and feet, you should consult a doctor. Back problems that are caused by congenital deformities or severe injuries will need the care of a physician. But if you have occasional or even regular general pain, you probably can rid yourself of that pain by following some basic rules and adopting a simple exercise program. I've found that one of the biggest challenges in controlling back pain is convincing the patient that simple measures, if adopted consistently, really will make a difference.

The spine is a finely tuned instrument, and its proper functioning depends on a complex system of muscles, ligaments, and bones. The spine is, in effect, a collection of more than thirty bones that are lined up like spools on a rod. The vertebrae—the "spool" bones—are separated by a spongy pad called a disk, which acts as a shock absorber. The term "slipped disk" is misleading: a disk never slips, but it sometimes bulges out and presses against a nerve in the spine, causing pain. Most pain in the lower back is caused by strained and torn muscles, ligaments, and tendons. Disk injury, which is less common, can be more serious. Sometimes the muscles that surround the injured back can go into spasms that effectively immobilize the back (nature's way of preventing further movement) but the spasms can also be severely painful. If you have pain that radiates down your leg, this is known as sciatica, caused by irritation of the sciatic nerve, usually due to pressure from a disk. If the pain is severe, see a doctor for an evaluation. Just remember that in many cases, natural remedies will work as well as medications or surgery.

What do you do when you suddenly feel that major ache in your back? If you're feeling discomfort, the best thing may be to take aspirin or a NSAID like ibuprophen to relieve pain. If you have a history of acid indigestion, heartburn, or ulcer symptoms, acetaminophen is the preferred pain reliever. (Remember that the use of pain relievers should be for the short term only. I recently had a patient who had taken so much ibuprofen to relieve his back pain that he suffered kidney damage. Fortunately, the damage was not permanent. NSAIDs can also irritate the stomach and exacerbate an ulcer.) It's also very helpful to take 1,200 mg. of calcium to help relax your back. Then you need to rest your back; this is best done in bed with your knees raised. While you are resting, you can begin simple stretching exercises: With one leg flat on the bed, pull the other bent knee to your chest. Hold it there for a few seconds and then release it and repeat with the other leg.

While you may need time to rest a back when you feel initial pain, too much bedrest is actually counterproductive; resting muscle fibers start to shorten and stiffen within days, and as little as two weeks of bed rest can cause demineralization of your bones; their return to normal can take many months. You should not spend more than a day or two immobilized. As soon as you feel able, you should start moving and begin the crucial exercises that will help you heal your back and avoid future problems. The key to a strong, healthy back is movement: Regular, correct movement will relieve pain, get you strong, and keep your healthy.

Marianne, a graphic designer, is one of my patients who has learned to conquer her back problems. Here is how she describes her backaches: "My back got really bad after my third baby. I'd always had occasional back twinges but nothing serious. Then after my daughter was born my back would go into spasms about every couple of months. I'd have to lie in bed for days until I could move again. Needless to say, with three children, this wasn't easy. Sometimes I'd feel pain for weeks at a time, and it affected every minute of my day. I'd get impatient with the kids, and I always felt tired.

"But now that I know how to treat my back, I haven't had an ache in two years. I always knew I should do exercises for my back, but I just never did. Now I do them every morning. They're simple and they take almost no time. I do back stretches, bent-knee sit-ups, and some pelvic tilts. That's it. Of course I'm careful about lifting and how I move and bend, and stretch regularly when I'm working at my desk. The relief of not having weeks of distracting pain is certainly worth a few minutes of exercises every morning."

Many people with back problems are aware that exercises might help, but they don't do them. I can't tell you how many patients have told me that they stopped back exercises because they seemed so simple they didn't believe they could really be making a difference and besides, their back was feeling okay. The truth is exercises make *all* the difference and they can help you banish back pain entirely. The key to avoiding back problems is developing strong limber muscles in the lower back and also in the abdomen.

In addition to the simple stretch you can do in bed, here are three exercises that you should do at least once, and probably twice a day.

- Bent-knee sit-ups: Lie on your back with your knees bent. With your arms extended toward your knees, do a sit-up. It is not necessary to actually sit up; in fact you should simply lift your head and shoulders off the floor. You'll feel the pull in your stomach. You should do twenty-five of these. When your stomach muscles are strengthened, you can cross your arms in front of your chest as you do the sit-up.

- Pelvic tilt: Lie on the floor and tilt your pelvis so that the small of your back is flattened into the floor. Press your back down while counting to ten. Repeat this exercise ten times.

- Wall press: Stand about 10 inches from a wall. Bending your knees, let your back rest against the wall (use your hands to guide you back so your back muscles won't strain). As in the pelvic tilt, press the small of your back hard into the wall, feeling the stretch in both your back and in the front of your thighs. Hold for a count of ten. Repeat two or three times.

This last wall-press exercise is very effective in stretching your back and in relieving pain. It's particularly useful if you work at a desk or in a sitting position. Most people aren't aware that sitting is the position that's hardest on the back. Even if you sit correctly in a well-designed chair, the pressure on your disks is twice that when you stand. And when you lie down, the pressure is half what it is when you're standing. If you sit for long periods, it's essential that you take frequent breaks. I tell my patients that they should break for a back stretch every half hour. Stand up, do a wall press or two, stretch the arms and neck.

In addition to these crucial back exercises, it's important that you get regular exercise that works the whole body. The best activities for back pain include swimming, cycling (providing you cycle in an upright position), walking (probably the best overall exercise), and rowing (if you are scrupulous about maintaining a straight back). Activities that are more risky because of back twisting and jarring include jogging, golf, tennis, bowling, football, basketball, baseball, and weight lifting.

Obesity can be a major factor in back problems. It stands to reason that a back that is carrying excessive weight can readily become strained. If you are overweight, you need to reduce.

Nutrition is important in maintaining a healthy back, and certain supplements can help relieve pain and strengthen tissue. Be sure to take vitamin C; also, calcium at bedtime to relax muscles.

If you have been told that your back pain is associated with arthritis, the fish oil supplement MaxEPA can be beneficial.

There are many tips that can help you with your everyday movements for times when your back is in pain and also to help you relieve back stress.

NATURAL PRESCRIPTION FOR BACK PAIN

- If you are in severe pain, if you feel tingling in your legs or feet, if your backache is due to a congenital deformity or an injury, you should consult a doctor. You may still be able to heal your back yourself with the exercises below, but you should confirm that nothing serious is wrong with your back first.

- If you're feeling pain in your back, try to rest it; if necessary, rest in bed. Do the knee-to-chest exercise described earlier, alternately lifting one knee to your chest, keeping the other leg flat on the bed. Do this every half hour or so while resting in bed.

- Do the four basic exercises every morning and every evening: the knee-to-chest stretch, the bent-knee sit-up, the pelvic tilt, and the wall press. You must do them religiously if you want to enjoy their benefits.

- Don't do any strenuous exercise first thing in the morning.

- When severe pain is improved, get regular aerobic exercise such as walking, cycling, and so on.

- If you sit for long periods of time, you must take regular breaks that include doing the wall press and overall stretching. Take a break every half hour. This includes stopping while on long car or plane rides to stretch.

- If you are overweight, you must lose weight to lessen the strain on your spine.

IN ADDITION TO YOUR DAILY SUPPLEMENTS, PAGE xxiv, TAKE

- Vitamin C: 500 mg. three times daily with meals.

- Calcium: 1,200 mg. at bedtime.

- Vitamin E: 400 I.U. daily.

- MaxEPA: 1,000 mg. three times daily (if you have been told that you have arthritis that contributes to your back pain).

HERE ARE SOME TIPS ON BACK-WISE WAYS TO GET THROUGH YOUR DAY

- Pay attention to your posture: Stand with your back straight, your pelvis tucked under, and your knees relaxed. Avoid any position that puts you in a swayback position.

- Never bend with the knees straight; always lift using your leg muscles, not your back muscles.

- When you work standing up, such as at a sink, rest one of your feet a few inches from the floor, say, on the base cabinet or a low stool. This keeps your pelvis tucked in rather than swaybacked.

- When sitting, try to keep your knees higher than your hips by resting your feet on an ottoman or a pile of books. This is especially important if you spend long periods of time sitting.

- Keep your car seat close to the steering wheel so your lower back is flattened and you're not leaning forward.

- Try not to sleep on your stomach, but if you must, try using a pillow under your hips to prevent a swayback position.

- Never bend forward without bending your knees and tucking your buttocks under.

IN ADDITION: I feel that acupuncture is the most effective treatment for lower back pain. This does not supplant the need for regular exercise, but it can help relieve pain and inflammation and make daily activity, including exercise, easier.

There is an antiinflammatory drug, colchicine, that seems to be helpful in relieving back pain for some people when injected intravenously. If natural treatments are not successful, you might discuss colchicine with your doctor.

•   •   •

BAD BREATH

MOST PEOPLE HAVE bad breath now and again; it's the constant or recurring cases of bad breath that can offend friends and loved ones and become a real social problem. There are a number of causes of bad breath and, fortunately, most of them are easily dealt with using simple natural techniques.

Whatever the cause of your bad breath I should tell you that the most common remedy is not only ineffective, it's counterproductive. I'm talking about mouthwashes. Mouthwashes are a combination of flavors, a bit of dye, and too much alcohol. (Children have been brought to the edge of death by drinking mouthwash!) While the claims that mouthwashes kill bacteria are true, it's also true that the bacteria quickly come back—and in greater force than before you used the mouthwash. But in addition to being ineffective, mouthwash can also be dangerous. Too much mouthwash is irritating to the gums, the palate, the tongue, and the mucous membranes of the mouth. And in a small percentage of people who are susceptible, and particularly if they smoke and drink, heavy use of mouthwash can cause certain types of cancer.

If you do want to use something to freshen your breath, you can put a few drops of peppermint oil in a glass of water and rinse (don't swallow it). You can get peppermint oil at a pharmacy.

Bad breath, or halitosis, has a number of causes, the most obvious being bad dental hygiene. If you don't brush your teeth regularly and well, bits of pieces of food will become lodged between your teeth and will decompose, causing a bad odor. You probably already know that you should brush your teeth carefully twice a day, but there are some other measures you can take to fight bad breath.

Brushing your tongue is probably the single most effective thing you can do. In studies, it has been shown that brushing the tongue alone is a better guard against bad breath than brushing only the teeth. Brushing both teeth and tongue can help reduce bad breath due to poor dental hygiene almost entirely. You don't need to scrub your tongue; just gently brush it with a soft-bristled brush to wash away the microscopic bits of food that become trapped in the tiny protuberances.

Flossing is also important for fresh breath. It liberates bits of food and gunk that could otherwise promote odor. Floss at least once a day, preferably just before brushing.

If you use dentures, don't forget to clean them regularly and thoroughly. Like natural teeth, they harbor food and bacteria that can cause bad breath.

Don't forget to change your toothbrush regularly. You should replace your old toothbrush about every two months. Not only does a fresh toothbrush clean more effectively, it also eliminates any buildup of bacteria that's begun to colonize your old one.

Brushing after every meal is a good way to fight bad breath, but most of us can't do it. Instead, just swish a mouthful of water around and spit it out along with bits of food that could otherwise invite bad breath microorganisms to grow on your tongue and teeth.

What you eat can sometimes help fight bad breath. Snacks like carrots, apples, and celery all help to fight the development of plaque on the teeth. Cleaner teeth mean fresher breath.

In addition to keeping your mouth clean, you have to keep it healthy. A twice-yearly visit to your dentist for a thorough cleaning and examination will eliminate other major causes of bad breath. Bleeding gums can cause bad breath and so can untreated cavities and abscesses. Your dentist can help you deal with these problems. See Periodontal Disease, page 272, for more information.

Of course poor dental hygiene is not responsible for all bad breath. Some foods are well-known offenders—garlic would probably be first on anyone's list. But there are others: Onions, hot peppers, cheeses including blue cheese, Camembert, and Roquefort, spicy oily meats including pastrami, pepperoni, and salami, and even anchovies can cause major breath problems. Drinks that can cause problems with your breath include coffee, beer, wine, and whiskey.

What do you do about these foods and drinks if you want to avoid bad breath? The bad news is that you just have to avoid them. The problem is that the food residue doesn't just lie on your teeth waiting to be brushed away: It goes into your digestive tract and into your bloodstream and eventually permeates your whole body so that every breath picks up the offending odor in your lungs and broadcasts it. This is why it can take up to twenty-four hours to get rid of some offending smells.

There are other causes of bad breath, some of which have to be dealt with by a physician. Constant postnasal drip from sinusitis (see Sinusitis, page 308) can cause bad breath. So can alcoholism, kidney failure, or liver disease, as well as certain medications. An ulcer can give you bad breath (see Ulcers, page 335), as can chronic indigestion (see Indigestion, page 212). If you have bad breath for more than a few days, your dental hygiene is good, and you haven't been eating or drinking offending foods, you should check with your doctor for other causes.

NATURAL PRESCRIPTION FOR BAD BREATH

- Avoid the use of commercial mouthwashes; instead rinse your mouth with a few drops of peppermint oil (from a pharmacy) mixed in a glass of water. Don't swallow the water.

- Brush your teeth carefully twice a day.

- Floss your teeth once a day, preferably before brushing.

- Clean dentures carefully.

- Change your toothbrush every two months.

- If you can't brush after meals, simply rinse your mouth with plain water.

- Snack on carrots, celery, and apples.

- Visit your dentist twice yearly for a thorough cleaning and examination and to eliminate other causes of bad breath: cavities, bleeding gums, abscessed teeth.

- Eliminate offending food and drink, including garlic, raw onions, hot peppers, anchovies, cheeses including blue cheese, Camembert, and Roquefort, oily meats including salami, pastrami, and pepperoni, and drinks such as coffee, beer, wine, and whiskey.

IN ADDITION: If, after following these recommendations, you continue to have bad breath, you should consult your doctor, as bad breath can also be a sign of indigestion, sinusitis, throat infection, lung infection, kidney disease, chronic alcoholism, or a problem with medications.

•   •   •

BODY ODOR

BODY ODOR CAN range from a minor embarrassment on a hot sticky day to a major chronic problem that causes social paralysis. One of the problems in dealing with body odor is that odors are very difficult to describe. I've had great success in my practice in dealing with different types of body odor, and the solutions are usually fairly simple.

First there's the body odor that comes from eating certain types of foods. Most people are aware that garlic can cause body odor—in some people the odor of garlic will persist for days—but there are other foods that can cause body odor such as cumin, curry, and even onions. Cigarettes can cause odor that the smoker is usually unaware of as the nose becomes desensitized to the smell. Alcohol can cause body odor, and drinking too much can definitely give you a certain scent the next day.

The solution to body odor that's caused by food or drink is obvious: Eliminate the same from your diet, or at least limit its consumption or eat the offending food at times when body odor won't be a problem.

Some people—and this is a rare condition—can develop a smell that's described as the odor of putrid fish as a result of eating foods that are high in choline, including eggs, beans, chicken, fish, and many other foods. This enzyme deficiency is called "fish odor syndrome." The problem is eliminated by excluding choline-containing foods and choline supplements from the diet. If you notice such an odor, you should be tested to see if you suffer from this deficiency.

More frequently, body odor is caused by a simple mineral deficiency. Many people who suffer from chronic body odor have found that magnesium and zinc give them total relief, an effect discovered accidentally when patients were being treated with the minerals for other conditions. No one is certain exactly how zinc and magnesium work to eliminate body odor, but it seems that a daily dose will not only help eliminate body odor but also help to sweeten the breath. Many of my patients report success by following this regime. It's helpful to take PABA (para-aminobenzoic acid) and vitamin B₆ at the same time.

In addition, many patients have been helped by taking chlorophyll capsules, which are available at health food stores.

While a garlic smell on your hands from cooking isn't really body odor, it can be annoying, so I'll pass along to you a trick I learned from a patient who is a chef: If you've been chopping garlic, hold your hands under running water while touching stainless steel—the sink if it's made of stainless steel, or a pot or pot lid. The odor vanishes immediately.

Almost all of my patients who suffer from candidiasis have a typically musty body odor. When the candidiasis is under control, so is the musty body odor. If you think that this could be the source of your problem, see Candidiasis, page 61.

A final source of body odor is poor hygiene. Inadequate or infrequent washing will cause body odor to develop on anyone, particularly in hot weather. The solution is obvious: A bath or shower at least once a day should eliminate the problem. In addition, washing with deodorant soap will help keep bacteria in check and thus help control body odor. A dusting with deodorant powder can help absorb perspiration. And wearing natural fabrics that let the body breathe and allow perspiration to dry is also helpful.

NATURAL PRESCRIPTION FOR BODY ODOR

- Eliminate from your diet foods and substances that are known to cause body odor including garlic, curry, cumin, onions, cigarettes, and alcohol.

- If you suffer from the enzyme deficiency that causes "fish odor syndrome" you must eliminate all foods containing choline from your diet including eggs, beans, chicken, and fish, as well as choline supplements.

- If you have a "musty" body odor, you might suffer from candidiasis. Once the condition is cleared up, the odor will disappear. See Candidiasis, page 61.

- Bathe or shower frequently, especially in hot weather, using a deodorant soap. Use an effective deodorant or antiperspirant. Wear natural fibers such as cotton that will allow for perspiration to dry.

- If you can't find a particular cause for your body odor, try taking the following supplements in addition to your daily basic vitamin/mineral supplements (page xxiv):

- Zinc: 50 mg. daily.
- Magnesium: 500 mg. daily.
- PABA: 50 mg. daily.
- Vitamin B$_6$: 50 mg. daily.
- Chlorophyll capsules:
  one three times daily.

•   •   •

BRUISING

SOME PEOPLE WILL take a hard hit on the arm or leg and develop a purple bruise that lasts a few days. Other people regularly develop black-and-blue marks on their body with just the slightest blow; the marks seem to linger, sometimes for weeks.

A common bruise that results from a blow is normal. It's simply blood under the unbroken skin that has accumulated because vessels have been damaged. These kinds of bruises are easy to deal with: To lessen the development of the bruise simply apply cold—an ice pack or even cold water—as quickly as possible to the affected portion of skin. Cold will constrict the blood vessels and thus allow less leakage into the surrounding tissue; you'll still probably get a bruise but it won't be as large or as painful.

But bruises that develop frequently from minor causes and seem to linger can be troublesome and not just from a cosmetic standpoint. One of my patients, a fifty-year-old woman named Marie, was concerned because she regularly developed bruises on her body and she couldn't remember any cause for them. In addition, it seemed that the most minor bump would result in a bruise that lasted for days. She was concerned that there was something seriously wrong with her and wanted help. We did a little detective work and soon came up with the answer.

When I quizzed Marie she said it had been about a year since she first noticed the bruises. She wasn't on any regular medication. Her nutrition was good. She had no other health problems. For a while I was mystified. And then she remembered that she and her husband had begun taking daily aspirin to lessen their risk of heart disease about a year ago. In her case that aspirin a day was enough to make her more susceptible to bruising. When she cut her dose to a baby aspirin (60 mg.) every other day, the bruising disappeared.

Medications are a common cause of easy bruising. Steroids, antidepressants, some asthma medications, and anticoagulant drug therapies may all cause easy bruising, as will the regular doses of aspirin that Marie and many people take to ward off heart disease. If you think your easy bruising could be caused by medications, discuss it with your doctor. That's probably no reason to change your medication, but at least you'll know the cause of your problem.

A poor diet will promote easy bruising. Vitamin C plays a major role in preventing the blood vessels from becoming leaky. If you bruise easily, you should increase your consumption of foods containing vitamin C, and you should take a daily supplement.

Also, I've had great success in eliminating easy bruising with quercetin, which is one of the bioflavonoids. It is derived from sea algae and has been shown to have a potent effect on the circulatory system. If you can't get quercetin, you can try the citrus bioflavonoids, which come from the white pulp of citrus fruits. Try one of these supplements for three months; if no improvement, discontinue.

Vitamin K is essential for blood to clot. Not many people are deficient in vitamin K, but, because the vitamin must be absorbed in fat, if you have a problem with fat absorption as in gallbladder disease, celiac disease, or ulcerative colitis, you could have trouble absorbing vitamin K. If you frequently use antibiotics such as penicillin and tetracycline, you could also have trouble absorbing vitamin K. If any of these conditions apply to you and you suffer from easy bruising, you should discuss the possibility of vitamin K supplementation with your doctor. You should take vitamin K *only* under a doctor's supervision.

NATURAL PRESCRIPTION FOR BRUISING

- To limit the development of bruises, apply cold to the site of a bump immediately.

- If you bruise easily, check your medications, including aspirin, steroids, antidepressants, asthma medications, and anticoagulant drug therapies, which all cause easy bruising. Blood thinners will also cause you to bruise. Discuss this problem with your doctor. If aspirin is causing the bruising, limit your intake to one baby aspirin (60 mg.) every other day (if you're taking them to fight heart disease). If you regularly take aspirin for some other reason, consult with your doctor.

IN ADDITION TO YOUR DAILY SUPPLEMENTS, PAGE xxiv, TAKE

- Vitamin C: 1,000 mg. daily.

- Quercetin: 600 to 900 mg. daily, or citrus bioflavonoids, 1,000 mg. daily. Take either of these supplements for three months; if there is no improvement, discontinue.

- Vitamin K: Use *only* under a doctor's supervision. See information above.

• • •

BURNING MOUTH AND TONGUE

THIS IS AN ODD condition that I've encountered a number of times among my patients who complain of a hot, burning feeling in the mouth and on the tongue. While it may seem like a small matter, it can be quite troubling to sufferers.

There are a number of causes for a burning mouth—or glossodynia, which means "tongue pain"—and you have to find the one that triggers your problem by a process of elimination. Here are the major causes:

In my experience, one of the most common cause is food allergies. To learn more about how to deal with them see Food Allergy on page 146. I've had a number of patients who have had dramatic results in eliminating their symptoms once they've eliminated hidden food allergies.

Some people can develop sensitivities to mouthwash and toothpaste, and this can cause burning mouth. Try brushing your teeth with plain baking soda and eliminating the use of mouthwash altogether (see Bad Breath, page 49) for a while to see if symptoms are relieved.

Dental amalgam fillings can cause a reaction in some people. If your symptoms began shortly after having dental work done, particularly if you've had fillings that contain amalgam, you should discuss the problem with your dentist.

Smoking can cause the symptoms of a burning mouth and tongue. Of course there are plenty of reasons to stop smoking, but maybe a burning mouth could be the one reason that gets you to stop.

Some people develop a burning mouth in response to alcohol. If you drink regularly, try eliminating alcohol entirely to see if that relieves your symptoms.

Dental plaque and poorly fitting dentures can cause a burning mouth. Also, if you wear dentures, the adhesive can cause a reaction in some people. Visit your dentist for a thorough cleaning and checkup.

Some medications can cause glossodynia. If you are taking any medications regularly, check with your doctor to see if a burning mouth can be a side effect.

Finally, there are vitamin and mineral deficiencies that can contribute to this problem. I'll simply list below the vitamins and minerals you should be taking.

NATURAL PRESCRIPTION FOR BURNING MOUTH AND TONGUE

- Investigate food allergies to see if they are the cause of the problem. See Food Allergy page 146.

- To see if your toothpaste is causing the symptoms, brush using only baking soda for a few days.

- Eliminate the use of mouthwash (see Bad Breath on page 49 for a fuller discussion of mouthwash problems).

- Stop smoking.

- Eliminate the use of alcohol for a few weeks to see if symptoms are related to that.

- Visit your dentist for a thorough cleaning, as plaque can sometimes cause these symptoms.

- If you wear dentures, have the fit checked and change the brand of adhesive you use, because some adhesives can cause reactions in sensitive people.

- If you have numerous amalgam fillings, or if you've recently had dental work done that includes fillings, you should discuss the possibility that your fillings are causing your symptoms. This is controversial, but some dentists are willing to allow for this possibility.

- If you take any medications regularly, check with your doctor to see if they could be causing your symptoms.

IN ADDITION TO YOUR DAILY SUPPLEMENTS, PAGE xxiv, TAKE

- Iron: 60 mg. daily (after checking with your doctor to see if you need it).

- B$_{12}$: 1,000 mcg. dissolved under the tongue daily.

- Folic acid: 800 mcg. daily.

- Zinc: 50 mg. daily.

IN ADDITION: Some patients with burning mouth and tongue are helped with injections of B$_{12}$, liver, and folic acid. You should discuss this with your doctor.

•   •   •

BURNS

MOST PEOPLE HAVE heard burns described in terms of "degrees" but they're not sure what that means. A first-degree burn is the most common type of burn. A sunburn, for example, is a first-degree burn. If you touch something hot or spill boiling water on your wrist you'll probably get a first-degree burn. This kind of burn will become red and may develop a scab that will eventually flake off. A second-degree burn means that a deeper layer of the skin has been affected. It will redden deeply and blister within a few hours or a day, but will ultimately heal and leave no scar. A third-degree burn is one in which the skin is burned through. It may be charred or may look white and will probably not be immediately painful. A third-degree burn is an emergency and should be treated immediately by a physician.

You can treat most first- and second-degree burns yourself at home. When should you see a doctor about a burn? When you have a third-degree burn; when a child is burned and the area of the burn is larger than a quarter; when the burn covers a large portion of the body, even if it's a first-degree burn (with the exception of sunburn, which can be treated at home except in extreme cases); when the burn is extremely painful. You should also consult a doctor if your burn does not heal in a few days or you have blisters that develop dark pus, which could signal infection.

The best first aid for a burn is the simplest: cool water. As soon as possible after the burn, submerge the affected skin in cool (not ice cold) water. (If clothing is in the way, take it off. If necessary, cut the clothing off, particularly if it is saturated with a hot substance like grease. If clothing sticks to the skin, leave it intact and see a doctor.) It's best to keep the whole burned area under water for a while. This can mean running the tap over a burned hand or wrist or submerging the whole body in a cool bath to treat a burned chest.

The cooling effect of water will not only relieve the pain of a burn but will also stop the actual burning of the tissue. I suggest keeping the affected area submerged for a half hour if possible.

If you do need to have a burn treated by a doctor, use a towel or pillowcase that has been soaked in cool water as a dressing until the burn can be treated. If you are going to seek medical treatment for a burn, don't use anything but cool water—no ointments or lotions—until the doctor has examined the burn.

It's important to remember never to put that old-fashioned remedy, butter or grease, on a burn. This will only serve to hold in the heat and prolong the pain and increase the damage. In addition, if your burn develops blisters you should never open them; let them heal on their own.

There are over-the-counter creams and gels that are designed to relieve the pain of a burn. There are also natural treatments that can be helpful. You can apply these treatments after you've soaked the burn in cool water. (If after soaking, the burn is not extremely painful and is not large, usually the best thing to do is simply keep it dry and clean. In this case a bit of vitamin E rubbed into the burn will prevent scarring.)

Apple cider vinegar splashed on a burn is a favorite remedy of mine. It helps to soothe pain. You can simply splash it gently on a sunburn or minor burn every few hours, or you can saturate a clean cloth with the vinegar and use it as a dressing on the burn for a half hour.

Tea-tree oil, which is a natural treatment available in health food stores, has been shown to be effective in relieving the pain of a burn. Apply it topically.

Aloe vera, either squeezed directly from the plant or used in the form of a gel, can be applied to a burn to relieve pain.

If you have been severely burned you will, of course, be under the care of a physician. But you should know that supplements can help promote healing and should be part of your recovery. I suggest you take the supplements listed below to ensure the most rapid possible healing.

NATURAL PRESCRIPTION FOR BURNS

- Gently splashing apple cider vinegar on a sunburn or any other type of burn every few hours can help reduce pain.

- Tea-tree oil, which is available in health food stores, is useful for relieving pain and promoting healing. It's applied topically.

- Aloe vera, squeezed directly from the plant or used in the form of a gel, can relieve pain.

- A vitamin E capsule stuck with a pin and squeezed onto the burn can help the healing process and prevent scarring.

- You can use aspirin or NSAIDs to relieve the pain.

TO HELP PROMOTE HEALING FOR ALL BURNS, TAKE, IN ADDITION TO YOUR DAILY BASIC VITAMIN/MINERAL SUPPLEMENTS (PAGE xxiv):

- Vitamin C: 1,000 mg. daily.

- Vitamin E: 400 I.U. daily.

- Beta-carotene: 10,000 I.U. daily.

- Zinc: 50 mg. daily.

• • •

CANDIDIASIS

CANDIDIASIS HAS BEEN around for thousands of years, but it's only since the advent of antibiotics that it has become a virtual epidemic. Antibiotics are a factor in the development of candidiasis because they kill off the friendly bacteria in our systems that keep the common yeast, *Candida albicans,* under control. When the *Candida* yeast overgrows its bounds, it causes a variety of symptoms that can range from general fatigue, gas, bloating, diarrhea, and frequent vaginal infections in women.

Candidiasis is difficult to diagnose. Many doctors don't acknowledge it as a systemic problem; they treat the variety of symptoms connected with it—like thrush and vaginal infections—and ignore the basic cause of what can be far more subtle and troublesome symptoms including depression, allergies, and inability to concentrate. An article in the *New England Journal of Medicine* reported, in effect, that there's no such thing as candidiasis. But physicians' responses to the article, criticizing its poor design and methodology, in addition to the countless cases of the syndrome I have seen, eliminated any doubts I might have had about the existence of this disease.

Mary is a thirty-two-year-old woman, an environmental engineer, who is a typical candidiasis patient. She came to me with a whole roster of complaints including general fatigue, inability to concentrate, digestive problems such as bloating, gas, and cramps, and recurring vaginal infections. Mary had no notion that these problems were connected. She had been to a number of doctors who had treated each problem individually, sometimes successfully at least for a time. But all the symptoms eventually returned. Mary was beginning to think that something was wrong with her entire system, and, in fact, she was right.

How can a simple yeast cause so many problems? In fact, the *Candida albicans* yeast is present in varying amounts in all of us, living in our gastrointestinal tract. The problem is created when the yeast begins to grow beyond its normal bounds, which often happens because of antibiotic use. It's also connected with the use of oral contraceptives, corticosteroids, drugs used for ulcers including Tagamet or Zantac, or even too much sugar in the diet. A woman who is on birth control pills, has had a few courses of antibiotics, and who eats too much sugar is the typical victim. Women with diabetes are more likely to develop candidiasis because the environment of their vagina is conducive to the overgrowth of the *Candida* yeast. But men can suffer from candidiasis, too, especially if they have a wife or girlfriend who has recurrent yeast problems.

Candidiasis has such a wide range of symptoms because it affects so many systems of the body—including the endocrine, gastrointestinal, genitourinary, nervous, and immune systems. The major clues I notice among my patients are:

- a white coating on the tongue
- recurring vaginal yeast infections
- digestive problems, particularly gas and bloating
- allergic rashes

A complete listing of the symptoms of candidiasis may include: general symptoms such as constant fatigue and loss of interest in sex, thrush (*Candida* overgrowth of the mouth), canker sores, sore throat and constant cough, constipation, intestinal cramps, bloating and gas, rectal itch, recurring vaginal yeast infections and bladder infections, general menstrual problems, depression and inability to concentrate, allergies, and low immune function.

One of the troubling aspects of candidiasis is that it can begin a vicious circle of poor health: Someone with a poorly functioning immune system can be vulnerable to *Candida* infections. In turn, the *Candida* infections increase the likelihood of a poorly functioning immune system. In addition, someone whose immune system isn't up to par is more likely to get a bacterial infection that would require treatment with antibiotics, which of course adds fuel to the fire by encouraging the overgrowth of *Candida albicans*.

Unfortunately, at this time, there is no simple test for candidiasis. There is a blood test for *Candida* antibodies, but if a woman has had recurrent vaginal yeast infections, the test will inevitably be positive; it is not a conclusive test for the syndrome. How do you know if your health problems are caused by candidiasis? I find that the cure is the identifying factor. That is, if you have a number of the symptoms; if you have been on medications that could affect yeast growth including cortisone, hormones (including birth control pills), or antibiotics; if you've tried other methods to deal with your symptoms without success, then it is worth the trouble to attempt the cure outlined here including a yeast-free diet and acidophilus supplements. If after two to four weeks on this regime, your symptoms improve, then you do have (or had!)

Candida. The relief can be quite dramatic. If you see no change in your symptoms, then *Candida* is not your problem.

When Mary came to see me she was not on antibiotics, but many patients are or they've just finished a course of antibiotics. If you suspect that you are suffering from candidiasis, you should try to eliminate the use of antibiotics and birth control pills. (You can resume taking birth control pills once your candidiasis is under control, but if it flares up again, I recommend you permanently stop the pill.) Mary was on birth control pills and had been for five years, but she agreed to use an alternative method of birth control while she cleared up the candidiasis.

The most important step to take to fight candidiasis is to modify your diet. I put my patients on a yeast-free, sugar-free diet for thirty days. Foods containing yeast that should be avoided include breads, baked goods, cheese, mushrooms, vinegar, soy sauce, fermented foods such as olives and pickles, and alcohol. I advise patients to avoid milk and milk products because of their high levels of milk sugar as well as the traces of antibiotics that they contain. Sugar should also be eliminated from the diet, as the yeast grows freely in a high-sugar environment. This means no candy, cake, cookies, ice cream, soda, diet soda, dried fruit, honey, chocolate, and sweeteners such as malt, barley, fructose, or fruit juice. If their symptoms diminish, I know that we're on the right track. If you have no relief after a yeast-free diet, you might investigate Food Allergy, page 146, or Hypoglycemia, page 202.

Mary went on the yeast- and sugar-free diet and told me that after four days she felt an enormous improvement. She no longer had regular digestive upsets, and her general vague feelings of fatigue were disappearing, too. In fact, she said that she had become so accustomed to feeling tired and worn out that she couldn't really remember feeling any different, until her treatment began to take effect.

There are additional steps Mary took to fight candidiasis, and because of the pervasive nature of the problem I advise all patients to make every modification they can to eliminate the problem, at least for a two-week period.

Garlic is known to be an effective antifungal agent, and you should add it to your diet either in its natural form or in the form of capsules that are available at health food stores.

Lactobacillus acidophilus, the live culture found in yogurt, is also beneficial in maintaining the healthy bacteria that fight *Candida.* You should add yogurt to your diet (be sure that the label says it contains live active cultures) or buy acidophilus supplements at a health food store.

I should mention that there is a naturally occurring fatty acid called caprylic acid that is helpful in fighting candidiasis. It is available under various names in health food stores. Potency varies; the labels will give the correct dosage.

NATURAL PRESCRIPTION FOR CANDIDIASIS

- If possible, after consultation with your doctor, eliminate antibiotics, birth control pills, corticosteroids, and ulcer drugs.

- Begin a yeast- and sugar-free diet and follow it strictly for at least thirty days. If your symptoms diminish, you know that you have been suffering from candidiasis. Depending on the severity of your symptoms, you'll have to follow the yeast-free diet for three to twelve months. Eliminate the following foods: bread, baked goods, cheese, mushrooms, vinegar, soy sauce, fermented foods, alcohol. Also eliminate sugar including all sweets: cookies, candy, ice cream, soda, diet soda, dried fruit, chocolate, and sweeteners including fructose, malt, barley, and fruit juice.

IN ADDITION TO YOUR DAILY SUPPLEMENTS, PAGE xxiv, TAKE

- *Lactobacillus acidophilus:* in natural form, in yogurt (make sure the yogurt contains live cultures, as indicated on the label), and in capsule form available in health food stores. Take one capsule three times daily.

- Garlic: in its natural form or in capsule form available from health food stores.

- Caprylic acid: follow the directions on the container as to dosage.

IN ADDITION: There is a prescription drug called Nystatin that can be of help to confirmed cases of candidiasis. If you try the yeast-free diet and your symptoms are alleviated but do not completely clear, then you might have had candidiasis for so long that you will require additional treatment in the form of prescription drugs. You should discuss Nystatin with your doctor.

• • •

CANKER SORES

CANKER SORES, or mouth ulcers, are a very common ailment. Most people just try to ignore them and, sure enough, eventually they go away. But some people are troubled constantly by these small, round sores that appear in the mouth. White in the center with a red, raised border, they can appear alone or in clusters. You can have them on your tongue, gums, or inside your cheeks and they can make chewing, drinking, and even talking uncomfortable.

No one is certain precisely what causes them, but we think that their appearance is due to a malfunctioning of the immune system as well as any trauma to the inside of the mouth. Certain factors can make you more disposed to developing canker sores: children with braces, for example, frequently develop them, as do people who chew the insides of their cheeks.

Two causes of canker sores that can be identified and remedied are nutrient deficiencies and allergies. I've had particular success helping people with recurring canker sores when their previously unrecognized allergies are treated. (More about this later.)

Canker sores can be painful and I suggest a few immediate remedies. First, there is an over-the-counter medication that contains carbamide peroxide. This combination of glycerin and peroxide helps soothe and heal the sore by killing the bacteria.

Many of my patients have found zinc applied topically to be extremely helpful. I suggest they take a zinc lozenge and let it dissolve directly on the sore. You can get zinc lozenges at a health food store in 50-mg. strength. Let one dissolve on the sore three times a day. It's okay to swallow the zinc. In addition, you can dissolve one or two zinc lozenges in hydrogen peroxide and water (half water, half hydrogen peroxide) and gargle four times a day with this solution. (Don't swallow this preparation.)

Lactobacillus acidophilus—the live bacteria found in yogurt—can also help. Whenever you feel a canker sore coming on, dissolve about ten capsules (they're available in health food stores) in water, and rinse your mouth out with this solution three times during the day. It's okay to swallow the solution.

If you have a problem with recurring canker sores, the first probable cause you should investigate is food allergies. I've had any number of patients claim that they had no problem with allergies only to remember upon questioning that they did have certain allergies as children or that they were colicky babies. Allergies can disappear and then come back in slightly different forms in later years. If you have a history of allergies in your family, if you had allergies as a child, if you have hay fever, skin allergies, rashes, or hives, you could be suffering from a hidden food allergy that's causing canker sores. You can investigate food allergies on your own. See Food Allergy, page 146, and remember that people with canker sores seem to be most vulnerable to a gluten allergy. Once you determine if you're having a reaction to a food and what the food is, you'll find that when the food is eliminated, the symptoms disappear.

Nutritional deficiencies also play a role in predisposing a person to canker sores. One study of 330 people with canker sores found that over half of them were deficient in iron, folate, or vitamin B_{12}, or some combination of these nutrients. When their diets were supplemented, almost all of them found that their canker sores disappeared. We've also found that a zinc deficiency can cause canker sores. If you have recurring canker sores, you should be sure that you're taking adequate amounts of iron, folate, vitamin B_{12}, and zinc.

A natural compound used in mouth ulcer therapy is a derivative of licorice known as deglycyrrhizinated licorice, or DGL, which stimulates the production of mucus to coat and protect the digestive tract. One study involving DGL found that 75 percent of the people studied had a 50 to 75 percent relief from pain within twenty-four hours after gargling with DGL. One man who had suffered from canker sores for ten years was completely symptom-free after two weeks. You can buy DGL in health food stores.

Many people find that continuing stressful situations will stimulate an outbreak. If you suffer from recurring canker sores, you should make a special effort to control the stress in your life.

NATURAL PRESCRIPTION FOR CANKER SORES

FOR IMMEDIATE RELIEF:

- Try an over-the-counter remedy containing carbamide peroxide. Apply to the sore according to the package directions.

- Use zinc topically by allowing a 50-mg. zinc lozenge to dissolve on the sore three times a day.

- Mix one half cup of hydrogen peroxide with a half cup of water, dissolve one or two zinc capsules in it, and gargle four times a day. Do not swallow.

- Dissolve ten capsules of acidophilus in water and gargle with this three times a day. It's okay to swallow this.

IN ADDITION TO YOUR DAILY SUPPLEMENTS, PAGE xxiv, TAKE

- Zinc: 50 mg. daily. (If you are dissolving zinc tablets directly on canker sores, don't take this extra supplement.)

- Vitamin C with bioflavonoids: 1,000 mg. on a regular basis. At the first sensation of a canker sore, take 1,000 mg. three times a day for the first three days.

- B_{12}: 1,000 mcg. under the tongue (it's best absorbed this way) once a day.

- Iron: 60 mg. daily (but only if you've had a blood test that indicates that you are iron-deficient).

- Folic acid: 800 mcg. daily.

- Vitamin E: 400 I.U. daily.

- DGL: gargle four times daily with 200 mg. of DGL mixed in a glass of water.

• • •

CARPAL TUNNEL SYNDROME

BETTY FIRST CAME to see me because she was having difficulty sleeping. It wasn't a problem with insomnia but rather a persistent burning pain in her wrist that kept waking her during the night. It turned out that the hand also bothered Betty during the day, but she said during the day she could live with it; at night she was driven to distraction by the tingling and burning. Betty was suffering from carpal tunnel syndrome. A typical victim of this disorder, she is a woman over thirty who had been working at a computer for a number of years. One theory on carpal tunnel holds that women around menopause are more liable to develop it because the change in hormonal levels encourages fluid buildup and thus swelling in the wrists. But women aren't the only sufferers. Men, particularly those who work at repetitive tasks with their hands such as carpenters or those who work at keyboards, are also liable to develop the syndrome. Certain conditions can predispose one to carpal tunnel syndrome, including arthritis, gout, diabetes, pregnancy, and thyroid problems.

Carpal tunnel syndrome results when pressure is put on the median nerve as it passes down the arm through the space formed by the wrist bones into the hand. The symptoms include weakness in the hand, pain, numbness, tingling, and aching that can radiate up into the arm and shoulder and is particularly troublesome at night. The first sign of the development of carpal tunnel syndrome is typically a tingling sensation in the thumb and forefinger; a feeling that they have "fallen asleep."

There is a simple test that may help you identify carpal tunnel: hold out the suspect hand, let's say it's the right hand. With the index finger of the left hand, tap the right wrist where it joins the hand. If you feel a tingling that shoots down into your right hand and fingers, you could have carpal tunnel syndrome.

When Betty came to see me she told me that she had been putting off seeing a doctor because her cousin had suffered from a similar pain and had had hand surgery with no real improvement in her painful wrist. While surgery for carpal tunnel syndrome may be successful, it's important to know that a recent study shows that two years after surgery, almost one third of the patients who had undergone the operation found that symptoms had returned.

Fortunately vitamin B_6 supplementation, the natural treatment for carpal tunnel syndrome, is simple, inexpensive, and usually very effective. Researchers have discovered that many people with carpal tunnel also suffer from a B_6 vitamin deficiency (which explains why many sufferers are pregnant women, menopausal women, or women on birth control pills, because these conditions deplete B_6.) Vitamin B_6 works to strengthen the sheath that surrounds the tendon and thus helps to relieve the pain. Two other B vitamins work in conjunction with B_6 to make the treatment more effective: B_2 and B_{12}. In addition, folic acid is beneficial.

I recommended that Betty begin supplementation immediately. As it takes six to twelve weeks for improvement to be felt, I cautioned patience. In the meantime, because her condition was quite painful, I suggested that she rest the hand completely for a week, using a simple splint to limit its motion. I also suggested that she use heat—either a heating pad or warm water soak—at least twice a day. After that first week, she could gradually go back to using the hand, but with caution.

It took seven weeks for Betty to really feel the effects of her treatment with a lessening in pain. After ten weeks she told me that all of her symptoms had completely disappeared. I warned her that if she discontinued the B_6 she might notice a return of symptoms.

If you work at repetitive tasks—at a computer keyboard, for example—you should stop at regular intervals while working to give your wrists a break. Making small gentle circles in the air with your hands will help restore circulation and ease pressure and can help prevent an attack of this syndrome.

NATURAL PRESCRIPTION FOR CARPAL TUNNEL SYNDROME

- You may want to use a simple splint—available at a pharmacy—to immobilize the hand and relieve pain until the other measures begin to take effect.

- A heating pad or warm moist compress can help relieve pain.

- If you work at repetitive tasks, stop occasionally and make slow circles with your hands to restore circulation and relieve pressure.

IN ADDITION TO YOUR DAILY SUPPLEMENTS, PAGE xxiv, TAKE

- Vitamin B$_6$: 300 mg. daily for *no longer than* three months; take 50 to 100 mg. daily as a maintenance dosage. Remember that it can take up to three months for the effects of the supplementation to be felt. *Warning: Vitamin B$_6$ can be toxic at high levels. Do not take more than the recommended amount.*

- Vitamin B$_2$: 100 mg. daily.

- Vitamin B$_{12}$: 1,000 mcg. daily in tablet form dissolved under the tongue.

- Folic acid: 800 mcg. daily.

IN ADDITION: Acupuncture treatments can be very helpful in eliminating the pain of carpal tunnel.

• • •

CATARACTS

CATARACTS ARE ONE of the major health problems troubling Americans. They are one of the leading causes of loss of sight in our country; four million people have some degree of vision impairment due to cataracts. These statistics are reflected in the queries from my radio audience; I receive more calls about cataracts than almost any other condition.

Cataracts are primarily a degenerative impairment, which is to say that if we live long enough, most of us will experience some degree of cloudiness in our vision. Cataracts can also be caused by disease, particularly diabetes, trauma to the eye, a congenital defect, or exposure to German measles during fetal development.

A cataract simply refers to the clouding of the lens of the eye. This lens, flexible, transparent, and crucial to normal vision, is located behind the pupil and the iris. Attached to muscles on all sides, it flattens or becomes rounded, enabling the eye to focus on objects near or far. Over time, certain factors cause the lens to become less transparent. When cataracts begin to develop, you might notice a slight cloudiness, which makes you want to use a brighter light for reading, or you might have difficulty driving at night because of the glare of oncoming headlights. You might find that bright sunlight adversely affects your vision. Cataracts may develop unevenly: One eye might be afflicted while the other is fine, or both may cloud but the degree of cloudiness may differ from one eye to the other. Cataracts may develop very quickly or very slowly over a period of years. In the case of a severe cataract, the pupil of the eye becomes white, but early cases show no change in the eye visible on inspection without instruments.

If cataracts have developed to the point where they severely impair your vision, surgery is the only course. Some people are frightened by the prospect of eye surgery, and this is understandable. But to be blinded or severely impaired because of fear of what is actually simple surgery is a tragedy. The surgery takes about a half hour and is done under a local anesthetic. You can be operated on in the morning and be home that same day.

There have been reports of natural remedies reversing cataracts, but I take a conservative route on this. I repeat, if your cataracts have compromised your vision to the point where you cannot carry on a normal life, you should arrange for surgery; natural treatments will probably not help.

If, however, your cataracts are in the very beginning stages or if you know that cataracts run in your family and you want to prevent them, natural remedies may both improve your current condition and prevent any further development.

As we age many of our body parts tend to "wear out." This seems normal and to be expected, and to some degree it is. But when we investigate the body on a microbiological level, we sometimes discover that when we understand what makes things wear out, we can prevent their degeneration. So it is with cataracts. Cataract formation is connected with an inability to maintain normal levels of sodium, potassium, and calcium within the lens of the eye. We now know that this occurs because damage to the "pumping system" that maintains these levels has occurred. Free-radical damage at the cellular level is the main cause of damage to the system.

If free radicals are a cause of cataracts, then the antioxidant vitamins E, C, beta-carotene, and selenium, which prevent free-radical damage, are crucial to preventing their development. One study found that those who took between 300 and 600 mg. of vitamin C daily had a 70 percent reduction in cataract risk; those who took 400 I.U. of vitamin E had a 50 percent reduction. Most significantly, people who took *both* supplements were almost entirely free of cataracts. Another fourteen-year study that involved 50,000 women found a 40 percent lower rate of cataract surgery among women whose diets were rich in vitamin A compared with those whose diets lacked the vitamin.

In addition, it's important to be sure that your diet is rich in food sources of antioxidants, specifically fresh fruits and vegetables. Try to follow the new guidelines that recommend five servings of fresh fruits and vegetables daily.

Inositol—part of the vitamin B complex—has been shown in experiments to be protective against the development of cataracts.

Recent research has pointed to a molecule called pantethine, which is present in all cells of the body, as helping in preventing the clumping of proteins in the eye that causes cataracts. Pantethine is the active form of pantothenic acid, one of the vitamins in the B complex.

Another factor in cataract development that we can control is exposure to ultraviolet light. Long-term exposure to ultraviolet light ultimately damages the lens of the eye by causing the release of free radicals. You can avoid the problem by wearing dark sunglasses and/or a brimmed hat whenever you're in the sun.

Recent research has also shown that cigarette smoke can lead to the development of cataracts and plays a significant role in worsening cataracts that have already developed. Smoking is a major risk factor in so many serious health problems, and here's just one more bit of evidence. If you smoke and are beginning to develop cataracts, perhaps this research will convince you to stop.

Finally, diets that are high in sugar have been implicated in promoting cataract development. For this reason, as well as others involving sugar and its connection to health problems, I recommend that you restrict your intake of sugar if you are developing cataracts or if cataracts run in your family.

NATURAL PRESCRIPTION FOR CATARACTS

- If impairment is severe, surgery is the only alternative.

- If cloudiness is just beginning, nutritional treatment can be successful and you should make sure that you get five servings of fresh fruits and vegetables daily.

- Avoid exposure to ultraviolet light by wearing dark glasses.

- Reduce your sugar intake.

IN ADDITION TO YOUR DAILY SUPPLEMENTS, PAGE xxiv, TAKE

- Vitamin C with bioflavonoids: 1,000 mg. daily.

- Vitamin E: 400 I.U. daily.

- Selenium: 50 mcg. daily.

- Beta-carotene: 10,000 I.U. daily.

- Inositol: 500 to 1,000 mg. daily.

- Pantethine: 300 mg. three times daily.

• • •

CELIAC DISEASE

CELIAC DISEASE, also known as celiac sprue and nontropical sprue, is a congenital, hereditary sensitivity to gluten, the protein found in wheat and other grains. It's an interesting disorder. When I was in medical school, celiac disease was considered rare; I don't know that I ever expected to diagnose a case of it in my practice. But over the years, I've encountered many cases of celiac disease, and I suspect that it has been considered rare because it's difficult to diagnose and is often overlooked.

Someone with celiac disease may have diverse symptoms. Chronic indigestion, gas, and bloating are the most common symptoms, but they may also include irritability, vomiting, loss of appetite, fatigue, pallor, and general symptoms including lethargy and depression. All these symptoms occur as a result of the destruction of the villi, or threadlike projections of the small intestines. The villi are damaged to the point where they are unable to transfer nutrients from food into the blood to nourish the systems of the body.

Some cases of celiac disease manifest themselves in childhood. The usual symptoms have different degrees of severity, and there can be different symptoms. Usually when a baby is introduced to cereals at the age of six months to a year the symptoms will first appear. Often one of the symptoms that parents notice with babies, in addition to increasing irritability, is a pale foamy diarrhea that has a particularly unpleasant odor. Sometimes there is a lag of a few weeks between introduction of the food containing gluten and the symptoms. In adults, symptoms often develop after overindulgence in foods that are rich in gluten—typically pasta or bread. Gas and bloating are the most common symptoms. Often a child will outgrow the reaction to gluten, but when an adult develops the reaction, it's there to stay.

The patients whom I later diagnose with celiac disease usually come to see me with vague digestive complaints, fatigue, and depression. I pinpoint their problem by process of elimination. There are various degrees of gluten sensitivity; some people are extremely sensitive while others are only mildly so. Many patients who I suspect suffer from celiac disease tell me that they become depressed after they eat foods that contain gluten. It's interesting to note that there's a connection between celiac disease and schizophrenia; researchers have long known that children of schizophrenics are much more likely to develop celiac disease than others. In any case, it does argue for the psychological symptoms of celiac disease.

It's difficult to diagnose celiac disease not because there's no reliable test but because it's often confused with other problems such as lactose intolerance, irritable bowel syndrome, and cystic fibrosis. A doctor usually has to have a high degree of suspicion to test for celiac disease. A biopsy of the small intestine used to be the definitive diagnostic procedure, but there is now a blood test—an antigluten antibodies test—that is highly accurate. Here are some questions I ask a patient who I suspect suffers from celiac disease:

- Do you have Irish, Scotch, English, or Scandinavian heritage? (Celiac disease is more common among people of these extractions; recent statistics reveal that 1 in every 215 Irish suffer from the disease.)

- Is there a history of intestinal disease in your family? Does anyone in your family experience similar symptoms including chronic gas, bloating, and indigestion?

- Have you ever had a blistery rash on the inside of your elbows, behind your knees, or at other body folds?

- Is your abdomen ever swollen?

- Is chronic fatigue a serious problem in your life, affecting your job performance and social obligations?

- Do you have frequent diarrhea or constipation?

- Does your family have a history of stunted growth or delayed maturity?

If the answers to these questions are primarily yes, celiac disease is a real possibility, and I suggest that you see a doctor for a definitive diagnosis.

The cure for celiac disease seems simple: Eliminate gluten from your diet. But the reality isn't that easy. Gluten is present in oats, rye, barley, wheat, and buckwheat as well as countless processed foods including breads, cereals, pasta, crackers, and most commercial baked goods. In addition, ice cream, puddings, desserts made from commercial mixes, cheese spreads, commercial salad dressings, meat, chicken, and fish products prepared with bread or breadcrumbs, soups, gravies, and sauces thickened with flour all can contain gluten as thickening agents, emulsifiers, stabilizers, and hydrolyzed vegetable protein. Malt, which is primarily used as a flavoring and coloring agent, can be a hidden source of gluten. It's present in beer and ale and most, though not all, dry breakfast cereals. Grape-Nuts contain a great deal of malt and is a good test food for gluten intolerance.

I think it's important to get guidance and encouragement on a healthy diet for those with celiac disease, and I encourage you to investigate sources of information including the National Digestive Disease Information Clearinghouse, Box NDDIC, Bethesda, MD 20892, (301) 468-6344, and the Celiac Sprue Association, 2313 Rocklyn Drive, Des Moines, IA 50322, (515) 270-9689. There are a number of cookbooks that are geared to a gluten-free diet, and these associations should help you find them.

When the diet is gluten-free, symptoms of celiac disease should clear up in a week or two. But that doesn't mean that gluten can be reintroduced. While children often begin to tolerate gluten after five years or so of a carefully monitored gluten-free diet, a doctor should be involved in trying to reintroduce gluten, and it's usually recommended that children stick with a gluten-free diet until they're fully grown. Adults who develop celiac disease later in life will usually have to remain gluten-free for life.

While suffering from the symptoms of celiac disease, it's important to hold to a lactose-free diet (see Lactose Intolerance, page 231), at least until the digestive system has a chance to recover. For the same reason, it is advisable to follow a low-fiber diet, and to avoid fatty foods at least until the symptoms disappear.

Vitamin and mineral supplementation is important for people who have celiac disease to replace the nutrients lost through diarrhea and also the nutrients that the villi of the small intestine were unable to absorb. It's therefore important to take a daily supplement as well as the supplements described below. Your doctor will tell you if you suffer from anemia, and, if so, you should take an iron supplement under medical supervision.

There is a skin disease called dermatitis herpetiformis closely associated with celiac disease. It usually develops over a period of time and it's characterized by tiny, blisterlike burning and itching hives on the elbow or knees, the back of the head, the base of the spine, or the buttocks. Like other symptoms of celiac disease, dermatitis herpetiformis will clear up once the sufferer adopts a gluten-free diet.

NATURAL PRESCRIPTION FOR CELIAC DISEASE

- Eliminate all foods containing gluten from the diet including:

Ale	Candy	Ice cream
Baby cereal	Canned meats	Ice cream cones
Beer biscuits	Coffee, instant	Infant formula
Bread	and brewed	Liquors
Breakfast cereal	Coffee substitutes	Macaroni
Cake mixes	Cookies	Milk, malted and
Cakes	Frankfurters	powdered

Noodles	Pudding mix	Tea
Pancake syrup	Salad dressings	Wheat flour
Pancakes	Soda crackers	Whipped cream
Potato chips	Spaghetti	substitutes

- While symptoms are evident: Follow a lactose-free diet (see Lactose Intolerance, page 231).

- Follow a low-fiber diet.

- Avoid fatty foods.

IN ADDITION TO YOUR DAILY SUPPLEMENTS, PAGE xxiv, TAKE

- Vitamin C: 1,000 mg. daily.

- Vitamin E: 400 I.U. daily.

- Beta-carotene: 10,000 I.U. daily.

- Calcium: 1,000 mg. daily along with 400 mg. of magnesium daily.

- Iron: 60 mg. daily if you have had a blood test that indicates you are iron deficient.

• • •

CERVICAL DYSPLASIA

CERVICAL DYSPLASIA refers to abnormal cells of the cervix, the lowest portion of the uterus. Most women learn about cervical dysplasia through the results of a Pap smear. If you've just gotten a report from your doctor that your Pap smear shows "abnormal" cells, you should know about the test itself, as there has been a great deal of controversy about Pap smears and the significance of their result.

A Pap test is a sampling of the cells of the cervix. It's the most common screening tool for cancer of the cervix, and it depends on the doctor's providing an adequate sampling of the cells and an accurate interpretation or analysis of the cells sampled. A Pap smear does not yield simple negative or positive results. In other words, both the lab analyzing the cells and the doctor interpreting the report from the lab must be competent. *The Wall Street Journal* recently reported on the scandalous inefficiency of some lab analyses of some Pap smears and the failure of prompt reporting to women who had levels of abnormality.

In addition, there has always been some confusion concerning what the various levels of abnormalities revealed by a Pap smear really mean. Under the system that's been in place for years, there are five different classifications: class 1 indicates normal cells and class 5 indicates cancerous cells. But the in-between classes—2, 3, and 4—are open to interpretation. For a woman to get a test result that tells her that she has a "class 3 Pap smear" is terribly confusing. Today there's a new system adopted by many labs for interpreting Pap smears called the Bethesda system. It uses uniform terminology and gives clear diagnostic results. Whether or not a laboratory adopts the Bethesda system is at its own discretion, so you might check with your doctor as to which test will be used next time you're having a Pap smear.

In addition to the confusion over Pap test results, there's also some dispute about their significance. In fact, only one in ten precancerous lesions of the type discovered in a Pap test is likely to develop into cancer if left untreated.

Despite this confusion, the Pap test is a valuable diagnostic tool that should be part of every woman's routine health care. The question is, How do you interpret any abnormal results? Of course, your doctor is your first resource. But here is what I tell my patients who ask about an abnormal Pap result. Most often an abnormal test is simply an alert; a follow-up test will be requested. Cervical dysplasia that has progressed will, of course, require surgery. But between the abnormal test and the follow-up, you have a chance to improve your condition by using nutritional medicine. Most women (and many doctors) take no action at all once they have an abnormal test result: They simply schedule another test. But you shouldn't be passive in this regard. If you've had an abnormal test, you should make every effort to improve your next reading, and a simple program, which I'll outline, can make the difference between another abnormal test and one that's perfectly normal.

There are a number of risk factors connected with cervical cancer including sexual activity at an early age, multiple sexual partners, long-term use of oral contraceptives, two viruses—the herpes II virus and the human papilloma (wart) virus—and smoking. There's nothing you can do about these factors (except smoking) at the time you get an abnormal Pap smear. But there is a great body of evidence that nutritional factors play an important role in the development of cervical cancer. Blood tests of cervical cancer patients have shown that 67 percent had at least one abnormal vitamin level.

Folic acid deficiency is closely linked to the development of cervical dysplasia. There have been reported cases of women who, after a diagnosis of cervical dysplasia, began taking folate supplements and subsequently had a completely normal Pap test.

Beta-carotene and vitamin A deficiencies are closely associated with the development of cervical dysplasia. In one study, women deficient in vitamin A were three times more likely to develop severe dysplasia. Vitamin A and beta-carotene supplements have been shown to improve cervical dysplasia to the point that no abnormal cells are in evidence.

Vitamin C is also important in controlling the development of cervical dysplasia. Women who consume less than 50 percent of the RDA of vitamin C can have ten times the risk of developing the condition.

If you've had an abnormal Pap smear, stop smoking, begin nutritional therapy as I've recommended, have a follow-up Pap smear at the time recommended by your doctor, schedule the second test for the middle of your menstrual cycle, don't douche before the test, and ask your doctor if the lab that will examine your test uses the Bethesda system.

NATURAL PRESCRIPTION FOR CERVICAL DYSPLASIA

- If you smoke, stop. This is important, as smoking is closely linked with the development of dysplasia.

IN ADDITION TO YOUR DAILY SUPPLEMENTS, PAGE xxiv, TAKE

- Folic acid: 5 mg. twice a day for three months or until your follow-up Pap smear. (Folic acid comes in 800-mcg. tablets; you need to take about nine a day, and you can take them all at one time.) Also increase your consumption of foods rich in folic acid, including raw deep green leafy vegetables such as spinach, beet greens, kale, turnip greens, broccoli, asparagus, and endive as well as liver, wheat germ, and lima beans.

- **Vitamin A: 50,000 I.U. daily for two months (do so only under medical supervision); then 10,000 I.U. daily or until follow-up Pap smear. Also increase your consumption of foods rich in vitamin A, including carrots, squash, sweet potatoes, dark leafy vegetables, and broccoli.**

- **Vitamin C: 1,000 mg. daily.**

IN ADDITION: If subsequent testing indicates that you do require surgery, the standard treatment is a cone biopsy, in which a cone-shaped piece of the cervix is removed. The procedure must be done in an operating room under general or spinal anesthesia. But there is a new treatment called Loop Electrosurgical Excision Procedure (LEEP), which was developed in Britain and is becoming increasingly available in this country. LEEP has many advantages over the cone biopsy in that it requires only local anesthesia, is fast, causes no post-op pain or discomfort, and the possibility for infection following the procedure is eliminated. Of course, your doctor is the best judge of which procedure is appropriate for your condition, but, if indicated, LEEP could simplify your treatment.

• • •

COLD SORES

COLD SORES, or fever blisters, are caused by the herpes simplex virus. We don't know exactly what stimulates the appearance of these blisters but they are commonly exacerbated by stress, sun, alcohol, sugar, a concurrent viral infection, or simply being run-down. They usually begin with a tiny red spot at the corner of the mouth or nostril, which quickly turns into small blisters. Sometimes there's just one; sometimes a whole cluster of blisters appears. After these blisters break, a scab forms that can take one or two weeks to heal.

It's estimated that 80 to 90 percent of the population harbors the herpes simplex virus that causes cold sores, but it's possible to have the virus and never experience an outbreak. On the other hand, some people are troubled by regular cold sores. The pain and discomfort can be considerable, but my patients often seem just as troubled by the embarrassment of their appearance.

There is no effective drug therapy that will cure cold sores, but the good news is that there are a number of very safe and effective natural remedies.

Two particular treatments have given my patients great relief and also act as a preventive: *Lactobacillus acidophilus* and lysine. In addition, zinc, used topically and as a supplement, can give immediate relief.

Lactobacillus acidophilus is the living culture that is used to make yogurt. You may have heard that yogurt can be beneficial for intestinal and digestive problems, and it's this connection that led to the discovery that acidophilus can help cold sores. A doctor using acidophilus to treat patients with severe diarrhea discovered that two of his patients suffering from cold sores found dramatic improvement in their sores as well as their diarrhea. Further research found that acidophilus capsules can not only help relieve existing cold sores but also help prevent new ones. You can buy acidophilus capsules at health food stores, but be sure that the tablets you buy contain living bacteria; they're usually kept refrigerated. Eating yogurt might be of some help, but there's no evidence that it can have the dramatic effect of the capsules.

Another aid in the relief of cold sores is the amino acid L-lysine, which is particularly effective in preventing recurrence. There is a hypothesis that lysine inhibits herpes activity, while another amino acid, arginine, promotes it. And studies have demonstrated that lysine treatment can be very beneficial to cold sore sufferers. In one study, forty-five patients who took lysine supplements were followed for two years. Forty-two of these patients had a dramatic reduction of cold sores. For most, pain disappeared overnight, and the initial sore did not spread, but the infection returned one to four weeks after stopping lysine.

The most effective pattern for taking lysine to prevent cold sores is to take a maintenance dosage as a preventive and then increase this dosage if you experience an outbreak of the infection. Be sure if you take lysine supplements that you watch your cholesterol levels, as there's some evidence that lysine may stimulate the liver to increase cholesterol production.

In addition to taking lysine as a supplement, it can be applied topically in the form of lysine cream, available in health food stores. I usually advise applying it topically twice a day, but check the directions on the label.

Since cold sores are stimulated by the imbalance of the amino acids arginine and lysine, it can also be beneficial to avoid arginine-containing foods. These foods include chocolate, peanuts and other nuts, seeds, and cereal grains.

Zinc used topically can help to heal cold sores. Zinc oxide—the stuff lifeguards used to put on their noses—won't work because it doesn't deliver the zinc. Instead, use a zinc lozenge—the kind used for sore throats—and let it dissolve on the lesions.

Both vitamin C with bioflavonoids and zinc supplements, particularly when taken in conjunction, can help cure cold sores. As with lysine, it's best to take a maintenance dosage and increase it in the event of an outbreak.

NATURAL PRESCRIPTION FOR COLD SORES

FOR IMMEDIATE RELIEF

- Lysine cream: Apply topically to lesions twice a day or as recommended on label.

- Zinc lozenge: let it dissolve on the lesion.

FOR PREVENTION:

- Avoid arginine-rich foods, including chocolate, peanuts and other nuts, seeds, and cereal grains.

IN ADDITION TO YOUR DAILY SUPPLEMENTS, PAGE xxiv, TAKE

- *Lactobacillus acidophilus:* three capsules a day, one with each meal.

- L-lysine: 3,000 mg. daily; 1,000 mg. with each meal at the first sign of a cold sore outbreak. After the symptoms lessen, reduce your intake to 500 mg. a day. If you break out on this maintenance dosage, increase your dose to 1,000 mg. a day to prevent recurrence.

- Zinc: 50 mg. a day.

- Vitamin C with bioflavonoids: 500 mg. a day.

•   •   •

COLDS

MANY PEOPLE THINK there's nothing they can do for a cold; they assume that they just have to tough it out. The fact is that there's good news about colds. While there's not a great deal you can do to stop a cold once you've caught it, there are natural remedies that can reduce its duration and severity. In addition, if you have frequent colds, you can take steps to reduce or completely eliminate their onset.

A cold is caused by a virus. You know you have a cold when you experience a stuffy nose and sneezing, a dry, sore throat, perhaps a slight temperature along with fatigue and headache. You can usually tell the difference between a cold and the flu: A flu may cause a higher fever and more severe symptoms including muscle aches and pains. And there will probably be news of a flu epidemic in your area.

The important thing to keep in mind about colds is that they are far more likely to attack when your resistance is down. If you get more than one or two colds a year, you could have a weakened immune system and you should adopt the measures in the Blueprint for Health, page xvii.

I've found that many of my patients develop colds when stress, particularly emotional stress, puts them over the top. They become generally run-down by working late, not eating properly, drinking too much caffeine and alcohol, and then they undergo a stressful incident that precipitates the cold: a project that's due and demands intense work, an emotional trauma involving a loved one, a professional setback, and so on. As stress reduces immunity, there's often one particular incident that they can point to that probably caused their cold. Obviously we can't avoid problems in our lives, but we can work to become as healthy as possible so that when something does come along to stress us we don't wind up in bed sick.

My approach to fighting colds is twofold: First strengthen your resistance to infection so that you won't catch a cold, then follow a course of action to lessen its length and severity.

You strengthen your immune system by following the recommendations in the Blueprint for Health, page xvii. In general, you must eat a wholesome diet, take a good daily vitamin, exercise regularly, control stress, and get enough rest. All these measures will go a long way to preventing colds.

One additional recommendation: If you are scrupulous about washing your hands frequently during cold season, you will considerably lessen your chances of catching a cold since a very common method of transmission of the cold virus is from your hands to your face. You shake hands with someone with a cold, you use a stair rail that someone with a cold has used, and soon you, too, are sick. So make a point of frequent hand washing, especially during the winter or when someone in your family or office is suffering from a cold.

To lessen a cold's symptoms and duration, you need to be willing to take the time—at least two days—to let your system fight it off. If you try to suppress the symptoms, you may feel better temporarily but, in my experience, the cold often lasts longer.

Unfortunately, the antibiotics that can be so effective against a bacterial infection will do nothing to help a cold. I've had patients beg for prescriptions of antibiotics because they're so conditioned to think that any pill is better than nothing. But the truth is that I believe no pill is best when it comes to a cold. That applies to over-the-counter remedies, too. Most of them contain ingredients that have uncomfortable side effects including nausea and drowsiness. Interestingly, a recent hearing sponsored by the Government Operations Subcommittee on Health attacked antihistamines as being useless for cold sufferers. As a cold is caused by a virus, it does not cause a release of histamines—the substances that antihistamines are designed to fight (and *do* fight in a runny nose caused by allergy). Studies have found that cold sufferers on antihistamines did no better than those given a placebo. And the antihistamines have potentially dangerous side effects. (I was amused to hear a "newsbreak" on TV, which heralded a new cold remedy that will reduce symptoms in most people about 20 percent. But the side effects were so serious —they included excessive bleeding, blurred vision, among others—that I can't imagine why anyone would prefer these problems to the cold itself.)

Vitamin C really can help reduce the length and symptoms of a cold. It enhances the immune system, including white blood cell production and antibody response, and can act as a natural decongestant. I suggest you take extra vitamin C for the duration of the cold, in addition to your regular daily supplement.

Vitamin A is a powerful infection fighter. It works to boost our immune system and more effectively rid our bodies of the cold virus. I suggest that people with colds take a vitamin A supplement daily for the duration of the cold.

One mineral that has been proven to lessen the symptoms and duration of a cold is zinc. Zinc gives a boost to the immune system and, like vitamin C, has a specific antiviral property. I have found zinc lozenges to be the most effective.

There's also an herb—echinacea—that's very effective in stimulating immune functions and fighting a cold. It also has antiinflammatory properties. Echinacea is commonly known as the purple coneflower, and it's native to the prairies of the midwestern United States. I have many patients who swear that it has reduced their cold symptoms dramatically. You can get echinacea in a capsule in health food stores, and one or two capsules twice a day, or as directed on the bottle, for up to two weeks can be helpful.

If your throat is sore, gargling with salt water will reduce the pain. Just mix a teaspoon of salt into a glass of half warm water and half hydrogen peroxide and gargle every hour or so.

Sleep and general bed rest will help speed the course of a cold. As I mentioned, many people feel they have to "tough" out a cold, and they wind up suffering from it for days and days. A day or two of rest could have made the difference. During the deepest levels of sleep our immune functions are greatly increased, functioning more effectively than during an active day. If at all possible, go to bed for at least the first day of a cold, when you're suffering the worst symptoms.

Fluids are important when fighting a cold, as a highly moistened respiratory tract will more readily repel the virus attacker. Liquids will also improve the function of the white blood cells and will flush out the virus in mucus. However, fruit juices are not the answer. Stay away from orange juice, apple juice, and other fruit juices. Anything with a high concentration of sugar—and that includes fructose and sucrose—will slow down the immune system. I suggest that you stick with water—with perhaps a slice of lemon—or seltzer or club soda either plain or with a *splash* of fruit juice. Warm beverages, including herb teas and soups, are the most effective liquids for fighting a cold.

If you are congested from a cold, a humidifier, especially one in your room at night, will help you breathe easier.

Many of my patients ask me if they can exercise with a cold. My recommendation is to stop exercising for the first day or two when the symptoms are worst. Don't push yourself; this will only weaken your immune system and prolong the cold. Wait until the third or fourth day when you are feeling "yourself" to resume exercise.

Many of my patients ask about taking cough or cold medications. As mentioned, I don't recommend them. Many have been proven to be ineffective, and most of them just mask symptoms. The only exception I make to this is if you have a cough that's keeping you awake at night. In that instance I think it's fine to take a cough medicine that will allow you to rest. If you tend to develop ear infections, using a decongestant at night, along with a humidifier, can help. I never recommend the use of nasal sprays, as they can cause a rebound effect. They temporarily stop your nose from running, but as soon as you discontinue them your nose runs even more than it did in the beginning. People sometimes get virtually addicted to these sprays, and I don't think they are of any real benefit.

One last tip: Alcohol swells your bronchial tissues, so if you do have a cold, it's best to avoid drinking so as not to exacerbate congestion.

NATURAL PRESCRIPTION FOR COLDS

FOR PREVENTION:

- Strengthen your immune system by following the recommendations in Blueprint for Health, page xvii.

- Wash your hands frequently during cold season or when someone in your household or office has a cold.

FOR TREATMENT:

- Get sufficient sleep and bed rest, especially for the first day or two. It really does make a difference in the duration of a cold.

- Drink plenty of fluids. Avoid any sugared drinks. Avoid fruit juices including orange juice, and rely on herb teas, warm soups, and vegetable juices.

- For sore throat pain, gargle with a teaspoon of salt dissolved in a glass of half warm water and half hydrogen peroxide. You can repeat hourly or as needed.

- Use a humidifier, particularly in your room at night.

- Don't exercise until the third or fourth day after the start of the cold, with the exception of light stretching exercises.

- If coughing is keeping you up at night, use an over-the-counter medication that will allow you to rest.

- Avoid the use of nasal sprays, because they can cause a rebound effect.

- Because alcohol swells your bronchial tissues, avoid drinking.

IN ADDITION TO YOUR DAILY SUPPLEMENTS, PAGE xxiv, TAKE

- Vitamin C: 500 mg. of vitamin C every four hours for the duration of the cold, not to exceed 2,000 mg. daily. If you develop diarrhea, reduce the amount.

- Zinc: one lozenge of zinc gluconate of 23 mg. every six hours for the duration of a cold. Discontinue after a week.

- Vitamin A: 25,000 I.U. daily for the duration of the cold. Discontinue after one week.

- Echinacea. This herb is available in capsule form in health food stores. Take one or two capsules twice a day, or as directed on the container, for up to two weeks.

• • •

CONGESTIVE HEART FAILURE

CONGESTIVE HEART FAILURE is a symptom of many serious diseases including high blood pressure (see Hypertension, page 194), heart valve disease, heart attack (see Angina, page 12), emphysema, congenital heart disease, and atherosclerosis (hardening of the arteries), among others. It's caused when the pumping action of the heart is impaired. Congestive heart failure differs from a heart attack or cardiac arrest in that the heart doesn't stop, it just becomes less and less efficient at pumping blood. As the heart loses its ability to pump blood, fluid accumulates in the veins that carry blood from the lungs, causing the lungs to become swollen and congested. The legs also become swollen with fluid. You may become breathless, particularly after mild exercise. You may have difficulty breathing when you lie down. You may have chest pain. You may lose your appetite and experience mental confusion. You may also experience frequent urination, particularly at night.

Usually the first symptom of congestive heart failure that patients notice is breathlessness and fatigue. If you have a "heart condition" or if you notice these symptoms or any of those described above, you should see your doctor. Anyone with any form of heart failure should be under the care of a physician. The first step in treating congestive heart failure is to determine exactly what's causing it. Is it high blood pressure? Heart valve disease? The result of a heart attack? Your doctor will of course determine the cause and prescribe the treatment.

You cannot depend on natural remedies to cure congestive heart failure. Where natural remedies can help you is in reducing the symptoms. I've had a number of patients who were on medication for heart failure —the common treatments being digitalis and diuretics and also a drug called Procardia—but were not getting sufficient relief from symptoms. These people have been greatly helped by adopting natural means. One of my male patients had great difficulty sleeping even though he was being treated with a variety of medications. Once he adopted a natural program, he found his symptoms relieved to the point where he sleeps as well as he ever has and rarely experiences shortness of breath.

The supplement coenzyme Q10 (or CoQ10) has been of enormous help to my patients with congestive heart failure. (Unfortunately, CoQ10 is on the FDA's "hit list," not because it's dangerous, but because the FDA claims that it has no benefit. Consumer groups are fighting to keep it in the stores since it has been found to be so helpful.) Coenzyme Q10, which is also known as ubiquinone, plays an important role in fat and energy metabolism. It's been shown to be of extreme benefit to people who suffer with any kind of heart disease, as it helps prevent the accumulation of fatty acids within the heart muscle. I'm aware of reports claiming that CoQ10 is ineffective, but my patients invariably find that the supplement reduces their symptoms. They usually see results in one to three weeks.

There's another nutritional supplement, an amino acid called carnitine, that improves the burning of fatty acids and thereby improves the heart muscle's exercise tolerance. Studies also reveal that in addition to helping to strengthen the heart muscle, carnitine aids in lowering total cholesterol and triglyceride levels and prevents irregular heartbeat. Carnitine is a substance natural to the body. As people age, they tend to become deficient in carnitine, which can have an adverse effect on the heart. I suggest that my patients with congestive heart failure take DL-carnitine (available in health food stores) daily.

There are other supplements that can help give relief. Beta-carotene, a powerful antioxidant, has been shown to have a significant effect in reducing symptoms (as well as the incidence of strokes, heart attacks, and sudden cardiac deaths). The most impressive evidence comes from a long-term study involving more than 22,000 male doctors who have been taking beta-carotene for an average of six years. The best effect is seen when the beta-carotene is ingested in the form of food, and I suggest that my patients make a serious effort to eat at least five half-cup servings of fruits and vegetables—primary sources of beta-carotene. This is not as difficult to achieve as you my think: A half cup is just an average serving of sliced carrots or a slice of cantaloupe. The best sources of beta-carotene are yellow/orange fruits and vegetables including carrots, sweet potatoes, apricots, peaches, and cantaloupes, and dark green leafy vegetables such as broccoli, spinach, kale, and arugula. I also suggest to my patients that they take a supplement of beta-carotene daily.

Magnesium is another mineral that's important for proper heart functioning. In fact, magnesium deficiencies have been found in over 20 percent of patients with congestive heart failure. In addition, patients with congestive heart failure are prone to irregular heartbeats in the form of premature ventricular contractions; magnesium has been used to control this condition.

Low levels of vitamin E have been implicated in the development of various heart problems. One World Health Organization study found low levels of vitamin E to be a major risk factor for death from heart disease.

Exercise is always important when discussing any kind of heart disease. A heart strengthened by exercise will be stronger and more resistant to failure. It's important that you discuss exercise with your doctor.

NATURAL PRESCRIPTION FOR CONGESTIVE HEART FAILURE

If you have congestive heart failure, you should be under the regular care of a physician. The following suggestions are meant to complement your doctor's recommendations.

IN ADDITION TO YOUR DAILY SUPPLEMENTS, PAGE xxiv, TAKE

- Coenzyme Q10: 30 to 60 mg. three times a day.

- DL-carnitine: 250 mg. three times a day.

- Beta-carotene: five half-cup servings daily of fruits and vegetables such as yellow/orange fruits and vegetables including carrots, sweet potatoes, apricots, peaches, and cantaloupes, and dark green leafy vegetables such as broccoli, spinach, kale, and arugula. Or you can take beta-carotene supplements in the amount of 10,000 mg. daily.

- Magnesium: 250 mg. twice daily.

- Vitamin E: 400 I.U. daily.

- Exercise: Discuss with your doctor.

• • •

CONJUNCTIVITIS

CONJUNCTIVITIS, OR PINK EYE, is a common infection. You know you have it when your eye becomes pink and feels itchy and gritty and when you wake up in the morning with crusted eyelids caused by a discharge. (Some people mistake the red eyes of an allergy with conjunctivitis: If you don't have a discharge, you don't have conjunctivitis.) Conjunctivitis, an inflammation of the conjunctiva, the membrane that lines the eye, is contagious, so if you do have the symptoms, avoid sharing washcloths or towels, and wash the ones you're using regularly in hot water.

If you get conjunctivitis routinely, you probably have allergic conjunctivitis. In my experience, people with this condition are almost always allergic to certain foods. Once they learn which food is the culprit and they eliminate it from their diet, the conjunctivitis clears up permanently. For more information on how to identify the cause of your allergic conjunctivitis, see Food Allergy, page 146. The other natural steps recommended in this section will help relieve discomfort until the allergen is eliminated.

When children get conjunctivitis they are commonly given antibiotic ointment or drops and, to avoid contagion, they must stay home from school until the redness clears up. Many adults, who are more careful with personal hygiene, find that they can treat conjunctivitis themselves. But if you have a case that isn't better in a few days or one in which the redness has been caused by something other than an infection (for example, an injury or trauma to the eye), you should consult a doctor.

The best approach in treating pink eye is to keep the eye as clean as possible and try to "wash" the infection away. You can use a warm-water solution (boil one quart of water with one tablespoon of boric acid) on a soft cloth or cotton ball. Let the moistened cloth rest on the eye for a few minutes to loosen any crusted discharge. Then rinse your eyes thoroughly but gently and pat dry with a clean towel.

If the discharge creates heavy crusts on your eyelids, you may need something more than a simple water wash. Try an over-the-counter preparation called I Scrub, a mild soap available at pharmacies that's safe for the eyes.

NATURAL PRESCRIPTION FOR CONJUNCTIVITIS

- Wash your eyes with a solution of one quart boiled water with one tablespoon boric acid (which you have allowed to cool) to clean your eyes. Put the solution on a clean washcloth or cotton ball three or four times a day, rinsing carefully and gently.

- Use I Scrub to wash your eyes in the morning and before bed to get rid of the crusts on eyelids and eyelashes.

- Don't share washcloths and towels. Change your bed linens, especially your pillowcase, frequently.

- If your conjunctivitis does not seem to be getting better in a few days, if the redness is due to an eye injury, if the discharge is becoming worse, or if there is pain or any change in your vision, see a doctor.

- If you experience chronic conjunctivitis, you might have allergic conjunctivitis. See Food Allergy, page 146, for more information on how to identify and eliminate food allergens from your diet.

•   •   •

CONSTIPATION

EVERYBODY THINKS THEY know what constipation is but you'd be surprised at the number of people who think they're constipated but are not. That's because bowel movement patterns are entirely personal: Whereas you may have a bowel movement every day, someone else might have one every second day. I certainly believe that more frequent bowel movements are preferable. The longer that waste sits in the bowel, the more likely it is to cause a range of health problems. For most people constipation can be described as a pattern of bowel movements that's changed from regular movements to irregular, infrequent (fewer than a movement a day), and/or difficult movements. When you are constipated, your stools are typically small and hard and difficult to pass.

If you notice a change in your bowel habits, you should not immediately reach for a laxative, but should try to determine what's causing the constipation. While there's a place for laxatives, too many people use them indiscriminately at the first sign of constipation. As constipation is a symptom and not a disease, the regular use of laxatives could be masking a more serious problem, or it could in fact *cause* constipation by promoting a "lazy" bowel that *requires* a laxative in order to function.

One of the major causes of constipation is insufficient fiber in the diet. It's relatively easy to remedy this, and you'll not only be helping your constipation but also reducing your chances of developing a host of other diseases. To increase fiber, add more fresh fruits, vegetables, and whole grains to your diet. For some people the simple addition of fiber from food sources—perhaps fruit for breakfast, a fruit snack in the afternoon, fresh vegetables at dinner, and a fruit snack in the evening, along with several prunes at bedtime—will solve the problem. For others the addition of bran to the diet will make the difference.

I'm a big believer in coarse miller's bran. Some people need just a tablespoon a day while others require up to a half cup. You can sprinkle it on fruit or yogurt or mix it in juice or cereal.

Remember that bran isn't for everybody: If it causes too much gas and bloating, you should try psyllium fiber, found in many over-the-counter products or available directly from your natural food store. (A reaction that involves lots of gas and bloating after using bran could indicate celiac disease, page 73) If you use a psyllium fiber product, make sure to take it with adequate water because it won't be effective if you don't and it also can cause a bowel obstruction if taken with insufficient water.

Aloe vera gel capsules, which you can find in a natural food store, are another good natural way to encourage a bowel movement.

Many people develop constipation because they don't drink enough water. A few of my patients have been scrupulous about heeding my recommendations to cut down on caffeine and diet sodas. But they forgot to increase their fluid levels to take up the slack and became constipated. You should drink from four to six glasses of water each day. If you tend to forget, keep a bottle of club soda or mineral water on your desk or in easy reach and drink from it regularly during the day.

Many busy people develop constipation with a change in routine such as a business trip, a new job, a move, or the like because they are so distracted that they're not taking the time to use the toilet. In order to have good regular bowel habits, you have to give your system a chance to work. You must regularly sit on the toilet and make an effort to have a bowel movement. I don't mean you should strain; this will cause hemorrhoids. But you should sit for at least a few minutes every day—preferably after breakfast—to let your bowels move. It sometimes helps to have a drink of something hot immediately followed by something cold, which helps stimulate bowel contractions. Remember also that if you feel the urge to move your bowels, you should not ignore it. This is another sure cause of constipation.

Regular exercise is a habit that will help fight constipation. Just a twenty-minute walk four or five times a week could make the difference, and, like adding fiber to your diet, regular exercise will help prevent a number of other diseases and promote general good health. Exercise makes your whole system work more efficiently and helps move food through your bowels faster.

Finally, if you've suddenly become constipated or can't even pass gas and you have abdominal pain and cramping, you should consult your doctor, as you may have developed on obstruction that could require immediate attention.

NATURAL PRESCRIPTION FOR CONSTIPATION

- Be sure you're getting adequate fiber in your diet. Eat plenty of fresh fruits and vegetables as well as whole grain cereals.

- Add bran to your diet. I recommend coarse miller's bran. Begin with one tablespoon in the morning and gradually increase by a tablespoon every several days until you achieve the desired result. You can mix it in juice or yogurt or sprinkle it on cereal. If the bran causes too much gas and bloating (it usually does cause some), cut down on the amount or try:

- Psyllium fiber stool bulking agent. Follow the directions on the package, and be sure to drink adequate amounts of water. Take one teaspoon in a glass of water and increase to two teaspoons a day if necessary.

- Drink plenty of fluids: four to six glasses each day.

- Develop healthy bowel habits. Give yourself time to use the toilet at least once each day, usually after breakfast. Drink something hot followed by something cold and then relax on the toilet. Don't strain. Be sure to go whenever you feel the urge.

- Try aloe vera gel capsules, which are a natural stimulant to move the bowels, and are available in natural food stores. Follow the directions on the package.

- If you must use a bowel stimulant/laxative, do so only occasionally.

•   •   •

CONTACT DERMATITIS

DERMATITIS MEANS INFLAMMATION of the skin. Any number of things can cause a skin irritation and sometimes the precise diagnosis is of less interest to the suffering party than the remedy, so I've tried to list ailments where you could most easily find them. Poison ivy is a type of contact dermatitis, but most people just think of it as poison ivy (see Poison Ivy, page 282). Eczema is a type of dermatitis; if you have a rash not described in this section, consult Eczema, page 132. Sometimes simple dry skin can be mistaken for something else. If you have a rash and it doesn't fall into any other category, consult Dry Skin, page 123).

Contact dermatitis is an allergy to something that touches the skin. Most cases involve a rash that can include itchy, red blisters, which can ooze and then develop a crust. In most cases, the rash will disappear when the allergen is removed, though sometimes if the allergen has been in contact with the skin for a while, the rash may continue for days or weeks after the allergen is removed.

The only way to cure a case of contact dermatitis is to remove the source of the allergen. In many cases, the patient knows exactly what caused the problem. I've had countless patients tell me that when they tried a new cosmetic or a new deodorant, they developed a reaction. When they stopped using the substance, their reaction disappeared.

The challenge is to help people discover the source of their reactions when they don't have a clue as to what caused them. Here is a list of body parts and common allergenic substances that can affect them. Remember, a rash will usually appear on or near the site where an allergenic substance was used.

SCALP: Often the rash will appear on the eyelids, neck, face, and ears and sometimes, especially when a substance was applied to the hair, on the hands. Sources are most commonly shampoos, hair dyes and rinses, permanent-wave treatments, dandruff treatments, soaps, bathing caps, wigs, combs and brushes made of materials that are irritating, curlers, and pins used in hair styling.

FOREHEAD: Most commonly seen as a rash spreading across the forehead. Sources are a hat band or hat linings, visors, helmets, cosmetics, suntan lotion, or anything worn on the forehead, like a sweatband.

EYES: Sources are cosmetics such as mascara or eyebrow pencil or eyeshadows, as well as pollens (see Hay Fever, page 167), soaps, hand lotions, insect sprays, and nasal sprays.

FACE: Usually cosmetics but could be from any substance used on the face including soap, suntan lotion, shaving cream, aftershave, or something that's on your hands and transferred to the face.

EARS: Usually from earrings. It can also be from perfume, hair dye, shampoo, eyeglasses or sunglasses, telephone receivers, or ear plugs.

NOSE: Nasal sprays, perfumes, paper tissues, eyeglass frames.

LIPS AND MOUTH: Cosmetics such as lipsticks, toothpastes and mouthwashes, cigarettes and cigars, denture adhesives, and candies.

NECK: Substances used on the scalp, for example, cosmetics, collars, scarves, certain dress or shirt labels, and fur or wool near the neck.

UNDERARMS: Soaps, deodorants, depilatories, antiperspirants, shaving creams, perfumes.

HANDS AND WRISTS: Dishpan hands are a common form of contact dermatitis caused by hands' being immersed repeatedly in soapy water. Regular use of vinyl gloves (not rubber, which can cause a reaction) is helpful, as is removing rings when wetting hands and wearing gloves when the weather is cold and windy. Soaps and cleansers used in showering or bathing, gloves, rings, bracelets, topical medications or creams, and most any substance that touches the hands can also irritate the skin. Wrists can develop a rash from the metal backing of a watch. Coating the back of the watch with clear nail polish can sometimes remedy this.

TRUNK: Clothing, bathing soaps or oils, and underwear.

FEET: Shoes, socks, shoe polishes, fur linings particularly in boots, ankle bracelets, medications, or detergents used on socks.

A few other common allergens that can cause symptoms in sensitive people include nickel, found in jewelry, which is often the cause of a red patch of skin that just won't go away. It can occur on the ears from earrings or the wrist from a watch or bracelet or on the neck from a necklace. Some people who have their ears pierced develop an allergy to nickel and must avoid it for the rest of their lives.

Perfume in any form can cause reactions in sensitive people. It's very difficult to identify exactly which chemical in a perfume is causing the problem as there are so many components to a fragrance. I suggest that if you have a problem with reactions to fragrances, or any allergic reactions to foods or instances of contact dermatitis, be especially careful when you use new products, including perfumes, shampoos, soaps, detergents, and the like. Try to introduce only one new product at a time and wait a week or so before introducing another; if you do have a reaction, it's easier to identify the cause and eliminate it.

What can you do if you develop a case of contact dermatitis? If you identify and remove the allergen, the rash should disappear in a few weeks. To relieve any itching in the meantime, you can use an over-the-counter cream containing 0.5 percent hydrocortisone. I tell my patients to use these creams sparingly; although they are quite mild, it's not a good idea to use them every day for more than a month as overuse can cause discoloration or thinning of the skin.

I also recommend taking nutrients that help maintain the health of the skin like MaxEPA, vitamin C, and vitamin A.

If your contact dermatitis doesn't clear up in a month, you should consult a doctor.

NATURAL PRESCRIPTION FOR CONTACT DERMATITIS

- Identify the cause of the reaction and eliminate the allergen.

- If you have contact dermatitis on your hands, use vinyl gloves in place of rubber gloves when using cleansers and chemicals and when washing dishes.

- To relieve symptoms while waiting for the rash to clear, use an over-the-counter cream containing 0.5 percent hydrocortisone. Use sparingly.

IN ADDITION TO YOUR DAILY SUPPLEMENTS, PAGE xxiv, TAKE

- MaxEPA: 1,000 mg. three times a day.

- Vitamin C: 1,000 mg. daily.

- Vitamin A: 10,000 I.U. daily.

• • •

COUGH/BRONCHITIS

BRONCHITIS IS A TERM that refers to an inflammation of the bronchial tubes—the main air passages that bring air to the lung tissue. When these passages become irritated they produce mucus, which stimulates a cough in our effort to clear the air passages. A cough is the primary symptom of bronchitis. Not all coughs are due to bronchitis, but bronchitis almost invariably causes coughing. Whether you suffer from bronchitis or a simple cough, you need to determine the cause in order to find relief.

If you have had a cough for a few weeks and it's becoming more severe; if you have an unexplained cough for more than three weeks; if you are having difficulty breathing; if you have a dry cough with no other symptoms, you should consult your doctor, as these types of coughs could be indications of a more serious problem.

If a cough is productive, that is, if sputum or phlegm is brought up, and the sputum is clear or white, then it's a cough you should probably endure for a few days. It's probably the result of a bout with a cold or flu and is the body's effort to rid itself of the sputum that has collected in your lungs as you fight off the infection. This kind of cough, which could be termed acute bronchitis caused by a viral infection, is annoying but necessary. If your throat is irritated by the cough, you can gargle with salt dissolved in warm water to ease any pain. In addition, a humidifier at night will help relieve the cough and encourage sleep (see Colds, page 83, for more information on fighting a cold).

If your cough is producing sputum but the sputum is yellow or green in color, you probably have an infection that will need to be treated with antibiotics, and you should consult your doctor.

If the cough is a dry or nonproductive cough, you need to determine the cause and eliminate it. Here are some likely causes of coughs.

Cigarette smoking is a primary cause. That's because the smoke is constantly irritating the bronchial passages. Many smokers wake in the morning with a cough that produces some sputum that's lightly tinged in color. Obviously the cure for this is to stop smoking. Some patients have complained to me that once they stopped smoking, their coughing actually got worse. This is because nicotine relaxes the cilia in the lungs, allowing smoke and toxins to enter. When you stop smoking, the cilia become reactivated, and any increased coughing is a good sign: It's the cilia cleaning out the lungs.

Many people suffer from a chronic morning cough. Often these people are also cigarette smokers and they come to believe that this morning cough is normal. But if it lasts for weeks at a time, particularly in the winter, and it recurs for at least two winters in a row, it could well be chronic bronchitis and you must visit your doctor for a definitive diagnosis. If you do have chronic bronchitis, the first thing you must do is stop smoking and avoid secondhand smoke.

Asthma can cause chronic coughing. Once you get the asthma under control, the coughing will diminish or stop entirely. See Asthma, page 23.

Sinusitis and a chronic postnasal drip can cause irritation when the mucus from the sinuses drips down into the bronchi at night. This usually results in morning coughing—though you can also experience coughing all day long—with clear to whitish phlegm. See Sinusitis, page 308.

I've had patients who have had persistent coughs for months following a cold. Seeing that the cough was no longer related to an infection, I tested for food allergies and, sure enough, the patients were allergic—in most cases to dairy products. Such an allergy, even one you have never noticed before, can manifest itself following a cold, when the immune system is weak. The cure is to eliminate the food that's causing the problem. In most cases, any allergenic food may be reintroduced in a few months, after the body has built up its immunity again (see Food Allergy, page 146).

Certain blood pressure medications can cause a chronic cough. The most common ones include Vasotec, Zestril, Capoten, and Prinivil. If you are on a medication to control blood pressure and are troubled by a persistent cough, talk to you doctor about changing your medication. If the drug was the problem, the cough will clear up in a few days.

Some people develop a cough as a result of acid reflux, which occurs when the contents of the stomach regurgitate into your esophagus. You also experience acid indigestion with this condition. A visit to your doctor and a series of x-rays can pinpoint this problem. If reflux is causing your cough, see Heartburn, page 173; H. Pylori, page 164; Ulcers, page 335.

Finally, it is possible to develop a cough after inhaling irritants such as cleaning fluids that contain ammonia, which can irritate your lungs. Of course such a cough will rapidly diminish and, assuming that you aren't exposed again to the irritating agent, should disappear in a few hours at most.

NATURAL PRESCRIPTION FOR COUGH/BRONCHITIS

DETERMINE THE SOURCE OF THE COUGH:

- If it's a productive cough with clear sputum and lasts for a day or two, it is usually due to a cold or viral flu. Relieve sore throat with a saltwater gargle (one teaspoon of salt dissolved in warm water) every few hours and allow the cough to continue to rid your lungs of sputum. See Colds, page 83.

- If the cough is a dry, nonproductive cough, see information above on the following causes: smoking, asthma, sinusitis, food allergy, blood pressure medication, acid reflux, or inhalation of irritants.

- If the cough is productive but the sputum is yellow or green, it's probably the result of an infection and may need to be treated with antibiotics. In that case, you should consult with your doctor.

• • •

CYSTITIS

CYSTITIS, A BLADDER INFECTION, is one of the most common ailments afflicting women. Almost half of all women will have a bladder infection at some point, and about 20 percent will have them repeatedly. Some women have anatomical conditions that predispose them to urinary tract infections, which a doctor would have to identify.

If, like some women, you develop bladder infections regularly or even occasionally, and you do not have an anatomical abnormality, you should know that there are very effective natural treatments that can help prevent these infections. You should also know that repeated treatments with antibiotics can actually increase your potential for infection, making the natural approach all the more desirable.

A bladder infection occurs when bacteria—usually from the bowel— travel the short distance to the urethra and into the bladder. Once there, the bacteria multiply and become an infection that you notice when you feel the frequent need to urinate accompanied by pain and/or burning. (If, in addition to these symptoms, you also have a fever, low back pain, and/or blood in your urine, you might also have a kidney infection, in which case you should consult your doctor. If your bladder infection has turned into a kidney infection, you should be sure, after it is treated, to follow the recommendations here to avoid future infections.)

Women are more vulnerable to cystitis than men because the anus is so close to the urethra, making it easy for the bacteria to reach the bladder. (In men, a bladder infection is usually caused by an enlarged and infected prostate, which should be examined by a doctor.)

There are a number of causes of cystitis including poor hygiene, vigorous intercourse, and infrequent urination. In the past, many women were embarrassed by the disease because they felt it was an indication that they were experiencing frequent sex. One woman who came to see me was puzzled by her frequent bladder infections because she was single and had no man in her life; she felt sure I wouldn't believe her. While it's true that bladder infections are sometimes referred to as "honeymoon cystitis," many women develop infections from improper hygiene—wiping back to front after a bowel movement. This brings bacteria into close contact with the urethra. It's important to keep the genital area clean and dry. In addition to proper wiping from front to back, you should avoid feminine hygiene sprays, douches, and bubble baths. Try to avoid tight clothes, and wear cotton panties.

Recent studies have shown that another practice can foster cystitis and may be even more important than poor hygiene or sexual activity, and that's failure to urinate frequently. We now know that women who "hold" their urine for a long time after they feel the urge to go are far more likely to develop a bladder infection than women who go immediately upon feeling the urge. Why? Because urine held in the bladder gives bacteria, which double in density every twenty minutes, more time to develop into an infection. If you want to stave off urinary infections, be sure to void regularly.

Of course if you want to void frequently, you should drink plenty of fluids, particularly water. One woman told me she stopped drinking fluids to avoid the burning that she experienced upon urinating, unaware that she was stimulating the development of the infection. Frequent emptying of the bladder flushes it of bacteria. So be sure to drink about six eight-ounce glasses of water daily.

In addition to voiding regularly, you should drink fluids before intercourse and urinate soon after. This helps to cleanse the urethra and prevent infections from developing. Of course, it's also helpful to wash the genital area thoroughly after intercourse.

If you've been through a bladder infection, you might have heard about the old-fashioned "cranberry cure." It was believed that the juice worked to acidify the urine, making an infection less likely to develop. Some doctors scoffed at the cranberry cure, saying that it was simply a matter of drinking so much fluid that the increased volume of urine flushed out the system and the bacteria. We now know that the cranberry cure *is* effective. It works because the juice contains a substance that makes it difficult for the bacteria to adhere to the lining of the urethra and bladder.

Cranberry juice should be part of your natural treatment. But as the types available in supermarkets usually have large amounts of sugar, it's best to buy cranberry juice in a health food store for the most beneficial results. As an alternative, ask for cranberry concentrate or cranberry concentrate capsules.

In addition to cranberry concentrate or capsules, I instruct my patients to take buffered vitamin C, a proven infection-fighter, as well as bioflavonoids, zinc, and vitamin A. Vitamin A encourages an antibacterial effect and helps to acidify the urine.

Antibiotics, while sometimes crucial to curing cystitis or, certainly, kidney infections, can sometimes create a problem. Patients have come to me complaining of persistent bladder infections that have been treated with antibiotics. While they have the symptoms of a bladder infection—urgent, frequent, and painful urination—repeat urinalyses do not reveal bacteria. In cases like these the previous courses of antibiotics kill the good bacteria as well as the bad bacteria leading to a yeast overgrowth. If you have recurring bladder infections or if you've been treated with antibiotics and have suffered from a bladder irritation subsequently, I suggest a yeast-cleansing program. This means you should follow a yeast-free diet for three months, avoiding foods containing yeast including bread, cheese, mushrooms, vinegar, soy sauce, fermented foods, alcohol, olives, and pickles. In addition, acidophilus supplements will aid the cleansing. If you are prone to frequent bladder infections, you might incorporate yogurt (with live cultures) into your regular diet. For more information on problems with yeast, see Candidiasis, page 61.

NATURAL PRESCRIPTION FOR CYSTITIS

FOR PREVENTION:

- Practice good personal hygiene: Wipe from front to back after having a bowel movement and keep the vaginal area clean and dry.
- Avoid feminine hygiene sprays, douches, and bubble baths.
- Avoid tight clothing, and wear cotton panties.

- Urinate frequently, as soon as you feel the urge. Never hold your urine.

- If bladder infections are persistent, but urinalysis does not reveal bacteria, try a yeast-cleansing diet by avoiding foods containing yeast including bread, cheese, mushrooms, vinegar, soy sauce, fermented foods such as alcohol and olives or pickles. In addition, take acidophilus supplements: one capsule three times daily. For more information on yeast, see Candidiasis, page 61.

- Drink lots of fluids: Try to consume at least six eight-ounce glasses of water daily.

- Drink fluids before intercourse and void soon afterward.

FOR TREATMENT:

- Cranberry juice concentrate or cranberry concentrate capsules. Take one capsule three times a day with an eight-ounce glass of water.

IN ADDITION TO YOUR DAILY SUPPLEMENTS, PAGE xxiv, TAKE

- Buffered vitamin C: 500 mg. every four hours for the duration of the infection and cut down to 1,000 to 1,500 mg. daily for a maintenance dose once the infection has cleared.

- Bioflavonoids: 1 g. daily.

- Vitamin A: 25,000 I.U. daily during the infection.

- Zinc: 50 mg. daily.

IN ADDITION: If you have regular infections, you should have a urologic exam and a specialized x-ray to see if there's any abnormality of the urethra.

•　　•　　•

DANDRUFF

DANDRUFF IS A VERY common complaint, which doesn't make it any less annoying if you have it. A scalp condition that involves lots of flaking of the skin and large scales, and is often accompanied by itching, dandruff is really a version of seborrheic dermatitis (see Seborrheic Dermatitis, page 303). In addition to the scalp, it may also affect the forehead, eyebrows, ears, and the crease that runs from the nose down to the mouth. It is caused by a yeast called *Pityrosporum ovale,* and it may be helped by eliminating yeast and yeast-promoting foods from the diet. That means giving up many popular foods, but the sacrifice is worth it for those with persistent dandruff. Forbidden foods include:

- All sugars and sweets that promote yeast and make the condition worse. See Blueprint for Health, page xvii, for information on sugar in the diet.

- All foods and beverages that contain yeast, such as bread and other baked goods, cheese, vinegar, soy sauce, fermented condiments such as olives and pickles, and all wines and alcoholic drinks. See Candidiasis, page 61.

A yeast-avoidance diet can help, but don't expect it to work immediately. It may take thirty days or so to notice improvement. In the meantime, use an antidandruff shampoo.

There are several over-the-counter shampoos with zinc pyrithione (ZPT) as the active ingredient. ZPT works by slowing down cell growth and discouraging the yeast organisms responsible for the condition. Coal-tar shampoos are also very effective, but use them cautiously if you are very fair, for some of them will darken your hair. Some dandruff shampoos contain an ingredient called salicylic acid, which can be effective for some people. If the shampoo you're using seems to be losing its effectiveness, switch to another with a different major ingredient for a time. Whichever shampoo you use, be sure to follow the directions, leaving it on for a full five minutes if that's what's called for.

If the over-the-counter shampoos don't seem to help, ask your dermatologist to prescribe an antifungal shampoo with ketoconazole as the active ingredient.

NATURAL PRESCRIPTION FOR DANDRUFF

- Follow a yeast-free diet for about a month to see if it reduces your symptoms.

- Try a dandruff treatment shampoo containing zinc pyrithione or ZPT. Try to use a dandruff shampoo as infrequently as possible to control your dandruff. If one shampoo loses its effectiveness, switch to another.

IN ADDITION: If you don't find relief with over-the-counter preparations, ask your doctor about prescription shampoo with ketoconazole. Nystatin/triamcinolone acetonide cream, sold by prescription under the name Mycolog cream, is very helpful for those resistant patches of dandruff at the edges of the hairline.

•   •   •

DEPRESSION

IT IS UNFORTUNATE that while the term "depression" is used commonly to refer to everything from a feeling of mild irritation to utter anguish, its real meaning is little understood and often trivialized. In fact, depression is the most common mental disorder suffered by Americans. Some estimates claim that roughly fifty million Americans will suffer from depression at some point in their lives.

There are two facts that are important to recognize about depression: First, it is not a "weakness"; it is an actual disorder. And if the depression interferes with normal functioning, attention and treatment are required. Actual depression is not a state of mind that you can "snap out of." In one large study conducted by the RAND Corporation and UCLA, depression was shown to be more disabling than many other ailments that are often taken more seriously including arthritis, ulcers, diabetes, or high blood pressure. Only arthritis proved more painful, and only advanced heart disease caused more days spent in bed. Moreover, doctors are beginning to recognize that depression affects both physical health and mortality. For example, in 330 men infected with HIV, the virus that causes AIDS, those who were depressed died at twice the rate of those who had no depression within the first three years after diagnosis.

Sometimes it's difficult to differentiate actual depression from sadness or melancholy. Those experiencing job loss, illness, or the loss of a loved one, for example, can feel overwhelming sadness but will retain their sense of self and their ability to function in the world. Other people will become clinically depressed, or as the American Psychiatric Association describes it, will experience "a loss of interest or pleasure in all or almost all usual activities and pastimes." While grief, sadness, and melancholy are a natural consequence of life's unhappy events, depression brings the normal round of activities to a halt.

Some people with a family history of depression are more prone to develop it. Some women suffer postpartum depression due largely to a fluctuation in hormones following the birth of a baby. Some women suffer a period of depression right before their menstrual cycle (see PMS, page 276). Chronic diseases and alcoholism can also cause depression, as can some infectious diseases, including hepatitis, mononucleosis, and tuberculosis, probably due to a biochemical reaction. And finally, there are medications that cause depression, particularly steroids and antihypertensives.

What can natural medicine do for someone who is depressed? There are many steps that can be taken to help resolve depression, but first it's important to recognize that some people who are suffering from depression need outside help before they can attempt to help themselves. Here are the warning signals that indicate this need:

- altered sleeping habits (insomnia, or waking at 4 A.M.)
- altered eating habits (loss of appetite and/or weight loss or gain)
- hyperactivity or underactivity
- loss of usual interests
- lethargy
- feelings of worthlessness and guilt
- inability to concentrate
- suicidal thoughts or attempted suicide
- overwhelming feelings of anxiety, sadness, and emptiness

If at least four of these symptoms are present for at least two weeks, you should seek professional help. You can contact the National Mental Health Association, 1021 Prince Street, Alexandria, VA 22314, phone (703) 684-7722, for the mental health association in your area that will in turn refer you to a specialist. It's very important to consult someone knowledgeable about severe depression. Many prescriptions for antidepressants are written by primary care physicians who don't have sufficient experience to be able to prescribe the right drug, the right dose, and the right duration of treatment. If the patient is unresponsive, it's then wrongly assumed that "drugs won't work." Most people with severe depression can be successfully treated with drugs, psychotherapy, or a combination of the two. Once a patient is in treatment with a professional, the measures outlined below, which have been proven to help, can be adopted. In addition, many cases of mild depression can be headed off by means of a sound nutritional program without the use of medication.

If you suffer from depression, either mild or severe, you should be certain that you are getting adequate nutrients. Many people with depression eat erratically, and inadequate nutrition actually exacerbates their depression. Deficiencies of vitamins B_1, B_2, B_6, B_{12}, and vitamin C are frequently found in people with emotional disorders. The vitamin/mineral compound recommended in Blueprint for Health, page xvii, should be an important part of your daily routine.

Some people who have problems with constant mild depression can be suffering from low blood sugar or hypoglycemia and do not need medication. Their eating habits are irregular, resulting in rapid fluctuations of the blood sugar levels, which can cause mood swings including depression. I've seen many mildly depressed patients with low blood sugar who eat too many sweets (sometimes they say they're "addicted" to sugar) and drink too much caffeine. These people need to eat regular meals at regular times; they need to have protein at lunch and dinner; and they must also eliminate caffeine, sugar, and refined carbohydrates from their diet. The mineral chromium is also extremely helpful in controlling low blood sugar. If you think that hypoglycemia could be causing your mood swings or depression, see Hypoglycemia, page 202.

Some people have hidden food allergies that can manifest as mental symptoms including depression. One study found that the incidence of allergy was about 33 percent in a group of depressed patients compared with only 2 percent in a control group of schizophrenics. Another study found that 85 percent of a group of depressed children and adults was allergic. In my experience, I've found wheat to be the most common cause of depression among people who are sensitive to it. If you suffer from hay fever, dust allergies, or allergies to pets, then food allergies may play a part in your symptoms (see Food Allergy, page 146).

There are two amino acids that have been shown to help some people suffering from depression. One of these is tyrosine. Depression has been associated with decreased activity of the neurotransmitter norepinephrine. But norepinephrine synthesis can be influenced by its amino acid precursor, tyrosine. Tyrosine (and ultimately norepinephrine) helps to promote positive moods as well as motivation and drive. Depressed patients who were given tyrosine improved their sleeping patterns, mood, libido, and other psychological and physiological patterns within a week.

Another amino acid that can help depressed people is D-phenylalanine, which is also involved in epinephrine metabolism. D-phenylalanine is converted into tyrosine by the liver.

There is a particular kind of depression that afflicts people only in the winter and only in the northern climes, where light is reduced. It begins in autumn as the days become shorter and peaks in January, subsiding in spring as the days once again begin to lengthen. The problem is exacerbated by the fact that in winter people tend to stay indoors, reducing the amount of light to which they're exposed. Called Seasonal Affective Disorder (SAD), it differs from the typical pattern of depression. People who suffer from SAD are four times more likely to be women. During the winter months they lose energy, suffer increased anxiety, lose interest in sex, oversleep, overeat, gain weight, and crave starchy foods. It has been estimated that 5 percent of the population in the North suffers from SAD and one in four people complains of having to suffer through the winter with similar, if less severe, problems. Sometimes people who have regular annual cases of the "holiday blues"—particularly around Christmas—are really suffering from SAD.

No one knows precisely what causes SAD. But we do know that when light enters the retina, electrical impulses transmit signals to the hypothalamus, which sends chemical and electrical messages to other parts of the brain as well as elsewhere in the body. This process is separate from the process of vision, and this explains why blind people can remain synchronized with the daily rhythms of light and dark. Melatonin, a hormone that promotes sleepiness when it grows dark, seems to be intimately involved in the development of SAD. Supplements of melatonin, available in health food stores, can help regulate sleep cycles and combat SAD.

Once disorders such as thyroid malfunction or the taking of medications have been ruled out, the treatment for SAD is simple and straightforward: daily exposure to bright fluorescent light. The treatment, known as light therapy, requires that you sit in front of a light box that contains full-spectrum fluorescent lights at eye level. You can read, knit, or stare into space, but your eyes must be open and near the light source. The light should be about 2,500 lux (a well-lit room is about 500 to 750 lux). Sources for light boxes are listed below, but I do recommend consulting a specialist before beginning treatment. You should expect to see results from the light therapy in two to three days.

Exercise can be a critical factor in treating depression. Most depressed people are not physically fit. One doctor reported treating depressed men who were unresponsive to standard drug and psychotherapy treatments with exercise regimes. As the men felt worse in the morning, the exercise was undertaken soon after rising. Some worked up to a daily half-hour workout on a stationary bike and a half-hour jog in the afternoon. The others worked up to a 3-mile brisk walk daily. Both groups subsequently responded to drug therapy. Many studies over the years have demonstrated the positive psychological effects of exercise, and I strongly recommend an exercise program—even if it's just a brisk daily walk—to my patients who complain of depression, whether they suffer from SAD, mild depression, or severe depression and are being treated with drugs and psychotherapy.

There's another natural approach you can take to fight depression: read. A recent study involving forty-five men and women suffering from mild to moderate depression recommended two self-help books to their patients: *Feeling Good: The New Mood Therapy* by David D. Burns and *Control Your Depression* by Peter Lewisohn. They were given four weeks to read one of their choosing. At the end of the study, significant improvement was reported by two-thirds of the readers, compared with only 20 percent improvement in the comparison group. A six-month follow-up revealed that the improvements were sustained in the group that had done the reading. Reliance on a good self-help book is especially useful for older people who might be reluctant to consult a psychotherapist.

NATURAL PRESCRIPTION FOR DEPRESSION

- Many cases of depression require outside help. See the list of signs in the text that indicate whether you should be seen by a professional specializing in depression. If necessary, get in touch with an appropriate specialist through the National Mental Health Association (address above, page 106) or a referral from your family physician.

- Low blood sugar, or hypoglycemia, is a common cause of depression. For information on the connection between depression and low blood sugar and information on how to use diet and supplements to control low blood sugar, see Hypoglycemia, page 202.

- Food allergies can cause depression. Avoid allergenic foods. For information on how to tell if food allergies cause your depression and how to control them, see Food Allergy, page 146.

- Exercise has been proven to help fight depression. I suggest a half hour of brisk walking at least five days a week as being the most simple and readily available. Other forms of exercise such as biking, swimming, and aerobics classes are just as effective.

- Avoid sleeping too much; sleeping exacerbates depression.

- Read *Feeling Good: The New Mood Therapy* by David D. Burns and *Control Your Depression* by Peter Lewisohn, both recommended as having been proven helpful for many depressed people.

- Some cases of depression are caused by Seasonal Affective Disorder (SAD). Light treatment can be extremely helpful for people who suffer from SAD. You can find someone experienced with SAD in your area by contacting the Society for Light Treatment and Biological Rhythms, P.O. Box 478, Wilsonville, OR 97070, phone (503) 694-2404. Sources for light boxes include: The Sunbox Company,

(301) 762-1786; Apollo Light Systems, Inc., (801) 226-2370; and MediLight Inc., (201) 663-1214. Other tips for people with SAD include:

Avoid sugar and caffeine, which exacerbate depression.

Take a walk at lunch.

Exercise regularly.

Take a winter vacation in a sunny place.

IN ADDITION TO YOUR DAILY SUPPLEMENTS, PAGE xxiv, TAKE

- Melatonin: 2 mg. at bedtime during the dark months, if you notice your symptoms are seasonal.

- Amino acid tyrosine: 500 mg. one or two capsules three times daily.

- Amino acid D-phenylalanine: 500 mg. one or two capsules three times daily.

• • •

DIABETES

DIABETES IS A DISEASE in which the body cannot properly convert food into energy, either because it does not produce enough insulin, or because the cells become insulin-resistant or incapable of absorbing it. Insulin, which is a hormone produced by the pancreas, regulates the level of glucose, or blood sugar, in the bloodstream. After a meal, carbohydrates pass through the liver, which stores part of them for later use, and releases the other part into the bloodstream as glucose for immediate use by the body organs, muscles, and red blood cells. When the blood glucose rises, the pancreas releases insulin, which promotes the absorption of glucose by the body's tissues.

In diabetes, this process breaks down, and glucose, instead of being absorbed as a nutrient, accumulates in the bloodstream. Where the normal range of glucose is 65 to 115 mg. per 100 dl. of blood, a diabetic's blood glucose can be three times as high. This triggers a harmful chain of events. The excessive glucose injures the delicate filtering mechanisms of the kidneys, causing increased urination. In the process, the body loses a lot of water, which is why two common symptoms of diabetes are frequent urination and excessive thirst. High blood glucose, as well as unused insulin, also affect several blood components, causing serious cardiovascular complications. People with diabetes have a much higher rate of heart attacks, strokes, and high blood pressure and cataracts than the general population. Because of poor circulation to the lower limbs, diabetics also experience various leg and foot problems. The nervous system may also be affected, with loss of sensation, burning, pain, sexual impotence, and feelings of weakness as a result. Another complication of diabetes that can lead to a medical emergency is ketoacidosis, which is a toxic accumulation of acidic by-products released into the bloodstream when the body, unable to utilize its glucose, starts burning its own fat and muscle for fuel.

There are two types of diabetes. Type 1, known as juvenile or insulin-dependent diabetes, usually starts in childhood or adolescence when the pancreas fails to produce insulin. Type 1 diabetics require regular insulin injections. Less than 15 percent of all diabetics have this form of the disease. Far more common is Type 2, adult-onset diabetes, which occurs most frequently in middle age or during pregnancy. Type 2 diabetics produce insulin, but are unable to utilize it properly, because their cells may lack an adequate number of "insulin receptors," or because of other unknown causes.

Diabetes appears to run in families. People who are overweight or sedentary are also prone to diabetes, and the likelihood of developing the disease increases with age. In the United States ten million people have diabetes, and it is estimated that an additional ten million have it without knowing it. Three hundred thousand people die from diabetes and its complications each year, making it the third leading cause of death in this country.

If you have juvenile or Type 1 diabetes, you will be taking injections of insulin under the supervision of your doctor.

Fortunately, most adult-onset, Type 2 diabetics can control the disease through a combination of weight loss, a diet high in fiber and complex carbohydrates, nutritional supplements, and adequate exercise. People who are at risk of diabetes because of family history or borderline elevated blood sugar can reduce the risk of getting the disease by following the same regimen.

If you have adult-onset or Type 2 diabetes, or suspect that you do, you have to recognize that it is both good and bad news. The bad news about adult-onset diabetes is that it makes you more vulnerable to a host of ailments. The good news is that this type of diabetes can be controlled with diet and lifestyle changes. Ironically, I have seen many patients who credit the development of diabetes as the single most important factor in improving their overall health: When they made the changes they needed to live successfully with diabetes, they felt better than they had in years.

Most of my patients with adult-onset diabetes were overweight when they first came to see me. I immediately placed them on a weight-reducing diet, which appears to increase the sensitivity of insulin receptors and thus lowers the blood sugar. Since proper nutrition is essential, I steer my patients away from crash diets and toward a diet they can follow over the long term. This should be a diet that is 60 percent fiber and complex carbohydrates, which will reduce the need for insulin and lower the fat levels of the blood. Whole grains, vegetables, fruits, and legumes are all appropriate complex carbohydrates. Avoid processed sugars, including those in cookies, candies, cakes, ice cream, sodas, diet sodas, honey, dried fruit, chocolate, and desserts. Keep fats down to 20 percent of your total calorie intake, and avoid high-fat foods such as butter, red meats, and other foods high in cholesterol. Monounsaturated vegetable fats, which include olive oil, are the best for diabetics, since they promote a healthy circulatory system. The remaining 20 percent of your diet should consist of protein such as fish or poultry.

I tell my patients to take their time over their meals. Don't gulp down your food, and eat three meals a day rather than one large one, to avoid a sudden surge of blood sugar. A snack of an apple or other fruit in midmorning or afternoon can also help to keep blood sugar stable. Apples and many other fresh fruits are also high in pectin fiber, which reduces blood sugar in diabetics. The more fresh salads you eat, the better, because these raw foods reduce sugar levels, perhaps because they take longer to digest.

In addition to eating a diet high in fiber, you can take fiber supplements, which have been shown to reduce blood sugar elevations and insulin requirements (fiber supplements should be taken before meals). The first one is guar, which comes in powder form. It's very important that you take guar with a large glass of water, so that you swallow it completely before it thickens. The second fiber is psyllium, which is available in the form of sugar-free Metamucil available at all health food stores. Don't take both guar and psyllium fiber at the same time—take one or the other, whichever is easier for you to get.

Another important supplement is the mineral chromium, which helps the body to respond to insulin, and reduces blood sugar. Chromium has also been found to promote a healthy cardiovascular system, which is an important consideration for diabetics. Nine out of ten Americans are estimated to consume inadequate amounts of chromium; in diabetics, this problem is compounded by the increased urinary loss of chromium common to diabetics.

Magnesium appears to stimulate insulin activity. In several studies, however, diabetics were consistently found to have below normal magnesium levels.

Diabetics are not particularly prone to zinc deprivation, but zinc supplements help control blood sugar levels, and I recommend taking them.

Vitamin C has been found to improve glucose tolerance and the functions of the liver, while vitamin E reduces cellular damage and promotes healing of lesions caused by diabetes. If you are a Type 1 diabetic on insulin, you might want to check with your doctor about vitamin E supplements. Since vitamin E may reduce insulin requirements, however, patients on insulin should start with doses of 100 I.U. of vitamin E, and monitor their insulin dosage closely, lowering it as they gradually raise their dosage of vitamin E.

Vitamin B$_6$ (pyridoxine) is also helpful, particularly in reducing damage to the extremities caused by poor circulation, and in improving delivery of oxygen to the tissues. It also helps prevent atherosclerosis, which diabetics are prone to develop.

Vitamin B$_{12}$ has also shown evidence of helping reduce the symptoms of diabetes.

Finally, it is important that you evaluate your entire lifestyle. If you smoke, you must give it up—not next month or next year, but immediately. Smoking, as you know, is dangerous for everyone, but particularly so for diabetics, whose circulatory systems are already at risk from the effects of high blood sugar and buildups of cholesterol. You should also give up caffeine, which impairs circulation and appears to accelerate the onset of diabetes.

Stress, if handled incorrectly, is also bad for you. We all have stress in our lives, and a certain amount of stress is inevitable and even useful. But try to avoid situations that escalate your level of anxiety and send damaging hormones racing through your system—it's not easy to do, but I have patients who have learned to control their emotional responses. (For more information on this see Stress Control, page 314.)

One of the best ways to control stress is exercise, which is also one of the most effective ways of preventing diabetes and controlling blood sugar levels. A study reported in the *New England Journal of Medicine* found that of the men in their study, those at highest risk of developing diabetes benefited the most from physical activity. Men who were very active, and burned 3,500 calories a week, cut their risk of disease by half. Other studies have found that both women and men benefit from exercise.

Exercise is also extremely helpful for those who already have diabetes, in that it decreases blood glucose while assisting the cells to absorb glucose in response to insulin. A word of caution: As with any new exercise regimen, get an all-clear from your doctor, and gradually build up to a regular routine.

NATURAL PRESCRIPTION FOR DIABETES

- Avoid processed sugars, including those in cookies, candies, cakes, ice cream, sodas, honey, chocolate, and desserts. Avoid dried fruit.

- Adopt a high-fiber, high-complex carbohydrate diet with a distribution of calories as follows:
    carbohydrates 60 percent
    proteins 20 percent
    fats 20 percent

- Eat three meals a day at regular times.

- Avoid drinks with caffeine.

- Eat apples and other fruits high in pectin.

- Eat a midmorning and afternoon snack of fruit (like an apple) to keep blood sugar stable.

- Take *either:* Guar fiber, 2 teaspoons a day with a large glass of water, before meals; or psyllium fiber, (eg. 3.4 g. sugarless Metamucil,) twice a day in a glass of water, before meals.

- Adopt a regular exercise program.

- Make a serious effort to control stress (see Stress Control, page 314).

- Avoid fatigue, emotional upsets, and use of tobacco.

IN ADDITION TO YOUR DAILY SUPPLEMENTS, PAGE xxiv, TAKE

- Chromium: 100 mcg. of trivalent chromium three times daily.

- Magnesium: 400 mg. a day.

- Vitamin C: 500 mg. two times a day.

- Vitamin E: 400 I.U. a day.

- Zinc: 50 mg. a day.

- B_6 (pyridoxine): 100 mg. daily.

- B_{12}: 1,000 mcg. in tablet form dissolved under the tongue.

IN ADDITION: Vanadium is another natural element that has worked for many diabetic patients. It's available in buffered form and it has insulin-like properties, increasing the uptake of glucose and protein by the muscles and liver. The recommended dosage is 2 mg. three times a day, to be taken with meals. Do not take more, as it can be toxic in large doses.

Some very recent research has suggested that cow's milk can be a possible trigger, putting susceptible people at greater risk of diabetes. While this certainly isn't a basis to eliminate cow's milk from a diabetic's diet, it is an argument not to use cow's-milk products early in life, especially if there is a family history of diabetes.

Recent studies have shown evening primrose oil to be helpful for diabetics. While the dose of 12 capsules daily used in the studies may be too expensive for many patients, it is speculated that a reduction of animal fat in the diet may make a lower dose effective.

• • •

DIARRHEA

DIARRHEA IS NOT really a disease; it's a symptom. Most commonly, diarrhea—loose, watery, unformed, frequent bowel movements—comes on suddenly. You'll feel some cramping and then find, in a case of acute diarrhea, that you have a bowel movement every hour or more frequently. It usually lasts for a day or two and can be stimulated by too much fruit in the diet, tainted food, the flu, or even extraordinary stress. In this type of diarrhea the body is trying to rid itself of toxins, and the best course to take is to let the body do what it wants, namely have frequent bowel movements. Most people immediately reach for a medication like Pepto-Bismol, Kaopectate, or Imodium A-D. This can help temporarily control the symptoms, but if at all possible you should wait at least twelve hours before taking over-the-counter medications so that your body has a chance to rid itself of the toxins that caused the problem. Make an effort to replace the fluids and nutrients lost through diarrhea. I tell my patients that the best diet for an occasional bout of diarrhea is a clear simple one.

- Drink plenty of fluids, particularly juices (although apple juice sometimes provokes diarrhea in children). Tomato juice or mixed vegetable juices like V-8 can be beneficial because they're rich in sodium and minerals lost through diarrhea.

- Avoid solid foods, even if you feel hungry, for the first day.

- Take clear soups, broths, and bouillon.

- Avoid caffeine; it can irritate the bowel.

- Avoid carbonated drinks because they can affect bowel contractions and worsen diarrhea. Instead, stick with herb teas such as chamomile or mint to help settle your stomach.

- Avoid "diet" foods—candy and gum—that are sweetened with sorbitol or mannitol; these artificial sweeteners can act as laxatives.

- After a day of a clear diet, you'll be ready to start some solid foods. Yogurt with live active cultures (check the label) is a good choice, as it can help restore the bowel flora.

- Bananas help restore minerals; they're an easily digested carbohydrate rich in pectin, which helps bowel function.

- Rice, applesauce, and mashed potoatoes are among the foods that are usually easily tolerated by the digestive system and are good foods to try once the worst of the diarrhea has passed.

If your diarrhea wasn't caused by the flu or by an intestinal "bug," there are other causes that you should know about. They include:

ANTACIDS: Antacids are the most common over-the-counter cause of diarrhea. Both Maalox and Mylanta contain magnesium hydroxide, which acts on your bowel like milk of magnesia.

ANTIBIOTICS: Antibiotics kill the good bacteria in your bowel along with the bad bacteria for which you're taking the antibiotic. Eating yogurt with live cultures or taking acidophilus tablets during the course of the medication will help. If diarrhea connected with antibiotics becomes troublesome, you should consult your doctor.

VITAMIN C: Too much vitamin C can cause diarrhea. Most people can tolerate up to 4 g. daily (not that everyone should be taking that much!), but if you're taking more than 1,000 mg., cut out the vitamin C to see if it has an affect on your symptoms.

MEDICATIONS: Various prescription drugs, in addition to antibiotics, can cause diarrhea. They include quinidine, lactulose, and colchicine. If you're taking a drug that seems to be causing diarrhea, discuss it with your doctor.

ARTIFICIAL SWEETENERS: Sorbitol and mannitol, artificial sweeteners found in diet foods, particularly candy and chewing gum, can act as a laxative when they're consumed in large doses. Many diabetics eat foods that contain sorbitol and are unaware that occasional bouts with diarrhea are caused by this ingredient.

If your diarrhea lasts for more than a couple of days or if it is accompanied by other symptoms including pain and/or fever or chills, consult your doctor.

What about "tourista" or traveler's diarrhea? You probably know that the best way to avoid it is to be scrupulous about what you eat when you travel—no unboiled water (including ice cubes), no unpeeled fruit or raw vegetables, no cooked food that has been sitting around. Do not drink milk or eat dairy products that have not been pasteurized. Do not eat food from street vendors. But if despite your best efforts, you still come down with a sudden case, the best thing to do is to use Pepto-Bismol. In more severe cases, Imodium A-D can be very helpful. By the way, Pepto-Bismol is used as a preventive by many savvy travelers, though no one is certain exactly why it works. Be sure that you are careful if you also take aspirin regularly: The salicylate in Pepto-Bismol added to the dose in your aspirin could cause such symptoms as ringing in the ears. Persistent traveler's diarrhea may be caused by an acute parasitic infection, which would need to be diagnosed and treated by a doctor.

If your diarrhea is not acute and is not due to the causes discussed above, you should not continue to take over-the-counter medications. They will only serve to mask the symptoms and can ultimately be dangerous. You need to get at the root of the problem and consult your doctor. The most common chronic conditions are:

LACTOSE INTOLERANCE. Many of my patients have found that when they deal with their lactose intolerance, their diarrhea disappears. See Lactose Intolerance, page 231.

INFLAMMATORY BOWEL DISEASE —ulcerative colitis or Crohn's disease.

FOOD ALLERGIES. A number of my patients who have suffered from chronic diarrhea have learned that they in fact have a food allergy. Once the allergy is identified and the offending food eliminated, the diarrhea disappears. See Food Allergy, page 146.

GLUTEN SENSITIVITY. See Celiac Disease, page 73.

PARASITIC INFECTIONS. See Protozoa Disease, page 287.

BENIGN OR MALIGNANT TUMORS, which must be identified by a physician.

NATURAL PRESCRIPTION FOR DIARRHEA

- If your diarrhea is acute—caused by a flu, tainted food, intestinal infection, and so on—let it run its course and treat with diet (see above) until it subsides. Sometimes the use of over-the-counter medications like Pepto-Bismol, Kaopectate, or Imodium A-D can be helpful only if used to control the most acute symptoms.

- Avoid antibiotics, antacids and other medications, excessive vitamin C, and artificial sweeteners, which can cause diarrhea.

- If your diarrhea is accompanied by pain, bloody stool, fever and chills (unrelated to a flu), jaundice, severe abdominal cramps, or severe weakness, or if it lasts more than a couple of days, you should consult your doctor.

- If your diarrhea is caused by something you ate or drank while traveling, Pepto-Bismol is an effective remedy, and it can even be used as a preventive in the course of your trip. (If you take regular aspirin doses, you should cut down when taking Pepto-Bismol, as they both contain salicylate and an overdose can cause symptoms like ringing in the ears.) Imodium A-D is also useful for more acute cases. If your traveler's diarrhea persists, see your doctor.

- If you regularly suffer from diarrhea and cannot determine the cause, you could be suffering from a chronic condition that needs to be treated; see your physician. The most common chronic conditions include: Lactose Intolerance, page 231; Irritable Bowel, page 220; Food Allergy, page 146; Celiac Disease, page 73; and Protozoa Disease, page 287.

. . .

DIVERTICULAR DISEASE

DIVERTICULOSIS used to be a rare disease; even today, it's almost nonexistent in certain parts of the world. But in the United States over half of the people over 60 have it, and most of them don't even know it. Diverticulosis is really a "lifestyle" disease that's easily prevented by dietary modifications. Unfortunately, by the time most people realize they have it, it's too late and the disease is established. But the good news is that simple changes in the diet will prevent it from ever becoming a serious problem.

Diverticulosis occurs when tiny sacs or pockets, somewhat like little balloons, form over time on the outer walls of the colon due to pressure from trying to pass stools that are hard and dry. As you would imagine, people who suffer from chronic constipation often develop diverticulosis. The reason it is so common today is that our diet contains so many refined foods lacking in fiber. Our digestive systems were made to process more bulk than most of us consume, so they work overtime to produce small, hard stools that ultimately stress the colon beyond endurance.

Some people with diverticulosis have no symptoms; others have chronic constipation alternating with diarrhea, gas, and sometimes pain in the lower left side of the abdomen.

Occasionally a bit of fecal matter will become trapped in the little sacs or outpouchings and become infected. This is the more serious stage of diverticulosis called diverticulitis. If this happens, you may develop fever, cramps, and rectal bleeding and you must be treated with antibiotics by a physician.

Some people learn they have diverticulosis when an x-ray is taken for some unrelated complaint, but most people discover it only when they develop diverticulitis. After their bout is cured with the help of antibiotics, they realize that they have to try to prevent diverticulitis from developing again. By taking the proper steps, they can.

Diverticulosis has a simple treatment: fiber. In the old days, even when I was in medical school, it was believed that people with this problem should eat a soft, bland diet so as not to tax the colon. We now know that a bulky diet high in fiber is one that will help the colon do its job.

Many studies have shown that increasing the fiber in one's diet can prevent surgical treatment in roughly 90 percent of patients. Bran supplementation is highly effective. Bran tablets, available in health food stores, are handy. Alternatively, you can use coarse miller's bran. Make sure you don't overdo it; too much fiber all at once can upset your system. Increase your intake gradually over three or four weeks. You can expect some gas in the beginning and perhaps some bloating.

Many of my elderly patients find bran difficult to tolerate. If you have trouble with bran tablets, try psyllium powders, which are available over-the-counter in pharmacies as well as in health food stores. Be sure to take them with plenty of water and adjust the amounts gradually to suit your needs.

It's important to drink lots of fluids—six to eight glasses of water each day—not only in conjunction with the bulking agents like psyllium and bran, but also to fight constipation.

If you have diverticulosis and particularly if you've ever had an attack of diverticulitis, you should avoid eating foods that contain nuts, seeds, and other hard particles such as popcorn. That includes seeds used as toppings on baked goods like poppy seeds and sesame seeds as well as seeds and hard particles inside the food itself like the seeds in zucchini or cucumbers or the grain particles in cracked-wheat bread. These tiny particles could become lodged in the sacs of the colon and become infected, bringing on an attack of diverticulitis.

NATURAL PRESCRIPTION FOR DIVERTICULAR DISEASE

- Adopt a high-fiber diet. This means lots of fruits and vegetables, whole grains, and cereals. Avoid eating processed food: substitute whole grain bread for white, a whole apple for apple juice.

- Add a fiber supplement to your diet. Take psyllium seed bulking agents. Follow the directions on the package and be sure to take with plenty of water.

- Avoid constipation and, if you do become constipated, don't use laxatives. If you do experience some constipation, increase your psyllium and water intake, and if this doesn't work add bran to your diet. You can take it in tablet form, available in health food stores. Take three tablets daily and increase by three tablets every few days until you achieve the desired result. You can also take bran in the form of coarse miller's bran—a teaspoon a day, increased by a teaspoon every few days. You can also sprinkle it on foods and cereals or mix it into baked foods like muffins and meatloaf. Increase bran intake gradually over the course of about a month. You can expect some gas and bloating when you first begin (see Constipation, page 92).

- Drink plenty of fluids every day: from six to eight glasses of water or other fluid.

- Avoid eating seeds, nuts, and foods with hard particles that could become lodged in the diverticular sacs. These include strawberries, figs, tomatoes, zucchini, cucumbers, baked goods that have cracked wheat, poppy, sesame, or caraway seeds.

•   •   •

DRY SKIN

DRY SKIN can be a real problem for some people, and it's not just a question of beauty. Some people get such flaky, itchy skin that they're uncomfortable and distracted, and if the skin cracks, it's vulnerable to infection.

Before you decide that your reddened, irritated skin is dry skin, check to be sure that you're not using a cosmetic that is giving you a case of contact dermatitis. Some people, in an effort to make their skin more supple, use a battery of moisturizers only to find that it gets worse. Usually these people complain to me in passing about their dry skin, and when I examine it I find that they have contact dermatitis from one or more ingredients in their moisturizers. A dermatologist can test which ingredient you might be allergic to, but alternately, you can simply stop using all moisturizers for a week or two: If the problem clears up, you had contact dermatitis and you should try a new, nonallergenic moisturizer, taking care to observe any reaction your skin might have.

If your problem is indeed dry skin, you're no doubt dealing with dry air. In normal humidity, most skin is naturally supple and moist. But when the air is dry, as in certain climates or in a heated house or office, the air leaches moisture from the skin. There are two ways to combat this process: You can humidify the air so it's not competing with your skin for moisture, and you can keep your skin from losing moisture by creating a barrier on the skin in the form of a lotion or moisturizer.

You must remember that if you have a dry skin problem it's not something that's going to go away with a single treatment. It requires that every day you are in a dry climate, house, or office, you add moisture to the air and to your skin.

The best way to humidify the air is with a cool mist humidifier. Set one up in your bedroom and keep it on at night. If your home is large you might also want to have one somewhere else in the house. Plants can help humidify the air and can be especially appropriate in offices where a humidifier might be impractical. One of my patients told me that the hot air in her office made her skin parched until she arranged a row of colored vases filled with water along her windowsill. Putting pans of water on top of radiators is a time-honored way of getting some moisture into the air.

If you've shopped for moisturizers, you know how confusing it can be. What really is the best moisturizer? The best, cheapest moisturizer is probably Vaseline. But most people don't want that slippery feeling. I tell patients to use Vaseline at night—on their hands, elbows, shins, arms, anyplace that's dry. It will protect against moisture loss all night. Doctors frequently recommend Crisco to people who have had work, such as a chemical peel, done on their faces. If you try it, use just the smallest amount and rub it in well. It's best used only at night. For the daytime, you'll want something lighter like Nivea or Lubriderm. Sea Breeze Moisture Lotion was rated highly by *Consumer Reports*.

The best time to use a moisturizer is when you're fresh from the bath or shower and are slightly damp. If you cover your damp skin with a moisturizer, it will help trap the additional water, giving your skin an extra boost.

If your hands are frequently wet, you should take two measures against dryness: Wear lined rubber gloves and keep a moisturizer on the sink to use each time you dry your hands.

If you have a severe problem with dryness, your doctor can prescribe a lotion called Lac-Hydrin. This lotion has to be used regularly; it actually changes the surface of the skin, increasing its ability to retain moisture. There are over-the-counter preparations called Lac-Hydrin Five and LactiCare that contain a lower percentage of the active ingredient in Lac-Hydrin—lactic acid—and should help severe dryness.

I've often heard that Bag Balm, an udder ointment sold in farm supply stores, can be helpful against dryness. It may be of great benefit to some people, but I have had patients who have had reactions to the lanolin in the product. A and D Ointment, Keri, and Lanoline are other preparations that contain lanolin. If you have a tendency to be allergic to wool, watch carefully to see if you have an allergy to lanolin in skin preparations.

Many people don't realize that water is really an enemy of dry skin— and not only for hands that work in water doing dishes or cleaning. Hot baths and showers can rob the skin of moisture, and soaps used for cleaning dry it further. If you have a dry skin problem, limit your bathing and showering—try to avoid taking a shower in the morning *and* after exercising if possible. When you do shower and bathe, use warm, not hot, water; the hotter the water, the more drying to your skin. And go easy on the soap. Dove is known as a good mild soap. Many people mistakenly think Ivory is mild, but it's really a strong, pure soap and thus drying. If you suffer from severe dryness, ask at your pharmacy for one of the preparations that are soap alternatives. They'll get you clean without the drying effect.

I've seen some patients who, because they're trying to control weight or cholesterol levels, have eliminated virtually all fat from their diet. They complain of dry, cracked skin. If they add just a small amount of olive oil (one or two tablespoons) to their diet, the dryness is often eliminated.

I've also found that people who take large doses of zinc—amounts greater than 100 mg. daily—often suffer from dry skin.

NATURAL PRESCRIPTION FOR DRY SKIN

- Be sure that your dry, reddened skin is not a case of contact dermatitis, especially if you've been using lots of different moisturizers. Use no moisturizers for a week or so to see if the redness clears up.

- Humidify the air with cool mist.

- Use Vaseline at night on dry areas.

- Use a moisturizer like Nivea or Lubiderm during the day.

- Try to use a moisturizer after bathing, when your skin is damp, to trap additional moisture.

- Protect hands from water by using lined rubber gloves.

- Keep moisturizer on the sink to use each time you dry your hands.

- Severe dryness problems can be solved with prescription Lac-Hydrin cream that actually changes the surface of the skin to help it retain moisture.

- Over-the-counter preparations like Lac-Hydrin Five and LactiCare can help dry skin.

- Bag Balm can be helpful for dry skin, but be sure you don't have an allergy to lanolin, one of its principal ingredients.

- Bathe or shower only as needed.

- Use warm, not hot, water.

- **If dryness is severe, use a nondrying soap alternative like Cetaphil for cleansing.**

- **If you are on an extremely low-fat diet, add one or two tablespoons of olive oil to your daily diet.**

- **If you are taking doses of zinc in excess of 100 mg. daily, reduce that amount.**

• • •

EAR INFECTIONS

MOST PARENTS of young children know more than they would like about ear infections. Too often babies and small children develop recurring cases of ear infections that cause them and their parents sleepless nights. One of the worst aspects of ear infections is that they always seem to occur in the middle of the night when there's nothing at hand to soothe the child.

Antibiotics are the routine treatment, but there is now some controversy about whether antibiotic use actually does any good: A number of studies have found that children who were given symptomatic relief but no antibiotics recovered completely from ear infections and had less recurrence than children who were regularly treated with antibiotics. In fact, in some countries children are never treated with antibiotics.

Even as I tell you this I know there are parents who would find it cruel and inhumane not to treat their child who is in the throes of a painful infection, particularly when they have learned through experience that the symptoms normally subside within twenty-four hours of the initial dose of antibiotics. If you or your child has an occasional painful ear infection, you'll probably elect to visit the doctor and get antibiotics prescribed. On the other hand (and this describes most of the patients who see me for this problem), if you or your child has regular recurring bouts with ear infections and is therefore taking antibiotics almost constantly during the winter months, you should probably look at a natural program of treatment and, more important, prevention of the infections. I have had great success, as many grateful parents can attest, in discovering hidden food allergies in children who suffer from recurring ear infections.

Prevention also avoids the possibility of a myringotomy in which a small hole is cut in the eardrum so that tubes can be inserted to drain accumulated pus. These tubes are as controversial as antibiotics, with some researchers claiming that they are of no benefit in preventing subsequent infections and may, in fact, promote them.

Ear infections are really inflammations of the middle ear or otitis media. They are more common in children because the eustachian tube, which normally adjusts the pressure in the middle ear and drains the fluid from it, is affected. In children this tube is much shorter than in adults and more likely to get clogged. The most common predisposing cause for a blocked tube is food allergy. Then, infection caused by either a virus or bacteria sets in. Because the tube is short, the infectious agent can easily travel along it into the middle ear where it collects, producing a sticky fluid that prevents the eardrum and middle ear bones from vibrating freely, thus inhibiting hearing. Usually if a middle ear infection is caused by a virus, it will clear up of its own accord, but if it's caused by bacteria, it will require antibiotics. The problem is that when a child is examined by a doctor who finds red, irritated ears, antibiotics are usually prescribed as a conservative measure.

There are some steps you can take to help relieve the immediate pain of an ear infection, one of which is to give acetaminophen. (Remember *never* to give aspirin to children.)

You can raise the head of the bed or crib to help the tubes drain naturally. (You'll notice that children rarely complain of pain in their ears during the day because they're upright and distracted and the tubes are draining freely. When they lie down at night, the tubes fill, causing pain.)

It's helpful to get your child to drink some fluids: The very action of swallowing helps the tubes to open and drain, and fluids will help fight an infection.

It's also helpful to use a vaporizer in the room at night. This will help to keep the air moist and encourage the thinning of fluids in the ear.

A warm, moist compress can relieve pain and can stimulate circulation to the area to fight infection.

There is an herb called echinacea that you can get in health food stores that can be helpful in fighting ear infections. Children can drink a glass of water containing a dropperful three times daily. This is safe for children over twelve months of age.

There is a natural supplement that can help reduce the severity of ear infections. N-acetylcysteine, which is derived from an amino acid, has been shown to be helpful in keeping mucus fluid and thus helping the ears to drain. It should be taken only during the acute stage of an infection. It's available at health food stores.

I don't like to recommend medications when something else will work, but this is one case where it really can be foolish to avoid them. Use a decongestant when you or your child suffers from a cold. Many ear infections begin with a cold. If you treat the cold vigorously with a vaporizer at night and a decongestant, especially at night, you can help stave off many ear infections. One mother whose son had a problem with recurring ear infections preferred to let things run their course, using a vaporizer but no medications. She recently reported to me that since she began using the decongestant, especially at night, her son's ear infections have been far less frequent and she no longer has to assume that if he gets a cold he will inevitably develop an ear infection.

There are plenty of reasons to avoid the regular use of antibiotics with recurring ear infections. They cause side effects including yeast overgrowth such as thrush and digestive upsets, and indeed may even be ineffective. For patients who come to me with this problem, I suggest a total program aimed at eliminating the major predisposing causes of ear infections.

Allergies are one of the major predisposing causes. Whether you are allergic to dust, dairy products, or pollen, once you or your child's respiratory passages become clogged in reaction to an allergen, they're more liable to harbor infection.

In a recent study presented to the American College of Allergy and Immunology, 104 children who suffered from frequent, serious ear infections were tested for allergies, and 78 percent were shown to have specific food allergies. After eliminating the offending food from the diet for eleven weeks, improvement was seen in 70 out of 81 children. This argues for trying to prevent allergies from developing in children by breast-feeding for as long as is possible (assuming that the mother avoids foods that she's allergic to during pregnancy and lactation), avoiding common allergenic foods during the first nine months of life including wheat, eggs, and dairy foods, and carefully introducing new foods into the child's diet while watching for adverse reactions.

If you or your child has recurring ear infections, you should check to determine if an allergy is the cause. In my experience, milk, cheese, and eggs are the most common culprits. Wheat, corn, oranges, and peanut butter are also common allergies. Usually, if a child is affected, one or both of the parents suffer from allergies as well.

You won't be able to cure an ear infection while it's in progress by eliminating allergenic foods and/or inhalants, but once the ear infection is under control you can try to determine the allergens. See Food Allergy, page 146, for a fuller discussion of this.

In addition to eliminating allergenic foods, it is most helpful to eliminate concentrated simple carbohydrates including sugar, cookies, candy, ice cream, sodas, chocolate, honey, dried fruit, and, particularly, concentrated fruit juice because these foods can make allergies worse. (See the list of simple carbohydrates' various names for sugar in Blueprint for Health, page xvii.) There are any number of children who live on peanut butter on whole-wheat bread, raisins, and endless amounts of fruit juice, and if these children have a tendency to allergies, they're eating the worst possible diet in terms of encouraging recurring ear infections.

One last thing to remember with small babies who are especially vulnerable to ear infections: Never let them drink a bottle while lying on their back. Milk can easily travel into their eustachian tubes and start an infection. Always hold the baby with its head at least partly upright when giving a bottle. Even if you're breast-feeding (which is preferable for the first year), try to elevate the baby's head to some degree while it's nursing.

And finally, if you or your child has a tendency to develop ear infections, you should avoid cigarette smoke, which has been shown to promote respiratory infections.

NATURAL PRESCRIPTION FOR EAR INFECTIONS

FOR IMMEDIATE RELIEF:

- Treat with acetaminophen (like Tylenol) to relieve pain.

- Elevate the head of the bed by resting the bed frame on books or lift the crib or bed mattress the same way. This will facilitate draining of the tubes and help relieve pressure and thus pain.

- Relieve pain with a warm compress held to the ear.

- Drink fluids to help keep mucus thin and flowing. The act of swallowing opens the tubes and encourages them to drain, and the fluids fight infection.

- Use a vaporizer in the bedroom at night.

- If you or your child has a tendency to ear infections, always use a decongestant at night when either one of you has a cold.

- Drink a dropperful of echinacea (available at health food stores) dissolved in a glass of water three times daily. This is safe for adults and children over a year old.

- During the acute stage of infection, take 200 mg. of N-acetylcysteine two times a day. (This is not recommended for babies under a year.)

FOR CHRONIC EAR INFECTIONS:

- Allergies are a major cause of chronic ear infections. Determine if you or your child has a food or inhalant allergy (see Food Allergy, page 146). The most common food allergens include wheat, eggs, dairy foods, corn, citrus, and peanut butter.

- To help prevent the development of allergies in babies, breast-feed for as long as possible.

- Introduce new foods carefully to babies, watching to see if a reaction occurs. Wheat, eggs, and dairy foods should probably not be introduced to babies in the first nine months of life, especially if there is a family history of allergies.

- Never allow a baby to drink from a bottle while lying down, as the fluid can collect in the ear. Even while breast-feeding, try to keep the baby's head somewhat elevated.

- While suffering from a cold or an ear infection, avoid simple carbohydrates including sugar, honey, cookies, candy, ice cream, sodas, chocolate, dried fruits, and fruit juices.

EARWAX

EARWAX, OR CERUMEN, is not just a nuisance; it's there to keep your ears clean. In most people, it works well. The wax traps dust, bacteria, and other tiny invaders, and as it works its way out of the ear, it takes the foreign substances with it. The problem occurs when too much earwax accumulates, blocks the ear canal, and ultimately causes deafness.

A fascinating study was reported in the *Journal of the American Medical Association* in 1970 concerning people in a mental hospital. Nearly half of these people failed a hearing test: Only about 10 percent of the general population fails such a test. Upon examination, doctors learned that most of the patients who had failed the hearing test had impacted wax in both ears. After removal of the wax, not only was hearing restored to most of the 1,700 patients, but 50 of them were rehabilitated to the point where they were discharged from the hospital.

I had one elderly patient who was becoming increasingly depressed and suffered from dizzy spells. Neurological tests had not revealed the cause of her condition. When I examined her ears, I saw that both ears were impacted with wax. Removal of the wax—a simple procedure—restored her spirits and relieved her symptoms of dizziness. It's common for people who have difficulty hearing to become withdrawn and depressed, and it's important to remember that the cause can be as simple as earwax.

If you know that you have excessive earwax, there are steps you can take to remove it. First of all, *never* put anything smaller than a banana in your ear (I'm tired of saying "your elbow"). Never use a cotton swab. These swabs can simply push wax farther into the ear canal, making it more difficult to remove. In addition, there are tiny hairs inside your ears to further protect them from foreign substances. When you use swabs to clean your ears, you push these hairs in so that they point in the wrong direction and offer little protection.

The best way to remove earwax is to use a softening agent, which you can buy over-the-counter at any pharmacy. You can also use hydrogen peroxide, glycerin, or mineral oil. Put a drop or two in the affected ear once a day for a few days, then use warm water to rinse out the wax. Some doctors recommend that you use a bulb syringe and *very gently* squirt some water into the ear, turn your head, and let the water drain out. If you feel comfortable doing this, that's fine. My patients most often prefer to use one of the softening solutions in their ears for a few days and then stand in the shower and let the water spray into their ears, turning their head afterward to be sure it drains out (along with the accumulated wax).

If you don't feel comfortable removing the wax yourself, by all means ask your doctor to do it. It's a simple procedure.

Once the wax is removed, take steps to keep your ears dry following bathing or showering. You can dry them with a soft towel or gently blow them dry with a hair dryer.

NATURAL PRESCRIPTION FOR EARWAX

- Never put anything smaller than a banana in your ear; don't use cotton swabs, or anything small, to clean your ears.

- To remove wax, use an over-the-counter preparation or a few drops of hydrogen peroxide, glycerin, or mineral oil. After using the drops for two or three days, rinse the ears using a bulb syringe and warm water, letting the excess water drain out along with the wax, or stand in the shower and let the warm water rinse your ear, turning your head to drain each ear thoroughly afterward.

- Dry your ears thoroughly after showering, using a soft towel or a hair dryer.

• • •

ECZEMA

ECZEMA, OR ATOPIC DERMATITIS, is a chronic, itchy skin disease that usually appears on the inside of the elbows and knees and on the face and the wrists. Infants are the most common sufferers of eczema, and most will be free of the disease by the time they're eighteen months old. But children as well as adults can develop it at any age.

Eczema is an allergic disease; it's more common in people who have other allergies, particularly asthma and hay fever. As you might guess, the best approach for controlling eczema is similar to that of controlling other allergies. The first step is to try to identify allergenic foods. I have seen patients improve dramatically when they eliminate allergenic foods from their diet: Eggs, milk, dairy products, chocolate, peanut, soy, potatoes, and the glutens found in wheat, oats, rye, and barley are common offenders. An allergen-free diet should be followed for four to six weeks in order to allow improvement. See Food Allergy, page 146, for a fuller discussion of this problem. In infants, cow's milk is the most common allergen, so it's important to breast-feed babies as long as possible. In addition, if the parents of a child are allergic to certain foods, the baby may carry that allergy as well, and those foods should be avoided. It's not uncommon for babies with eczema to develop chronic ear infections.

One recent well-controlled study found that the food additive tartrazine can provoke eczema in some people, though the reaction is not common (sometimes it's difficult to make a connection between eczema and a particular cause because the symptoms can vary from one day to the next). It was reported that of the twelve children studied, one showed severe eczema symptoms after the ingestion of tartrazine. Tartrazine, or FD&C Yellow Dye No. 5, is found in many foods. For a complete list, see the section on food colorings in Hives, page 191.

There's a great deal of evidence that people with eczema have a problem with their digestion of essential fatty acids. Over half of eczema sufferers improve when they take evening primrose oil—as a supplement as well as topically. Evening primrose oil can relieve the symptoms of eczema and help to normalize the digestion of essential fatty acids.

Fatty fishes, a natural source of the oils that help relieve the improper fatty acid digestion, are a great aid to people with eczema. MaxEPA is a form of fish oil supplement that I recommend. I also tell my patients to have fatty fish like herring, salmon, or mackerel at least twice a week.

Vitamin C and bioflavonoids are extremely useful in controlling this condition, and I discuss a natural source of bioflavonoids in Food Allergy, page 146.

Vitamin A is very important to the health of the skin and can be very useful in the treatment of eczema.

Zinc is especially helpful for people with eczema. Many eczema sufferers have been found to be deficient in zinc, and, in fact, zinc is an important mineral in the fatty acid metabolism.

In addition to supplements, there are some practical measures that you can take to relieve the symptoms of eczema, outlined below.

NATURAL PRESCRIPTION FOR ECZEMA

- Identify food allergies and eliminate the offending foods from your diet. See Food Allergy, page 146. Eggs, milk, cheese, chocolate, peanuts, soy, potatoes, and the glutens in wheat are common allergenic foods. It will take four to six weeks for the results of an allergen-free diet to be observed, so be patient.

- Breast-feed infants for as long as possible if there is any sign of eczema. While breast-feeding, the mother should avoid any foods to which she has had an allergic reaction.

- Investigate the possibility of the food additive tartrazine contributing to the eczema, and if it does, eliminate it from the diet.

- Eat fatty fish like salmon, herring, and mackerel at least twice a week.

IN ADDITION TO YOUR DAILY SUPPLEMENTS, PAGE xxiv, TAKE

- Evening primrose oil: 1,000 mg. three times daily, and then reduce the dose to 500 mg. daily.

- Evening primrose: topically to the affected skin twice a day.

- MaxEPA fish oils: 1,000 mg. three times daily.

- Vitamin C and bioflavonoids: 1,000 mg. of both daily.

- Vitamin A: 10,000 I.U. daily

- Zinc: 50 mg. daily.

SOME STEPS TO RELIEVE SYMPTOMS:

- Do not use hot water for bathing and showering. Use warm water.

- Use bath oil to soften skin. Use a nondrying soap substitute instead of soap.

- Do not use over-the-counter ointments that contain benzocaine or antibiotics.

- Avoid lanolin in skin lotions, cosmetics, cleansers, and the like.

- Try to avoid temperature extremes and any activity that will involve excessive sweating.

- Aerobic exercise is beneficial to eczema and other skin ailments. Just be sure to take a warm shower after exercise to wash away sweat.

- Avoid any oily or greasy ointment that prevents skin from breathing.

- Try to wear cotton and other natural fibers next to your skin with the exception of wool, which you should avoid.

- As stress can exacerbate eczema, practice stress reduction techniques.

• • •

EYE PROBLEMS

THERE ARE THREE common eye problems that people consult me about, and, since their names are unfamiliar, I've discussed them together.

Before I outline the simple problems you can deal with yourself through natural means, I should mention symptoms that should send you directly to your doctor. They include:

- Something in your eye that you can't remove after flushing with water.
- An injury to your eye that involves a cut or a puncture or a blow that causes pain or affects your vision.
- A chemical in the eye that causes pain after flushing with water.
- Unusual sensitivity to light.
- Eye inflammation during a bout with cold sores or herpes.
- Sudden loss of vision or the appearance of halos around light sources.
- Pain in connection with the use of contact lenses.

Now, here are the symptoms you can deal with yourself using natural methods.

DRY EYES

Dry eyes are eyes that are tired, burn, and sometimes ironically are also watery. Dry eyes are a common problem of older people. About 30 percent of people over forty—unaccountability, most of them are women

—suffer from dry eyes. As we age, the quantity and quality of tear production simply slows down and/or the oil produced in the eyelid gland isn't as copious. Sometimes people can have dry eyes or insufficient tear production as a side effect of a drug that they're taking. Diuretics and antidepressants can cause them and so can antihistamines. Sometimes vitamin B_6, which is a natural diuretic, or DLPA or tyrosine, which are natural antidepressants, can cause dry eyes. Sometimes dry eyes are associated with thyroid problems, rheumatoid arthritis (see Rheumatoid Arthritis page 18), or Sjögren's syndrome, a connective-tissue disease.

If your eyes are dry, your first step should be consulting your doctor to find out the cause. Once you're sure it's not an eyelid abnormality, infection, or systemic disease, you can treat the problem naturally. There are products on the market that mimic natural tears and can be used as eyedrops. You can buy these products over-the-counter at any pharmacy. Just avoid brands that contain "vasoconstrictors." These substances constrict the blood vessels in the eyes, thus exacerbating the problem.

Some of my patients have had success with evening primrose oil used as a supplement. Because dry heat in winter can further irritate dry eyes, use a humidifier. One simple thing to keep in mind is to protect your eyes from sun and wind. If you don't already wear glasses, wear sunglasses.

NATURAL PRESCRIPTION FOR DRY EYES

- Check with your doctor to learn the cause of your dry eyes and to be sure that it's not a symptom of some other condition that needs attention, such as an infection.

- Use artificial tears, which are available over-the-counter. Avoid brands containing vasoconstrictors.

- Use a humidifier during dry seasons or when indoor heat is on.

- Protect your eyes from sun and wind by wearing sunglasses.

IN ADDITION TO YOUR DAILY SUPPLEMENTS, PAGE xxiv, TAKE

- Evening primrose oil: 500 mg. three times a day.

BLEPHARITIS

Most people have never heard of this problem, even if they have it! Blepharitis is a condition that causes scaly red eyelids. It looks and acts like dandruff of the eyelids; in fact, it's usually connected with dandruff and is commonly a form of sebhorrheic eczema. Sometimes bacteria will exacerbate the situation, and in the worst cases, small ulcers may develop on the eyelids and lashes can fall out. Some people with blepharitis are prone to conjunctivitis because flakes fall into the eye and irritate it (see Conjunctivitis, page 90).

The best approach to treating blepharitis is to keep the eyelids clean by washing them twice a day with soap and warm water, or with a solution of baking soda or salt in warm water.

You can also try the shampoos formulated for dandruff that are available in any pharmacy. The ones with ZPT or zinc pyrithione as the active ingredient are quite effective; just be very careful to keep the shampoo out of your eyes.

Finally, if your blepharitis just won't seem to clear up, or if it clears up but keeps coming back, you might have a hidden food allergy that's causing the problem. For more information on how to cope, see Food Allergy, page 146.

NATURAL PRESCRIPTION FOR BLEPHARITIS

- Wash the eyelids twice a day with either warm soap and water, a solution of one cup warm water to one tablespoon baking soda, or a solution of one teaspoon salt to a cup of warm water.

- Try using an antidandruff shampoo with ZPT or zinc pyrithione as the active ingredient, such as Selsun Blue.

- If you have a recurring problem with blepharitis, you could have a food allergy that's causing the condition. For more information on this see Food Allergy, page 146.

IN ADDITION: If your eyes don't clear up in about two weeks, you should see your doctor who can prescribe an ointment that will help. Certain prescription antifungal creams can be very effective if your blepharitis is due to eczema, but you must be careful not to get it in your eyes. However, do not use cortizone cream around your eyes. Nizoral, a prescription shampoo, can also help.

FOREIGN BODIES IN THE EYE

It is no mystery when there's something in your eye: It hurts! Before you do anything about it, look in a mirror and try to see what is causing the pain. If it looks like an object or speck is really imbedded in your cornea, you should see a doctor or go to an emergency room. If you've determined that the problem is something on the surface of the eye, you can proceed. You may feel the urge to rub your eye. Don't. If what you have in your eye is gritty or sharp, rubbing can imbed it and cause further problems. Instead, pull your upper eyelid over the lower, and roll your eye. This motion will help to dislodge the foreign body. If that doesn't work, try rinsing the eye with plain water.

Sometimes, if you blow your nose, the foreign body can be dislodged.

If none of these techniques seems to help, you should go to a doctor or to an emergency room.

NATURAL PRESCRIPTION FOR FOREIGN BODIES IN THE EYE

- Don't rub your eye; you might scratch the cornea.

- Pull your upper eyelid down over the lower lid and roll your eye.

- Try rinsing your eye with plain water, using an eye cup (available at pharmacies) or by cupping clean water in your clean palm and holding it against your eye.

- Blow your nose.

- If nothing else works, see your doctor or go to an emergency room.

•   •   •

FIBROCYSTIC BREAST DISEASE

FIBROCYSTIC BREAST DISEASE, also known as cystic mastitis, is a sometimes painful, but benign, cystic swelling of the breasts. It is important to know that it is not a disease; it is a condition that is an inconvenience and a discomfort but not a serious health problem. Some 60 percent of all women suffer from fibrocystic breast disease, in which the breasts are sometimes cystic, or lumpy, and become swollen, typically before menstruation. Some women find that their breasts become so painful that they can't bear to touch them and have trouble sleeping at night. The condition is not medically dangerous, and is not a precursor of cancer, but it does complicate breast self-examination as it is difficult to identify a new lump among the existing ones. Consequently, regular mammograms are essential, particularly if there is a family history of breast cancer.

The inflammatory processes of cystic mastitis appear to be aggravated by estrogen, both in its natural form and in birth control pills. The fluctuating levels of estrogen account for the cyclic nature of the inflammation and swelling. (For further information about premenstrual symptoms, see PMS, page 276.) Diet also has an effect on the formation of painful lumps. In my experience, caffeine in coffee and colas, theophylline in tea, and theobromine in chocolate have all been shown to contribute to the inflammation and should be eliminated from your diet. Some asthma medications that contain caffeine can also aggravate the condition. Although there have been studies that claim giving up caffeine and related compounds did not work, these studies only reduced caffeine in the diet, they did not eliminate it entirely. For a list of substances containing caffeine, see Blueprint for Health, page xvii.

There is also evidence that what you eat and the regularity of your bowel movements have a direct bearing on cystic mastitis. Women having fewer than three bowel movements per week are 4.5 times more likely to have the condition than women who have at least one a day. In addition, women on a vegetarian diet excrete two to three times more detoxified estrogens than women who eat meat, who tend to reabsorb estrogens. A diet high in vegetables and fruits will regulate bowel function and help reduce the severity of the inflammation.

Vitamin E has provided dramatic results in controlling cystic mastitis. Eighty-five percent of the patients in one study showed remission of lumps, while the remaining 15 percent showed clear improvement. The vitamin E used in this study was natural vitamin E, so be sure to check the label. (The synthetic vitamin E was found ineffective.)

Vitamin A, taken in high doses, also stimulates complete or partial remission of cystic mastitis. However, some people developed headaches in high-dose vitamin A studies and had to withdraw. Beta-carotene, with similar activity, has been used by my patients with success.

Primrose oil has been used successfully in Europe to reduce the size of cysts, and is now available in health food stores in the United States. I recommend it regularly.

NATURAL PRESCRIPTION FOR FIBROCYSTIC BREAST DISEASE

- Eliminate coffee, tea, chocolate, and caffeinated sodas from your diet. Check labels on over-the-counter medications because many diet preparations, analgesics, pain relievers, diuretics, and cold and allergy remedies contain caffeine. Also, prescription drugs can contain caffeine.

- Avoid animal fats.

- Eat lots of fresh fruit, vegetables, nuts, and berries.

- Eat fish and other seafood rich in iodine.

- Have regular mammograms. Check with your gynecologist regarding frequency.

IN ADDITION TO YOUR DAILY SUPPLEMENTS, PAGE xxiv, TAKE

- Vitamin E: 400 I.U. a day.

- Beta-carotene: 10,000–25,000 I.U. a day.

- Primrose oil: one or two capsules three times a day.

IN ADDITION: There is experimental evidence linking iodine deficiency in animals with cystic mastitis. Some doctors have had good results prescribing kelp supplements for patients, but this isn't something you should do on your own: Your doctor will want to test you for thyroid activity before making a decision. If your intake of iodine is low because you are cutting back on iodized salt, you can compensate by eating seafood, which is rich in iodine, and by taking kelp daily.

•   •   •

FINGERNAIL PROBLEMS

FINGERNAILS REVEAL A LOT about you and your state of health. Many people are careless about their nails. They use them instead of tools, they immerse them in harsh soaps and detergents, they hit them or snag them accidentally, they overexpose them to the elements. But even people who take good care of their nails often have problems with brittle, cracked, and breaking fingernails, conditions that may be helped by diet or nutritional supplements.

Fingernails, which protect the multiple nerve endings in the fingertips, are composed of a protein called keratin. They grow at the rate of about one-eighth inch a month, which means it can take up to three months to grow a new nail. The healthy nail should be smooth, and the nail bed underneath should be pink, indicating a healthy blood supply. A very pale or blue nail bed, or nails streaked with either white or red may be indicative of poor circulation or disease. If you're in overall good health but your nails keep breaking and splintering, try to determine the reason for their poor condition.

The most frequent cause for problem fingernails is overexposure to the elements and harsh chemicals. Every time your nails get wet they swell, then shrink again when they dry off. This swell-shrink cycle, when repeated often enough, leaves your nails brittle and fragile. Cold weather and dry, heated rooms cause a variety of problems, from brittle nails to dry skin and cuticles. Harsh nail products such as nail polish remover and the glue used to attach artificial nails can also be harmful. You should try not to use nail polish remover more than once a week and look for one that contains acetates, which are less drying than acetones. A manicure itself, if it involves cutting the cuticle, can cause lasting damage to the nail as well as the nail bed, which relies on the cuticle for protection against damage and infection.

The best thing you can do for your nails is use a pair of rubber gloves for any project that involves soaking your hands in water or cleansers. If you do get your hands wet, dry them off thoroughly and apply a moisturizing lotion, rubbing it in around the fingertip and nail area. Lotions that contain at least 10 percent urea (this will be indicated on the tube) work particularly well. Apply more lotion before putting on your winter gloves, and again before going to bed. In addition, rub in some cuticle cream, available in pharmacies, whenever you have the chance, massaging the nail area to stimulate circulation and growth.

I had a patient who was a copywriter for a major advertising agency. She was generally in good health, but she mentioned in passing that her nails drove her crazy because they were brittle and her cuticles were rough. I gave her advice about lotions and cuticle creams. When I saw her a few months later, her nails were in perfect condition. She'd developed the habit of keeping a tube of cuticle cream next to her computer. Whenever she was stumped or waiting for something to print, she'd rub a bit of cream on her nails. She told me that she also kept some cream in the glove compartment of her car: When her husband was driving, she worked on her cuticles. She was delighted with the results, and I pass her tip along to you: Keep some cuticle cream in any spot where you're likely to have time or opportunity to use it.

It will take several weeks of these new patterns to bear fruit: Remember that it takes up to three months for a new nail to grow in. If there is no improvement, your nails may not be receiving the nutrients they need. There is some controversy on this point, but I have found supplements very helpful, particularly for pregnant women or people on a low-calorie diet. Before I recommend supplements I examine my patients for other signs of nutritional deficiency, since poor, brittle nails may be the first outward sign of more serious problems. For instance, poor nail condition, when accompanied by thinning hair and overall feelings of fatigue, may be indicative of a weak thyroid. Or, when taken together with bloating and burping after meals, and possible constipation, brittle nails may be indicative of insufficient stomach acidity for proper digestion. The body is not absorbing nutrients for lack of sufficient acid. When these conditions are present, they must be corrected before adequate nutrition and supplements can help.

Most deficiencies, however, are simply the result of insufficient nutrients. Protein, for instance, is very important: If you don't get enough protein, the calcium in your nails is not properly utilized. You should eat at least 8 ounces of fish, chicken, or turkey each day.

Calcium is also very important, and supplements may be helpful, particularly for pregnant women, women past menopause, and people on a restricted-calorie or low-fat diet. Take 1,200 mg. of calcium once a day (I recommend calcium citrate as it is the calcium form best absorbed by the body).

Biotin, a water-soluble B vitamin, is necessary for healthy skin and hair. In fact, it's sometimes known as "the hair vitamin." It plays a role in nail health, too. You can buy it at a health food store or pharmacy.

Iron deficiency is one of the most common causes for brittle nails. According to a study in England, researchers found that among five women suffering from iron deficiency anemia, all five had brittle nails. But, after the women took iron supplements, the nails weren't brittle any longer. Too much iron can be as troublesome as too little, so be sure to have your blood tested before taking supplements.

Zinc deficiency is sometimes highlighted by white spots on the nail or the nail bed. People on restricted-calorie diets often suffer from zinc deficiency, as do many women just before their menstrual period.

Finally, silica is a trace mineral that I've found useful for nails.

NATURAL PRESCRIPTION FOR FINGERNAIL PROBLEMS

- Protect you nails whenever possible from water and chemicals by wearing rubber gloves.

- Moisturize your hands, paying particular attention to nails and cuticles whenever possible.

- Use cuticle cream whenever possible.

- Make sure you are getting adequate protein in your diet.

IN ADDITION TO YOUR DAILY SUPPLEMENTS, PAGE xxiv, TAKE

- Calcium: 1,000 mg. per day, 1,200 mg. if you are pregnant or postmenopausal. Use calcium citrate.

- Biotin: 2,500 mcg. daily.

- Iron: 60 mg. a day (after having a blood test to determine if you are deficient).

- Zinc: 50 mg. a day

- Silica: amount as described on package label.

FLATULENCE

MANY PEOPLE THINK that if their digestive system is normal, they won't have any gas unless they eat a particular food, like beans. The fact is that normal people on an average diet expel nearly a quart of intestinal gas each day. Most of us aren't aware of this. It's when we become aware of the gas that it can become uncomfortable and embarrassing.

Gas is formed when certain foods reach the large intestine without being completely and adequately digested. When they arrive, bacteria that reside there go to work to digest them and in the process produce gas. This is a normal process; in most cases, intestinal gas is not a sign of a disease. Today, when we're eating more high-fiber foods and fruits and vegetables—which can be sources of intestinal gas—the problem of flatulence is more common.

The major cause of occasional excess flatulence is gas-promoting foods. Most people know that beans are a major suspect, but there are other foods that will put you at risk including apricots, bananas, broccoli, Brussels sprouts, cabbage, cauliflower, eggplant, radishes, and onions.

Obviously the first step in reducing flatulence is avoiding the foods that give you gas. But remember that people react differently to various foods. Some people have found that corn, oats, and even bagels give them gas. You have to make a point of noticing which foods give you problems. Of course, even when you identify the foods, it may not be practical or even sensible to give them up.

There are ways to reduce the amount of gas produced by one of the main offenders: beans. Soaking beans in water for at least twelve hours and then cooking them well will help reduce their gas-producing properties. Make sure that you discard the soaking water. Rinse beans thoroughly and be certain to cook them thoroughly until they are completely tender with no "bite" left.

There are other methods to help reduce gas while still eating problematic foods. The most effective one seems to be a new product called Beano. You use it as a condiment, adding a few drops to your first spoonful of offending food. It has a mild soy sauce–type flavor that usually works well with beans and other gas producers.

Some people find that activated charcoal tablets, which are available at health food stores, help cut down on their gas production. The charcoal absorbs the problem odors. If you try activated charcoal tablets, be careful to avoid taking them within two hours of any other medication.

Because they are so effective at absorbing chemicals, they can absorb your medicines and make them unavailable to your body.

It is not uncommon to experience intestinal gas and bloating when on antibiotics. As I've discussed, antibiotics kill off good as well as bad bacteria in your system, and an overgrowth of yeast can result. Yeast overgrowth is a common cause of flatulence and can be easily remedied by following a yeast-free diet (see Candidiasis, page 61) as well as taking acidophilus tablets available in health food stores.

Many people are unaware that milk products can be a cause of flatulence but, in fact, lactose intolerance is probably the major cause of chronic excessive gas and bloating. I've had a number of patients who have developed lactose intolerance and complained of gas and bloating. Fortunately, it's not hard to deal with this problem. There's a product available called Lactaid, which is available at any pharmacy and even some supermarkets. It helps break down the sugar in milk, which causes the problem. If you suspect that you are lactose intolerant, avoid all dairy products including milk, cheese, and the like for ten days to see if your symptoms are alleviated. Acidophilus is also helpful. For more information, see Lactose Intolerance, page 231.

There are also some dietary and lifestyle changes that can help. Smoking, chewing gum, drinking carbonated drinks, and drinking from water fountains can all introduce excess air and gas into your system, thus promoting flatulence.

If you have chronic flatulence it's possible that you're suffering from something other than a simple case of gas. Check the following conditions for more information: Celiac Disease, page 73; Diverticular Disease, page 120; Irritable Bowel, page 220; Protozoa Disease, page 287; and Food Allergy, page 146.

NATURAL PRESCRIPTION FOR FLATULENCE

- Avoid gas-promoting foods, including beans, broccoli, Brussels sprouts, cabbage, cauliflower, eggplant, radishes, and onions.

- When you cook beans, be sure to soak them for at least twelve hours in cold water. Discard the soaking water, rinse carefully, and cook thoroughly until the beans are tender.

- Sprinkle Beano on your first bite of a gas-promoting food. Beano is available at pharmacies.

- Try activated charcoal tablets, available at health food stores, which absorb odors. Follow the directions on the package. Don't take them within two hours of any medication.

- If you are lactose intolerant, use Lactaid, a product that helps digest the sugar in milk. Take one acidophilus tablet three times a day.

- Avoid the following, which introduce excess air and gas into your system: smoking, chewing gum, drinking carbonated drinks, and drinking from water fountains.

- If you have chronic flatulence, check the following for more information: Celiac Disease, page 73; Diverticular Disease, page 120; Irritable Bowel, page 220; Protozoa Disease, page 287; Food Allergy, page 146.

• • •

FOOD ALLERGY

FOOD ALLERGIES HAVE BECOME one of the most common undiagnosed health problems today. Some researchers speculate that more than half of the people in the United States suffer from symptoms brought on by food allergies. When you consider the wide range of symptoms that food allergies can cause and the number of bodily organs and systems they can affect, it's not hard to believe that every other person you know could have a food allergy.

Why have food allergies become so common today? There are a variety of possible explanations: greater stress on our immune systems caused by pollution of our air, water, and food, a tendency among many people to eat a limited and repetitive diet, the trend toward weaning babies early and putting them on solid foods early, and finally, the fact that some of our food sources, including both plants and animals, have been genetically manipulated causing who-knows-what challenge to our tissues. Why one person develops food allergies while another does not seems to be, for the most part, a question of genetics. Some people are simply more prone to react to foods in a negative way. In addition, children whose mothers' diets are high in allergenic foods during pregnancy or who are weaned early are more likely to develop a reaction to certain foods.

Food allergy is sometimes used as a general term to cover a variety of negative reactions to food. Not all of these reactions are true food allergies. A true food *allergy* results from a reaction of your immune system to a component of a certain food, often a protein. A food *intolerance* comes from adverse reactions to foods that don't involve the immune system. This would include lactose intolerance, which results from an enzyme deficiency (see Lactose Intolerance, page 231). Some people are *sensitive* to a food, a food additive such as a coloring, or a chemical like monosodium glutamate (MSG) or sulfite or salicylates (pain relievers) including aspirin. For a detailed list of additives that can cause reactions in sensitive people, see Hives, page 191.

Because many reactions to foods are not simple allergies, classic allergy testing will often give negative results. Occasionally doctors are so insistent that food allergies are primarily a myth or psychologically induced that they'll ignore the fact that a certain food causes a symptom and that when it's removed the symptom is gone, too. I've found with my patients that eliminating symptoms from negative food reactions, whether true allergies, intolerances, or sensitivities, is more important than "proving" a food allergy. Therefore from this point on we will use the term "food reaction" instead of "food allergy."

One difficulty in pinpointing food reactions is that the symptoms they cause are so varied. One person may develop headaches and fatigue from eating corn products while another person could get chronic diarrhea or eczema from eating the same thing. The perplexing fact about food reactions, from the standpoint of a diagnostician, is that any organ, from your brain to your colon, can be a target. Many people are unaware of their food reactions, and I've sometimes diagnosed them incidentally— when people came to me with a specific complaint and in the course of investigating its source I realized that food reactions played a role.

Certain foods seem to be more reactive than others. The most likely culprits include milk, eggs, and peanuts, followed by wheat, corn, fish, shellfish, berries, nuts, peas and beans, and certain spices.

Here's a rundown of some of the symptoms that can be caused by food reactions: acne, arrhythmia, arthritis, asthma, anxiety, back pain, bed-wetting, bursitis, chronic infections, chronic diarrhea, chronic bronchitis, chronic bladder infections, eczema, depression, ear infections, fatigue, gas, gastritis, headaches, hives, hyperactivity, hypoglycemia, inability to concentrate, insomnia, irritable colon, itchy nose and/or throat, joint pain, migraines, sinusitis.

As you can see, it's a pretty exhaustive list. How can you determine whether your symptoms might be caused by a food reaction? This simple list of questions can point you in the right direction.

- Do you feel worse after eating?
- Do you feel better when you don't eat?
- Is there a history of food reactions in your family?
- Did you have allergies when you were younger?
- Do you now have recurrent, unexplained symptoms?

If you answered yes to most of these questions, you should investigate whether food reactions are causing your symptoms.

There are also some typical physical characteristics of people who have food reactions. They often have dark circles under their eyes (known as "allergic shiners"), their eyes are puffy, they have a few horizontal creases in their lower eyelids, they suffer from irregular fluid retention, and they often suffer from swollen glands.

One way to determine the source of your reactions is to be tested. I have no faith in skin testing. I also don't think the pure water fast followed by food challenges to be very practical. In my experience, a blood test for antibodies to specific foods is the most convenient testing method. But since many food reactions may not show up on this test or other classic allergy tests, it's often best to determine what you're reacting to on your own by means of an elimination diet followed by a "food challenge." Sometimes this is a very simple process. You may quickly discover that you're reacting to milk or eggs or fish. But sometimes it's more difficult, especially if you're reacting to a food additive. You must be patient and meticulous as you go about the process.

The best way to begin an elimination diet is to start a food diary and keep it for two weeks before beginning the diet. In it you note everything you eat throughout the day, along with any symptoms you might have and precisely when those symptoms occur. This will give you clues as to the foods that could be causing your reactions.

In the elimination diet, you will omit for at least seven days any food that you eat more often than twice weekly, as well as common allergenic foods. You should continue to take any regular prescribed medications while on the diet, but it's best to eliminate vitamins, minerals, and OTC medications like laxatives. The basic elimination diet for adults and children allows all vegetables save corn and all fruits but citrus fruits, fresh meats (free of preservatives), drinks such as water and juices of the fruits allowed, all nuts but peanuts, honey, pure maple syrup, safflower and sunflower oils, noniodized salt, rice, and oats.

See the tables listing all foods allowed on an elimination diet as well as foods to be avoided.

ELIMINATION DIET: ACCEPTABLE FOODS

(Foods marked with a * should be avoided by people who suffer from headaches.)

MEATS & SEAFOOD
Beef
Chicken
Clams
Cornish hens
Crab
Deer
Dove
Duck
Fish (all)
Frog legs
Goose
Lamb
Lobster
Oysters
Quail
Pheasant
Pork
Rabbit
Scallops
Shrimp
Squirrel
Turkey
Veal

NUTS & SEEDS
Almonds
Brazil nuts
Butternuts
Cashews
Chestnuts
Filberts
Hazelnuts
Hickory nuts
Macadamia nuts
Pecans
Pistachios
Pumpkin seeds
Sesame seeds
Sunflower seeds
Walnuts

VEGETABLES
Artichokes
Asparagus
Avocado *
Beets
Broccoli
Brussels sprouts
Cabbage
Carrots
Cauliflower
Celery
Cucumber
Eggplant
Greens (all)

Jicama
Kale
Okra
Olives
Onions (all)
Parsley
Parsnips
Potatoes (all)
Pumpkin
Radish
Rutabaga
Spinach
Squash (all)
Turnips
Watercress

BEVERAGES
Bottled water
Juices from allowed
 fruits
Sparkling water

FRUITS
Apples
Apricots
Bananas *
Berries (all)
Cherries

Coconut

Dates

Figs * (fresh)

Grapes (green, red *)

Kiwi

Mango

Melons (all)

Nectarines

Papaya

Peaches

Pears

Persimmon

Pineapple *

Plums *

Pomegranate

Prunes *

Rhubarb

Raisins *

OILS

Safflower

Sunflower

Olive

MISCELLANEOUS

Amaranth

Buckwheat

Noniodized salt

Oats

Quinoa

Rice

Vinegar

E L I M I N A T I O N   D I E T :   F O O D S   A N D   F O O D   P R O D U C T S   T o   A v o i d

MILK PRODUCTS

Breads

Butter

Candies

Cheese

Cookies

Ice cream

Lunch meats

Margarines

Milk

Processed foods

Soups

EGG PRODUCTS

Cakes

Cookies

Ice cream

Macaroni

Noodles

Pancake mix

Pies

Salad dressings

WHEAT PRODUCTS

Batters

Bread

Candies

Cereals

Cookies

Crackers

Gravies

Lunch meats

Processed foods

Salad dressings

Soups

CORN PRODUCTS

Bacon

Breads

Candies

Cereals

Corn chips

Corn oil

Corn starch

Corn syrup

Ketchup

Pastries

Peanut butter

Popcorn

SUGAR PRODUCTS

Candies

Cookies

Honey

Ketchup

Maple syrup

Salad dressings

Soft drinks

Sucrose and dextrose

CITRUS PRODUCTS

Citrus flavoring

Grapefruits

Lemons

Limes
Oranges
Soft drinks

CHOCOLATE &
COLA
Candy
Cereal
Desserts
Snack foods
Soft drinks

ADDED
INGREDIENTS
Flavorings
Colorings

Preservatives
including:
butylated
hydroxyanisole
(BHA)
butylated
hydroxytoluene
(BHT)
Monosodium
glutamate (MSG)
Karaya and other gums
Nitrite
Sulfite

DRINKS
All alcoholic beverages
Carbonated beverages

Coffee
Tea (except herbal tea)

ADDITIONAL PRODUCTS
Aspartame
Beans
Black pepper
Canned foods
Mustard
Peanuts
Processed and preserved meats
Saccharin
Salt
Soy products
Spices
Yeast, baker's and brewer's

When you have followed the elimination diet for seven to ten days, you should see a reduction in your symptoms if they are food related. To pinpoint which foods are problematic for you, you then need to do a food challenge, introducing foods, one at a time, to see if you react to them. You should keep a detailed food diary when you begin to try the food challenges and note any symptoms you experience. These symptoms, of course, indicate which new or challenge foods are causing trouble. Here are the foods to use—one at a time—for a challenge following seven to ten days of the elimination diet.

- Wheat: cream of wheat, shredded wheat, or puffed wheat
- Corn: corn on the cob or popcorn
- Eggs: boiled or scrambled
- Milk: as beverage or as shake with allowed fruit
- Citrus fruit: as fruit or pure juice
- Peanuts: as nut or unadulterated butter
- Oils: sautéed with acceptable vegetables
- Chocolate: cocoa mixed with honey*
- Yeast: mixed in tolerated fruit juice*
- Sugar: mixed in tolerated fruit juice*

- Food coloring: mixed in tolerated fruit juice*
- Monosodium glutamate (MSG): sprinkle Accent on stir-fried vegetables*
- Preservatives: frankfurters, ham, or bologna, if tolerated*
- Aspartame or saccharine: mixed with juice*

The foods you use for challenges should be in their purest form (such as yeast mixed directly in fruit juice) so that you can more readily pinpoint precise sources of reactions. The foods that you should challenge with last are those most likely to cause symptoms. These usually include those foods eaten most frequently. It's usually best to add only one challenge food per day, though you can eat that food several times on that day if there is no reaction. Most food reactions occur a few minutes to twenty-four hours after the food is eaten; if a reaction does occur, don't challenge with any other foods until the reaction clears.

If you make a connection between a symptom and a particular food, that food should be eliminated from your diet for six to eight months. You can then reintroduce the food and see if you're still sensitive. Sometimes reactions will disappear when the foods are eaten infrequently. If you don't have any symptoms, you can eat the food occasionally. Of course, if symptoms recur, the food should be eliminated.

There's another reaction you might notice and one that will help you identify troublesome foods: a rapid pulse. In his book *The Pulse Test,* Arthur Fernandez Coca described how some people will get a high pulse rate after eating foods to which they have a reaction. You might try taking your pulse after meals to see if it's elevated.

I've discovered that one of the reasons for food reactions among my patients is a limited, repetitive diet. Many of my patients are busy, active people with myriad responsibilities and little time. One of the first casualties of these demands is a varied diet. I've had patients who claimed to eat a "very healthy" diet who eat the same meals virtually every day: bran cereal with skim milk for breakfast, apples several times a day for snacks, a tuna sandwich on whole wheat for lunch, chicken cutlet and a vegetable for dinner. While this is a fine menu for one day, to repeat it every day can create problems.

Some reactions are really a kind of addiction: When you first eat the offending food, you usually have a strong negative reaction—a severe headache or a rash, for instance—but you may never connect it with the

---

* These foods are not recommended for daily diet regardless of allergy.

food. The next time you eat the food, your reaction is milder and your body gets a bit of a buzz. Eventually your reaction becomes a chronic symptom. If you discontinue the food, you go through a period of withdrawal. That's why patients often say that when they eliminate a known reactive food from their diet, they go through a period of feeling worse than ever. This can last up to five days. Eventually, they'll recover and feel much better after their body adjusts.

The point is that repeating the same foods day in and out can make you more vulnerable to developing an allergy and then establishing that allergy as a regular part of your body's systemic reaction to a certain food. It's very important to vary your diet. Try not to eat the same things every day. Don't get into a "same breakfast–same lunch" pattern. My rule of thumb is not to repeat the same foods two days in a row. You'll help your body to avoid reactions.

NATURAL PRESCRIPTION FOR FOOD REACTIONS

- As there is no "cure" for food reactions, elimination of the offending food or substance is critical. Keeping a food diary and following an elimination diet followed by "food challenges" as described above is the most effective way to pinpoint allergenic foods. Once you've noticed a connection between a food and a symptom, eliminate the food from your diet for at least six months. See the listing in Hives, page 191, of common food additives to which people are often sensitive.

IN ADDITION: If you have no success in pinpointing food reactions with an elimination diet followed by a food challenge, but you still feel that your symptoms are connected with food, you may have to consult a doctor who specializes in nutrition to help you identify your troublesome foods.

•   •   •

GALLBLADDER DISEASE

THE OLD-FASHIONED APPROACH to gallbladder disease was to ignore the pain until it was so severe the patient couldn't stand it any longer and then operate to remove the gallbladder. Once upon a time this made a certain kind of sense, but today there are other alternatives.

The truth is that I've been seeing fewer and fewer patients with gallbladder disease, probably because diet plays such an important role in preventing it and in general my patients are conscious of eating a healthy diet.

The disease typically causes symptoms including regular or occasional digestive distress, bloating, gas and nausea, usually after a fatty meal, which result from the irritation and spasms of the gallbladder. Sometimes these symptoms are ignored until the patient experiences intense abdominal pain, a result of passing a gallstone. Sometimes there are no warning symptoms—just the intense pain that some people confuse with appendicitis or duodenal ulcer. You may have an irritated gallbladder with or without stones. The symptoms and treatment will be identical.

The gallbladder is a pear-shaped organ located just under the liver and behind the bottom right rib. Bile, a substance produced by the liver, is stored in the gallbladder for release into the gut to help digest fat. When you eat fatty foods, the bile becomes saturated with cholesterol, one of the components of bile. Eventually, the excess cholesterol separates from the bile and begins to calcify, forming stones. Gallstones can be formed from substances other than cholesterol, but in the United States about 80 percent of them are composed primarily of cholesterol (about 20 percent are formed from minerals, particularly calcium salts).

The stones themselves may not be the problem. In fact, many people without symptoms are surprised to learn from an ultrasound sonogram or x-ray that they have gallstones. By age forty nearly 20 percent of the population has gallstones. The problems begin when the stones begin to move from the gallbladder into one of the small bile ducts leading to the liver. The pain of a gallstone attack comes when the stone blocks the duct and the duct contracts, most commonly after a fatty meal.

Of the gallbladder patients I have treated in the past, Lucille comes to mind immediately. From an English background, nearly sixty pounds overweight, she was a typical gallbladder victim. Gallbladder disease strikes women twice as often as men and is most common among Asians, Latin Americans, Indians, and the English.

Lucille had regularly suffered from indigestion, but the day she came to see me she had awakened with a severe pain in the upper right-hand corner of her abdomen—a much sharper and more powerful pain than any she had experienced before. An ultrasound sonogram revealed gallstones.

Lucille thought that her only option following her gallbladder attack was surgery. But as recovery from gallbladder surgery is often painful and as many people never have subsequent attacks, I thought that in Lucille's case it was worth trying a natural approach. Her health was suffering from the very factors that were causing her gallstones: obesity and a very high cholesterol count. Lucille followed the recommendations outlined below, and six years later she still has her gallstones but is free of the symptoms of gallbladder disease.

Gallstones are much easier to prevent than to cure. If you have a history of gallbladder disease in your family and/or if you have had some mild symptoms of gallbladder problems such as regular indigestion, bloating, and gas following a fatty meal, you should immediately adopt these guidelines, which might well keep you free from ever developing full-blown gallbladder disease.

Gallbladder disease, including gallstones and an inflamed gallbladder, is closely connected with a Western diet: high in refined carbohydrates and animal protein and low in fiber. The first step in avoiding gallstones, and preventing an attack if you already have them, is to eliminate aggravating (fatty) foods. In order to digest them, your gallbladder will go into overdrive and might force a stone into the duct, causing a gallbladder attack. For more details on cutting fat from the diet, see Blueprint for Health, page xvii.

There's been a great deal of research that indicates a low-fiber diet is a primary cause of gallbladder disease. Increasing the fiber in your diet is also critical in avoiding gallstones. Water-soluble fiber such as that found in vegetables and fruits, pectin, and oat bran is the most important.

There's another interesting theory that links food allergies and gallbladder attacks. In 1948, Dr. J. C. Breneman began using a very successful regime to prevent gallbladder attacks based on his work with food allergies. Dr. Breneman holds that eating allergy-causing foods stimulates the swelling of the bile ducts. The swelling reduces the flow of bile from the gallbladder and causes the pain and other symptoms connected with a gallbladder attack. In one study, 100 percent of gallbladder patients were totally free from symptoms when they followed a basic allergy-elimination diet. The foods that most commonly produced symptoms in decreasing order of occurrence include eggs (93 percent of the patients reacted to eggs), pork, onions, fowl, milk, coffee, citrus, corn, beans, and nuts. Lucille found that eggs, corn, and citrus gave her symptoms and eliminated them entirely from her diet. The connection between food allergy and gallbladder attacks could account for the numerous people who have gallbladder surgery and are then dismayed to find that their symptoms are still a problem: Though the stones have been removed, the allergy-causing foods promote the swelling of the ducts and the symptoms.

If you have symptoms of gallbladder disease, you should definitely try going on an allergy-elimination diet to see if it will eliminate your symptoms. As you gradually reintroduce foods to your diet, watch carefully for reactions. It could well be that once you find the offending foods and cut them from your diet, you'll be entirely free from symptoms (see Food Allergy, page 146).

If you are overweight, your chance of developing gallstones soars. If you are 20 percent overweight you double your susceptibility to gallstones. The proper diet for preventing gallstones—a low-fat, high-fiber diet—is also a diet that will help you lose weight. I must stress that recent research has shown that a very-low-calorie diet—a crash diet and in particular the "protein" power diets—can actually promote the formation of gallstones, so be sure that you are on a sensible weight-reduction program.

A minor but potentially significant step is to be sure to drink six to eight glasses of water each day. This fluid is necessary to maintain the water content of the bile and help prevent the formation of stones.

Interestingly, it has been found that women who skip breakfast or have only coffee have a much greater incidence of gallstones.

There is also evidence that taking aspirin can prevent the formation of gallstones. In one study, all the regular users of NSAIDs avoided a recurrence of gallstones compared with 32 percent who did not use aspirin regularly. I tell my gallstone patients to take one baby aspirin a day for this reason.

There is one nutritional supplement that can help gallstone sufferers. Lecithin has been recognized as a substance that will promote the ability of bile to keep cholesterol in solution and may prevent stones from forming.

NATURAL PRESCRIPTION FOR GALLBLADDER DISEASE

- Eliminate any possible food allergies (see Food Allergy, page 146).

- Avoid aggravating foods, including all fatty and fried foods. See Blueprint for Health, page xvii, for more information on eliminating fat from the diet.

- Increase your fiber intake, particularly more of the following foods: fruits, vegetables, whole grain breads and cereals, and oat bran.

- If you are overweight, lose weight on a sensible diet. Do *not* go on an extremely low-calorie diet, as this can exacerbate gallstones.

- Be sure to drink six to eight glasses of water daily.

- Eat a healthy breakfast daily.

- Avoid caffeine.

IN ADDITION TO YOUR DAILY SUPPLEMENTS, PAGE xxiv, TAKE

- Lecithin: 500 mg. three times a day.

IN ADDITION: Surgery is the traditional route for gallstones that are persistent and troublesome. But there are some new techniques that are being used in lieu of conventional surgery: a drug that dissolves stones; a new surgical technique using laparoscopic (microsurgical) instruments that require small incisions; a shock wave lithotripsy that "crushes" the stones. These techniques have their advantages and disadvantages and should be discussed with your doctor.

A recent report in *Lancet,* a respected British medical journal, made a connection between gallstones and fair-skinned people who suntan. In general, people who enjoy sunbathing have twice the risk of gallstones; fair-skinned people who sunbathe are at twenty times more risk than nonsunbathers of developing gallstones. This research is in its preliminary stages, but it could be significant for fair-skinned sun lovers.

●　　　●　　　●

GLAUCOMA

GLAUCOMA, A DISEASE of the eye that can lead to blindness, occurs when normal drainage of eye fluid is blocked, causing increased pressure within the eye and consequent damage to the optic nerve. There are two types of glaucoma. Acute glaucoma, which is relatively rare, causes severe, throbbing pain, blurred vision, and is often accompanied by nausea and vomiting. Acute glaucoma is a medical emergency that requires immediate medical attention.

Far more common—and insidious—is chronic glaucoma. Of the two million Americans who have glaucoma, 90 percent have this form of the disease. Symptoms include mild headaches and visual disturbances, such as seeing halos around electric lights. Frequent changes in eyeglass prescriptions may also be indicative of glaucoma. But most people with chronic glaucoma have no symptoms until they start losing their vision, which is why I urge my patients to have an annual eye examination, particularly if they are over forty-five or have a family history of glaucoma. The examination should be conducted by an optometrist or an ophthalmologist, as glaucoma pressure readings may be misleading and need to be interpreted by an experienced practitioner.

Glaucoma is usually inherited, though parents may be carriers without developing the disease. Other people at risk include those with diabetes and myopia (nearsightedness). People who strain their eyes with prolonged close work may also be at risk of increased eye pressure. Recent studies indicate that there is also a correlation between glaucoma and nutrition, which affects collagen metabolism. Collagen, which is the most abundant protein in the body, is also the key building block of eye tissue. When collagen metabolism is abnormal due to poor nutrition or general ill health, the eye becomes vulnerable to various abnormalities.

Treatment for glaucoma ranges from topical medication to eye surgery. The most common treatment is eyedrops, which reduce fluid formation in the eye and encourage increased outflow. Eyedrops, however, can produce systemic side effects such as low heart rate and blood pressure, asthmatic wheezing, bronchial cough, light-headedness, and fatigue. For this reason, they are generally not prescribed until the pressure within the eye becomes acute enough to damage the optic nerve. By the way, if you use such drops, be sure to let your doctor know. Many people, thinking that eyedrops will have only a localized effect, forget to do this. If they develop side effects from the drops, their primary care physician may be unaware of the cause of the problem.

The good news about glaucoma is that there are natural remedies that can help reduce elevated eye pressure, and in some cases bring it back to normal. Whether you have glaucoma or are at risk of developing the disease, you may benefit greatly from nutrients and supplements.

It's important to remember that glaucoma is not an inevitable effect of aging and heredity. In Nigeria, where glaucoma has reached epidemic proportions, researchers found that improved nutrition was a much better cure for glaucoma than drugs. In one study, a doctor treated a group of patients by giving them large doses of vitamins A, B, C, and E, as well as additional amounts of protein. For most of these patients, he reports, the eye pressure was reduced to within normal limits within a week.

Even in the United States, where malnutrition is not the severe problem that it is in Africa, vitamin and mineral deficiencies have been found to contribute to eye abnormalities, including glaucoma. Vitamin C plays a lead role in its prevention and treatment. People with low blood levels of vitamin C have been found to have significantly higher eye pressure than those who took 1,000 mg. of vitamin C daily. In one experimental controlled study, a group of people were given 500 mg. of vitamin C twice a day. After one week, their eye pressure readings were significantly lower, but returned to previous levels one week after vitamin C was discontinued.

In the treatment of chronic glaucoma, vitamin C dosage varies from patient to patient. Some patients have responded to as little as 1 g. (1,000 mg.) a day, while others require higher doses. Since individual tolerance varies, however, you should not exceed 3 g. (3,000 mg.) of vitamin C a day without talking to a physician.

Recent studies have demonstrated that rabbits who are given daily doses of cod liver oil have a lower incidence of glaucoma than rabbits who are not treated. Though studies are still needed to relate these findings to humans, I still think it's prudent for people with glaucoma to take a fish oil supplement like MaxEPA daily.

Rutin, which has been found useful in restoring normal collagen metabolism and normalizing eye tissue, is also helpful in prevention and treatment. Rutin is available in supplement form at a health food store.

Chromium, zinc, and the B complex of vitamins, particularly thiamine, also appear to play a role in the prevention and treatment of glaucoma. People with elevated eye pressure have been found deficient in these elements; a supplement is indicated for anyone at risk.

There are also some things you must avoid if you have glaucoma or a strong family history of the disease. Tobacco, of course, is one of them. Smoking and secondhand cigarette smoke can irritate glaucoma. Corticosteroids, which destroy the collagen structure in the eye, should also be avoided, both in the oral and topical form.

You should also stay away from any substances to which you are allergic. It has been determined that allergic reactions precipitate increased pressure within the eye. People who already have elevated pressure readings must avoid the risk of further elevation and consequent damage to the optic nerve. Identify food and drink to which you may be allergic and avoid it (see Food Allergy, page 146). It's more difficult to identify—and avoid—airborne allergens. Dust, dander, and various air pollutants are difficult to escape entirely, but try to keep these irritants to a minimum (see Hay Fever, page 167).

Finally, as I tell my parents, no health regime can be complete without adequate exercise, which is particularly important in glaucoma prevention and treatment. In a recent study, a group of sedentary patients with elevated eye pressure started a course of aerobic exercise training. After three months, their eye pressure decreased by an average of 20 percent. Three weeks after exercise was discontinued, however, the pressure readings returned to previous levels.

NATURAL PRESCRIPTION FOR GLAUCOMA

- Adopt a regular exercise program.

- Avoid the use of corticosteroids if possible.

- Avoid smoking and secondhand cigarette smoke.

- Keep food and inhalant allergies under control (see Food Allergy, page 146, and Hay Fever, page 167).

IN ADDITION TO YOUR DAILY SUPPLEMENTS, PAGE xxiv, TAKE

- Vitamin A: 10,000 I.U. per day.

- Vitamin C: 1,000 to 3,000 mg. daily, in divided doses.

- Vitamin E: 400 I.U. daily.

- Chromium: 100 mcg. of trivalent chromium two times daily.

- Zinc: 50 mg. a day.

- Fish oil: 1,000 mg. three times daily of MaxEPA.

- Rutin: 50 mg. three times daily.

• • •

GOUT

GOUT SNEAKS UP on its victims quietly. Many patients are first stricken in the middle of the night with an aching, throbbing, and exquisitely painful big toe. Usually the afflicted joint is swollen, red, and tender and, if the attack continues, the victim can develop fever and chills. Many people later realize that their first attack was stimulated or at least preceded by a bumped toe, surgery, too much alcohol, overeating or fasting, or medications such as penicillin, insulin, or certain "water pills" or diuretics. In fact, all or some of these factors can be implicated.

Most gout victims are male. In fact nearly 90 percent of people who suffer from gout are men over the age of thirty. But women are not immune, particularly if they are taking medications, such as those for hypertension, that can predispose them to the condition.

Gout is caused by an increased concentration of uric acid in the fluids of the body. When the uric acid forms crystals and the crystals deposit in joints (like the big toe), tendons, or other tissues, they cause pain, inflammation, and eventually damage. You can have elevated uric acid without having the "gouty arthritis" attacks, as they are more precisely described.

If you develop gout when you are young and/or if you suffer from severe attacks, you should be under the treatment of a physician who can, if necessary, administer drugs to control the levels of uric acid in your body. A physician can also help alleviate the severe symptoms of an acute attack. But you should know that the medications do have side effects, some of them serious. They tend to be toxic to the digestive tract and can cause problems for people with stomach or intestinal difficulties. If you are on medications for gout and/or if you've had your first attack and are wondering if you can stave off future attacks, it's worth trying the following preventive measures.

Obviously, if you're on medication, you should consult your doctor on when and how best to reduce the medication to see if the natural treatment is working. If you're on certain medications for high blood pressure, it is possible that the medication is precipitating your gout. In that case, you should ask your doctor if it's possible for you to change or reduce your medications (see Hypertension, page 194).

If you suffer from an acute attack of gout, you will probably want to take pain relievers. Be sure to use the right one. Aspirin can actually worsen your symptoms by inhibiting the excretion of uric acid. The best over-the-counter pain reliever for gout is ibuprofen, available by various names including Nuprin and Advil. Ibuprofen reduces inflammation and is more effective than other pain relievers including acetaminophen. If your symptoms persist, consult your doctor.

The first step to take to reduce gout attacks is reducing the amount of uric acid–rich foods—or foods with high purine levels—in your diet. These foods increase the levels of uric acid in your blood and therefore can precipitate attacks. If you're on medication, by the way, the medication is doing that job; if you want to try to eliminate the medication, you have to reduce the uric acid through diet. Foods rich in uric acid include anchovies, shellfish, smoked meat, meat extracts, mincemeat that contains real meat, kidneys, liver, brains, sweetbreads, sardines, mackerel, yeast (baker's and brewer's), asparagus, mushrooms, and dried peas. While you are eliminating these foods from your diet, you should eat more fruits and vegetables, as they will reduce the acidity of your urine and decrease the likelihood of uric acid buildup.

People who are obese are more likely to suffer gout attacks than those with normal weight. Of course, if you are overweight you already know that you should lose weight for other health reasons. Remember that it's crucial to lose weight gradually: no more than one or two pounds a week. A quick weight-loss diet can actually stimulate increased gout attacks.

You should also eliminate alcohol. Alcohol increases uric acid production and reduces its excretion—two of the worst things that can happen to a person with gout. For some people, eliminating alcohol can actually prevent recurrence of attacks.

Drinking adequate amounts of fluids is important. Not only will fluids dilute your urine and lessen the chance of uric acid crystals forming, but they will also help to prevent the formation of kidney stones. About 10 to 20 percent of gout victims develop kidney stones, so trying to prevent them before they form is important. You should aim for 2 quarts of fluids each day.

Stress can exacerbate gout. When I tell my patients this they tend to roll their eyes and I know they're thinking there's no way they can reduce stress because it's built into their jobs, their families, and their lifestyles. It's true you can't get a stress-free job, but you can make an effort to control the stress in your life through exercise and stress-reduction techniques. See Stress Control, page 314.

Vitamin A in large amounts can exacerbate gout. Make sure you take no more than 5,000 I.U. daily. If you are having attacks, you should stop all vitamin A intake.

Niacin can also raise uric acid levels and thus aggravate gout. You should therefore limit your niacin intake (which you might be taking to help control cholesterol) to no more than 100 mg. daily.

The final natural treatment is one I have never had experience with though I have read about it in the literature and have heard good reports about it. In the fifties, a doctor named Ludwig Blau accidentally discovered a remedy for his terrible gout that had confined him to a wheelchair. One day he ate a handful of cherries and noticed that the next day the agonizing pain in his toe was gone. If he continued to eat cherries, he was pain-free, but a relapse of even a day would bring back his pain. It is reported that you can use sweet or sour cherries and they can be fresh, frozen, or even canned to achieve Dr. Blau's results. Cherries (and blueberries and other dark red or blue berries) are rich sources of substances that have a powerful ability to prevent collagen destruction. It is certainly worth a try. About a half-pound of cherries daily for a week could give you some positive results.

NATURAL PRESCRIPTION FOR GOUT

- Check your medications to see if they're having any effect on your gout attack. Discuss them with your doctor.

- For pain relief rely on ibuprofen (Nuprin, Advil, etc.) but not aspirin (which can worsen symptoms) or acetaminophen (which is less effective). If you need a stronger antiinflammatory, consult your doctor.

- Adopt a low-purine diet, that is, one that eliminates foods that promote the production of uric acid, including anchovies, shellfish, smoked meat, meat extracts, mincemeat that contains real meat, kidneys, liver, brains, sweetbreads, sardines, mackerel, yeast (baker's and brewer's), asparagus, mushrooms, and dried peas.

- Maintain an optimum weight. If you are obese, you should lose weight, but be sure to do it gradually.

- Increase your fruit and vegetable consumption.

- Eliminate alcohol from your diet.

- Be sure to drink adequate fluids: 3 quarts liquid daily.

- Adopt stress-reducing techniques.

- Eat one-half pound of cherries each day, either canned, frozen, or fresh. If you don't notice reduction of symptoms in a week or two, discontinue.

- Eliminate or reduce niacin. Don't take more than 100 mg. daily.

- Don't take more than 5,000 I.U. of vitamin A daily, and if attacks continue, eliminate vitamin A intake entirely.

• • •

H. PYLORI

H. PYLORI IS NEITHER a disease nor an ailment but rather the cause of an ailment, and this entry is not typical of others in this book in that H. pylori cannot be treated by natural means. I am, however, including information on H. pylori because I think it will be useful to the many people who are searching for information and to those who suffer from gastric complaints, including ulcers, and haven't been able to find relief.

H. pylori is an abbreviation for a bacterium called *Helicobacter pylori*, which has been implicated in the development of both duodenal and peptic ulcers as well as other gastric complaints including esophagitis, hiatus hernia, and acid indigestion. Recently there have been headline articles in various newspapers linking the *H. pylori* bacterium to stomach cancer.

H. pylori is commonly found in the lining of the stomach and usually doesn't cause symptoms. In the United States about half of all people over the age of fifty have the bacterium in their stomach. In some people —and no one knows why—the bacterium is involved in the development of stomach disorders including ulcers, gastritis, and stomach cancer. It seems that 70 to 75 percent of patients with gastric ulcers and 90 to 100 percent of patients with duodenal ulcers harbor the *H. pylori* bacterium. Ulcers were long considered to be a kind of organic breakdown that results in an overproduction of acid. Recognizing a bacterium as the cause of ulcers was a dramatic breakthrough. And we know that unless *H. pylori* is eliminated, ulcers will continue to recur. The exciting news is that ulcers, previously believed to be incurable, can now be permanently cured if the *H. pylori* can be eliminated.

A blood test can confirm whether you have *H. pylori*. Unfortunately, eliminating *H. pylori* can sometimes be a frustrating procedure. I have not found any effective way with natural means. A doctor must treat you, as you must take two prescription drugs: usually an antibiotic such as amoxicillin, along with the drug metronidazole. Bismuth (e.g., Pepto-Bismol) has also been found helpful. The treatment usually continues for three weeks; sometimes it needs to be repeated.

Treatment for *H. pylori* can be helped by acidophilus supplements. *Lactobacillus acidophilus* is the substance used to culture yogurt; you can buy it in capsule form in health food stores. I usually recommend taking one capsule three times daily. Make sure the capsules you buy contain living cultures. They're usually kept refrigerated.

For more information on ulcers, see Ulcers, page 335.

• • •

HANGOVER

I HOPE YOU'RE NOT expecting me to give you a sure-fire natural hangover remedy that will allow you to drink all night and feel great the next morning—there's no such thing. If you drink too much, you're going to pay the penalty the next day. Though I no longer drink myself, I can empathize.

The truth is, the only way to avoid hangovers is to avoid drinking. Indeed, a hangover is not the only problem you're likely to have if you overindulge. Most people don't realize that even though they might feel okay after a night of drinking, their performance ability is impaired. Many studies have shown that no matter how you feel in the morning, if you've been drinking more than a drink or two the night before, your reaction times are slowed and your other facilities are not up to par. So if you are required to give a peak performance the next day, the best advice is to avoid drinking entirely.

If you are going to drink, there are ways to help prevent a hangover. First, there's some evidence that vitamin C can help clear alcohol out of your system faster than otherwise. This doesn't mean that vitamin C will cure or prevent a hangover; it does mean that some vitamin C before drinking will help you recover more quickly.

You should be sure to drink on a full stomach because food will help to slow the absorption of the alcohol. It's those few drinks at the cocktail hour before dinner that can really do damage by rushing into your bloodstream and destroying any resolve you have not to drink too much.

It also helps to drink slowly. Five drinks spread over four hours have a very different effect than the same amount of alcohol consumed in an hour. Pace yourself by paying attention to the amount you're drinking in relation to the passage of time.

If you did have too much to drink, have two aspirins, ibuprofen, or some Alka-Seltzer before bed. They can help to eliminate the symptoms of hangover the next morning. And if you forgot to take them before bed, they'll still help in the morning by relieving your headache.

Black coffee won't help you get back to normal, but fruit juice can. The fructose in fruit juice helps the body burn alcohol faster and replenishes the fluid your body loses from drinking. So a large, cold glass of orange or apple juice will help you get back on track. One of my patients told me whenever he felt "fragile" from too much to drink, he started the next day with two tall glasses of orange juice mixed half and half with seltzer: It makes the juice lighter and gives the body extra fluid.

Another patient told me that every time he has a hangover he feels a craving for a bowl of chicken soup made from a dried mix, no doubt because these soups have a high sodium content. Chicken soup is really therapeutic—a big steaming bowl will help replace lost salts and potassium as well as lost fluids.

Finally, there is a theory that the symptoms of hangover are caused by substances called congeners. It's said that because vodka is so low in congeners, it doesn't cause the wicked cognac or whiskey hangovers. Congeners are absorbed by activated charcoal, so if you take some activated charcoal tablets before bed, you can expect to absorb at least a portion of the congeners before they do their damage. I have never tried this, but some of my patients have told me that it works for them.

NATURAL PRESCRIPTION FOR HANGOVER

- Avoid drinking to excess.

- Take 1,000 mg. of vitamin C before drinking.

- Drink only on a full stomach.

- Drink slowly.

- Take two aspirins or some Alka-Seltzer before bed.

- Try taking two or three tablets of activated charcoal before going to bed.

- Drink two large glasses of fruit juice spritzer the next morning.

• • • •

HAY FEVER

HAY FEVER IS ACTUALLY the common name for an allergic reaction to an airborne substance. Usually the substance is pollen, but it can be a fungus, mold, mildew, dust mites, or even pet dander or, believe it or not, cockroaches. Hay fever has nothing to do with hay: It got its name because long ago British farmers noticed that their symptoms of headache, irritability, and runny nose and eyes occurred during the season of the spring hay harvest, and so they connected it with hay. In fact, the irritation came from grass that pollenates in the spring.

Hay fever, or allergic rhinitis (the official name for most inhalant allergies), can plague people all year round. In the early spring, tree pollens are the major offenders, then in mid-May there are the grass pollens, followed by ragweed pollen in mid-August. And don't forget the airborne fungus spores that are common from early spring to late fall— for some people there's no respite whatsoever. One study found that more than a third of people with other allergies are also hypersensitive to cockroaches and even 12 percent of people without any histories of allergies are allergic to some roaches. And some people are sensitive to cleaning products and will develop a reaction whenever exposed to them. To make things even more complicated, some people are allergic to more than one thing and can suffer both seasonal reactions to pollen and perennial reactions to other allergens.

People usually recognize hay fever immediately, as the symptoms are pretty obvious: watery eyes, runny nose, body aches, sneezing, coughing, wheezing, sore throat, ear pain and pressure, fatigue, and irritability. But I've had patients with vague seasonal symptoms of fatigue and sore throat who have gone for years not knowing the cause of their discomfort. If you have any of these symptoms but can't figure out the cure, try keeping a "health log." Jot down what the symptoms are and when they occur and any potential allergenic situations you might have been exposed to such as a seasonal change, pets, a damp garage, use of certain chemicals, or a camping trip, for example. This will help you isolate any possible allergens.

Traditionally, hay fever symptoms have been treated with antihistamines, drugs that fight the histamines, the symptom-provoking substances that supposedly cause allergic symptoms. There are many over-the-counter preparations, but most of them cause drowsiness—the prescription drugs Seldane and Hismanal are quite popular because they do not. Soon one or both of them will be available over-the-counter, but they are not without side effects. Just recently it was found that Seldane can cause rapid heartbeat, particularly when used in conjunction with certain antibiotics.

Usually people use decongestants in conjunction with antihistamines. The antihistamines subvert the irritating effect of the histamines, and the decongestants shrink the swollen nasal passages, allowing freer breathing. But regular use of decongestants can cause headaches, irritability, and dizziness. And you can suffer from the rebound effect where your body begins to rely on the decongestant so that when you stop taking it your nose becomes stuffier than ever.

What can you do about hay fever without relying on drugs and possible side effects? The only completely effective solution is, as with other allergies, avoid the allergen. Of course, for most people who can't move to another part of the country, that's impossible. Fortunately, there is a more moderate, natural route that will help relieve your symptoms and allow you to live with your allergies.

The first thing to investigate is the possibility of hidden food allergies, which can make inhalant allergies worse. Some patients have real problems with hay fever until they eliminate milk and cheese products from their diet. Dairy products are common sources of hidden food allergies. For a more complete discussion of these allergies see Food Allergy, page 146.

No matter what the cause of your hay fever, there are natural supplements you can take that can dramatically alleviate your symptoms. I suggest that my patients take four supplements, and in many cases they report great improvement.

Vitamin C is, among other things, a natural antihistamine, and some allergic people seem to have a greater need for it than others. To see the best results, it needs to be taken in relatively large doses during the allergy season.

Bioflavonoids, closely related to vitamin C, have been found to have anti-allergy effects. Bioflavonoids are most easily procured from the pulp, rind, and juice of oranges, lemons, and grapefruit. A simple way to consume them is to cut orange and/or lemon peels into strips and cook them with some honey until they're soft. Eat one or two teaspoons daily. You can also get bioflavonoids at a health food store or buy vitamin C tablets that contain bioflavonoids.

Pantothenic acid, one of the B vitamins, is especially important in eliminating the symptoms of hay fever. Some people find that a dose of pantothenic acid will clear their stuffy nose within a half hour. It doesn't work for everyone, but for those who report success it seems like a miracle. I suggest you take pantothenic acid daily, along with vitamin B complex.

Evening primrose oil is another natural substance that has just recently gotten attention for its powerful antinflammatory action that has proven helpful in fighting bronchial congestion. I suggest that patients take evening primrose oil three times daily.

There are two other natural steps you can take. There is mounting evidence that salicylates, substances found in certain foods as well as in aspirin and ibuprofen products (like Advil or Motrin), can inhibit an enzyme that helps fight many ailments including the symptoms of hay fever. Some people are particularly sensitive to salicylates. It is in a number of over-the-counter medications, and it also occurs naturally in almonds, apples, apricots, blackberries, boysenberries, cherries, cucumbers and pickles, currants, dewberries, gooseberries, grapes or raisins, nectarines, oranges, peaches, plums or prunes, raspberries, strawberries, and tomatoes. I tell my hay fever patients to avoid salicylates in foods and medications, and to try to stick to a low-fat diet.

NATURAL PRESCRIPTION FOR HAY FEVER

- Avoid aspirin and ibuprofen as well as foods containing salicylates including almonds, apples, apricots, blackberries, boysenberries, cherries, cucumbers and pickles, currants, dewberries, gooseberries, grapes or raisins, nectarines, oranges, peaches, plums or prunes, raspberries, strawberries, and tomatoes.

- Stick to a low-fat diet.

IN ADDITION TO YOUR DAILY SUPPLEMENTS, PAGE xxiv, TAKE

- Vitamin C: during hay fever season 2 g. (2,000 mg.) of the ester-C form daily.

- Citrus bioflavonoids: 1,000 mg. daily or cut strips of orange and lemon peel and cook in honey until soft. Eat a teaspoon or two a day.

- Pantothenic acid: 200 to 300 mg. daily.

- Evening primrose oil: 500 mg. three times a day.

IN ADDITION TO THE NATURAL REMEDIES I'VE OUTLINED, HERE ARE SOME PRACTICAL STRATEGIES. IN GENERAL, WHENEVER POSSIBLE:

- Avoid cigarette smoke, which can make your symptoms much worse.

- Avoid car exhaust.

- Arrange your vacation to coincide with your area's worst allergy season. A cruise—no plants, no pollen!—is ideal.

- Remember that alcohol swells your bronchial tissues, so it's helpful to avoid drinking during allergy season.

- Use a dehumidifier in your basement if it is damp.

- Try to get rid of any old, damp articles that may clutter your basement, garage, attic, yard, or deck, particularly old upholstered furniture, cushions, carpets or rugs, stuffed animals, and stacks of magazines and newspapers.

- Keep rooms dry and clean: Use space heaters to dry damp rooms. Keep closet doors open during the day to dry them and closed at night with a low-wattage light burning inside them if possible. Don't keep wet shoes or boots in your bedroom.

- Limit the number of houseplants and terrariums in your home and office.

- Vent your clothes dryer to the outside.

- Install a bathroom fan that's vented to the outside and use it whenever you bathe or shower.

- Don't let damp clothes sit in the washer; dry them immediately.

IF YOU'RE ALLERGIC TO DUST

I've noticed that people whose symptoms are worse in the morning are usually allergic to dust and house dust mites. In addition to the things I've outlined, there are steps you can take if this is your problem.

- A mattress cover can be of enormous help in avoiding dust mites. Use an allergen-proof plastic cover along with a pillow made of hypoallergenic material like dacron or polyester (you'll see it noted on the pillow label). Be sure to vacuum the mattress before putting the cover on. You can get a mattress cover from a department store or from a surgical supply house. Here are two that will ship: Allergy Control Products (800) 422-DUST [or in Connecticut (203) 438-9580]; The Janice Corporation (800) 526-4237 [in New Jersey (201) 691-2979].

- Don't store anything under your bed, as this can encourage the accumulation of dust mites.

- Try to avoid rugs and carpets, possible breeding grounds for mites.

- Don't vacuum yourself, and try to be out of the house when someone else vacuums. On the other hand, be sure your living areas are wet-mopped and vacuumed frequently. There are vacuums that come equipped with allergen-absorbing filters.

- Consider installing a high-frequency particulate-arresting filter (HEPA filter) on your furnace. They're expensive but extremely effective. Consult with a heating expert for more information.

- There are chemical agents for testing and for eliminating dust mites. You can discuss this with your doctor.

IF YOU'RE ALLERGIC TO POLLEN

- Try to stay indoors between 5:00 A.M. and 10:00 A.M. when the pollen levels are the highest.

- Dry your clothes and bedding inside rather than outside, where they'll collect pollen.

- When outside, wear glasses or sunglasses to keep your eyes free of pollen.

- Try to keep windows in your car and home closed during pollen season.

- Keep air-conditioner filters and dehumidifiers scrupulously clean. Many people have reported a reduction in their symptoms when they clean these filters regularly. Don't forget the filter on your humidifier if you use a room humidifier in the winter.

- Mow your grass low to prevent it from blooming and producing pollen. Be sure to wear a mask when mowing or gardening.

- During pollen season, it's helpful to wash your hands and rinse your eyes with fresh water every time you come in from outdoors.

IN ADDITION: If the natural remedies suggested here don't work, you may have to consult with an allergist for medications and possibly allergy desensitization.

• • •

HEARTBURN

IT CAN FEEL LIKE a weight on your chest or a bra that's much too tight, but usually it's a burning pain that begins in the pit of the stomach and spreads in waves upward to the back of the throat. Some people get it occasionally after an unusually heavy meal; others get it regularly, almost daily. It's heartburn, and it's no surprise that it makes you feel like something in your chest is burning: heartburn can occur when stomach acid containing hydrochloric acid (the stuff they use to clean metal!) moves up from the stomach into the esophagus, the tube between your stomach and your mouth. The stomach has a lining that protects it from the effect of the powerful acid digestive juices, but the esophagus has no such lining. When the acid hits, it burns.

This type of heartburn can be an occasional event caused by over-eating, spicy foods, too much alcohol, or medication. This is simple acid reflux. This occasional type of heartburn is usually remedied by an antacid. But repeated episodes of acidic reflux may lead to certain complications including esophagitis (the inflammation of the esophagus), esophageal ulcers, and a narrowing of the esophagus. These conditions would have to be identified and treated by a doctor.

There are other conditions that can cause heartburn, and they must be remedied to relieve the symptom. For information on dealing with your heartburn when it is not simple acid reflux, see these sections of this book: Ulcers, page 335; H. Pylori, page 164; Hiatal Hernia and Esophagitis, page 186.

• • •

HEAVY PERIODS

FOR SOME WOMEN, heavy periods are an irritating inconvenience. For others they become a source of serious concern when a doctor suggests that hormone therapy or surgery—typically a hysterectomy—is the only remedy. A number of patients have come to me when faced with the dilemma of whether to have a hysterectomy. Fortunately, there is some help for women who suffer heavy periods, or menorrhagia, in the form of nutritional therapy which is both safe and effective.

If you have extremely heavy periods, meaning periods that last for more than five days during which you bleed excessively, your first step should be a visit to your gynecologist to rule out conditions that should be treated with traditional medicine. These include cysts, tumors such as fibroids, or a troublesome intrauterine device (IUD). If you've been checked and no particular problem has been discovered, you should try the following regime of natural treatments.

The most common and well-known nutritional aid to regulate heavy periods is vitamin A. In fact, vitamin A is so closely tied to normal hormone production, and thus period regulation, that laboratory-induced deficiencies of vitamin A in animals can completely suspend the menstrual cycle. It's long been known that women who bleed heavily have lower levels of vitamin A in their blood than women with normal periods. Women on the pill have higher levels of vitamin A than normal, and some of my patients have found that when they discontinue the pill they begin to have heavy periods. (One of my patients was terrified that her heavy periods were a sign of cancer. In fact, heavy periods in premenopausal women are rarely connected with cancer.) Supplementation can be the answer. I tell my patients discontinuing the pill to take vitamin A daily with meals.

Bioflavonoids can also make a remarkable difference. Found in the inner peel and white pulpy portion of citrus fruits, bioflavonoids are important in maintaining the strength of the blood vessels.

You might be aware that heavy periods can cause iron deficiency anemia; in turn, iron deficiencies can actually cause heavy periods. Iron supplementation can help relieve symptoms of iron deficiency anemia such as tiredness as well as the cause of the anemia itself. Make sure that your doctor tests your blood to determine if you are anemic. If you are, take a daily dose of elemental iron with meals. Be aware that iron supplementation can cause dark bowel movements and/or constipation.

You should also take a zinc supplement because low levels of zinc have also been shown to contribute to heavy periods.

Some of my patients tell me that when they take either aspirin or vitamin E, they bruise easily. As both aspirin and vitamin E are known to have an effect on blood clotting, I suggest you stop taking both for a month or two to see if your heavy periods improve.

NATURAL PRESCRIPTION FOR HEAVY PERIODS

- Check with your doctor to see that there is no serious cause for your heavy periods such as a tumor, including a fibroid tumor, cysts, or an IUD.

- Discontinue both vitamin E and aspirin for a month or two to see if your periods become less heavy.

IN ADDITION TO YOUR DAILY SUPPLEMENTS, PAGE xxiv, TAKE

- Vitamin A: 25,000 I.U. daily for three months, then 10,000 I.U. for six months. If there is no improvement, discontinue.

- Bioflavonoids and vitamin C: 1,000 mg. of bioflavonoids plus an equal amount of vitamin C twice a day.

- Iron: If a blood test has revealed that you are anemic, take 60 mg. daily with meals. (Iron can cause constipation and/or dark bowel movements.)

- Zinc: 50 mg. a day with meals.

• • • •

HEMORRHOIDS

FOUR OUT OF FIVE Americans will develop hemorrhoids at some point, so if you're a victim you're certainly not alone. Hemorrhoids, similar to varicose veins, are simply veins located in the anus that have become stretched and weakened. Many people find the problem is exacerbated by long hours of sitting, heavy lifting, or pregnancy and childbirth.

Most of my patients who complain of hemorrhoids first report them when they notice bright blood in their stool. While alarming, this symptom is usually just an indication that the pressure of defecation has abraded the hemorrhoid and caused it to bleed. On the other hand, rectal bleeding can be a symptom of a serious disease—colon cancer or colitis. If you have doubts as to the source of the bleeding, it's best to have a doctor check it out.

Many people rightly connect hemorrhoids with constipation: Straining on the toilet causes pressure that can create hemorrhoids. Unfortunately, some people think that the remedy is laxatives. This approach can exacerbate the problem by ignoring its real cause. Most cases of hemorrhoids can be eliminated by natural remedies and simple lifestyle changes that also promote better overall health. I've had great success with patients who have been plagued by hemorrhoids. The simple steps I recommend will also help you avoid diverticular disease, constipation, and other health problems.

It's interesting to note that hemorrhoids are virtually unknown in undeveloped countries. Because the diet of those people is bulky and fibrous. Our Western diet is usually so limited in fiber that the resulting stools are small, hard, and dry. Year after year of straining to eliminate, coupled with too much sitting and too little exercise, results in rectal tissue that is severely strained and ultimately weakened so that hemorrhoids are inevitable.

If you're suffering from hemorrhoids right now, you want immediate relief. What about all those over-the-counter remedies? Just last year the FDA clamped down on the manufacturers of these products, and some of them are being removed from the market because they've never been proven to be effective. Others must limit their claims. Those that claim to shrink tissues must carry a warning because people with diabetes or heart disease, for example, shouldn't use them. In the final analysis, while you may get some temporary relief from these products, you could do as well by applying zinc oxide, petroleum jelly, or witch hazel, which are just as effective and far cheaper.

In addition to applying a topical ointment, a sitz bath (soaking in a warm bath in three or four inches of water with your knees raised) can give relief by drawing blood to the area and helping to shrink the swollen veins. If you do a lot of sitting on the job, an inflatable "doughnut," which you can buy at a pharmacy, will give you relief from pressure.

Many people aren't aware that wiping themselves with harsh tissue paper can aggravate their problem. Use premoistened towelettes—make sure they're the kind with no added ingredients that can irritate—to soothe and help avoid further irritation.

The most important step you can take to avoid and *cure* hemorrhoids, as opposed to just relieving symptoms, is to improve your diet. A high-fiber diet will create a stool that is soft and bulky and therefore much easier to eliminate. A high-fiber diet simply means an emphasis on fruits, whole grains, and vegetables. Don't immediately switch your diet to one

consisting largely of roughage; this could cause diarrhea and wo[...]
problem. Make a gradual change: Over a week or two, increase[...]
amount of fruits and vegetables you eat and start eliminating some [...]
the refined, processed foods. I advise my patients not to rely on bran
supplements—they can become irritating. And it's important to increase
your liquid consumption. Eight glasses of water a day should be your
goal. Start the day with eight pennies in your right pocket; each time
you drink a glass of water, put a penny into your left pocket. Alcohol, coffee, and nuts can aggravate hemorrhoids for some people. If
you notice worsening symptoms after consuming them, avoid them
completely.

My patients often ask me about stool softeners or bulking agents like
psyllium. These substances act as natural laxatives by attracting water
and creating a larger, softer stool. I think that they're fine to take when
you first notice symptoms and if dietary changes do not produce soft,
nonconstipated stool.

There is one nutritional supplement that has been of great help to my
patients. Rutin, part of the C complex, is a bioflavonoid that is thought
to help strengthen the capillary system.

NATURAL PRESCRIPTION FOR HEMORRHOIDS

- For immediate relief, apply a topical over-the-counter ointment or use zinc oxide, petroleum jelly, or witch hazel.

- Take two or three sitz baths daily: Sit in a warm bath with your knees raised for five to fifteen minutes.

- If you must sit for long periods of time, or if you simply need immediate relief from painful hemorrhoids, buy a "doughnut" to relieve the pressure of sitting.

- Shift the emphasis of your diet to high-fiber, complex-carbohydrate foods. Gradually increase the amounts of fruits, vegetables, whole grain breads, beans, and other high-fiber foods. Gradually eliminate highly refined foods.

ener or psyllium powder—1 teaspoon in water once
when you first notice symptoms or if hard stool is not

wel habits: Don't strain; move your bowels only
e urge. Limit the time you spend on the toilet—don't
use the bathroom as a library!

- Don't use harsh toilet paper. Use premoistened towelettes and wipe gently.

- Avoid lifting heavy objects, as this puts a stress on your circulatory system.

- If you are pregnant, it can help to lie down on your left side and rest for about a half hour two or three times a day. It also helps to lie on your left side at night, if you're comfortable in that position, to relieve the pressure of the fetus on the veins serving the lower half of the body.

IN ADDITION TO YOUR DAILY SUPPLEMENTS, PAGE xxiv, TAKE

- Rutin: 100 mg. three times daily.

IN ADDITION: If, after a while, you find that an improved diet, use of a stool softener, better bowel habits, and topical applications don't solve your problem, it is possible that you will need surgery. Surgical techniques for hemorrhoids are relatively simple today; consult your doctor.

•   •   •

HEPATITIS

HEPATITIS IS AN INFLAMMATION of the liver, which can be caused by a virus, alcohol, and some drugs. Some cases of hepatitis have no known cause. Viral hepatitis, also known as infectious hepatitis, will cause the following symptoms in its acute stage: You will feel very tired and listless. Your skin and the whites of your eyes will develop a yellowish tinge. You may feel nauseated and have no appetite, and if you are a smoker you will be put off cigarettes.

There are several types of viral hepatitis:

Hepatitis A is caused by a food-borne virus, found in contaminated shellfish, or food and water exposed to unsanitary conditions. Many people with hepatitis A have no symptoms, while others may experience flulike symptoms including fever, headache, aching muscles, loss of appetite, nausea, and vomiting; they may develop jaundice.

After a person is exposed to the virus, during the asymptomatic incubation stage, hepatitis A is infectious for two weeks. The acute phase lasts for three to four weeks, and most patients recover without any lingering effects and without specific medical treatment. If you believe you've been infected with hepatitis A, your doctor may give you a shot of gamma globulin to enhance your immunity and decrease the severity of the infection. A vaccine is now available for hepatitis A, and you should consider it if you're planning to travel through possible problem areas.

Hepatitis B is caused by a blood-borne virus, and transmitted sexually or through contaminated needles. Some 10 percent of patients with hepatitis B develop chronic hepatitis, which can cause severe damage to the liver. Pregnant women infected with hepatitis B risk passing on the infection to the fetus, with potentially fatal consequences. There is an effective vaccine for this virus, which is routinely given to health-care workers. For those who are not vaccinated, hepatitis B immune globulin can give temporary immunity if taken immediately after exposure. There is no cure for chronic hepatitis B. While interferon is used to fight hepatitis, no long-term studies on its effectiveness have been done. Some temporary improvement has been seen with the drug, but many patients' liver function returns to the pretreatment state when the drug is stopped. The general recommendation for people who might be exposed to hepatitis B is to have the vaccine, which is given in three shots over eight months. The following people are candidates for this vaccine:

- intravenous drug users
- health-care workers
- anyone living with someone infected with hepatitis B
- homosexual men who are sexually active
- heterosexuals who have multiple partners
- recipients of certain blood products
- children of immigrants from areas where hepatitis B is common, such as Southeast Asia
- infants born to infected women

- travelers who are going to spend six months or more in a region with a high incidence of the disease

Hepatitis C (which used to be called non-A, non-B hepatitis) is similar to type B, but is transmitted through blood transfusions or infected needles. Fortunately, since this virus has been identified, it has been screened out of blood used for transfusions. Recent studies on hepatitis C point to it as being the most common cause for chronic hepatitis; some people harbor the hepatitis C virus for twenty years. Some infected people have few symptoms while others experience all the symptoms typical of chronic hepatitis. Interferon is used to treat hepatitis C, but, as with hepatitis B, only a percentage of patients respond positively, and many relapse.

Most people who have infectious hepatitis are diagnosed by their doctors: They have obvious symptoms and are given a liver function test, which identifies their disease. But there are people who suffer from a type of hepatitis that is not infectious but from poor health habits. This virtually self-inflicted hepatitis is the type I see most frequently. People with this type may not have any symptoms; their hepatitis is discovered by a routine blood test and then a liver function test. I most commonly see this type of hepatitis in patients who drink alcohol regularly (some of them as little as two drinks a day), and who are generally run-down and have a poor diet. Occasionally, this hepatitis may develop from taking medication—large doses of aspirin and ibuprofen may prove toxic. Tylenol when combined with alcohol has been known to have extremely toxic effects on the liver. Long-acting niacin can also cause liver damage, mostly in large doses exceeding 2,000 mg. a day, though some people have been affected by as little as 500 mg. a day.

Whether you are being treated by your doctor for infectious hepatitis, or you have developed noninfectious hepatitis, you can help restore your liver to normal through natural means. Indeed, there is no drug treatment to cure hepatitis; antibiotics and other drugs are ineffective against the virus. The goal of treatment is to ease the symptoms and promote self-healing. The first step, of course, is to give up anything that may further damage the liver. This means all alcohol, including wine and beer, until liver functions have been restored to normal. Medications such as aspirin, ibuprofen, and Tylenol should kept to a minimum. Keep in mind that everything you eat and drink is processed through the liver, and that a high-fiber diet will help to eliminate bile acids and toxic substances from the system. Avoid fried food and animal fats, and keep saturated fats and simple carbohydrates to a minimum, as they place extra stress on the liver.

Exercise is a natural way to promote a healthy liver. An interesting study involving ten dogs showed the effects of exercise in minimizing fatty buildup in the liver. All the dogs were fed a diet rich in lard and cholesterol, and all ten were kept confined in small cages. But five of the dogs were exercised on a treadmill for one hour each day. By the end of the study, three of the unexercised dogs had died of liver disease, and two had fatty, cirrhotic livers. The exercised dogs, on the other hand, had essentially healthy livers, in spite of the high-fat diet.

Vitamin C is very helpful in improving hepatitis. It's interesting to note that only 2 g. proved effective in preventing hepatitis B in hospitalized patients, who are vulnerable to the disease. While 7 percent of the control patients developed hepatitis B, none of the treated patients did.

Vitamin B_{12} and folic acid have been found somewhat helpful in shortening the recovery time of hepatitis. The B_{12} should be taken in tablet form dissolved under the tongue (which is how it's best absorbed).

NATURAL PRESCRIPTION FOR HEPATITIS

- Eliminate all alcoholic beverages.

- Avoid animal fats and saturated fats and fried foods.

- Keep simple carbohydrates to a minimum.

- Eat a diet rich in complex carbohydrates.

- Establish a daily exercise routine.

IN ADDITION TO YOUR DAILY SUPPLEMENTS, PAGE xxiv, TAKE

- Vitamin C: 2 to 3 g. (2,000 to 3,000 mg.) daily.

- Vitamin B complex: 50 mg. daily.

- Vitamin B_{12}: 1,000 mcg. daily in tablet form dissolved under the tongue.

- Folic acid: 800 mcg. daily.

IN ADDITION: There's an herb called silymarin, which is actually the common milk thistle, that is reported to be enormously helpful in fighting the effects of cirrhosis of the liver and particularly alcoholic cirrhosis. It is commonly used in Europe and is finally being studied in the United States. Catechine is another botanical that can be helpful. Both are available in health food stores. Discuss these treatments with your doctor.

People suffering from chronic infectious hepatitis may also be helped by thymic hormonal replacement, which has great potential for treating immune system diseases, from allergies to lupus, cancer, and AIDS. The thymus, a gland within the chest which is thought to control the immune system, is large in children but becomes atrophied around age twenty. A doctor at Wayne State University in Detroit, Michigan, found in controlled studies that 75 percent of his patients who were treated with thymosin injections were cleared of hepatitis B. A study is in progress to discover more about the effectiveness of thymus replacement.

•   •   •

HERPES

YEARS AGO, BEFORE AIDS, genital herpes was in the forefront of the news as a sexual scourge. While it is no longer in the headlines, it is still very much a part of many peoples' lives: It's the most common venereal disease in the United States. Roughly twenty million Americans are infected, with about 500,000 new cases each year. Unfortunately, there is as yet no cure for herpes, but there are natural steps you can take to minimize the number and severity of outbreaks, and there is a drug that your doctor can give you that will also help to limit your outbreaks.

Herpes is among the many diseases caused by herpesvirus, a family of viruses with five different strains that cause ailments including chickenpox and shingles. The most common strain, herpes simplex, has two variations: type 1, which is usually associated with cold sores around the mouth, and type 2, which generally infects the genitalia, buttocks, and thighs with painful sores and blisters. But the two types of herpes can overlap: The genital infection can be acquired through oral sex with a partner who has an active cold sore. Typically, after the initial infection, the herpesvirus becomes dormant in the nerves and recurs following a minor infection such as a cold, a trauma, an emotional or environmental stress, or sun exposure.

Genital herpes is spread through sexual contact with someone who has an active outbreak of herpes; there is about a 75 percent chance of infection as the result of contact. Infected men who are suffering an outbreak will have blisters and sores on their penis and scrotum while women will typically exhibit sores on their vulva. Unfortunately, because a woman can have a painless outbreak or can have sores hidden inside the female genitalia, she could unwittingly pass the virus on to a sexual partner. In addition, there have been cases of herpes being passed on by a man who has no visible signs of an outbreak. The obvious prevention is extreme care in sexual contact. And of course if you do have herpes, you have an obligation to inform and protect any sexual partner.

One of the potentially serious complications of herpes is that it can endanger a child born of a mother who is suffering from an active infection. If you have herpes or have been exposed to the virus and you are pregnant or planning to become pregnant, you should discuss your infection with your obstetrician.

If you have been exposed to herpes and you become infected, you will typically feel symptoms about four or five days after your initial contact. If you do develop burning, itching, and/or pain at the site of contact, I recommend that you call your doctor immediately because there is an antiviral drug, acyclovir (Zovirax), that will shorten the symptoms of the first attack, which generally is the worst. The most severe symptoms can include fever, headache, muscle aches, fatigue, and flulike symptoms.

No one can predict when a second herpes attack will occur, but there's a great deal of evidence that you can help prevent attacks by natural means and, while I think it's sensible to take acyclovir to treat the initial, severe attack, it's important to take steps to boost your immune system, modify your diet, and take appropriate supplements to prevent future outbreaks.

For immediate relief of an outbreak, do not use any ointment or cream on your sores unless under a doctor's guidance. Many of the ointments that you have in your medicine cabinet will only worsen your symptoms. It's important to keep herpes lesions clean and dry. This means washing them with soap and water, avoiding binding clothes, wearing cotton underwear, and avoiding any creams or ointments that will smother the blisters and prevent drying. Some people find warm baths are soothing. Ice wrapped in a clean cloth and applied to the lesions for about ten minutes on and five minutes off can relieve pain. Some people find that drying their genitals with a hair dryer on low heat can be soothing.

Remember when you, or anyone, has active lesions, you should not touch the affected area and then touch your mouth, face, or eyes, as this can spread the infection.

Stress is a major stimulant of recurrent herpes outbreaks. You cannot eliminate the stress in your life, but I believe that it's critical for you to control that stress. For more information, see Stress Control, page 314. I tell all of my herpes patients that they must adopt the relaxation response exercise described in the chapter on stress at least twice a day. Many have reported fewer outbreaks when following this regime.

Certain nutrients can help prevent herpes outbreaks. Beta-carotene strengthens the immune system and can help inhibit viruses. Both vitamin C and zinc are helpful in inhibiting herpes attacks. And vitamin E has been shown to be helpful in relieving the pain of the herpes outbreak and also in shortening the duration of the attack.

In my experience, the most effective aid in the relief of herpes is the amino acid L-lysine. There is a hypothesis that lysine inhibits herpes activity (while another amino acid, arginine, promotes it). Studies have demonstrated lysine's usefulness. A maintenance dosage can be taken as a preventive and then increased if you experience an outbreak. If you take lysine supplements, be sure that you watch your cholesterol levels, as there's some evidence that lysine may stimulate the liver to increase production of cholesterol.

In addition to taking lysine as a supplement, it can be applied topically in the form of lysine cream, available in health food stores. I usually advise applying it topically twice a day, but check the directions on the label of the package.

Following the hypothesis that herpes outbreaks are stimulated by the imbalance of the amino acids arginine and lysine, it can also be beneficial to avoid arginine-containing foods while taking the lysine supplements. The foods to avoid include chocolate, peanuts and other nuts, seeds, and cereal grains.

Lactobacillus acidophilus, the living culture used to make yogurt, can be helpful in fighting herpes. It can help relieve the symptoms of an outbreak as well as prevent future outbreaks. You can find *Lactobacillus acidophilus* in capsule form in health food stores. Be sure to buy capsules that contain living cultures. They are usually kept refrigerated.

NATURAL PRESCRIPTION FOR HERPES

- At the first signs of an initial outbreak—pain, burning, and itching at the site of contact four to five days after encounter with an infected partner—call your doctor to confirm diagnosis and get a prescription for acyclovir (Zovirax), which will lessen the severity of the initial outbreak.

- Keep affected area clean and dry.

- Do not use over-the-counter ointments or creams on the lesions, unless prescribed by a doctor.

- To keep the area dry, wear cotton underwear and nonbinding clothes.

- Warm baths—two or three daily during an outbreak—can give relief.

- Relief from pain can be achieved with the use of an ice pack or ice covered with a clean cloth. Apply for ten minutes to lesions and then remove for five minutes. Repeat three or four times.

- Remember not to touch the lesions and then touch your face, mouth, eyes, and so on, as this can spread the infection.

- Adopt a method of stress control. See Stress Control, page 314.

- Avoid arginine-rich foods, including chocolate, peanuts, nuts, seeds, cereal grains such as oatmeal, gelatin, carob, and raisins.

IN ADDITION TO YOUR DAILY SUPPLEMENTS, PAGE xxiv, TAKE

- L-lysine: 3,000 mg. daily; 1,000 mg. with each meal at the first sign of a cold sore outbreak. After the symptoms lessen, reduce your intake to 500 mg. a day. If you break out on this maintenance dosage, increase your maintenance dose to 1,000 mg. a day to prevent recurrence.

- Lysine cream: apply topically to lesions twice a day or as recommended on label.

- *Lactobacillus acidophilus:* three capsules a day; one with each meal.

- **Zinc: 22.5 mg. a day.**

- **Vitamin C with bioflavonoids: 1,000 to 2,000 mg. a day.**

- **Vitamin E: 400 I.U.**

- **L-lysine: 500 mg. daily.**

• • •

HIATAL HERNIA AND ESOPHAGITIS

HIATAL HERNIA REFERS TO the bulging of a portion of the stomach above the diaphragm. This condition can be caused by a stretching of the diaphragm muscle, which normally fits snugly enough around the esophagus to keep the stomach from pushing up into the chest cavity. Oftentimes a hiatal hernia will cause heartburn. When the hiatal hernia causes an irritation of the esophagus—esophagitis—it may need to be corrected by surgery; but if commonsense natural means are employed, this can often be avoided.

How can you differentiate hiatal hernia from an ulcer? If your symptoms are worse when your stomach is empty, it is more likely to be an ulcer. If your symptoms are worse when you eat and drink too much, when you eat and lie down, or when you eat and bend over, then it's more likely to be hiatal hernia.

Heartburn and hiatal hernia symptoms can sometimes mimic heart problems. Obviously, you don't want to mistake a heart attack for heartburn. If you have these other symptoms with heartburn you should immediately get in touch with a doctor or go to a hospital:

- shortness of breath
- light-headedness or dizziness

- pain radiating into your neck and shoulder
- pain when swallowing

If you notice any of these symptoms, get immediate help. Don't worry about feeling foolish if the emergency room staff tells you it's only heartburn; it's better than the coroner telling your survivors that it wasn't heartburn!

What do you do when you feel that burning in your chest and you know it's heartburn from hiatal hernia or esophagitis? Most people reach for an antacid, which can help relieve the symptoms. Occasional use of antacids is probably not harmful (though I don't advocate it, as I prefer to get at the cause of the symptoms). The problem is that many people take antacids constantly and some of these products have ingredients that could potentially be harmful. Many of the most popular antacids contain both magnesium and aluminum. While occasional consumption of these minerals probably won't do any harm, regular consumption could. Magnesium can cause diarrhea. Occasionally a patient who complains of heartburn and diarrhea will realize, after a consultation, that he is simply taking too much antacid or the wrong kind of antacid.

It's the aluminum in antacids that I think poses the more serious problem because of the possible link between aluminum and Alzheimer's disease. Autopsies on patients who suffered from Alzheimer's disease have shown much higher than normal concentrations of aluminum in their brains. There's still controversy about the cause/effect relationship between aluminum and Alzheimer's, but I think it's wise to err on the prudent side and avoid regular consumption of anything containing aluminum.

Plenty of antacids on the market are aluminum-free, and many have the extra benefit of adding calcium to the diet. Tums, Tums Extra Strength, Advanced Formula Di-Gel, Chooz, and Titralac tablets and liquid are among the products that I suggest to my patients. And don't take antacids right after eating. That's when you need the stomach acid to do its digestive work. Wait about thirty minutes.

A drawback to antacids is they only treat the symptoms, not the underlying problem. There are a number of things you can do to remedy the cause. The first is to eat smaller, more frequent meals. It stands to reason that a smaller meal will produce less stomach acid and is less likely to fill your stomach to the point where acid will back up.

Cutting down on fatty foods will help reduce the amount of stomach acid. Fatty foods remain in the stomach longer than others, thus delaying the emptying of the stomach and allowing for production of more stomach acid.

In addition to fatty foods, certain other foods will increase acid production in your stomach. These foods, including coffee and tea (both decaffeinated and regular), citrus fruits, and tomatoes, should be avoided. Onions are particularly troublesome.

People with heartburn often drink milk to try to soothe the burning feeling. But this may be counterproductive; while the milk may feel good going down, it is a fatty food that will cause the stomach to produce a good quantity of acid. Then you're right back where you began.

Don't bend, stoop, or lie down right after eating. Many people love to eat a big meal and then collapse on the sofa or in a lounge chair. Some people go to bed right after eating. The problem with this is that your stomach is fighting gravity. You're much more likely to have acid flushing back into your esophagus when you're lying down. I had one patient who would wake every night with terrible heartburn. When he told me that he ate dinner at around 10 P.M., I knew the source of his trouble. As soon as he started eating earlier, his heartburn disappeared.

If you tend to get heartburn during the night, elevate the head of your bed by lifting the bed frame two to three inches. By keeping your head higher than your feet, you'll be helping to prevent the acid from flushing back out of the stomach.

Your sleep position can also promote heartburn. Lying on your right side encourages stomach acid to wash into the esophagus, triggering a burning sensation. Switching to your left side will eliminate the problem.

Stop smoking. We know that smoking releases the tension in the muscle separating the esophagus from the stomach. Because of this, regular smokers are much more likely to develop heartburn than non-smokers.

Drinking alcohol is also likely to promote heartburn. Cut down or eliminate your alcohol consumption.

Sometimes taking one or two acidophilus capsules, available at health food stores, can relieve your symptoms.

Stress can also aggravate heartburn; learning to control it can help relieve symptoms.

Finally, tetracycline and other antibiotics, slow-release potassium, aspirin, and nonsteroidal antiinflammatory drugs (NSAIDs) can irritate the lining of the stomach. If they're taken at night, they can irritate the esophagus when you lie down. In some patients, they can actually cause gastric ulcer or bleeding.

NATURAL PRESCRIPTION FOR HIATAL HERNIA AND ESOPHAGITIS

- Eat smaller, more frequent meals, and be sure not to eat right before bedtime.
- Cut down on fatty foods.
- Avoid coffee and tea (regular *and* decaffeinated), chocolate, liqueurs, citrus fruits and juices, onions, tomatoes.
- Avoid bending down or lying down right after eating.
- Elevate the head of your bed two to three inches and sleep on your left side if you tend to get heartburn at night.
- Stop smoking.
- Eliminate alcohol.
- Use methods of stress control. See Stress Control, page 314.
- Take one or two acidophilus capsules to relieve symptoms.
- Avoid tetracycline and other antibiotics, slow-release potassium, aspirin, and nonsteroidal antiinflammatory drugs just before bed.
- Antacids can help on an occasional basis, but avoid ones that contain aluminum or magnesium. Try Tums, Di-Gel, Chooz, or Titralac, for example.
- Don't take antacids immediately after eating. Wait a half hour.
- Investigate other possible causes of heartburn. See Ulcers, page 335, and H. pylori, page 164.

• • •

HICCUPS

LIKE SOME OTHER unlucky people, I seem to have a propensity for hiccups, and I once suffered through two full days of them while in medical school. If I laugh a lot or if I laugh and cough at the same time I can count on a spell of hiccups. Swallowing too much air seems to be a common cause, but no one has ever come up with the precise physiological cause of hiccups. And what's worse, no one has ever come up with a definitive cure.

A hiccup is really a spasm of the diaphragm. It's rarely caused by a serious disorder; it's most often simply annoying or even exhausting. Most hiccups disappear on their own in a short while, but a few people have had cases that lasted for years! If your hiccups are really troublesome—for example, following surgery—you can take a drug to get them under control. For the garden variety of hiccups you'll just have to try the home remedies that the world has relied upon for generations.

My own favorite remedy and the one that seems to be the most effective for the widest range of people is the sugar cure. Take a teaspoon of sugar under your tongue and then very, very slowly drink a cup of water. This usually gives immediate relief: The diaphragm relaxes and the hiccups are gone.

NATURAL PRESCRIPTION FOR HICCUPS

VARIOUS TIME-HONORED REMEDIES INCLUDE:

- The sugar cure: Put a teaspoon of sugar under your tongue and then very, very slowly drink a cup of water. Some people find it works just as well to let a teaspoon or two of sugar dissolve in the mouth.

- Fill a glass of water, hold your breath, and drink the water from the other side of the cup; in other words, drink the water upside down.

- Blow in and out of a brown paper bag held securely to your lips. Make sure you blow with great vigor and do it at least ten times.

- Inhale ground black pepper until you sneeze.

- Soak a lemon wedge in angostura bitters and then suck on the wedge. Several patients have told me they've used this technique with success.

- Take a deep, deep breath and then, holding your nose, drink a glass of water.

- Press against the roof of your mouth with a cotton swab.

HIVES

HIVES ARE AMONG the most common kind of skin allergies. Hives usually appear in the form of one or more raised light red patches called wheals. They have clearly defined edges, and they itch. Sometimes they join together to form larger patches. Hives are annoying, even embarrassing, but they are usually harmless and often disappear within a few hours. The only time hives demand serious immediate attention is when the tissue around the larynx swells and breathing is obstructed.

While everyday hives, also called urticaria, are not life-threatening, they can be disruptive and, when they occur frequently, you should investigate to learn the cause. A number of things can cause hives, the most frequent in adults being medication or foods whereas children most often develop them in reaction to foods and food additives or to infections. Some people develop hives from exposure to cold, sunlight, heat, or even water.

Medications, particularly aspirin and penicillin, are common causes of hives. Most people who are allergic to aspirin will develop a reaction immediately after ingesting it. The same thing will happen with penicillin except that sometimes people don't realize that the source of the penicillin is not the pharmacy but the dinner table. Penicillin found in minute amounts in milk, soft drinks, and frozen dinners has been the cause of hives in particularly sensitive people. Obviously, if you develop hives after taking penicillin or any medication, you should let your doctor know. If you have recurring hives and can't pin down the cause, particularly if you know that you're allergic to penicillin, you should consider your food, especially dairy food, as a possible source.

I've found in my practice that people who regularly suffer from hives have developed them as a result of hidden food and food additive allergies. Milk, soy products, and yeast products are common culprits. Often the offending food is easy to recognize, as the hives appear a few minutes after ingestion. Shellfish, strawberries, milk, fish, beans, and nuts are common allergenic foods. Obviously, if one of these foods gives you hives, you should avoid it (see Food Allergy, page 146).

Sometimes people can suddenly have a reaction to a food that they've eaten in the past without problem. I had one very dismayed patient in her mid-forties who began to develop hives whenever she ate lobster, a food that she'd often enjoyed in the past. She was eager for some medication that would enable her to go back to her favorite seafood, and I had to disappoint her and tell her that she must give up lobster.

Some patients have come to me because they have recurring hives that they can't connect with any particular food. Many people develop hives in reaction to food additives. Here are some common additives that can cause hives in sensitive people.

FOOD COLORINGS: Tartrazine (FD&C Yellow Dye No. 5), a food dye, has long been known to cause hives, particularly in children. This dye is added to nearly every packaged food as well as to some drugs. People who are sensitive to aspirin are especially likely to be sensitive to tartrazine. Foods that commonly contain tartrazine include ice cream, margarine, cake mixes, cloves, jam and jelly, bakery goods except plain bread, Jell-O, candies, gum, hot dogs, oil of wintergreen, toothpaste, mint flavors, lozenges, mouthwash, and lunch meats such as salami and bologna. The following liquids also commonly contain tartrazine: cider and cider vinegars, wine and wine vinegars, Kool-Aid and similar beverages, soda and soft drinks, gin and all distilled alcoholic beverages (except vodka), all tea, beer, diet drinks and supplements, and birch beer.

FLAVORINGS include those found in puddings, cake mixes, ice cream, chewing gum, and soft drinks. Sometimes vanilla, cinnamon, menthol, and the artificial sweetener Aspartame can cause hives.

SALICYLATES, found in aspirin and some over-the-counter drugs, are also naturally occurring substances found in foods. Salicylates commonly cause reactions in people who are also sensitive to tartrazine (above). Foods containing salicylates include almonds, apples, apricots, blackberries, boysenberries, cherries, cucumbers and pickles, currants, gooseberries, grapes or raisins, nectarines, oranges, peaches, plums or prunes, raspberries, strawberries, and tomatoes.

FOOD PRESERVATIVES: Benzoic acid and benzoates, the most commonly used food preservatives, are likely to cause hives. BHT and BHA can also be allergenic. Sulfites added to many processed foods and most beers and wines can also cause hives. Sulfites and benzoates are commonly used on fish and shrimp to help keep them fresh, which explains why so many people develop hives after eating these foods.

EMULSIFIERS AND STABILIZERS: These substances are used in processed foods to ensure that the oils and solids don't separate. The polysorbate in ice cream and the vegetable gums found in other foods including acacia, gum arabic, tragacanth, quince, and carrageenan can be allergenic.

If you are a woman with a history of frequent vaginal yeast infections and chronic hives, *Candida albicans* can be the cause. For a full discussion of this problem, see Candidiasis, page 61.

Children can sometimes develop hives from bacterial infections. The child may have a fever and be obviously ill but suddenly hives appear, frightening the parent as well as the child. Hives in this case are nothing to worry about (as opposed to the bacterial infection), and they'll disappear when the ailment is treated.

There's no practical way to subvert the effects of allergens that cause hives: Elimination is the only sensible approach. If you have an occasional case of hives, you should simply be alert to the probable cause and eliminate the offending food or medication. If, however, you regularly develop hives, you should seriously investigate the possible causes in a systemic way, watching your diet and medications for a reaction, eliminating as many problem foods as possible along with food additives and preservatives, and then gradually reintroducing them.

Finally, vitamin C and vitamin E and selenium can help cases of chronic hives.

NATURAL PRESCRIPTION FOR HIVES

- As common hives usually disappear in an hour or two, there's no immediate treatment needed. For long-term treatment, the only answer is avoiding the trigger that causes your hives. Investigate the following possibilities:

  Medications such as aspirin and penicillin

  Food allergies

  Food additives and preservatives

  Candida albicans

  In children: infections

- As tension and stress usually make hives worse, practice relaxation techniques. See Stress Control, page 314.

- Chronic hives may be helped by taking the following in addition to your daily basic supplements:

> Vitamin C: 1,000 mg. daily.
>
> Vitamin E: 400 I.U. daily.
>
> Selenium: 100 mcg. daily

IN ADDITION: Benadryl, an antihistamine available without prescription, can provide temporary relief from the itching of hives. Seldane, a prescription medication, is also helpful.

• • •

HYPERTENSION

HIGH BLOOD PRESSURE, or hypertension, is one of the biggest medical challenges we face in this century. If you have high blood pressure (along with sixty million other Americans), your risk of heart attack is three times greater and your risk of stroke seven times greater than that of people with normal blood pressure levels. Hypertension is called "the silent killer" because it damages many organs without ever causing pain, and the longer the condition exists, the greater the damage and the risk of cardiac disease.

There are two types of hypertension: primary, or essential, hypertension and secondary hypertension. Secondary hypertension, which accounts for only 10 to 15 percent of all cases, is precipitated by an identifiable cause, such as kidney disease or a tumor. In these cases, once the cause is treated, the pressure returns to normal. We are concerned here with primary hypertension, which has no known or specific cause.

There are a number of drugs that are used to control blood pressure, and sometimes there's no other alternative than to take one of them. But most of these drugs have side effects that can include increased fatigue, depression, and impotence in male patients. Generally speaking, the higher your pressure, the higher the dose you'll have to take and the more likely you are to suffer side effects. An additional problem is that many elderly people taking medication for blood pressure are also taking medication for other conditions, which increases the risk of drug interaction.

Natural measures can be of enormous help in controlling hypertension, enabling you to reduce and possibly eliminate your medication and its side effects.

Blood pressure refers to the force exerted by the blood against the blood vessel walls. A blood pressure reading contains two numbers. The first number, which is ordinarily the higher of the two, refers to the systolic pressure or the pressure when the heart is contracting to pump the blood. The second number is the diastolic pressure, or the pressure when the heart is resting between beats.

Here is how the National Institutes of Health currently classify these numbers:

SYSTOLIC PRESSURE (if diastolic pressure below 90)

- Less than 140: normal. Recheck within two years.
- 140–159: borderline isolated systolic hypertension. Confirm within two months.
- 160 or higher: isolated systolic hypertension. If systolic pressure is below 200, confirm within two months. If reading is 200 or more, refer for care within two weeks.

DIASTOLIC PRESSURE

- Less than 85: normal. Recheck within two years.
- 85–89: high normal. Recheck within one year.
- 90–104: mild high blood pressure or hypertension. Confirm within two months. Whether or not treatment is indicated in this range is controversial, particularly when the numbers are between 90 and 94.
- 105–114: moderate hypertension. Refer for care within two weeks.
- 115 or higher: severe hypertension. Refer for immediate care.

Everyone's blood pressure varies during the course of the day. As you'd expect, it's lower when you're resting or relaxed and higher after activity, especially a sudden burst of activity. Some people have what's referred to as "white coat syndrome," which simply means that the experience of having their blood pressure taken in a doctor's office will boost their reading. For this reason, most prudent doctors will not prescribe pressure-lowering medication after the first high reading; they'll wait until they've seen a pattern of several high readings before thinking about medication.

Before you begin to worry about your blood pressure reading, be sure that you're getting a number that reflects your real pressure. Certain drugs can elevate your pressure. For example, phenylpropanola-mine (PPA), an ingredient which is commonly found in many over-the-counter medications including cold remedies, decongestants, and appetite-suppressants, can elevate your pressure, as can caffeine. An alarmingly high reading can result from taking a decongestant and two cups of coffee an hour before a reading.

The big questions today are determining when hypertension needs to be treated with medication and how much the pressure should be reduced by means of medication. There's been considerable controversy about this. Years ago researchers linked hypertension with an increased rate of heart attack and stroke. Yet studies that tried to demonstrate the value of reducing blood pressure produced a decrease only in the number of strokes while the number of heart attacks remained the same. The key seems to be that if the pressure is reduced either too much or too little, the danger of heart attack is still present. The latest studies recommend moderate reductions in the range of 7 to 17 mmHg for people with mild to moderate hypertension. This provides yet another incentive to avoid medication, as blood pressure controlled naturally is less likely to be reduced either too much or too little. If you've got severe hypertension, you will no doubt need drug therapy. But if your diastolic pressure is between 90 and 104, you may well be able—depending on your family history and other lifestyle factors—to avoid drugs and rely on natural means to get your pressure under control.

If you already know that you have high blood pressure and are on medication, you should not stop taking it. Instead, after consultation with your doctor, adopt the measures I recommend, and then after a sufficient trial period—say a month or two—get a pressure reading that will indicate if the new steps you're taking are having an effect. It's quite likely that your pressure will be lower and you'll be able to reduce your medication.

If you have a "high normal" pressure reading, you're in a great position to profit from the help that natural medicine can offer. By adopting the suggestions below, you'll probably be able to lower your pressure naturally and avoid medication entirely.

While we don't know precisely what causes hypertension, we do know that it's primarily a lifestyle disease that's found almost entirely in developing nations. People who live in remote areas of the globe including parts of China, the Solomon Islands, and New Guinea, for example, show virtually no evidence of hypertension, nor do they have a rise in blood pressure as they age.

The first step in reducing blood pressure is changing your diet, particularly if you are overweight. In one study where various means of treatments were tried in an effort to lower pressure, weight loss was by far the most effective. Some people are discouraged when they hear this because they've tried dieting and found it difficult. But you don't have to get down to your ideal weight in order to reduce your pressure. If you're overweight, even a small drop can lower your pressure significantly. So don't feel overwhelmed by having to lose twenty or fifty pounds: Just aim for five or ten pounds. You may well want to go on and lose additional weight, if need be, once you achieve this goal.

A vegetarian diet has been shown to be prophylactic against hypertension. Most vegetarians enjoy lower blood pressure readings than meat eaters. The reason is that the components of a vegetarian diet—more fiber, vitamin C, vitamin E, magnesium, calcium, potassium, and significantly less salt and less total fat, saturated fat, and cholesterol—help to fight hypertension. I don't advise my patients to become vegetarians. Many people don't do well as vegetarians; they feel tired and run-down on a vegetarian diet, especially if they have been eating sugar and have low blood sugar. And for many people it's impractical to go a strictly vegetarian diet. But some of my patients are vegetarians and are quite robust and healthy. While strict vegetarianism may not be sensible for many patients, I do advise them to adopt as many of the aspects of a vegetarian diet as possible, particularly the reduction of saturated fat and cholesterol. Studies have been done with Finns, who eat more saturated and less polyunsaturated fats compared with Americans, and who have a higher incidence of hypertension. When their saturated fat intake was decreased, despite the fact that their sodium intake was unchanged, they experienced an average pressure drop of 7.5 mmHg systolic and 2.8 mmHg diastolic. When their previous, high saturated fat intake levels were resumed, their pressure once again went up.

Sodium or salt has always been an issue for people with hypertension. In the past it was assumed that if you had high blood pressure you had to eliminate salt from your diet. Today we know that not everyone with hypertension is salt sensitive. In fact, only about 30 to 40 percent of the population is sensitive to salt. If you have heart or kidney problems in addition to high blood pressure, you should definitely avoid salt, because your body doesn't properly eliminate sodium. But if you're restricting sodium solely for hypertension, you might want to test yourself to see if sodium restriction is doing you any good. After having your pressure taken, follow a diet that is as sodium-free as possible for two weeks.

Have your pressure taken again. You can do the opposite if you've been avoiding salt: Try two weeks of a diet that does include salt and see what effect, if any, it has on your blood pressure reading.

If, however, you are salt sensitive, you should probably restrict your salt intake and increase your potassium intake. Many people who are salt sensitive not only consume too much salt but also get too little potassium in their diet. This causes an increase in fluid volume and an impairment of the blood pressure regulating mechanism. You can either rely on potassium supplements or you can make a concerted effort to get it from food sources. In one study, people were able to reduce medications for hypertension by half simply by consuming a diet rich in potassium. Particularly good sources are fresh fruits and vegetables such as potatoes, peas, peppers, eggplant, pears, squash, lima beans, tomatoes, and bananas.

A diet that is low in fiber will promote hypertension as well as a host of other chronic ailments. The benefits of a high-fiber diet are dramatic in someone whose pressure is high. I don't recommend taking fiber supplements, but I do think an emphasis on fresh vegetables, fruits, and whole grain cereals, breads, and pastas is important. Another good way to increase your fiber intake, which I recommend to my patients, is to have a bowl of oat bran cereal or other high-fiber cereal for breakfast.

Recent research has proven that celery can have a beneficial effect on hypertension. It lowers the blood pressure by relaxing smooth muscles in the blood vessels themselves. Despite the fact that celery is often forbidden to people with hypertension because of its high sodium content, its benefits are now recognized. Four stalks of celery daily will provide sufficient amounts of the active chemical that causes the desired effect. Don't overdose on celery because it can be toxic in extremely large amounts. And don't take it if you are sodium sensitive. But I think it's worth trying a week of three or four daily stalks of celery before a pressure reading to see if it works for you.

If you drink alcohol, you're much more likely to suffer from hypertension. In men, 5 to 11 percent of hypertension has been attributed to alcohol. One hospital survey showed that over half of the admitted men whose daily alcohol consumption exceeded the equivalent of four pints of beer, had hypertension. Despite the reports that "moderate" alcohol intake has a certain protective effect, I tell patients with any degree of hypertension that they should completely eliminate alcohol from their diet. I believe that the alcohol's possible protection from coronary artery disease isn't worth the definite myocardial damage and risk of hypertension. Fortunately the negative effects of alcohol on your blood pressure will disappear when you stop drinking.

There are also a number of supplements that can be helpful. The first pair to look at are calcium and magnesium. I mention them together because they work together in the body and because low levels of both these minerals have been found to be associated with high blood pressure. We know that there's a relationship between calcium and blood pressure, though there is some controversy about exactly what the relationship is. It may be calcium's interaction with magnesium and particularly sodium that affects the pressure. In any case, some studies have shown definite benefits for some patients who take calcium and magnesium, and no change in others. I suggest that you take both calcium and magnesium supplements on a trial basis for two months. If you see a reduction in your pressure, you should continue with the supplements; if not, discontinue.

Coenzyme Q10 is a supplement that's been extremely helpful for many people with cardiovascular disease, including hypertension. It's believed that CoQ10 improves the function of the blood vessel wall and thus helps regulate blood pressure. In one ten-week trial, hypertensive patients taking CoQ10 experienced a mean systolic and diastolic pressure reduction of 10.6 and 7.7 mmHg, respectively, during their treatment, while the group taking a placebo had no change.

We know that there's a connection between fish oil and the omega-3 fatty acids in fish oil and regulation of blood pressure. Many studies have shown reduction of pressure when taking fish oil either in the form of a supplement, an increase in fish consumption, particularly mackerel (which is high in omega-3 fatty acids). I think the best way to supplement with omega-3 fatty acids is through MaxEPA (a trade name for a fish oil preparation), which is available at health food stores.

Garlic has been shown to decrease the systolic pressure by 20 to 30 mmHg and diastolic pressure by 10 to 20 mmHg. I tell my patients to enjoy garlic in food as often as possible. As you need to take two to three cloves of fresh garlic daily to get a therapeutic benefit, many people prefer to take supplements, available in an odor-free form at health food stores.

Vitamin C, so useful for so many metabolic functions, has also recently been found to help regulate blood pressure. While studies haven't yet shown it effective at reducing diastolic pressure, it definitely can help reduce the systolic reading.

Exercise can be extremely effective in treating hypertension. In one recent study, people with moderate hypertension lowered their pressure using only exercise. These people adhered to a six-month program of a half hour of aerobic exercise three or four times a week. After this regime, their average systolic drop was 5 mmHg and the average diastolic drop was 8 mmHg. Exercise not only has a physiological effect but also reduces stress and therefore is of enormous benefit to the cardiovascular system. I tell all my hypertensive patients that they must make a commitment to exercise, even if they only walk briskly for a half hour three or four times weekly. If you are under a doctor's care for hypertension, review your exercise program with your physician to be sure that it's safe for you. Avoid exercises such as weight lifting, which causes a temporary rise in blood pressure.

Stress control can make a big difference in lowering high blood pressure. One study, which used a controlled trial of yoga and biofeedback, demonstrated a highly significant reduction in blood pressure with stress control treatments (see Stress Control, page 314).

Smoking is very closely associated with hypertension as nicotine stimulates the adrenal glands, which ultimately act to increase blood pressure. If you smoke, add hypertension to all the diseases you're promoting.

NATURAL PRESCRIPTION FOR HYPERTENSION

- If you are taking medication for hypertension, do not discontinue. Consult your physician, adopt the changes recommended here, and get a pressure reading two to three months later to see if your pressure has lowered and if you can reduce your medication. If your pressure is "high normal," adopt the recommendations below and you will probably be able to avoid the use of medication entirely.

- If you are overweight, lose weight. This change alone can sometimes lower your pressure into the normal range. Just five to ten pounds can make a difference.

- Lower your fat intake (see Blueprint for Health, page xvii).

- Adopt as many relevant features of a vegetarian diet as possible including more polyunsaturated fat, fiber, vitamin C, vitamin E, magnesium, calcium, and potassium (see recommendations below for vitamin/mineral doses), and reduce total fat, saturated fat, and cholesterol.

- Determine if you are salt sensitive. If sodium is affecting your blood pressure, eliminate it from your diet (see text).

- If you are salt sensitive and therefore must reduce sodium in your diet, increase your intake of potassium-rich foods such as peas, peppers, eggplant, and pears.

- Adopt a high-fiber diet. Try oat bran cereal, or some other high-fiber cereal, for breakfast. Increase your intake of fresh fruits and vegetables, and whole grain cereals, breads, and pastas. Do not take fiber supplements in connection with hypertension.

- If you are not sodium sensitive, try eating three or four stalks of celery daily a week before a pressure reading to see if it helps. (Don't eat celery in extremely large amounts, as it can be toxic.)

- If you drink alcohol, stop.

- Adopt an exercise program. Exercise for a half hour three to four times weekly. A brisk walk is excellent.

- Adopt a stress control program. See Stress Control, page 314, for more information on how to do this.

- If you smoke, stop.

IN ADDITION TO YOUR DAILY SUPPLEMENTS, PAGE xxiv, TAKE

- Calcium: 1,200 mg. of calcium at bedtime for a trial period of two months.

- Magnesium: 250 mg. two or three times daily for a trial period of two months.

- Coenzyme Q10: 30 mg. three times daily.

- MaxEPA: 1,000 mg. three times daily.

- Garlic: Increase consumption of garlic and other foods in the onion family. You can try garlic supplements, available in health food stores. Take one 300-mg. long-acting, odor-free capsule daily.
- Vitamin C: 1,000 mg. daily.

HYPOGLYCEMIA

LOW BLOOD SUGAR is caused, paradoxically, by eating too much sugar. When the sugar reaches the blood, which happens within seconds after you eat it, the body produces insulin to normalize the blood-sugar level. In a person suffering from hypoglycemia, the body produces too much insulin. The blood-sugar level is decreased so rapidly and thoroughly that the person suffers distressing symptoms including headaches, fatigue, depression, anxiety, dizziness, lack of mental alertness, and rapid mood swings.

A number of years ago hypoglycemia became "popular," and many people decided that they suffered from it. Reacting to this fad, many doctors have dismissed the disorder entirely, claiming it doesn't exist. I believe the truth is somewhere in between: Not everyone who claims to have hypoglycemia suffers from it, but many people have some degree of difficulty in handling refined sugar in their diet and they commonly experience symptoms.

In my practice I see many people with blood-sugar problems. They may be chronically fatigued, headachy, or depressed; feel tired in the morning; have trouble concentrating; and suffer late afternoon fatigue. And their symptoms are exacerbated by not eating. Many of them have been to doctors and have been told that they had no specific medical problem, yet when they follow the program for hypoglycemia outlined here, their symptoms disappear. If you suspect that your vague symptoms as described are caused by low blood sugar, it is well worth following the recommendations to see if you feel better. You can get a good indication of whether you could have an adverse reaction to sugar, if you suffer any of the above symptoms shortly after eating simple sugar or two to four hours after an all-carbohydrate meal.

How can too much sugar cause so many symptoms? Sugar gives your body a temporary lift, but over the long haul it puts the body under great stress. When you eat too much of it, refined or otherwise, the sugar levels in your blood rise to abnormal heights. In an effort to return things to normal, your pancreas produces insulin, the hormone that regulates sugar levels. If you don't have hypoglycemia—or if you don't regularly eat too much sugar—your pancreas can easily handle isolated overdoses of sugar. But if you are a virtual sugar addict, your pancreas goes into overdrive at every rise in blood-sugar levels: It overreacts, flooding your body with insulin, which makes your blood-sugar level take a nosedive. In response, the adrenal glands release antistress hormones that in turn release the sugar stored in the liver for emergencies. The result? Everything gets worn out—the pancreas, the adrenal glands, and the liver. And your symptoms are nervousness, palpitations, anxiety, headaches, butterflies in the stomach, and so on.

Eventually, someone who has experienced this pattern will find that their symptoms are constant. They complain of chronic irritability and constant fatigue, unrelieved by sleep. By this time, they notice they cannot go very long without eating or their symptoms get worse.

Why do blood-sugar fluctuations seem to affect the brain, causing the symptoms associated with anxiety? The brain requires a constant adequate level of blood sugar to function properly. It is more dependent on blood sugar, or glucose, than any other organ. Low glucose levels resulting from the severe dip after a high sugar intake tax the brain and cause the headaches and other symptoms that plague sugar addicts.

Americans consume more than eighty pounds of sugar per person a year or about thirty teaspoons a day. In addition, we eat large quantities of refined carbohydrates—white flour, for example, which is turned into glucose in the body. Even if you don't own a sugar bowl, half of your sugar intake is probably hidden in the foods you buy. Cookies and ice cream are obvious sources of sugar, but most people are unaware that catsup, prepared frozen meals, and salad dressings also contain sugar.

Simple changes in your diet plus a few supplements can make an enormous difference in how you feel. Many of my patients have found that by following this program for hypoglycemia they not only are relieved of their symptoms but also have more energy and enthusiasm for life and, in many cases, they've lost weight.

I recommend that *all* my patients—not only those suffering from hypoglycemia—eliminate or cut way down on their sugar intake. Sugar has so many negative effects on the body that you don't need to feel the symptoms of hypoglycemia to be suffering on some level from overconsumption of sweets.

To fight hypoglycemia you must of course cut out the obvious: sugar, honey, cakes, candies, cookies, ice cream, sodas, sweetened cereal, canned fruit, frozen desserts, honey, and other sweetened foods. You must also learn to read labels carefully. Here are the most common sugar additives you'll find listed on a food label:

corn syrup	glucose	molasses
sucrose	lactose	maple syrup
fructose	maltose	sorghum

Ingredients on a label are listed in descending order of amounts used; a product that counts sugar as its second ingredient probably has an enormous amount of sugar in it. Just as bad are products where two or three types of sugar are listed. Though they may be near the bottom of the list, leading you to think that there isn't a great deal of sugar in the product, if you could add up all the different types of sugar as a percentage of total ingredients you may find that sugar is in fact the main ingredient! Look carefully and you'll find that many brands of soup, spaghetti sauce, catsup, mayonnaise, cranberry sauce, and peanut butter contain sugar. You can find comparable products that don't contain sugar, but you may have to search for them.

Avoid simple carbohydrates and refined and processed foods such as instant rice and potatoes, white flour, soft drinks, and alcohol. Instead stick to a diet high in complex carbohydrates and fiber, both of which help to stabilize blood sugar. Whole grain products should be a large part of your diet. Stick to the most natural, unprocessed form of a food: An apple is better than apple juice.

Eat regular meals at regular times. You would be amazed at how many of my patients, who should certainly have known better, used to skip meals. Regular meals are especially important for people with hypoglycemia because regular food intake keeps the blood sugar stable. If you miss a meal you're much more likely to crave a sweet snack to relieve your symptoms. Don't skip breakfast. Don't have a late lunch. Don't have a late dinner. Try to eat your meals at nearly the same time each day if at all possible.

It's important to have protein at both lunch and dinner. Protein tends to produce much less of an insulin response than do carbohydrates. Don't have just a salad at lunch. I suggest fish (water-packed tuna is good), chicken, or turkey as the best choices for protein.

Some doctors recommend that people who suffer from hypoglycemia have frequent small meals—six to eight meals throughout the day. Most of my patients find that this is too difficult to arrange, so I recommend that in addition to your regular meals, you routinely eat midmorning, midafternoon, and bedtime snacks such as a piece of fruit. Some of my patients like to have a piece of whole-wheat toast with fruit butter at bedtime. A few whole-wheat crackers (check to be sure they don't contain sugar), popcorn (of course without butter), and rice cakes can also make handy snacks.

It's important for people with blood-sugar problems to avoid caffeine, alcohol, and smoking. All of these cause precipitous changes in blood-sugar levels. I've found that caffeine, alcohol, and smoking also make it more difficult for my patients to give up sugar. Because they cause rapid fluctuations in blood-sugar levels, they create cravings for sweets and/or more caffeine, tobacco, or alcohol. I do think that it's acceptable to have one caffeinated beverage a day. (Remember to watch out for caffeine in soft drinks and in over-the-counter medicines.) Many of my patients have a cup of coffee in the morning, but I tell them that they should have some food in their stomach before that first sip and, of course, they don't continue to drink coffee throughout the day. Most people find this a relatively easy change to make, even those who were drinking up to six or seven cups of coffee daily.

Many patients ask me about artificial sweeteners. I'm against them, particularly for people with blood-sugar problems. There are a variety of health problems associated with artificial sweeteners. While the risk for most people is low, I think the more important issue is that they encourage people with a sweet tooth to continue having sweet cravings. Many of my patients have been surprised to find that when they eliminate sugar from their diet, even if they were heavy sugar users, within a few weeks their taste for sugar diminishes. If you continue to use artificial sweeteners, you prevent this from happening.

There is a nutrient that I use with hypoglycemic patients and it has proven to be something of a miracle in controlling blood sugar and reducing sweet cravings. Chromium, a trace mineral, is essential to the proper functioning of insulin. Unfortunately, the average American diet is deficient in chromium. I've found that the trivalent form of chromium taken three times a day before meals is most effective for controlling sweet cravings, reducing appetite, and keeping energy levels up between meals.

NATURAL PRESCRIPTION FOR HYPOGLYCEMIA

- Eliminate sugar from the diet. This also means no cakes, candies, cookies, ice cream, sweetened cereal, canned fruit, and frozen desserts. In addition, you must learn to read food labels to find hidden sources of sugar. See text on how to assess a food label.

- Avoid simple carbohydrates and refined and processed foods such as instant rice and potatoes, white flour, soft drinks, and alcohol.

- Eat a diet high in complex carbohydrates and fiber, both of which help to stabilize blood sugar. Try to stick to the most natural, unprocessed form of a food.

- Eat regular meals at regular times. Don't skip meals. Don't eat late meals. Have protein at both lunch and dinner.

- Eliminate alcohol and smoking.

- Limit your caffeine intake to one caffeinated beverage—coffee or tea —daily. Watch out for caffeinated soft drinks and over-the-counter drugs.

- Eliminate the use of artificial sweeteners.

IN ADDITION TO YOUR DAILY SUPPLEMENTS, PAGE xxiv, TAKE

- Chromium: the trivalent form in dosages of 100 mcg. three times a day before meals.

• • •

IMPOTENCE

IN MY PRACTICE over the years I've noticed that men complain of two distinct sexual problems: lack of desire and impotence. Patients often confuse the two problems and describe both as "impotence," but they're distinctly different.

Many men, and the numbers seem to be increasing over the years, suffer from what can be termed lack of desire. They no longer seem to have much interest in sex. They'd really rather watch TV or go to the gym, and they begin to wonder if what they're experiencing is an early sign of impotence. While lack of desire may precede impotence, it's not the same thing. Lack of desire usually stems from stress, fatigue, and/or depression.

Abe, a youthful fifty-year-old patient, was seriously worried about his sex life. He was convinced that he was becoming impotent because he hadn't had relations with his wife of twenty-five years in nearly six months. He still loved her and was happy in his marriage, but he no longer felt the drive to have sex. Abe said he had two children in college and he felt enormous financial pressure. He was working harder than ever, but despite his excellent job performance, a younger man in his office was assuming more and more responsibility and seemed to be breathing down his neck.

Abe's story is typical of what many of my male patients experience. At a point in their lives when they might begin to notice a decreased ability to develop and maintain an erection, they are also feeling enormous pressures in other areas of their lives. They begin to think that sex is something that they no longer do very well, so why do it at all? With more and more time lapsing between sexual experiences, anxiety and avoidance build.

What Abe was experiencing was lack of desire. While his erection was probably slightly slower to build and less engorged than his erection of twenty years ago, he was not impotent. He was able to achieve intercourse but was avoiding it or ignoring it. He simply needed to get his sex life jump-started. By thinking about sex in a positive way, making stress-free time for sex, and, in Abe's case, avoiding too much alcohol before sex, he found he was able to enjoy a satisfying sex life again.

But there are other psychological problems that can trigger impotence. One is the notion that sex is an athletic event. Obviously most men can't compete at sixty the way they could at twenty. And so they begin to lose confidence in their ability to perform. Their anxiety sets off a self-perpetuating problem: They're afraid to engage in sex and so they don't, until they finally try, and, paralyzed by anxiety, they can't. Counseling and reassurance can reverse the problem.

Impotence, while it sometimes mimics Abe's problem, is more complicated than lack of desire and, in fact, more easily defined. Impotence is simply a permanent or temporary inability to have or maintain a sufficiently rigid erection to achieve intercourse.

Many men are confused by changes in their sexuality as they age and ascribe their problem to impotence. Here are some changes that most men can expect as they grow older:

- By age sixty, many men notice that it takes longer to reach an erection.

- As they age, many men notice that their lubrication prior to ejaculation lessens or even disappears.

- Older men produce a smaller amount of semen and thus feel less of a desire to ejaculate.

- Most older men notice that it takes them longer to achieve an erection after ejaculating.

All of these changes are normal and do not indicate impotence.

If you do suffer from actual impotence, there may be a variety of contributing factors. A number of natural remedies have proven helpful, and there are other remedies a physician may prescribe that may be the answer if you have a problem that won't respond to the natural solutions.

Alcohol is implicated in numerous impotence problems. The solution is obvious: If you drink too much, you are probably going to have trouble achieving and maintaining an erection. Contrary to what you might think, those three or four or five drinks that "get you in the mood" sabotage your performance.

Many men believe that reduced male hormones cause their impotence. While it is true that adequate testosterone is essential to achieving an erection, it's not common for a man to be deficient unless he has had prostate surgery for cancer and his testes have been removed. Your doctor can check your hormone level to reassure you: You may be one of the few who does need hormonal injections to restore potency.

One possible cause of diminished hormones is heavy smoking, which leads to large amounts of carbon dioxide in the blood, reducing the hormonal levels and contributing to impotence. Not only does smoking affect hormonal levels, it also can contribute to the clogging of penile arteries, which can cause impotence even in younger men. One study found that men as young as thirty-five suffered impotence connected with smoking. Men who smoked a pack a day for twenty years were four times more likely than nonsmokers to become impotent as a result of clogged arteries.

Vascular problems can cause impotence. When the flow of blood is impaired, you may not get sufficient blood into the penis to engorge it sufficiently. High blood pressure and high cholesterol are problems that can cause some level of impotence. If you have any of these problems, please read the sections on them in this book: It's quite possible that by remedying these problems you can eliminate impotence.

Some men develop adult-onset diabetes as they age, without knowing it. If this happens, in addition to impairing the blood flow to the penis, it can wreak havoc with blood-sugar levels; this, too, can contribute to impotence (see Diabetes, page 111).

A major cause of impotence is illness. Sometimes the illness itself causes the problem, but more often the illness creates fear concerning intercourse. Many men who've suffered a heart attack worry about sex and its effect on their heart. In fact, regular sexual activity can reduce the risk of another heart attack. Countless studies have shown that sexual intercourse causes stress comparable to climbing several flights of stairs or other normal activities. For most people, by the time they are released from the hospital, they are able to resume normal activities including a normal sex life. The publicized cases of men dying of heart attacks while having intercourse often involve men who are having extramarital affairs (a cause of considerable stress) and who are also suffering from the effects of alcohol, overeating, and/or drugs.

If you have had a heart attack, it's possible that your partner also is nervous about sexual activity. I strongly suggest that you discuss this with your doctor. Cardiologists are used to dealing with this problem and can give you the best advice concerning your particular case.

Medications are thought to be responsible for about one quarter of all cases of impotence. Some prescription drugs can interfere with the autonomic nervous system as well as with the production and action of sex hormones. Bill came to see me because of high blood pressure. He had been on medication for his condition for nearly three years, and while his blood pressure was under control, he was looking for a way to reduce his medication. On his second visit, he rather sheepishly mentioned that he had been having some sexual problems. His blood pressure prescription was causing impotence, but he had never made the connection. Too embarrassed to mention it to anyone before, he spent three years agonizing over this—a simple change of medication restored his ability to enjoy sex. The natural treatment for reducing blood pressure can also, in many cases, reduce the need for medications.

Surgery can cause impotence. Prostate surgery (prostate problems are quite common in men over fifty) can impair the ability to achieve erection. Major abdominal surgery can also cause impotence. Both types of surgery can compromise the nerves and/or the blood supply serving the penis. If surgery has caused your impotence, only your doctor can tell if it is possible to repair the damage and restore your ability to achieve erection.

If you can think of no explanation for your impotence—if you can eliminate medications, illness, surgery, hormonal levels, diabetes, high blood pressure, elevated cholesterol, and psychological problems as the source of your problem—there are natural remedies that you should try.

Zinc is a mineral that is crucial to the production of testosterone, the male sex hormone. We now know that if you are even marginally deficient in zinc, your potency can be affected. Zinc supplementation has been helpful for many men. Incidentally, patients on kidney dialysis —70 percent of whom have some degree of impotence—are helped enormously by zinc supplements. I suggest that patients take 50 mg. of zinc daily.

There are two natural substances that offer great promise for impotent men. The first is the herb *Ginkgo biloba,* which can be helpful for men whose problem stems from diminished blood flow to the penis. You should hope to see some improvement in about two months; some patients regain full potency within six months. You can get ginkgo at health food stores. There are no known harmful side effects.

Another natural remedy for impotence is yohimbine, a substance that is derived from the bark of the yohimbe tree in Africa. Yohimbine (available by prescription) is known to dilate surface blood vessels and stimulate the release of norepinephrine. The usual dose is three 5.4-mg. tablets a day; you should see some results in two to three weeks. By the way, yohimbine can increase your heart rate and make you feel slightly nervous as well as raise your blood pressure, so if you experience any of these reactions, you should lower the dosage and gradually increase it to the prescribed amount.

Finally, there is a mechanical device that's useful for men who have found no other solution. It's known as a vacuum constrictor device (VCD), available by prescription. The device consists of a tube into which the penis is inserted. A vacuum is then created by means of a small pump, which encourages blood flow into the penis and thus an erection. A flexible ring is then slipped onto the base of the penis to maintain the erection. The device is safe and effective for most men, and if nothing else has been helpful you might want to ask your urologist about it. One of my patients has a ninety-two-year-old father who has a fulfilled and happy sex life by means of the pump.

NATURAL PRESCRIPTION FOR IMPOTENCE

- Stop smoking.

- If you suffer from high blood pressure or elevated cholesterol, you should try to remedy these problems, as they can affect potency.

- If you suffer from atherosclerosis, diabetes, or high blood pressure (see Atherosclerosis, page 31; Diabetes, page 111; Hypertension, page 194), your impotence could be connected to these problems. Make sure that you are following appropriate measures to keep them under control.

- Check any medications you take to see if they affect potency. Ask your doctor to check the *Physicians' Desk Reference*, a listing of all prescription drugs (also in the library), to learn about side effects of your medications.

- If you have had a heart attack or other major illness, you should discuss with your doctor its effects on your sex life. Usually fear about sex following a heart attack or health problem is unfounded.

- If you've had surgery—prostate or abdominal—it's possible that you've had nerve or vascular damage that can be reversed. Check with your doctor.

- If you sense that your impotence has a psychological basis, make an effort to get counseling.

IN ADDITION TO YOUR DAILY SUPPLEMENTS, PAGE xxiv, TAKE

- Zinc: 50 mg. daily.

- *Ginkgo biloba:* one 40-mg. capsule or tablet daily for up to six months. If you've seen no results by then, discontinue.

IN ADDITION: Try yohimbine—a natural extract available only by prescription. Take three 5.4-mg. tablets daily of the generic form (it's cheaper than the brand names) daily for about two months. If no results, discontinue.

If other efforts have failed, ask your doctor about a vacuum constrictor device or VCD, a mechanical aid that can be of help and/or penile injections.

•   •   •

INDIGESTION

WE ALL KNOW what indigestion is—sort of. It's like heartburn, only different. Actually, indigestion refers to any disturbance of the upper part of the gastrointestinal tract, which includes the esophagus, stomach, and gallbladder. Heartburn is one of the usual symptoms of indigestion. Gas, bloating, and belching are also common symptoms.

If you suffer from indigestion after eating or drinking too much or as a result of stress, you need to investigate the various possibilities. Here are the most common causes of indigestion and where you can find more information about each:

Candidiasis, page 61
Food Allergy, page 146
Gallbladder Disease, page 154
H. Pylori, page 164
Heartburn, page 173

Hiatal Hernia and Esophagitis,
   page 186
Lactose Intolerance, page 231
Ulcers, page 335

Most people who suffer from chronic indigestion have been to doctors and have been tested for various conditions. If this describes you, and if you have read about the above ailments and still can't find the cause of your indigestion, there are two other possible causes that are not widely known:

Deficiency of hydrochloric acid
Deficiency of pancreatic enzymes

If you suffer from deficiency of hydrochloric acid or lack of gastric acid secretion, you may experience:

- bloating, belching, burning, and flatulence right after eating
- diarrhea or constipation
- a feeling of overfullness after eating
- food allergies
- nausea caused by nutritional supplements

Over half of people over the age of sixty suffer from low gastric acidity. If you've consulted your doctor about indigestion, taken antacids, and tried the prescription drug Tagamet and there has been no improvement or in fact you have felt worse, your problem could stem from a lack of hydrochloric acid. A physician can use a diagnostic test to confirm this problem, but there is also a simple test you can perform at home. Take a tablespoon of apple cider vinegar or lemon juice when you are experiencing indigestion. If this eliminates your symptoms, then you may be deficient in stomach acid. If it makes your symptoms worse, you have an overproduction of stomach acid. If the vinegar helps, you can take it with meals or you can take hydrochloric acid (HCL) supplements (these often contain pepsin), which you can buy at health food stores. Please note that hiatal hernia, gastritis, and duodenal ulcer are caused by overproduction of stomach acid, and HCL supplements can make these conditions worse. Therefore, it's important to rule out hyperacidity before treating yourself with HCL supplements.

Other people suffer from a lack of pancreatic enzymes. The pancreas produces enzymes that are essential to the digestion and absorption of food. The enzymes include lipases that digest fat, proteases that digest proteins, and amylases that digest starch. I've noticed that patients with low blood sugar are more prone to a problem with pancreatic enzymes. This may be because both insulin, which controls blood sugar, and the pancreatic enzymes are produced by the same organ, the pancreas. If the pancreas is out of whack, low blood sugar and lack of enzymes could result.

A lack of pancreatic enzymes will lead to trouble when you ingest fatty foods: You may experience bloating or belching an hour after a fatty meal, or your may have a feeling of fullness.

If you lack pancreatic enzymes, there are supplements that can help. Preparations of pancreatic enzymes isolated from animal sources are used with other enzymes including bromelain, which comes from pineapple, to aid digestion. These supplements are available at health food stores.

NATURAL PRESCRIPTION FOR INDIGESTION

- Rule out all the disorders listed above, including cardiac trouble, as possible causes.

- If the discomfort is caused by lack of gastric acid secretion as determined by the self-test recommended above, take hydrochloric acid (HCL) supplements. *Please note you should never take hydrochloric acid at the same time as aspirin, Butazolidin, Indocin, Motrin, or any other antiinflammatory medications. If you experience stomach irritation, discontinue.*

  Begin treatment by taking one hydrochloric acid capsule (10 grains) at your next large meal. At every large meal after that take one more capsule. For example, one capsule at your next meal, two at the meal after that, three at the meal after that, and so on. Continue until you reach five capsules or until you feel your digestion has improved, whichever comes first. When you've discovered the dose you need, continue to take it with meals. You can reduce the number of capsules you take when the meals are small.

  Your stomach may regain the ability to manufacture stomach acid. If this happens, you can reduce the number of capsules taken.

- If your indigestion stems from a lack of pancreatic enzymes, you should take pancreatic enzymes and bromelain, available at health food stores. Take two to four tablets of pancreatic enzymes with meals—"8X USP" is the type to look for. Take bromelain in doses of 250 to 500 mg. with meals.

•   •   •

INSOMNIA

MANY PEOPLE HAVE experienced insomnia at some point in their lives. Sometimes it's because of that late cup or two of coffee. Sometimes it's because of a job interview the next morning. And sometimes you just can't figure out why you're having trouble getting to sleep. If insomnia, an inability to fall asleep and stay asleep, troubles you occasionally, you can usually identify the cause and avoid it. But some people suffer so regularly with insomnia that it interferes with their normal functioning.

I believe that one of the real dangers of insomnia is not the ailment itself—most people can perform better than they think with less sleep and eventually the body will catch up. The real problem is with the traditional treatment: sleeping pills. Most sleeping pills are miraculously effective—at first. And then, after several weeks, their effectiveness diminishes. Too often people take one or two extra pills to recapture the deep sleep they enjoyed when they began the medication. Before they know it, they're taking far too many, reducing any hope they have of getting a good night's sleep without them.

Sleeping pills interfere with normal sleep. They often increase nightly wakings. They interfere with deep sleep and they continue to interfere with normal sleep for up to five weeks after they've been discontinued. So, unless you're experiencing a temporary, unusual situation and your doctor agrees that a few nights of pill-induced sleep won't harm you, don't even think about getting into the sleeping pill habit. Instead rely on the natural treatments I've outlined here; many of my patients have enjoyed success.

I've found insomniacs are divided into two groups: those who can't fall asleep and those who can't stay asleep. Sometimes the causes for the two patterns are the same. People who can't fall asleep at night often are simply too wired. They have a lot on their minds and their thoughts are racing. Perhaps they do work or get involved in a challenging project before bedtime or even exercise too strenuously late in the evening. They can be suffering from stress and tension, but they can also be ingesting too much sugar and sweets, alcohol, or caffeine, or perhaps they smoke —all stimulants.

The solution for this group of insomniacs is to limit these stimulants at bedtime. They must develop good sleep habits, which I'll discuss in a minute. And they should adopt an exercise program if they don't have one, being careful not to exercise an hour or so before bedtime.

The second group is people who wake in the middle of the night and can't get back to sleep. They often have problems with low blood sugar, drink alcohol in the evening, consume caffeine late at night, overeat, or suffer from depression.

A common cause of insomnia that many patients fail to identify as the source of their problem is caffeine. Some people aren't aware of how much caffeine they consume. I had one patient who drank roughly six cups of coffee a day—mostly at the office—and drank two or three cans of (caffeinated) cola in the afternoon. She was exhausted at the end of the day and fell soundly asleep at bedtime but regularly woke in the middle of the night and couldn't get back to sleep. When she cut down her caffeine to one cup a day and eliminated sodas and diet sodas, her problem disappeared. If you have any problem with insomnia, keep track of exactly how much caffeine you consume. A cup of coffee or tea may be okay, unless you're unusually sensitive to caffeine, but anything more than that should be eliminated. Don't be surprised if you have withdrawal symptoms when cutting down—caffeine is an addictive substance. But within a week you should be back to normal and sleeping well. See Blueprint for Health, page xvii, for information on eliminating caffeine.

There are any number of medications that can cause sleepless nights. Many cold remedies that contain phenylpropanolamine (PPA), some blood pressure medications, appetite suppressants, Inderal and other beta blockers, and Dilantin for the prevention of seizures can all cause insomnia. Check with your doctor to see if any medications you are taking could interfere with your sleep. Or check the label on the medicine itself. Obviously, if the drug is causing insomnia, you should discuss it with your doctor.

Many of my patients who wake in the middle of the night suffer from low blood sugar. One man would have dinner each evening with his family at about six-thirty, followed by dessert or sweets later that evening. He would go to bed at 11:00 P.M. and fall soundly asleep, but at 3:00 A.M. he would be wide awake. He ate his dinner so early that his blood sugar fell as the evening went on and, by the middle of the night, he would wake up. He solved this problem by having a light snack before bed, a piece of fruit or crackers. If you have some fatigue in the morning and also are tired and irritable at about four in the afternoon, you could have a blood-sugar problem that affects your sleep, and a snack should help. For more information on low blood sugar, see Hypoglycemia, page 202.

You should know that insomnia is closely associated with depression. Indeed, about half of all cases of insomnia have some psychological cause. If you have had major surgery, have had a major life change like a divorce, death of a loved one, job loss, or recent move, or if you are simply worried about your tax return, you could develop insomnia. If your problem is a major one, you should seek help (see Depression, page 105), but you can still find that the techniques I'll outline can help.

If none of the above is your problem, then it could be that you don't have good sleep habits. Sleep really is a habit, and it's important to set up a pattern that you follow each night to settle your body and mind. It's amazing how many people will sit down at 10 P.M. to catch up on paperwork, pay bills, or figure out their taxes, and then be surprised when they don't readily fall asleep an hour later. I advise patients who have trouble with insomnia to avoid any demanding work for two hours before bedtime. Read a novel, watch television, listen to music, or simply arrange your clothes for the next day.

It might seem obvious, but some people are unaware that a nap in midafternoon will probably make it harder for them to sleep at night. Elderly people often have a problem with this. I had a patient who would come home from work exhausted—she was a primary school teacher—and would often take a nap for about forty-five minutes in the early afternoon. She then found that she had trouble sleeping at night. The nap also seemed to set up her body to demand naps every afternoon: She said that even on weekends, she felt the desire to nap. When she began taking a half-hour walk after school instead of a nap, she found that her sleep became restful and satisfying. No matter how tired you may feel during the day—unless you're sick or have experienced some major disruption of your schedule—don't nap.

One of the most important habits for good sleep is going to bed at the same time every night. Many people who stay up very late one night are surprised to find that the following night, when they thought they'd sleep like a baby, they have insomnia. One of my women patients had this problem at the beginning of every week. She had a mild case of insomnia on Monday and Tuesday nights. It turned out that she stayed up very late on Friday and Saturday nights and sometimes Sunday night as well, and she slept as late as she possibly could on the following mornings. When Monday evening came she was exhausted and fell asleep early but always woke up during the night and had trouble getting back to sleep. When she regulated her hours—getting to bed earlier and getting up earlier on the weekend—the problem disappeared.

One remedy for insomnia that has proved extremely helpful in the past is an amino acid supplement called L-tryptophan. You may have heard about it a few years ago when people using it became ill. It was revealed that a batch of the supplement was contaminated and the problem had nothing to do with toxicity of tryptophan itself. I believe that tryptophan will one day become available again, but until it does you can rely on naturally occurring tryptophan in foods like milk and turkey and tuna fish. The time-honored glass of warm milk before bed really does induce sleep because it's rich in tryptophan, and it's worth a try if you have a problem.

I've had great success with some of my insomniac patients when they take a calcium supplement at bedtime.

There's an herb—valerian—that has been used for years as a sedative, and some of my patients have had success with it. Valerian depresses the central nervous system and relaxes smooth muscle tissue. It's available in natural food stores as a nutritional supplement.

There is another herb that when made into a tea can be helpful in inducing sleep. Passionflower, which is a sedative and an analgesic, is available in natural food stores in various forms.

In addition to taking herbs and supplements and eliminating the sources of bedtime stimulation, there is one more important thing that you can do to encourage restful nights, and that's exercise. While it's not a good idea to exercise in the evening as it can be too stimulating, exercise at any other time of the day will help defuse tension and relax your body so that sleep will come more easily at night. Daytime walks can serve this function, as can any other mild regular exercise.

Exercise helps to reduce tension, but some insomniacs need a more specific program of relaxation. There are a number of theories about how best to induce relaxation. You can buy tapes on self-hypnosis, and many books are available on relaxation techniques. Many of these methods are a variation on the simple time-honored trick of counting sheep. One technique that helps my patients is to imagine lying on a warm beach and breathing in and out slowly in time to the rhythm of the waves. You can also think about breathing in through your fingertips, following the path of the breath up into your shoulders, down into your lungs, through your legs and feet, and out your toes. If you concentrate on images like these, you'll find that your muscles relax, and you'll begin to feel pleasantly warm and drowsy. Herbert Benson's *Relaxation Response* has excellent detailed information on how to develop these techniques.

Natural Prescription for Insomnia

- Check your medications. Some common medications can cause insomnia.

- Do not overeat at dinner; avoid late meals.

- Eliminate caffeine, Including all caffeinated beverages—don't forget colas and other soft drinks—as well as chocolate. You can try one caffeinated beverage in the morning but nothing more.

- Stop smoking or at least don't have a cigarette within a few hours of bedtime as it's a stimulant.

- Avoid stimulation at bedtime, including any work or reading that is likely to produce anxiety.

- Don't take naps even if you're tired at a certain point in the day. Try to exercise at this time instead.

- Develop regular sleep habits, going to bed and getting up at virtually the same time every day.

- Until and unless the natural supplement L-tryptophan comes onto the market again, rely on natural sources including turkey and tuna or a glass of milk before bed.

- Try the herb valerian: two capsules one hour before bedtime.

- Take a cup of passionflower tea before bedtime.

- Get regular daily exercise, avoiding exercise close to bedtime.

- Try relaxation techniques at bedtime.

IN ADDITION TO YOUR DAILY SUPPLEMENTS, PAGE xxiv, TAKE

- Calcium: 1,200 mg. at bedtime.

IN ADDITION: Another supplement that can be helpful in promoting sleep is melatonin. The latest research is encouraging. Some researchers have found it to be as effective as tryptophan in promoting sleep. As it's without side effects and safe, you might give it a try. It's available in 2-mg. capsules; take one a night for two weeks. If no results, discontinue.

• • •

IRRITABLE BOWEL

IRRITABLE BOWEL SYNDROME, also known as spastic colon or nervous indigestion, is a common and frustrating problem. In simple terms, IBS is a condition in which the large intestine fails to function as it should. Normally, regular muscular contractions of the large intestine move waste from the small intestine to the rectum, at which point it's evacuated. But when IBS is present, excessive muscular contractions of the large intestine result in cramping and diarrhea, and the lack of contractions results in constipation and cramping. The range of symptoms associated with IBS includes abdominal pain and distension; frequent painful bowel movements; diarrhea; constipation; excess mucus in the colon; flatulence; and depression.

IBS is so common that gastroenterologists report that nearly half the patients they see suffer from it. Most sufferers are women, but that may be because women are more likely than men to seek medical help. Some estimates conclude that roughly 15 percent of the population suffers from IBS. You should know that IBS is not dangerous or life-threatening, though it certainly can range from troublesome to debilitating depending on its severity.

The diagnosis of IBS will have to be made by a doctor because the symptoms can also indicate a number of other intestinal disorders including colitis, Crohn's disease, diverticulitis, food sensitivity, parasitic infection (protozoa disease), and cancer. (If you think you might have IBS, you should read the following sections in addition to this one, as these conditions are sometimes associated with IBS: Lactose Intolerance, Diverticular Disease, Candidiasis, and Celiac Disease. Identifying IBS is usually a process of elimination once a complete history has been taken. Its cause varies. Though some doctors will prescribe antispasmodic drugs, this will give relief only to some people. I think it's far preferable to work with dietary changes before taking drugs: In many cases natural measures will give great relief.

One of the first steps in controlling IBS is to increase dietary fiber. At one time, the medical community believed that too much fiber *caused* IBS, but we now know this isn't the case. You can increase dietary fiber by eating more fruits and vegetables. Psyllium fiber is also a good way to increase fiber when taken as a daily supplement. Increase your consumption of fiber, particularly fiber supplements, gradually so as not to cause too much gas and bloating. Additional fiber in the diet will not only help people with constipation, but can be helpful for those who suffer from diarrhea.

IBS is often associated with food sensitivities. One study of two hundred patients found that roughly half of them were sensitive to one or more foods, and when they avoided these foods, their symptoms were alleviated. Other studies have demonstrated that approximately one third of people with IBS are sensitive to certain foods. The most common problematic foods include dairy foods and grains. Because most people with IBS suffer from a food *sensitivity* rather than a true allergy, many food allergy tests are inconclusive. The best way to learn if a food sensitivity is causing your IBS is to go on an allergy-elimination diet for a week. This is further described in Food Allergy, page 146. Keep in mind the pulse test mentioned in that chapter, as a rise in pulse can indicate a food that causing a reaction. It's important for patients with IBS to keep a food diary both to record the elimination diet described in Food Allergy and also to help pinpoint other causes of IBS including stressful events and hormonal changes associated with menstruation.

Dairy products are often the cause of IBS symptoms; therefore, I recommend that all patients who may have IBS eliminate them for a week or two to see if that has any effect. For more information on this see Lactose Intolerance, page 231.

In addition to identifying food sensitivities and eliminating dairy products, it's important to cut down or eliminate gas-producing foods to which people with IBS seem particularly vulnerable. This means avoiding beans, cabbage, Brussels sprouts, broccoli, cauliflower, and onions.

Fatty foods can stimulate excessive muscle contractions and are therefore best avoided. Cut out all fried foods, cream sauces, cheeses, butter and margarines, and most red meat.

Caffeine, because of its bowel-stimulating properties, can also cause trouble. I suggest that patients completely eliminate caffeine from their diet and that includes coffee, tea, caffeinated soft drinks, and over-the-counter drugs containing caffeine.

For some people artificial sweeteners, particularly sorbitol, can create digestive problems. Some people who claim they don't use artificial sweeteners do use sugar-free gum. I've had patients who chewed two or three packs a day of this kind of gum and had digestive problems to show for it. If you use artificial sweeteners, completely eliminate them for one week: If your symptoms are better you should cut them out permanently; if you see no change then it's probably okay for you to use them.

Nicotine, like caffeine, can cause bowel disturbances. If you smoke, it could be affecting your symptoms and you really should quit. But remember that nicotine gum, while it may help you break the addiction of cigarettes, will not relieve your IBS symptoms because of the nicotine content of the gum.

While we don't know precisely what causes IBS, we do know that the yeast *Candida*, always present in the intestinal tract, can exacerbate IBS when overgrown. For more information on this, see Candidiasis, page 61. If indicated, I tell some of my patients with IBS to make every effort to eliminate candida from their systems.

Many studies have pointed to psychological disturbances as playing a role in IBS. Some studies have shown that people with IBS have higher levels of anxiety than normal and also a greater tendency to depression. But other studies have pointed out that these patients were assessed *after* the development of the disorder. IBS can be such a troubling and disruptive syndrome, it should come as no surprise that people who suffer from it would find that their mental health suffers. I think it is critically important for people with IBS to work on controlling stress and to short-circuit any tendency to anxiety or depression as a part of their overall program.

If you have IBS you need to adopt two strategies: you need to use specific stress-reducing techniques as described in Stress Control, page 314, and an exercise program. Some of my patients have started aerobic walking. Just a half hour four or five times a week will go a long way not only in controlling stress but also in reducing symptoms. In addition to aerobic exercise like walking, there are exercises that can help relieve bowel contractions. Bent-knee sit-ups, which bend the colon back and forth, can encourage normal intestinal contractions and can thus help regulate the bowel.

Peppermint oil, a natural substance commonly used in Europe, has been shown to be helpful in relieving intestinal contractions as well as gas. In order for the oil to work it must reach the colon. You need to buy it in enteric-coated capsules, which you should be able to find at a health food store. The coating will prevent the oil from being absorbed until it's needed in the large intestine and colon. If, after taking the capsules, you feel a burning in the rectum when you move your bowels it's because some of the menthol in the oil hasn't been absorbed. This is not dangerous, merely uncomfortable, and an indication that you need to reduce your consumption of the capsules.

Ginger's ability to relieve gastrointestinal upset can be helpful in reducing the symptoms of IBS. Some patients have had great results with ginger capsules while others have not, but it's certainly worth a try.

NATURAL PRESCRIPTION FOR IRRITABLE BOWEL

- Diagnosis of IBS must be made by a doctor. If you suspect you suffer from it, you should read about Lactose Intolerance (page 231), Celiac Disease (page 73), Protozoa Disease (page 287), and Candidiasis (page 61), to see if your symptoms could be connected with these problems.
- Investigate the possibility of food allergies or food sensitivities as the cause of your symptoms. Read Food Allergy, page 146, and try an elimination diet.
- Try eliminating dairy products from your diet for a week (see Lactose Intolerance, page 231).
- Increase your fiber intake by eating more fresh fruits and vegetables and whole grains.
- Take a psyllium fiber supplement daily. Take one teaspoon in water once a day, and every three to four days increase this amount by another teaspoon in another glass of water until you reach four teaspoons in four glasses of water daily.
- Avoid wheat bran as a fiber supplement; many people have reactions to wheat.
- Cut down or eliminate gas-producing foods including beans, cabbage, Brussels sprouts, broccoli, cauliflower, and onions.
- Cut out all fried foods, cream sauces, cheeses, butter and margarines, and most red meat.

- Eliminate caffeine from your diet including coffee, tea, caffeinated soft drinks, and over-the-counter drugs that contain caffeine.

- Eliminate artificial sweeteners, including sorbitol, from your diet for a week to see if it alleviates your symptoms.

- Eliminate nicotine in the form of cigarettes or nicotine gum.

- Use stress-reducing techniques as described in Stress Control, page 314.

- Adopt an exercise program and/or walk for a half hour four to five times a week.

- Do bent-knee sit-ups to exercise the colon and relieve spasms.

- Take two to three enteric-coated peppermint oil capsules between meals. If you notice burning in the rectum when you move your bowels, reduce your dosage.

• • •

JET LAG

ALMOST EVERYBODY who has flown has experienced jet lag. It's that "out-of-sync" feeling you have when you cross one or more time zones. You're tired, you're irritable, you're hungry at the wrong times, you can't get to sleep at the right times. Many people believe that jet lag means they need to catch up on their sleep. In fact, jet lag is the result of the disruption of more than one hundred different bodily functions including those that govern hormone levels, body temperature, heart rate, and others.

When you appreciate how intimately your regular bodily functions are tied to a clock, you can see that an abrupt change would take a major adjustment and would require something more than just extra sleep. For example, it can take up to twelve days for normal body temperature patterns to readjust after a westerly flight that crosses six time zones. Reaction times after the same trip can take six days to return to normal. For reasons no one understands, it's more difficult to adjust to time changes following an eastward trip than a westward one.

There is no way to avoid jet lag unless you do what Lyndon Johnson did when traveling the world as president: He stayed on his own home time for the duration of his visit. But there are a number of ways you can mitigate the effects of jet lag and speed your recovery.

The best way to avoid jet lag is to make sure that you establish regular sleeping habits before your trip. If you have no regular bedtime, establish one: It's much harder to adjust to a time change if you don't have a regular schedule at home. For at least two days before your trip, get to bed early—fifteen minutes to a half hour before your regular bedtime.

It's easier on your system to fly during the day, if at all possible. The ideal scenario is to arrive at your destination in the early evening, go for a stroll, have a light dinner, and get to bed by 11 P.M. local time.

Drink plenty of fluids on the flight. Pressurized airplane cabins are terribly dry, and you'll be better able to combat jet lag if you're well hydrated.

Don't drink alcohol on the flight. For one thing, it's a diuretic and will exacerbate the problem of the dry airplane cabin. Moreover, alcohol combined with a high altitude will greatly increase your fatigue: Two or three drinks consumed in a cabin that's pressurized to 5,000 feet have the effect of three or four drinks at sea level.

When you get to your destination, avoid napping. If you can't see straight and must nap, limit your sleep to one hour. Longer naps will delay your adjustment.

If it's sunny, get out and enjoy it. The sun signals the body that you're in an active phase and will help you adjust to the different time.

One patient of mine swears by exercise. She claims that by sticking to her workout routine, she bounces back from jet lag much more quickly than she used to. Just fifteen or twenty minutes can make a big difference, and it can help you get to sleep at the appropriate time.

There's a fascinating diet called the Anti-Jet-Lag Diet, which was developed by Dr. Charles Ehret at the Argonne National Laboratory. The military has used this diet to prevent jet lag in troops moving around the world, and I've heard many reports of its remarkable effectiveness. Here it is:

1. Determine your breakfast time at your destination on the day of arrival.

2. *Feast-fast-feast-fast* on home time: Start three days before departure day.

On day one, *feast:* Eat heartily, with a high-protein breakfast and lunch and a high-carbohydrate dinner. No coffee except between 3 and 5 P.M.

On day two, *fast:* Eat light meals of salads, light soups, fruits, and juices. Again, no coffee except between 3 and 5 P.M.

On day three, *feast* again.

On day four, departure day, *fast.* If you drink caffeinated beverages, take them in the morning when traveling west or between 6 and 11 P.M. when traveling east. Going west, you may fast only half the day.

3. Drink no alcohol on the plane. Sleep until the normal breakfast time at destination but *no later.* Break your final fast at destination breakfast time. *Feast* on a high-protein breakfast. Stay awake, active. Continue the day's meals according to mealtimes at destination.

In general: *Feast* on high-protein breakfasts and lunches to stimulate the body's active cycle. Suitable meals include steak, eggs, hamburgers, high-protein cereals, green beans, and the like.

Feast on high-carbohydrate suppers to stimulate sleep. They include spaghetti and other pastas (no meatballs or meat sauces), crepes (no meat filling), potatoes, other starchy vegetables, and sweet desserts.

Fast days deplete the liver's store of carbohydrates and prepare the body's clock for resetting. Suitable foods include fruit, light soups, broths, skimpy salads, unbuttered toast, half pieces of bread. Keep calories and carbohydrates to a minimum.

NATURAL PRESCRIPTION FOR JET LAG

- Establish a regular routine, including regular bedtime and rising time, at least two days before your trip.

- Get at least fifteen minutes extra sleep for two nights before your trip.

- If possible, fly during the day instead of at night.

- Drink lots of fluids on the flight.

- Don't drink alcohol on the flight.

- Don't nap when you reach your destination; try to stay up until what would be a slightly early local bedtime. If you must nap, limit your sleep to one hour.

- If possible, get out into the sun when you arrive.

- Exercise. Maintain your regular routine, or if you don't have one, do simple calisthenics in your room, or better yet, walk for an hour, exploring your destination.

- Try the Anti-Jet-Lag Diet.

IN ADDITION: There is some interesting recent research on a hormone, melatonin, that shows it can be extremely useful for fighting jet lag. In one study involving seventeen people who used melatonin prior to a flight west to east across the United States and across the Atlantic, no one was affected by jet lag. They took one capsule at bedtime for three nights preceding their flight and one capsule on the travel day two hours before sleep and for the next three days before sleep. I suggest you take 2 mg. at bedtime a week before travel and every night on your trip. It's most effective for eastward travel.

•   •   •

KIDNEY STONES

FEW AILMENTS ARE as painful as kidney stones. The pain is caused by the passing of the stone as it blocks the flow of urine and causes stretching of the ureters and the kidney pelvis. The kidney pelvis is like a funnel that directs urine into the ureters, the tubes that lead to the bladder. Typically, the pain of a kidney stone starts at the flank, and then moves to the front and down toward the groin. It may take weeks or even months for a stone to pass, with the pain coming in intense periodic waves. Many stones pass by themselves. When there are complications or the pain is too intense, a nonsurgical procedure, like ultrasound, which shatters the stones, can be used.

The most serious complication of kidney stones is infection caused by the blocked flow of urine. Chills, nausea, and a high fever are all signs of infection, an emergency that requires immediate medical attention. Even when no infection is present, your doctor may prescribe medication to help manage the pain, and may order a urinalysis and x-rays to support the diagnosis.

Kidney stones are very common in the United States, and one out of every four people is expected to suffer from them in his or her lifetime. Once you have kidney stones, the odds are you'll form them again and again every two or three years—a bleak prospect of repeated pain and possible infection. There are drugs available to improve the odds, but they are not without side effects, and most people don't relish the thought of being on daily medication for the rest of their lives. Fortunately, the most effective way to discourage kidney stones is a simple modification of your diet.

Kidney stones develop when calcium oxalate, or uric acid, in the urine are present in such high concentrations that they form crystals. You can prevent kidney stones by dietary modifications and increasing fluid intake. The goal is to dilute concentrations so that crystals no longer form.

To begin, increase your fluid intake. Eight glasses of water a day is recommended, but keep in mind that is only an average. Your weight may require a greater liquid intake, as can heat or exertion that makes you sweat. An interesting study showed that Israeli soldiers in the desert, who were prone to kidney stones, decreased crystal formation in direct proportion to their increase of fluids. You should drink enough liquids to produce two to three quarts of urine each day.

Eat a low-protein diet, while increasing the amount of vegetables and fiber. Limit your protein to 3 ounces at both lunch and dinner. Protein increases the levels of uric acid and calcium in the urine, both of which can form stones. The incidence of kidney stones is highest in countries where people eat diets high in animal protein. Vegetarians rarely have kidney stones. Don't eat large meals late at night, as they tend to promote crystal-forming concentrations. Also, avoid sugar and salt, caffeine and alcohol, all of which increase the amount of calcium in the urine.

As high levels of vitamin C can be involved in the creation of stones, I suggest that you limit your daily vitamin C intake to under 2,000 mg.

Magnesium has been found to be very important in the prevention of stone formation. Eat foods rich in magnesium, such as barley, bran, corn, buckwheat, rye, oats, brown rice, potatoes, and bananas.

Additional diet modifications and supplements depend on your specific kidney stone, as determined by chemical analysis. Here are the common conditions and the modifications you should make connected with them:

HYPERCALCIURIA occurs when there is too much calcium in the urine but a normal amount in the blood. You may be ingesting too much calcium, either through supplements (for example, Tums or other antacids), or through stomach acid medications, or even your drinking water. But calcium is very important, so you can't restrict it entirely. Reduce your calcium intake to the minimum required amount, which is about 600 to 1,000 mg. daily. (See calcium table in Osteoporosis, page 264.)

Remember that mineral waters can contain calcium. The bubbles in naturally carbonated water come from dissolved limestone high in calcium. It's best to avoid mineral or naturally carbonated waters entirely if you're prone to kidney stones.

As sodium can contribute to excess calcium excretion, it's best to follow a low-salt diet.

Avoid coffee, which increases the amount of calcium in the urine.

Add rice bran to your diet. Rice bran contains phytin, which binds to calcium in the intestine and reduces urinary calcium in the process. A study in Japan showed that patients given 10 g. of rice bran twice a day after meals had a decided decline in the formation of kidney stones.

HYPEROXALURIA occurs when there is too much oxalate in the urine. Avoid foods high in oxalate, which include tea, chocolate, spinach, beans, instant coffee, peanuts, parsley, and rhubarb. Take a supplement of vitamin B_6, 50 mg. daily.

HYPERURICOSURIA occurs when there is too much uric acid in the urine. This condition is associated with too much protein in the diet. In addition to limiting your protein, take a supplement of potassium of 100 mg. daily. Also avoid foods high in uric acid as listed in Gout, page 161.

NATURAL PRESCRIPTION FOR KIDNEY STONES

- Drink a minimum of eight glasses of liquid a day.

- Don't eat large meals late at night.

- Keep vitamin C supplementation below 2,000 mg. daily.

- Avoid naturally carbonated and mineral waters; their calcium content can be high.

- Eat foods that are rich in magnesium such as barley, bran, corn, buckwheat, rye, oats, brown rice, potatoes, and bananas.

- Reduce animal protein in the diet to 3 ounces at lunch and 3 ounces at dinner.

- Reduce foods rich in calcium such as milk and cheese.

- Cut back on salt, sugar, caffeine, and alcohol.

- Eat lots of fruits and vegetables.

- Determine the type of stone formation you suffer from (hypercalciuria, hyperoxaluria, or hyperuricosuria) by means of a chemical analysis and see text for more details concerning natural remedies for your particular problem.

IN ADDITION TO YOUR DAILY SUPPLEMENTS, PAGE xxiv, TAKE

- Magnesium: 400 mg. daily.

- Vitamin B_6: 50 mg. daily.

- Potassium: 100 mg. daily.

•　•　•

LACTOSE INTOLERANCE

LACTOSE INTOLERANCE, which is the inability to properly digest milk and milk products, can cause symptoms ranging from mild abdominal discomfort to flatulence, bloating, stomachache, and diarrhea. Many people who suffer from these symptoms never learn what's causing them. I've had any number of patients who were surprised to learn that they were lactose intolerant and were delighted when a few simple measures ended their symptoms.

Lactose, the name of the carbohydrate in milk, is digested with the help of an enzyme called lactase. Almost all babies have lactase in their digestive system. Shortly after being weaned, however, many people start producing less and less lactase. Nearly 70 percent of all adults are lactase deficient. Only people of Western European descent tend to maintain high levels of lactase through life. This does not mean that all lactase-deficient people will develop symptoms from drinking one glass of milk or eating a cheese pizza, because the natural bacteria in their intestines will process lactose when the lactase enzyme is missing. It's only when people consume too much lactose for the natural bacteria to handle (or when the natural bacteria have been destroyed by antibiotics, which kill the "good" bacteria along with the "bad") that they develop gas, cramps, and diarrhea.

Here's how one of my patients discovered she suffered from lactose intolerance. Because of a dental problem, Mary was on antibiotics for a while, and she noticed that her regular breakfast of oat bran cereal seemed to be causing gas and bloating. Mary is very health-conscious, and she guessed that the natural bacteria in her system had been killed by the antibiotics so she took acidophilus to replenish the missing organisms. The acidophilus relieved the symptoms, but even after she discontinued the antibiotics her digestion didn't return to normal. Mary described these symptoms to me and I realized that her problem was being caused by more than just an antibiotic reaction. Suspecting that lactose intolerance played a role in her digestive problems, she gave up all dairy products for a week and her symptoms were completely relieved.

Unfortunately, many people with lactose intolerance don't realize that is what they have. They feel bloated and uncomfortable, and may have terrible cramps and diarrhea. They may have gone to a succession of doctors and gotten very little help, because the symptoms of lactose intolerance mimic those of irritable bowel or spastic colon. There is a test for lactose intolerance, which consists of ingesting a large amount of lactose and then checking the blood to determine how much sugar was absorbed. But the test is not necessary for most people. If you have gas, bloating, or flatulence here's my simple recommendation: Try giving up all milk products for two weeks. Watch out for hidden sources of milk, such as cream sauces or salad dressings. Unfortunately, lactose is frequently used as a filler in many pharmaceutical preparations, both those available by prescription and over-the-counter. Check the labels for lactose, or, in the case of prescription medication, ask your doctor or pharmacist to rule out the presence of lactose in the drug.

If the symptoms clear up, your problem was probably due to lactose intolerance and you should limit your intake of milk and dairy products. You can experiment with various milk products such as cheese or yogurt to determine your tolerance level and see if some milk and dairy foods can be reintroduced into your diet. Remember, not all foods have the same levels of lactose. Milk, for example, has a lot; cream cheese has a little; ice cream is in the moderate range. Try one food at a time, and wait two or three days to see if the symptoms reappear. If not, go on to the next food, and so on.

Some people with lactase deficiency can drink as much as a glass of milk or its lactose equivalent (9 to 14 g.) without side effects, and most dairy products contain less lactose than a glass of milk. Hard cheese, for instance, contains just 1 g. of lactose for a 1½-ounce serving, and two tablespoons of sour cream contain 1 g. Yogurt, while high in lactose (5 to 19 g.), is easier to digest than milk, because the bacteria that turn milk into yogurt digest some of the lactose as the milk is fermented and stored, and continue to digest it once it's in your small intestine. But frozen yogurt doesn't act the same way, because most of the bacteria are destroyed in the freezing process.

While some people can tolerate certain amounts of lactose, others are unable to tolerate any, and just a little Parmesan cheese sprinkled on pasta will give them gas and bloating. Everybody's sensitivity is different and you'll learn by trial and error exactly how much your own body can tolerate. The chart shows how much lactose is in a variety of common foods.

LACTOSE CONTENT OF COMMON DAIRY FOODS

(The amounts shown for lactose vary because ingredients in products can vary, affecting the lactose content.)

PRODUCT	LACTOSE IN GRAMS
Whey, dry (1 oz.)	19–21
Milk, acidophilus skim (1 cup)	11
Yogurt, whole milk (1 cup)	10–12
Milk, whole (1 cup)	9–14
Buttermilk (1 cup)	9–12
Ice Milk (³/₄ cup)	8
Yogurt, lowfat (1 cup)	5–19
Velveeta cheese (1¹/₂ oz.)	4
Ice Cream (³/₄ cup)	3–8
Orange sherbet (³/₄ cup)	1–2
Half and Half, cream, or sour cream (2 Tbs.)	1
Most hard cheeses (1¹/₂ oz.)	1
American cheese, pasteurized processed (1¹/₂ oz.)	0–6
Ricotta cheese (¹/₂ cup)	0–6
Cottage cheese, creamed (¹/₂ cup)	0–4
Cream cheese (1¹/₂ oz.)	0–1
Butter or margarine (1 Tbs.)	0

While experimenting with your tolerance level, you can try a lactose-reduced milk such as Lactaid, or take lactase in capsules along with the milk. Acidophilus capsules, which contain lactic acid bacteria similar to those used for fermenting yogurt, will also relieve the symptoms by supplementing the natural bacteria in your intestines.

If you decide to stay away from all milk products, be sure you are getting enough calcium by eating foods such as sardines, salmon, tofu, broccoli, and kale. In addition, take a calcium supplement each day.

NATURAL PRESCRIPTION FOR LACTOSE INTOLERANCE

- Reduce your consumption of milk and milk products.

- Try yogurt or lactose-reduced milk, but avoid acidophilus milk (which is not lactose-free).

- Try acidophilus capsules; three capsules daily.

- Try lactase capsules as directed on package.

- If you reduce your milk intake because of lactose intolerance, you should be careful to take calcium supplements. Monitor how much calcium you get from other sources (salmon, sardines, tofu, broccoli) and then take supplements to equal about 1,200 mg. calcium daily.

• • •

LEG CRAMPS

EVERYONE EXPERIENCES muscle cramps from time to time. Perhaps your neck gets cramped after a day at your desk or you get a leg cramp after exercise when you've been sedentary for a long time. Some women get leg cramps after wearing high heels. The solution to most of these common cramps is to stretch the muscles regularly, and, in the case of high heels, avoid them.

There is another, more troubling kind of cramp that my patients often ask about: nocturnal leg cramps. Just as you've fallen into a deep, comfortable sleep, you're wakened by a severe and painful cramping of your calf muscle. Most people leap out of bed and hop around on the affected leg until the cramp goes away. But occasionally it returns. Sometimes the cramp is in the thigh; sometimes in the foot. In any case, it's annoying and painful.

The first thing to check if you have leg cramps is your prescription drugs. Some can cause cramping; your doctor can tell you the side effects of your medication. Diuretics taken for high blood pressure or heart disorders, for example, can cause an imbalance of your potassium and magnesium levels. A blood test can tell you if this is a problem, and if it is, supplements of the appropriate mineral will alleviate the symptoms.

The most common cause of nocturnal leg cramps is calcium deficiency. If you are postmenopausal, trying to lose weight, or don't consume enough calcium, you are vulnerable to developing leg cramps. It's quite alarming to realize the extent of calcium deficiency in our population, particularly among women. While leg cramps are just an annoyance, another result of calcium deficiency—osteoporosis—is a crippling disease that can be prevented. To relieve leg cramps and prevent the long-term problems associated with calcium deficiency, begin now to increase your calcium consumption. If you're avoiding fat, try nonfat yogurt and skim milk. In addition, I've had great success with patients who complain of leg cramps by advising them to take a calcium supplement at bedtime.

Pregnant women are sometimes vulnerable to leg cramps, which usually occur with the changes in their calcium metabolism. Calcium supplements can help. Taking calcium daily should give relief. Please check with your obstetrician before beginning the supplement and check to see what amount of calcium, if any, there is an any pregnancy vitamin you may be taking.

Another help for nocturnal leg cramps is vitamin E. In one study of 125 patients with nocturnal leg and foot cramps, all but 2 had complete or nearly complete relief from their symptoms when they took vitamin E supplements. In most cases, the symptoms returned when the supplements were discontinued.

If neither calcium nor vitamin E gives you relief, you may benefit from magnesium, potassium, or vitamin A.

Because as it has been shown that sugar and caffeine reduce the absorption of vitamins and minerals, particularly calcium, I advise patients with cramping problems to eliminate as much sugar and caffeine from their diets as possible.

NATURAL PRESCRIPTION FOR LEG CRAMPS

- Eliminate as much sugar and caffeine as possible from the diet.

IN ADDITION TO YOUR DAILY SUPPLEMENTS, PAGE xxiv, TAKE

- Calcium: 1,200 mg. at bedtime. If no results, you can discontinue but be sure that you are getting 1,200 mg. of calcium daily through diet and/or other supplements. For pregnant women: Check with your doctor before beginning supplementation.

- Vitamin E: 400 I.U. twice a day after meals for two weeks. If symptoms are relieved, cut down to 400 I.U. once a day. If symptoms recur, up the dosage until symptoms are relieved but never take more than 1,200 I.U. daily.

- Magnesium: 400 mg. daily.

- Vitamin A: 10,000 I.U. daily.

- Potassium: 100 mg. daily.

• • •

MACULAR DEGENERATION

I GET MORE CALLS about macular degeneration on my radio show than almost any other ailment. At the same time, many people have never heard of it. I suppose it's one of those ailments you're unaware of until it strikes you or someone you know. This is a shame, because it's also one of those ailments that can be prevented, or at least slowed, through good nutrition and the regular use of supplements.

Macular degeneration is the degeneration of the macula, which is the part of the retina that provides sharp central vision. Unlike glaucoma, which causes loss of peripheral vision in its beginning stages, macular degeneration causes loss of central vision at the start. As it progresses, it can cause blindness. In fact, macular degeneration is the second major cause of blindness in the United States.

Macular degeneration is primarily a disease of aging. People with high blood pressure, diabetes, and cardiovascular disease are at higher risk than others for developing it (see Hypertension, page 194; Diabetes, page 111; and Atherosclerosis, page 31). Macular degeneration occurs because the tiny blood vessels that surround the eye become broken or impaired. The macula is then deprived of blood and oxygen. The patient begins to see a black spot in the middle of his field of vision. While peripheral vision may be unaffected for some time, ultimately blindness may result.

This is a frustrating disease to treat. I always want to say to patients, "I wish you would have come to see me before you developed this condition." That's because I believe that you can help prevent macular degeneration with good nutrition and supplements, but once the macula has begun to degenerate, you can't revitalize it. There's no real cure for the disorder, but it can be slowed with the use of natural remedies.

The latest research points to free-radical damage as the major cause of macular degeneration and the natural treatment is geared to increasing antioxidants, particularly vitamins C and E, which fight free radicals. Increase the fresh fruits and vegetables in your diet. This will increase the amounts of vitamins C and E—the known antioxidants. Supplements of vitamin C and vitamin E have proven to be helpful as well.

Supplements of beta-carotene—the antioxidant that the body turns into vitamin A—will help to repair the damage that the free radicals inflict.

Another nutrient that will help slow the development of macular degeneration is zinc. In one study patients who ranged in age from forty-two to eighty-nine years were given zinc supplements and showed significant improvement in the acuity of their vision following treatment.

In addition to nutritional supplements there is another botanical medicine that has been shown to offer great promise in halting the progress of macular degeneration. For reasons unknown, its effects seem to be much more specific for the function of the eye than the other supplements mentioned above. The botanical is called *Ginkgo biloba,* and it's available at health food stores.

NATURAL PRESCRIPTION FOR MACULAR DEGENERATION

- Increase the amount of fresh fruits and vegetables in the diet.

IN ADDITION TO YOUR DAILY SUPPLEMENTS, PAGE xxiv, TAKE

- Vitamin C: 1,000 mg. daily.

- Vitamin E: 400 I.U. daily.

- Beta-carotene: 25,000 I.U. daily.

- Zinc: 50 mg. daily.

- *Ginkgo biloba:* 40 mg. three times daily.

IN ADDITION: There is now a procedure—krypton laser treatment—in which a point of light aimed at the vessels in the eye stops the bleeding and prevents or at least retards blindness. This treatment is not suitable for everyone, but you might want to discuss it with your doctor.

•   •   •

MEMORY LOSS

ONE OF THE MOST tiresome joke genres is the forgetfulness of middle-aged and elderly people. With all the press that Alzheimer's disease has gotten in recent years, this humor has taken on an anxious edge as people begin to wonder if their forgetfulness regarding the whereabouts of their glasses and the name of the friend they just ran into is an early warning sign of Alzheimer's.

People really do begin to lose some of their short-term memory as they age. There are various speculations as to why this is so. Some research has indicated that women who are undergoing menopause may be more likely to experience forgetfulness as their bodies adjust to reduced supplies of estrogen. Blood pressure medicine, antihistamines, or even diet pills can compromise memory. Alcohol can affect memory, too.

How can you strengthen your memory? If your memory loss isn't due to medication or alcohol consumption, there are any number of books that suggest methods for improving a faulty memory. These books can be helpful for many people, but there are also ways of improving your memory through nutrition. I don't mean to claim that a vitamin will improve your memory, but it is true that a less than adequate nutritional intake can compromise your memory. If you are troubled by memory loss, read the section on Alzheimer's disease (page 7). And I'll repeat here the nutrients that you should be taking to help memory function at maximum levels.

The natural herb *Ginkgo biloba* has helped many of my patients with their memory and concentration. In fact, it's one of my favorite recommendations because it works so well.

NATURAL PRESCRIPTION FOR MEMORY LOSS

IN ADDITION TO YOUR DAILY SUPPLEMENTS, PAGE xxiv, TAKE

- *Ginkgo biloba:* 40 mg. three to four times daily.
- Choline: 650 mg. three times daily.
- Vitamin C: 1,000 mg. daily.
- Vitamin E: 400 I.U. daily.
- Beta-carotene: 10,000 I.U. daily.
- Selenium: 50 mcg. daily.
- Vitamin B_{12}: 1,000 mcg. daily dissolved under the tongue.
- Zinc: 50 mg. daily.

• • •

MENIERE'S SYNDROME

MENIERE'S SYNDROME is a perplexing problem that usually has no known cause. It usually appears in attacks that are characterized by ringing in the ears, extreme dizziness, hearing loss, a sense of pressure in the ears, and sometimes nausea and vomiting. Attacks can come and go and their severity can vary, but sometimes they can become so frequent and so intense that the victim is virtually incapacitated.

It's always frustrating to deal with a syndrome for which there is no known cause: You just don't know precisely what you're trying to change to bring about a cure and you're left with treating the symptoms. But there is some good news: Recent research indicates that there's a connection between blood-sugar levels and Meniere's syndrome. One study found that 42 percent of patients with Meniere's syndrome showed evidence of hypoglycemia in the course of a five-hour glucose tolerance test. This is compared with only 15 percent of patients with other diseases.

Some doctors have been recommending high-protein, low refined-carbohydrate diets for people with the syndrome because they've found that their patients have high insulin levels, insulin being the hormone that controls blood sugar. We now speculate that it's not only the high insulin levels that are causing the problem but also the impaired circulation that occurs as a result of the high insulin levels combined with other factors such as overweight, poor diet, smoking, drinking, and high cholesterol levels.

The best way to control blood sugar is to adjust your diet: Eat a low refined-carbohydrate diet, adequate protein, regular meals at regular times, and, most important, avoid sugar. Eating sugar in the form of candy, cakes, cookies, ice cream, and dried fruits will initially boost your blood sugar and then cause it to fall precipitously. This is a cycle that is hard to break unless you avoid sugar entirely. (See Hypoglycemia, page 202.)

Another factor in controlling blood sugar is maintaining a proper weight. If you're overweight, diet. I know this is easier said than done, but it's important if you want to be able to control your blood-sugar levels.

A nutritional aid to controlling blood sugar is the mineral chromium. I have been using chromium for years with patients who need help regulating blood-sugar levels, and it's been very effective. I suggest that patients take the trivalent form of chromium.

Alcohol, smoking, and caffeine can send blood-sugar levels soaring, only to subsequently crash. If you want to maintain a stable blood-sugar level, it's important that you avoid alcohol, quit smoking, and cut down on your caffeine intake. I don't think it's essential to completely eliminate caffeine; one cup of coffee or tea a day is not going to be a problem. But if you habitually drink caffeine throughout the day you need to cut way down. (See Hypoglycemia, page 202.)

If efforts at controlling insulin levels are not helping your symptoms, consider food allergies, which can cause symptoms that mimic Meniere's syndrome (see Food Allergy, page 146).

NATURAL PRESCRIPTION FOR MENIERE'S SYNDROME

- Follow a low refined-carbohydrate diet (with an emphasis on complex carbohydrates including whole grains, fresh vegetables, and so on) with adequate protein, being sure to eat regular meals at regular times.

- Eliminate sugar from your diet. This includes candy, ice cream, cakes, cookies, frozen yogurt, sodas, diet sodas, honey, chocolate, and dried fruit.

- If you are overweight, lose weight.

- Take 100 mcg. of the trivalent form of chromium three times a day before meals.

- Eliminate alcohol, smoking, and caffeine (except for an optional single cup of coffee or tea daily) from your life.

- See Hypoglycemia, page 202, for more information on controlling blood sugar.

- Check for hidden food allergies to be sure that they're not what's causing your symptoms (see Food Allergy, page 146).

IN ADDITION: Recent studies have shown that, in addition to your daily basic vitamin/mineral supplements, the following have been helpful: fish oils (1,000 mg. three times daily) and ginkgo biloba (40 mg. three times daily).

• • •

MENOPAUSE

THERE IS A GREAT deal of confusion about menopause these days. I guess it's better than the ignorance of years ago, but it's still troublesome for the woman who's trying to make sense of what this inevitable marker in her life will mean. Menopause used to be a virtual mystery; before the 1900s most women died around the age of fifty, a few years before the average onset of menopause. As women lived longer, there were doctors who denied that menopause was anything but a psychological problem. Tranquilizers were thought to be the solution. Today, most women are familiar with the well-known symptoms of menopause: hot flashes, headaches, sleep disturbances, and changes in sexual function and desire. But there are other, long-term results of menopause that are the source of today's controversy. At the heart of the controversy is whether menopause and its physical changes should be viewed as a natural event to be endured (or simply ignored by the many women who experience few symptoms), or whether it is an evolutionary mistake that can be corrected by the use of drugs.

Menopause, which usually occurs around the age of fifty, is, like puberty, a dramatic change in a woman's body. At menopause, the ovaries, which have been releasing eggs since puberty, shut down and stop producing the hormone estrogen. (If a woman has had her ovaries removed surgically, she will experience menopause immediately due to the reduction in estrogen, no matter what her age.) Menopause does not happen overnight; for most women the process will play out over one to five years with gradually diminishing menstrual periods. During this time the amount of estrogen decreases, and it's this decrease in estrogen that causes the typical symptoms of menopause.

The first sign of menopause for most women is irregular periods. The cycle may shorten or lengthen; the menstrual flow may increase or decrease. A woman can be fertile even if she's been without a period for a year. After a woman experiences irregular periods for a year to five years, menstruation will stop. A year to a year and a half before a woman's periods end, she may experience hot flashes, during which her temperature will rise and fall as much as 9 degrees. These flashes may be accompanied by sweating, heart palpitations, nausea, and, not surprisingly, anxiety. Hot flashes can contribute to insomnia; some women complain of waking frequently and having to change damp bedclothes. And some women also notice irritability, headaches, short-term memory loss, lack of sexual desire, and inability to concentrate. Some of these symptoms are not due to estrogen loss, but are simply a result of hot flashes and lack of adequate sleep.

When you realize that more than three hundred types of tissues throughout the body have receptors for estrogen—which is to say that they're affected in some way by the hormone—it's not surprising that its decrease would cause physical changes. Estrogen affects the genital organs (vagina, vulva, and uterus), the urinary organs (bladder and urethra), breasts, skin, hair, mucous membranes, bones, heart and blood vessels, pelvic muscles, and the brain. It's the loss of estrogen to these organs that causes the ultimate changes of menopause, including dry skin and hair, incontinence and susceptibility to urinary tract infections, vaginal dryness, and, most important, the diseases osteoporosis and heart disease. These diseases are at the center of the controversy concerning menopause: Because estrogen plays a role in preventing these diseases, should you replace the estrogen lost at the time of menopause with a synthetic version?

Before exploring this question, I just want to mention that not all women suffer the symptoms and diseases mentioned above. Many women sail through menopause with minimal discomfort. A few women never have a hot flash, some experience one or two hot flashes a month, and others have several an hour. Just as some women experience debilitating symptoms of PMS while others are symptom-free in relation to their menstrual cycle, so it is with menopause. Don't *expect* to have symptoms; you may be one of the lucky ones who have none at all.

Estrogen replacement therapy, or ERT, and whether or not to take it, is an option that women facing menopause will have to consider carefully. You should not rely on anyone, including your doctor, to make this decision for you. There are too many variables that affect your best course of action, and you alone can decide. Here are some of the factors to consider:

BENEFITS

- Prevents osteoporosis
- Prevents heart attacks and strokes
- Prevents hot flashes
- Improves energy and mood
- Eliminates insomnia

- Prevents vaginal atrophy
- Prevents weakening of pelvic muscles

RISKS

- Possible increase of endometrial cancer
- Possible increased risk of breast cancer
- Blood clots or hypertension
- Gallstones
- PMS-type symptoms including breast pain and tenderness
- Frequent medical monitoring involving increased costs and potential for surgical procedures

Reviewing these benefits and risks will help you decide on the wisdom of ERT for you. For example, if you have a family history of breast cancer or endometrial cancer, these factors argue against ERT in your case. But a strong family history of osteoporosis might incline you toward ERT. All of the facts concerning your background should be weighed and discussed with your doctor.

Remember that the decision concerning ERT need not be forever. Some women take ERT for a year or two or three to get them through a highly symptomatic time of their menopause and then discontinue it.

Whatever you decide concerning ERT, there are natural means you can employ to minimize the discomforts of menopause.

Hot flashes are, for some women, the most troublesome symptom of menopause. They cause insomnia, resulting in irritability, and they can be uncomfortable and embarrassing. In my experience with my patients, drops in blood sugar can be the single most common precipitating cause of hot flashes; once the blood sugar is controlled, the incidence of hot flashes diminishes. In fact, by following the suggestions outlined in Hypoglycemia (page 202), particularly eliminating sugar, reducing caffeine, eating meals at regular times, eating protein at lunch and dinner, and taking the supplement chromium, many women have told me that their hot flashes were dramatically relieved.

There are foods that can reduce menopausal symptoms. These foods, including soy flour, tofu, and other soy foods as well as linseed oil, contain substances called phyto-estrogens that can help compensate for the body's loss of estrogen at menopause. Interestingly, in some societies, half of the dietary intake includes foods that contain phyto-estrogens; our typical diet contains less than 10 percent. In one study of healthy menopausal women who increased their intake of soy products or soy-containing foods for a period of six weeks, significant improvement was seen in the results of vaginal smears following the increased phyto-estrogen consumption.

The mineral boron has also proved helpful for my patients. Boron naturally elevates estrogen levels, and I originally recommended it to help fight osteoporosis. Many women told me that it had an immediate beneficial effect on their hot flashes.

Vitamin E has been helpful for many women who suffer from hot flashes, and sometimes when supplemented with vitamin C, it completely eliminates the symptom. Vitamin E is also useful because it decreases the tendency of blood platelets to clump together in menopausal women, which can contribute to heart attacks and strokes.

Many women complain of anxiety, irritability, and depression during menopause. As I've mentioned, these symptoms can be exacerbated by loss of sleep. Calcium supplementation generally has worked for all my patients, including menopausal patients, in helping them get to sleep and stay asleep. The mineral magnesium can also be helpful in relieving these symptoms.

Osteoporosis, which should be a concern for all women, becomes a pressing issue during menopause, when the estrogen supply diminishes and promotes increased bone loss. The most critical steps to take are to increase your calcium intake, in the form of foods and supplements, and to exercise. For more information, see Osteoporosis, page 264.

Heart disease also becomes a threat. Prior to menopause, estrogen plays a protective role in relation to heart disease, but as estrogen production diminishes, the risk of heart disease increases. Ten years after menopause, a woman has nearly the same risk as a man of dying of heart disease. The major cause of this increased risk is a rise in the LDL ("bad") cholesterol and a lowering of the protective HDL cholesterol resulting in vulnerability to atherosclerosis. In addition, the lack of estrogen causes the blood vessels to become less flexible, so blood clots can form more readily. Improved diet, exercise, and the use of supplements can all be helpful in preventing heart disease. For more detailed information, see Atherosclerosis, page 31.

There is also an herb that can be helpful in relieving menopausal symptoms including hot flashes and depression. Dong quai (*Angelica sinensis*) has been proven to affect estrogen activity, and many women find it beneficial.

One of the most critical steps you can take to reduce the symptoms of menopause is to exercise. Countless studies have demonstrated that regular exercise can benefit menopausal women by fighting depression and anxiety, strengthening bone mass and lessening the risk of osteoporosis, reducing the risk of atherosclerosis, and improving one's overall quality of life. I strongly recommend that all menopausal women adopt an exercise program.

Many women find that walking is a form of exercise that they can fit into their lifestyle easily and do on a year-round basis. There are a number of excellent books available on walking programs that will inspire you. Of course other forms of exercise such as swimming, aerobic classes, cycling, and dance are good choices, too. But exercise must be done regularly if it's to be of benefit. I suggest that you exercise for a half hour five times a week.

One last note: In addition to the myriad problems associated with cigarettes, smoking encourages an early menopause. Women who smoke experience menopause four to five years earlier than women who do not smoke. Smoking also increases your risk of many of the symptoms of menopause, including osteoporosis and heart disease.

NATURAL PRESCRIPTION FOR MENOPAUSE

- Discuss the advisability of estrogen replacement therapy with your doctor. See text for a full discussion of this.

- Control blood-sugar levels in an effort to reduce hot flashes. See Hypoglycemia, page 202.

- Increase your intake of soy-containing foods, including tofu and soy flour, as well as linseed oil (which is available in capsule form in health food stores) in the amount of 500 mg. three times daily.

- Reduce your risk of developing osteoporosis. See Osteoporosis, page 264.

- Reduce your risk of heart disease. See Atherosclerosis, page 31.

- Adopt a program of regular exercise—at least 30 minutes, five times a week.

IN ADDITION TO YOUR DAILY SUPPLEMENTS, PAGE xxiv, TAKE

- Boron: 2 mg. daily.

- Calcium: 1,200 mg. daily in the form of calcium citrate.

- Magnesium: 400 mg. daily.

- Vitamin E: 400 to 600 I.U. daily.

- Chromium: 100 mcg. three times daily.

- Dong quai, a Chinese herb available in health food stores. Take according to the package directions.

• • •

MIGRAINE HEADACHES

IF YOU SUFFER from migraine headaches, you know how truly debilitating they can be. My migraine patients tell tales of being out of commission for days at a time, often when they can least afford to be. Most people know if their headaches are everyday tension headaches or migraines, but if you're unsure read Tension Headaches, page 325. There are typical symptoms of migraines that help identify them. If you experience at least three of the following, your headaches are probably migraines:

- You've had more than one attack.

- Only one side of the head is affected.

- You experience an "aura" of flashing lights, blind spots, or a feeling of irritability or depression immediately before the headache.

- You experience stomach distress possibly with nausea and vomiting along with the headache.

- Someone in your immediate family also suffers from migraines.

Natural approaches can help; unfortunately, once a migraine starts you may have to rely on drugs for pain relief. But there are ways of avoiding migraines once you learn some of their causes.

Migraine headaches usually come at intervals, with complete freedom from pain between attacks. They can last anywhere from a few hours to a few days. The pain is severe and can be incapacitating. For many people, the headache is preceded by feelings of depression and irritability, as well as increased sensitivity to light and noise. A classic migraine is preceded by a characteristic "aura," during which the person feels light-headed, has a reduced field of vision, and may see flashing lights. The headaches usually starts on one side of the head, (the word *migraine* is derived from the Greek for "half a skull") and is accompanied by nausea, abdominal discomfort, and sometimes vomiting.

Nearly 20 percent of all women and 10 percent of all men suffer from migraines, and most of them have a family history of the disorder. Some people may have daily attacks, others one every several months. The intensity and duration of the attacks may vary from one time to another. Though the symptoms vary, migraines always involve an abnormal constriction and swelling of the blood vessels in the head—constriction in the early warning phase, swelling concurrent with the pain.

Inherited instability of the vascular system is one of the causes of migraine. Migraine patients are more prone to fainting when standing up suddenly than other people, and they are also more sensitive than other people to the vasodilatory effects of physical and chemical agents. Blood platelet disorder has also been implicated, with the platelets of migraine sufferers aggregating more readily than normal platelets in response to neurotransmitters such as serotonin and adrenaline, the "stress" hormone. The nervous system itself may also be implicated, as it releases specific neurotransmitters, possibly in response to chronic stress.

Medications used to prevent the onset of migraines have had limited success, and, as do all medications, they have harmful side effects when used over the long range. Medications to reduce the pain can be of some help if taken immediately after the migraine starts. Once the headache takes hold and severe nausea sets in, the stomach shuts down, so oral medications can't be properly absorbed. While biofeedback techniques and acupuncture can give relief for some people, I find that my patients have the most success by learning to recognize the triggers that cause migraine headaches and then avoiding those triggers.

Of course everyone is different: what causes your migraines may be completely different from what causes someone else's.

Certain foods contain chemicals—amines—that dilate the blood vessels, causing a rebound vasodilation and may thus precipitate an attack.

The most common foods implicated in migraine attacks as a result of amines include:

avocado	plum	wine
banana	potato	beer
cabbage	tomato	aged or
eggplant	cheese	cured meat
pineapple	canned fish	yeast extract

Other people are sensitive to foods containing MSG, the flavor enhancer, or nitrates, which are commonly found in bacon, hot dogs, and other preserved meats.

Some people are sensitive to artificial sweeteners like Aspartame, which is found in Nutrasweet.

When I give my migraine patients this list of offending foods, they're usually overwhelmed. How can they figure out which of these things could be causing their headaches:? It's not as difficult as it seems, although it does take some diligence. The first step is to keep a headache diary for two to three weeks (or for longer if you don't get migraines frequently). Note not only when you get headaches but also when you eat any of the listed items. Many of my patients will see a migraine pattern that's connected to their eating habits. Obviously, once you identify the causative substance, you must avoid it. One of my patients who drank enormous quantities of diet soda noticed a possible connection between her soda consumption and her headaches. When she eliminated all artificial sweeteners from her diet, her headaches occurred far less frequently.

Many women find that certain stimulants such as alcohol which have no effect on them regularly can trigger an attack if they're consumed just before a menstrual period or at the time of ovulation. If you are a menstruating woman who suffers from migraines, be sure to make note of your menstrual cycle on your headache diary. Check to see if headaches occur just before you begin to menstruate or when you ovulate, and note any triggers during those times. If you are a postmenopausal women on estrogen therapy, you may find that a change in your hormone treatment will help your headaches. Discuss this with your doctor.

While the food triggers listed above are common causes of migraines, there are a host of other foods that can cause migraine symptoms as a result of an allergy or sensitivity. Here is a list of some of the most common allergenic foods connected with migraines (see also Food Allergy, page 146).

apple	goat's milk	soy
beef	grapes	tartrazine
benzoic acid	oats	tea
caffeine	onion	tomato
cane sugar	orange	walnuts
corn	peanuts	wheat
cow's milk	pork	yeast
egg	rice	
fish	rye	

Food is not the only cause of migraines. Low blood sugar caused by fasting or irregular meals often brings on a headache, which, for the average individual, quickly disappears following a meal. But for people prone to migraines, the low blood sugar may start off a chain reaction that a belated meal will not stop. Balanced meals eaten on a regular schedule are a must for those suffering from migraines. Some of my patients find that they must eat something every few hours to prevent headaches. Chromium, as recommended in Hypoglycemia (page 202) can help stabilize the blood sugar.

There's an additional factor that could explain why women suffer from migraines so much more frequently than men. Recent research has pointed to fluctuating levels of estrogen as a factor in their development. For these women, headaches can disappear during pregnancy, when estrogen levels are constant. If you get a headache every month just before your period, it could be because your blood-sugar levels are dropping. Again, chromium can remedy this. Muscle cramping can also contribute to period-related headaches—calcium and evening primrose oil are helpful. Menopause can bring complete relief from headaches, or, for some women, make them worse. Birth control pills affect migraines as well.

Stress, anxiety, and excitement promote the release of hormones and neurotransmitters, which can provoke a migraine attack. While it may be difficult to avoid stress, it can be alleviated through exercise. A doctor at the Neurology Department of the New Mexico School of Medicine reported that several of his patients became migraine-free after jogging 7 to 9 miles a day, at a speed of seven to nine minutes per mile. Of course jogging is not suitable for everyone, but even moderate exercise can relieve tension and stress. I recommend that all my migraine patients adopt a regular exercise program even if it's just a brisk half-hour walk four or five days a week.

Other factors that have been known to precipitate migraines are changes in routine, such as late rising on a holiday or change of working hours; changes in climate, high winds, loud or high-pitched sounds; bright sunlight and bright artificial light, such as fluorescent; and prolonged staring at television, movie, or computer screens.

Identifying the factor responsible for your migraine may be complicated by the fact that there may be more than one. For instance, skipping breakfast may not affect you most days, but it may trigger a headache if you are also tired and under stress. Getting up unusually early may normally be no problem, but if you rise before dawn on the day before your period it may plunge you into a migraine. Keeping a diary of activities, including what and when you eat, is really the best way to pinpoint the causes of your migraines.

An herbal migraine treatment that has long been popular in Europe and is now available here is feverfew. A double-blind study of patients who reported they had been helped by feverfew was performed at the London Migraine Clinic. A test group was given a placebo to determine if their symptoms worsened. They did, increasing in both the frequency and severity of the attack.

Feverfew has some of the same antiinflammatory effects as aspirin, without aspirin's side effects. It must be taken for several weeks before the effects are felt.

One aspirin taken every other day has also been found to reduce the risk of migraine, presumably by preventing the platelets in the blood from clumping together. These bunches of platelets form serotonin, a neurotransmitter that has been linked to migraines. They can also form blood clots that lead to heart attacks, which is why aspirin is helpful in preventing recurrences of heart attacks.

Fish oils (omega-3's) are beginning to be widely recognized for their antiinflammatory properties, and have proven effective for a variety of conditions including migraines.

Magnesium is also helpful as low brain magnesium has been identified as an important factor in the mechanism of a migraine attack.

One last thing: Sometimes people go for long periods thinking that they're suffering from migraine headaches when, in fact, they have chronic sinusitis, which can cause regular painful headaches (see Sinusitis, page 308).

NATURAL PRESCRIPTION FOR MIGRAINE HEADACHES

- Try to identify the cause of your migraine by keeping a daily food or activity diary. Especially note foods listed here as possible triggers of migraine headaches. You may be sensitive to a chemical in a food or you may have a food allergy that triggers your headaches. See if you can establish a pattern between something you ate or some unusual activity that caused your headache (see also Food Allergy, page 146).

- Other migraine causes include changes in routine, such as late rising on a holiday or change of working hours; changes in climate, high winds, loud or high-pitched sounds; bright sunlight or bright artificial light; and prolonged staring at television, movie, or computer screens. Keep these in mind when you compile your diary.

- If you are a woman, pay particular attention to the hormonal fluctuations of your menstrual cycle to see if your migraines are connected to changing estrogen levels. Headaches caused by low blood sugar can be helped by chromium—100 mcg. of the trivalent form three times daily (see PMS, page 276, and Hypoglycemia, page 202).

  Headaches caused by muscle cramping can be helped by evening primrose oil and calcium. The dose for evening primrose oil is four 500-mg. capsules in the morning and four 500-mg. capsules in the evening for five cycles; if no improvement, discontinue; for calcium, 1,200 mg. at bedtime.

- If you are postmenopausal and on estrogen replacement therapy, your medication could be a factor in your migraines. Discuss this with your doctor.

- Eat regular meals at regular times to avoid low blood sugar. Never skip meals (see Hypoglycemia, page 202).

- Keep stress under control with stress-reducing techniques (page 314).
- Adopt a regular exercise program.

IN ADDITION TO YOUR DAILY SUPPLEMENTS, PAGE xxiv, TAKE

- One aspirin every other day.
- The herb feverfew: 150 mg. twice a day or as directed on package.
- Fish oils: 1,000 mg. three times a day.
- Magnesium: 250 mg. twice daily.

IN ADDITION: Sumatriptan, a medication used widely in Europe, has recently been approved for use in the United States. It is self-injected to help stop a migraine headache. Consult with your physician to determine if this may be helpful to you.

• • •

MITRAL VALVE PROLAPSE

MITRAL VALVE PROLAPSE is generally considered a benign heart valve abnormality, although some authorities hold that because it is so common it is merely a normal variant in heart structure. The mitral valve controls the blood flow in the heart between the left atrium and the left ventricle. In a person with mitral valve prolapse, the valve billows back toward the atrium each time the ventricle contracts. This billowing is often accompanied by a leaking of blood across the valve. For most people this leaking is minimal, but for others it could be harmful or even life-threatening, particularly if the leak is substantial.

Mitral valve prolapse is actually a common condition: One study found that 17 percent of the young women studied had evidence of prolapse. No one is certain why more women today seem to have this condition; this same study found that only 1 percent of the female population over the age of eighty has a prolapse, despite the fact that the abnormality does not change with age; it is permanent. Interestingly, it seems to be most common in young women of slender build who have long fingers and a relatively shallow chest from front to back.

I want to emphasize that *you cannot diagnose your own mitral valve pro-*

lapse nor can you treat it on your own. Symptoms that can accompany the abnormality include chest pain (which can last for a few hours or a few days and is not brought on by exertion,) palpitations, headaches, weakness, anxiety, and panic attacks, but in the majority of cases, mitral valve prolapse does not cause symptoms at all. A doctor would suspect a mitral valve prolapse if a murmur and/or click is heard. An echocardiogram is then done. The doctor who interprets the echocardiogram will recommend a course of treatment if necessary. The most common recommendation to people with mitral valve prolapse is to take preventive antibiotics when undergoing surgery or a dental procedure that could involve bleeding, therefore allowing an infection to develop in the valve. An infected wound would also require antibiotics for the same reason. If you have a mitral valve prolapse, it should be checked periodically, as the valve is subjected to the deterioration brought on by more than three billion contractions (which is the average for a lifetime).

If you do have mitral valve prolapse, there are natural means you can take that may help prevent damage to the heart.

Coenzyme Q10 (which the FDA is threatening to make unavailable) can be very helpful for people with MVP as well as people with other heart conditions. In fact, in one study it was found that 50 to 75 percent of people who showed evidence of heart disease had a coenzyme Q10 deficiency. CoQ10 increases exercise tolerance and in general strengthens the heart.

Magnesium is an important supplement for people with mitral valve prolapse. It is useful for people with palpitations, as it helps to regulate the heartbeat.

Most of my patients with MVP think that they're suffering from symptoms of that condition while in fact they're suffering from low blood sugar. I'm not saying that there's a connection between MVP and low blood sugar; only that sometimes people mistake the symptoms of one for the other. For more information on low blood sugar, see Hypoglycemia, page 202.

Stress control is important for people with MVP. Sometimes, people become so alarmed by their diagnosis (without reason, I might add) that they begin to have panic attacks and palpitations. Be sure that you get adequate exercise to help control stress and that you are familiar with stress-reduction techniques such as progressive relaxation (see Stress Control, page 314).

NATURAL PRESCRIPTION FOR MITRAL VALVE PROLAPSE

- Your MVP will have been identified by a doctor who will recommend appropriate treatment.
- Be sure that any symptoms you have are not a result of low blood sugar.
- Adopt a regular exercise program to reduce stress, and learn stress-reducing techniques.

IN ADDITION TO YOUR DAILY SUPPLEMENTS, PAGE xxiv, TAKE

- Coenzyme Q10: 30 mg. three times daily.
- Magnesium: 400 mg. daily.

• • •

MORNING SICKNESS

MANY OF MY pregnant patients who are seeing me about other problems complain about nausea. There are a few natural therapies that can give a great deal of relief.

Many women experience some degree of nausea during early pregnancy. Some have symptoms only when they wake in the morning (thus the term "morning sickness"), but others suffer all day long. Fortunately the symptoms usually disappear by the end of the first trimester. But when you're suffering from a bad case of nausea, two months can seem a lifetime to wait for relief.

Severe nausea and vomiting, by the way, should not be ignored. If you can't keep any food down for more than three days, see your doctor.

Three simple remedies can help the nausea of pregnancy.

The first thing to try, and the approach that's helped many of my patients, is taking B_6 supplements. Many recent studies have shown that B_6 has been effective in relieving nausea and vomiting in the early stages of pregnancy. Please note that B_6 supplementation can affect nursing, so I don't recommend taking it after the first three months of pregnancy.

Another approach that's helped some of my patients is taking ginger supplements. People have long relied on ginger for upset stomachs; it's also useful for seasickness. It's particularly appealing to pregnant women because it has none of the side effects that drug treatment can have. You can get ginger capsules at health food stores.

There are acupressure points on the wrist that are called "neiguan." Located on the inside of the wrist, about three finger-widths toward the elbow, they can be used in preventing nausea. If you apply constant firm pressure to these points, you can relieve feelings of nausea. Some people find this technique more effective than others, and it's certainly worth a try. You can buy "seasickness straps," elastic wristbands that have little bumps that press on the correct points and can be worn at any time. They're available at marine supply stores and some pharmacies and health food stores.

There are a few things you can do in relation to diet that can give relief. Avoid greasy foods—they're hard to digest and can cause digestive upset. Try to keep your stomach full—an empty stomach in the morning and late afternoon can make symptoms worse. Have frequent protein snacks, as protein takes longer to digest. Keep some crackers at your bedside for a snack in the morning before you get out of bed.

NATURAL PRESCRIPTION FOR MORNING SICKNESS

- Avoid greasy foods.
- Have frequent protein snacks.
- Keep your stomach full.
- Apply pressure to the acupressure points on the wrist. Measure three finger-widths up the inside of the wrist from the crease and press for several minutes or purchase a seasickness band from a marine supply store.

IN ADDITION TO YOUR DAILY SUPPLEMENTS, PAGE xxiv, TAKE

- 50 mg. of vitamin B$_6$ daily for seven days. If no relief, discontinue. In any event, discontinue after the first three months of pregnancy, as B$_6$ can later cause difficulty in nursing.
- Ginger capsules: 250 mg. three times daily.

MOTION SICKNESS

MOTION SICKNESS is surely one of the worst feelings in the world. First you feel weak, then you get dizzy, then nauseated, then you throw up. Some children get motion sick virtually ever time they go for a car ride. Some adults experience motion sickness for the first time when they go on that luxurious cruise—and spend the first three days confined to their cabin. Almost anyone can be vulnerable to motion sickness, though some people are more vulnerable than others: In one study where just over half of Caucasian and black subjects suffered from motion sickness, virtually all Chinese people got sick.

While motion sickness feels like it begins in your stomach, in fact it begins in your inner ear. Just recently we've learned that it's the disparity between what the eye reports seeing (a stable environment like the cabin of a ship) and what the inner ear knows is happening (the constant moving, rolling, and pitching of a moving ship) that causes the problem. The body reacts to this stress with an overproduction of hormones that eventually precipitates the dizziness, sleepiness, fatigue, headaches, and nausea of motion sickness.

Fortunately there is a good natural remedy for motion sickness: ginger. Ground gingerroot capsules, which you can find in any health food store, will help prevent motion sickness for most people. In fact, in some tests, ginger was proven more effective than Dramamine and, unlike Dramamine, has no side effects. I tell my patients who are prone to motion sickness or who are going on a sea voyage for the first time to lay in a store of ginger capsules. Take two or three an hour or so before leaving and one or two every three or four hours after that. You can also make a ginger tea by steeping peeled, chopped fresh ginger in boiling water for a few minutes. Iced ginger tea makes a good drink for any boating party.

There are also practical steps to combat motion sickness. For example, because foods that are hard to digest will challenge your stomach regardless of where you are, they are to be avoided when you might be facing motion sickness. Instead, stick with small, low-fat starchy meals before you travel.

Position matters: The more still you are, the better you are able to combat motion sickness. On a ship, stay in the middle where there's less motion. In a car, ride in the front seat where the view helps fight the confusion of the inner ear. Try to get fresh air: On a ship, don't stay below deck; on a plane turn on the vent so the air blows directly on your face.

If you're on a small boat, help with the boat handling if at all possible. People who are active and busy are less likely to develop motion sickness. Most people get sick if they read while in motion, so put off reading until you're back on firm ground.

Stay calm. Worry and anxiety can stimulate the same hormonal reactions that cause nausea. Use stress-reduction techniques to help you relax (see Stress Control, page 314).

Watch out for disagreeable smells or strong odors. I was once on a sailing trip that went well until the captain anchored and pulled out pickled herring and offered it all around. Most of the sailing party lunged for the rail. The same goes for fatty foods which are hard to digest and a challenge for a stomach that's already in trouble.

Try to occupy your mind. Studies have shown that people who are asked to solve tricky problems while in motion experience less motion sickness.

I've heard a great deal about acupressure bands worn on the wrist that press on the "neiguan" acupressure points inside each wrist. There are studies in progress to determine how effective these bands are for seasickness. Some patients swear by them.

NATURAL PRESCRIPTION FOR MOTION SICKNESS

- Eat a small, low-fat starchy meal before you travel. Avoid fatty, greasy foods both before and during travel.
- Try to stay as still as possible; the middle of a ship experiences less motion than forward or aft; in a car, ride in the front. Get fresh air by staying outdoors or using a vent to blow air directly on your face.
- Keep busy but don't read.
- Use stress-reduction techniques (see Stress Control, page 314) to combat anxiety.
- Avoid disagreeable smells or strong odors.
- Keep your mind occupied.

> **IN ADDITION TO YOUR DAILY SUPPLEMENTS, PAGE xxiv, TAKE**
>
> - Two or three ground gingerroot capsules before your journey and additional capsules every three or four hours. Alternatively, drink ginger tea made by steeping peeled, chopped ginger in boiling water.

IN ADDITION: If natural remedies don't help you, you can get a patch from your doctor that's worn behind the ear. It releases scopolamine through the skin into the blood and helps relieve motion sickness. Some people suffer from side effects from this treatment.

• • •

MULTIPLE SCLEROSIS

MULTIPLE SCLEROSIS, or MS, is a chronic, slowly progressing disease of the brain, the spinal cord, and the optic nerves. About 250,000 Americans are diagnosed with MS annually, with women being affected slightly more often than men. In about two thirds of patients, the disease begins between the ages of twenty and forty. The most common initial symptom is the sudden loss of vision in one eye and/or a tingling or feeling of numbness in an arm or leg. Weakness in the limb can cause fumbling or an unsteady gait. Other symptoms include mental changes, slurred speech, and difficulties with bladder control.

Typically, the first symptoms disappear in a few weeks or months. Some people go for years—five, ten, or even more—before having another attack. A few people never have a second attack. The fact that MS can be so erratic in its development is one reason that discovery of a cure has been elusive: If a certain approach works is it because it's really effective or because the patient went into remission? The diagnosis of the disease is usually made after a series of attacks give a high probability of MS. An examination of the spinal fluid helps give a conclusive diagnosis. It's important to remember that not everyone is crippled by the disease. Many people have mild symptoms and lead an essentially normal life.

Anyone who suffers form MS should, of course, be under the care or a neurologist. There is, as yet, no cure, but there are drugs that can help relieve symptoms. There are also natural treatments that are primarily of help in retarding the progression of the disease. No matter what treatment or drug is used in fighting the disease, it is very important for MS patients to adopt a generally healthy lifestyle with an adequate diet, good stress control, and sufficient sleep (see Blueprint for Health, page xvii).

The cause of MS remains a mystery. We know what happens—the myelin sheath that surrounds the nerves is destroyed—but we don't know precisely why. Interestingly, people from higher latitudes are at higher risk for developing the disease: High-risk areas include the northern United States, Canada, Great Britain, Scandinavia, Northern Europe, New Zealand, and Tasmania. The intriguing exception to this geographic distribution is Japan, where MS is rare. The peculiar geographic spread of the disease has led researchers to study environmental factors as contributing to MS. There does also seem to be evidence that diet plays a part. Studies point to a high correlation between a high animal-fat diet and development of the disease.

Viruses have long been studied for their relation to MS. Recent research in Norway proposed a connection between exposure to a virus such as Epstein-Barr at a critical age—between thirteen and twenty—and the development of the disease, the speculation being not that the Epstein-Barr virus causes the disease but that it acts as a trigger. The measles virus has also been implicated in this way.

Lately a great deal of scrutiny has been placed on MS as an autoimmune disease, that is, a disease in which the body does not recognize its own cells and sends out antibodies against them. In MS the speculation is that the antibodies are attacking the myelin that covers the nerve fibers. A recent and exciting discovery seems to confirm the autoimmune connection: Researchers have identified two types of white blood cells that are thought to cause MS by attacking the nerve tissue. Earlier studies with animals demonstrated that a peptide made specifically to react to the white blood cells could block them from attacking the nerve tissue. Studies are under way to determine whether the same process will be effective with humans.

In the meantime, we are left with some natural means that have proven helpful in retarding the progress of the disease. I should mention that all of the suggestions I am about to make have been found to be most effective when started early on in the development of the disease. Someone who has suffered from MS for a long time and is severely symptomatic will probably have less success with natural methods than someone newly diagnosed.

One of the most comprehensive treatments devised for patients with MS was created by Dr. Roy Swank in 1948. Dr. Swank believes that a diet that is low in animal fat can "arrest the disease in a high proportion of cases," as he says. And he has had great success over the years in working with patients on his program. His basic recommendations include:

- Saturated fat intake of no more than 10 g. (about a half ounce) daily.
- A daily intake of 40 to 50 g. of polyunsaturated oils (margarine, shortening, and hydrogenated oils are forbidden).
- A supplement of one teaspoon of cod liver oil daily.
- Normal protein intake of 6 to 10 ounces daily.
- Consumption of fish three or four times weekly.

In addition, Dr. Swank recommends avoiding physical, emotional, and mental strain and fatigue as well as getting plenty of rest. For sixteen years 146 patients followed his program; their attacks were reduced by 95 percent. Dr. Swank points to longer, more fruitful lives for people with MS who follow his program, and he also says that when the treatment is started early, "Ninety to ninety-five percent of the cases remained unchanged or actually improved during the following twenty years." For detailed information on his program, you can refer to his book *The Multiple Sclerosis Diet Book* (Doubleday, 1977). As to why the diet is effective, it seems that three factors come into play. The diet promotes less platelet aggregation, it reduces the autoimmune response, and it normalizes the decreased essential fatty acid levels found in the serum, red blood cells, platelets, and, probably most important, in the spinal fluid in patients with MS.

Some researchers have found a connection between MS and allergies. Dr. Herman Weinreb at New York University Medical Center, who noticed that the changes in the nervous system of patients with MS resembled the changes caused by allergies, worked to eliminate all allergens in an effort to reduce MS attacks. His treatment had positive results, with bedridden patients becoming wheelchair-bound, wheelchair patients becoming ambulatory, and some patients becoming symptom-free. While food allergies are not a cause of MS, if we accept that it is an autoimmune disease it follows that eliminating any allergens, which also stimulate an autoimmune response, would be very helpful. I believe it is useful to review the potential for allergic reactions and to eliminate as much as is possible any allergen sources. For more information, see Food Allergy, page 146, and Hay Fever, page 167.

The connection between MS and allergies may be the reason that the MacDougall treatment is effective for some people. Roger MacDougall was severely affected by MS. Confined to a wheelchair and almost blind, he created a diet and, over the course of years, became virtually free of symptoms. His diet forbids all gluten-containing cereals such as wheat, oats, rye, and barley. (For more information on avoiding gluten-containing foods see Celiac Disease, page 73.) Like Swank, MacDougall recommends severely limiting saturated fats and strictly forbids dairy products including butter, cream, and cheeses. In addition he recommends taking vitamins and minerals including the B complex vitamins as well as vitamins C and E, calcium, magnesium, and zinc.

It appears that treatment with high levels of antioxidants can be helpful. The antioxidants include vitamin C, vitamin E, beta-carotene, and selenium. These antioxidants should be taken every day for the rest of your life.

There have been reports, beginning in the early 1970s, and particularly by Dr. Harold Millar in Belfast, Northern Ireland, that diets high in linoleic acid can be helpful for MS patients. Patients who supplemented their diet with linoleic acid had longer remissions and reduced the severity of their attacks. The best sources for linoleic acid in supplement form include black currant seed oil and borage oil, both available at health food stores. Sunflower seed oil is also rich in linoleic acid and can be used in cooking. Boosting the linoleic content of the diet is most effective when it's done in conjunction with a diet that severely limits the intake of saturated or animal fats.

There is a great deal of evidence that certain trace minerals including calcium, magnesium, selenium (mentioned above as an antioxidant), and zinc can be helpful for MS patients. No one knows why calcium, for example, is helpful for MS patients, but studies have shown that daily supplements of calcium can help relieve symptoms.

NATURAL PRESCRIPTION FOR MULTIPLE SCLEROSIS

- Patients with MS should be under the care and follow the recommendations of a neurologist.

- Reduce the amount of saturated fat in the diet. This includes severely limiting all dairy foods, including whole milk, eggs, and cheese, and meats high in fat such as red meats.

- Increase intake of polyunsaturated oil including vegetable oils, safflower oil, sunflower seeds, pumpkin seeds, wheat germ, wheat germ oil.

- Make every effort to eliminate any allergens from your diet and environment. See Food Allergy, page 146, and Hay Fever, page 167.

IN ADDITION TO YOUR DAILY SUPPLEMENTS, PAGE xxiv, TAKE

- Vitamin C: 1,000 mg. daily.

- Vitamin E: 400 I.U. daily.

- Vitamin B_{12}: one 1,000-mg. tablet dissolved under the tongue daily.

- Beta-carotene: 10,000 I.U. daily.

- Selenium: 100 mcg. daily.

- Zinc: 22.5 mg. daily.

- Calcium: 1,200 mg. daily.

- Magnesium: 400 mg. daily.

- One teaspoon of cod liver oil daily.

- Supplement with linoleic acid. Sources include black currant seed oil and borage oil. Take one 1,000-mg. capsule three times daily.

IN ADDITION: Because we are still uncertain of the precise cause of MS, new theories and treatments are constantly proposed. Though I don't specialize in MS, I have investigated some of these new treatments on behalf of my patients and here are several I think have merit:

- Dr. Hans Neiper in Germany has been working with MS patients for years and has had some remarkable success with his treatment regime that includes supplements such as magnesium, potassium, and special forms of calcium. You can get more information on Dr. Neiper's treatments by contacting HansA Referral, P.O. Box 32, Viroqua, WI 54665 (608) 637-3030.

- There is evidence that injections of colchicine (an antiinflammatory compound extracted from a common herb, meadow saffron) can be effective in relieving symptoms and in promoting general stamina. Oral colchicine can also be used. In a preliminary clinical trial, 75 percent of MS patients who took colchicine improved or stabilized; my patients with MS have had comparable results. While there are side effects including gastrointestinal symptoms, they can usually be managed by altering the dose. As existing drugs for MS can be quite toxic, the use of colchicine is a promising alternative, and patients should be able to take it safely throughout their lives.

- B_{12} injections have been found to be helpful to patients with MS.

- A preliminary study has indicated that injections of myelin protein, extracted from the brains of cows, may be a promising treatment for MS.

- There is a new beta-interferon drug, Betaseron, that is about to be approved by the FDA. While not a cure, it seems to reduce symptoms among some patients.

•   •   •

OSTEOPOROSIS

TOO MANY PEOPLE think of osteoporosis as a relatively minor problem that makes you somewhat more liable to break your arm or leg. There is bad and good news about osteoporosis. The bad news is that nearly half a million older people—particularly women—take a fall each year that lands them in a hospital or nursing home with a broken hip that broke at least in part because of the effects of osteoporosis. Only three in four ever go home again. The others eventually are confined to nursing homes for the rest of their lives. This is a heavy price to pay for a preventable problem.

The good news is that until very recently it was believed that supplements were of no use in preventing bone loss in postmenopausal women. But the latest research shows that supplements can indeed stop bone erosion completely: If you are over the age of fifty-five, you can keep your bones strong by consuming the amount of calcium found in three glasses of milk every day and by taking certain other measures.

Osteoporosis, or loss of bone density, is a crippling affliction of the elderly. It causes older people to lose strength in their bones, to lose inches in height, and to suffer fractures and breaks that can lead to hospitalization and, ultimately, complete lack of mobility. Sometimes the bones become so fragile that a powerful cough breaks a rib, or a slip that should have been a misstep fractures a hip.

Who is vulnerable to osteoporosis? Women are at higher risk than men because they have less bone mass to begin with, and, because of hormonal changes, they lose it faster. But some women are more at risk than others. Women at highest risk include:

Asian women
white women, especially blond or redheaded women of Northern
    European ancestry
postmenopausal women
underweight women
women with small bone structure
heavy alcohol users
heavy caffeine users
smokers
women on a high-protein diet
women with a family history of osteoporosis
women who have experienced menopause before age forty
women who are diabetic
women with thyroid disease
women with asthma or other lung diseases
women who take glucocorticoids (for example, cortisone or predni-
    sone prescribed for rheumatoid arthritis)

If you fit several of these descriptions, you should be all the more vigilant about taking steps to prevent osteoporosis. The key to avoiding it is prevention: Every woman should monitor her calcium intake throughout her life. Beginning in her teens, she should consume at least 1,200 mg. of calcium daily. When she reaches menopause (or if she's nursing), she should increase her intake to 1,500 mg. The reason calcium intake is affected by menopause is that the process of depositing calcium in the bones is very much dependent on the female hormone estrogen, which is diminished after menopause.

I think that one reason osteoporosis has become such a problem today is that the major source of calcium—dairy products—are also high in calories and saturated fat. Many people, particularly women, are avoiding these foods for the sake of weight control and cholesterol. In addition, controversy about the value of calcium supplements has kept women from using them.

When the diet is deficient in calcium, the body "steals" the essential mineral from the bones for other metabolic processes, making them brittle and thin. When a woman is consuming under 500 mg. of calcium a day (half of what her body needs), which describes one quarter of American women, she simply doesn't have enough of the mineral present in her body to carry on normal functions. Every day, her bones are losing a degree of strength and resiliency.

I recommend to all my women patients a daily supplement of calcium in the doses mentioned. It's very important that you take the right kind of calcium. There are a variety of calciums available as supplements including calcium lactate, calcium phosphate, calcium gluconate, and calcium carbonate. All of these calciums have disadvantages, the primary one being that the amount of calcium that the body can absorb from them is small. The best, widely available calcium is calcium citrate. It's very well absorbed, even by people with poor digestion, and it is not particularly expensive. Research has shown it's best absorbed when taken at bedtime. I also suggest that women increase their calcium consumption through their diet. This can mean more nonfat yogurt, skim milk, low-fat cheeses, greens, and sardines with bones. Bok choy and broccoli are among the best vegetable sources of calcium.

SOURCES OF CALCIUM

FOOD	MILLIGRAMS OF CALCIUM
Whole milk, 8 oz.	291
1% milk, protein fortified, 8 oz.	349
Nonfat dry milk, ¼ cup dry	377
Yogurt, plain, low-fat, 8 oz.	414

Yogurt, plain, nonfat, 8 oz.	452
Cheese, cheddar, 1 oz.	204
Cheese, cottage, creamed, 4 oz.	68
Cheese, goat, hard, 1 oz.	254
Cheese, goat, semi-soft, 1 oz.	84
Cheese, feta, 1 oz.	140
Cheese, mozzarella, part skim, 1 oz.	183
Cheese, muenster, 1 oz.	203
Collard greens, frozen, cooked, 1 cup	357
Kale, frozen, cooked, 1 cup	179
Broccoli, cooked, chopped, 1 cup	178
Chard, cooked, chopped, 1 cup	102
Mustard greens, cooked, chopped, 1 cup	150
Spinach, frozen, cooked, 1 cup	278
Calcium-enriched orange juice, 8 oz.	225
Salmon, canned, with bones, 3 oz.	203
Sardines, with bones, 3¼ oz.	351
Oysters, 1 cup	111

Source: U.S. Department of Agriculture

The mineral magnesium, which is involved in calcium metabolism, also plays a crucial role in helping to avoid the development of osteoporosis. One study demonstrated this by supplementing postmenopausal women with half the recommended amount of calcium and twice the recommended amount of magnesium. These women gained bone density at a rate sixteen time greater than women who simply had nutritional counseling with no supplements.

Deficiencies of vitamin D can promote bone loss. Please note that if you're taking a good multiple vitamin, it may well contain 400 I.U. of vitamin D, and in that case there's no need to take more.

In addition, the mineral boron seems to reduce the loss of calcium from the body. In one study boron supplementation significantly reduced the excretion of calcium in postmenopausal women.

Reduced calcium consumption isn't the only factor that affects bone loss. Certain dietary factors actually cause the body to lose calcium. A diet high in protein increases calcium excretion and therefore bone loss. Many people today are restricting their protein intake by eating less meat, and I recommend this. Of course meat isn't the only source: Fish and chicken are also high in protein. The point is to reduce your overall intake. Six ounces per day—the equivalent of a small chicken breast or a small fish fillet—is enough.

Caffeine can also cause calcium loss from the body. If you drink more than one cup of coffee or tea per day, you're ingesting a chemical that's actually acting to leach calcium from your bones. Limit coffee consumption to no more than one caffeinated drink per day. And be sure that any carbonated drinks you consume don't have caffeine as an ingredient.

Alcohol can also leach calcium from your body, so limit your consumption. I believe that to maintain optimum health, it's best to avoid alcohol entirely, but certainly don't have more than two to three drinks per week.

Did you need to know another bad thing about cigarettes? Well, they lower estrogen levels in women, thereby increasing the risk of osteoporosis. Moreover, smokers have been found to have double the risk of hip fractures of nonsmokers.

Excess salt and sugar in the diet have both been linked to depletion of calcium stores.

Exercise is absolutely crucial to prevent bone loss. Whereas lack of exercise can promote the loss of bone density, you can rebuild density by becoming active. Many women think that by taking some calcium supplements they're fighting osteoporosis. Taking the supplements is better than nothing, but exercise will compound the benefits. You don't have to take up windsurfing; a simple program of a half-hour walk every day or even every other day will help tremendously.

NATURAL PRESCRIPTION FOR OSTEOPOROSIS

- Increase foods containing calcium, including nonfat or low-fat dairy products. You can add dry, powdered milk to certain recipes— puddings, meat loafs, muffins, and baked goods—to boost calcium content.

- Reduce your protein intake (limit to 6 ounces daily) and your salt intake (avoid the salt shaker and use sparingly in cooking).

- Eliminate caffeine, sugar, and alcohol from your diet.

- Stop smoking

- Adopt a program of regular exercise.

IN ADDITION TO YOUR DAILY SUPPLEMENTS, PAGE xxiv, TAKE

- Calcium: 1,200 mg. of calcium citrate at bedtime.

- Magnesium: 400 mg. daily.

- Boron: 2 mg. daily.

- A good multiple vitamin that will provide 400 I.U. of vitamin D.

IN ADDITION: There is a new drug that's being used to treat osteoporosis, though it hasn't been approved by the FDA for that purpose (it has been approved to treat another bone disorder). The drug is called Etidronate, and it's taken in conjunction with calcium. If your problem with osteoporosis is severe, discuss this drug with your doctor.

• • •

PARKINSON'S DISEASE

PARKINSON'S DISEASE occurs when an area of the brain known as the substantia nigra is damaged, and can no longer make dopamine, the neurotransmitter that carries movement orders to various parts of the body. Patients in the advanced stages of Parkinson's are stiff, have tremors, and walk with a slow shuffling gait.

There are a number of warning signals for parkinsonism, which I'll list here, but I want to emphasize that Parkinson's disease is not something that you diagnose and treat on your own. If you or a parent or loved one has symptoms that indicate Parkinsonism, it's important that you get a specific medical diagnosis from a qualified doctor—probably a neurologist. In days past it was believed that Parkinson's disease was untreatable and had to run its course, but now there are treatments—drug treatments combined with natural measures—that might help prevent the disease from progressing and greatly increase the quality of life for anyone with Parkinson's. The sooner the disease is identified and treated, the better the prognosis. Here are some warning signals of the development of Parkinson's disease:

- a constant "pill-rolling" motion of the fingers
- a tendency to hold an arm with the elbow bent
- a tendency to turn the foot inward
- difficulty in chewing or swallowing
- stiffness in limbs
- trembling in the limbs only when they're at rest
- masklike expression
- handwriting that becomes smaller than usual

The following symptoms are also associated with Parkinson's disease, although they're also common to other disorders and aren't definitive of Parkinson's:

- easy fatigue
- dizziness when standing
- excessive sweating
- increased consumption of sweet foods
- constipation and frequent urination

Some half a million Americans have Parkinson's, most of them elderly. The disease is not inherited and its precise cause is not known, though all evidence points to a toxic reaction in the brain as the important trigger. The degeneration of the message-sending part of the brain most likely comes either from environmental pollution or medications that accumulate over the years until they reach a toxic level. Some drugs, such as certain ones used for schizophrenia, can cause symptoms that resemble Parkinson's.

Parkinson's is most commonly treated with a chemical called L-dopa, which closely resembles dopamine, the missing neurotransmitter. L-dopa is used in conjunction with other drugs like Sinemet. No matter what the name of the drug, be sure to check on any food/drug interactions you should be aware of: Many drugs for Parkinson's require you to avoid alcohol, antacids, vitamin B6, or to increase fiber intake.

Natural supplements cannot take the place of medication the physician will prescribe. However, there's mounting evidence that certain supplements along with certain dietary practices may slow the progression of the disease and add to the patient's well-being and general quality of life. In addition, most people with Parkinson's are not on medication all the time, as the medications tend to gradually lose their effectiveness. The typical pattern is a period of medication followed by an unmedicated period.

Patients with Parkinson's should make every effort to maintain good overall health with a high-quality diet, a good daily multivitamin, effective stress control, and even an exercise program. They should also follow a low-protein diet, because excessive protein will interfere with the absorption of most of the drugs used for treating the disease. About four ounces of high-protein food a day is fine. Fish and chicken are the best sources.

Since both undernutrition and constipation are a problem with Parkinson's, it is important to follow a diet high in vegetables, fruit, fiber, and sufficient calcium. Miller's bran and psyllium fiber can help fight constipation.

Both vitamins C and E seem to be helpful in delaying the progress of the disease. In an interesting study, Dr. Stanley Fahn of the Department of Neurology at Columbia University put a number of his patients on megadoses of these vitamins. He found that the patients taking them stayed free of symptoms for two and a half years longer than the patients of other physicians who were not taking vitamins C and E. Foods especially rich in vitamin E include salad oil or dressing, walnuts, sunflower seeds, and plums.

It's important with Parkinson's, as with all chronic ailments, to take only the basic recommended amount of supplements unless additional amounts have been *proven* helpful. In the case of Parkinson's, there are supplements that can actually worsen symptoms. Those to be avoided include choline, B_6, and manganese, which have been found to aggravate the disease.

There are some exercises, usually recommended by a doctor, that can help patients gain better physical control.

- Patients who stoop should line up their spine against a doorjamb or wall several times a day.

- Patients who shuffle should raise their feet over books placed at regular intervals along the floor.

- Patients who have trouble getting out of chairs should stand up by leaning forward 45 degrees and pushing up with their hands.

- Patients who have trouble speaking can benefit from reading aloud.

NATURAL PRESCRIPTION FOR PARKINSON'S DISEASE

- If you suspect Parkinson's disease, you should consult your physician and a neurologist to direct an informed course of treatment.

- It's important to maintain good overall physical and emotional health by observing the general recommendations in Blueprint for Health, page xvii.

- Limit protein intake to 4 ounces of chicken or fish daily because a diet high in protein will interfere with the absorption of many drugs used to treat Parkinson's (check with your doctor).

- Fight constipation by increasing foods high in fiber, especially fruits and vegetables (see Constipation, page 92).

- Limit the intake of manganese to no more than the minimum daily requirement.

- Use the exercises described to gain better physical control.

IN ADDITION TO YOUR DAILY SUPPLEMENTS, PAGE xxiv, TAKE

- Vitamin E: under your doctor's supervision, gradually increase to 2,000 I.U. daily and eat foods rich in vitamin E such as salad oil or dressing, walnuts, sunflower seeds, and plums.

- Vitamin C: under your doctor's supervision, increase to 3 g. daily and eat foods rich in vitamin C.

• • •

PERIODONTAL DISEASE

PERIODONTAL MEANS "located around a tooth," and periodontal disease refers to any disorder of the gums and jawbone. The first stage of periodontal disease is gingivitis, an inflammation of the gums that causes them to become red, soft, and shiny, and to bleed easily, particularly when the teeth are brushed. Gingivitis is caused by accumulations of plaque, which attract the bacteria that destroy the tissues of the gum. Too many soft foods in the diet and the lack of proper nutrients also cause gingivitis. If left untreated, the bacteria cause abscesses, or pockets in the gum, which then pulls away from the tooth. Eventually, the damage progresses to the bone, softening it and weakening its support of the teeth.

Gum disease in its various stages has reached epidemic proportions in the United States. Three out of four adults suffer from some form of the disease, which often starts in childhood. The American Academy of Periodontology estimates that the majority of children suffer from gingivitis, which if unattended can progress into the more destructive stages of periodontal disease with loss of gums, bone structure, and teeth.

Since the main cause of gingivitis is tartar buildup, the main prevention and treatment is flossing at least once a day: Flossing after each meal, though not always practical, would be even better. Brushing alone does not remove the food particles that accumulate between the teeth and gums.

In case you're fuzzy on how to floss, here's a refresher: Take about 20 inches of floss and wind the bulk of it around the middle finger of one hand, winding the rest around the middle finger of the other hand, leaving a few inches free between the fingers: This is the working part of the floss. Holding the floss tightly, slip it between the teeth, gently moving it back and forth until it reaches the gums. Curve the floss around one of the adjacent teeth and, sliding it back and forth, move it toward the biting edge of the tooth, freeing any debris. Then curve the floss around the other tooth and repeat the motion. When you're finished with one tooth, unwind a bit more floss from the finger with the bulk of the floss, wind the used floss onto the other finger, and continue flossing the next tooth. Floss each tooth in turn and don't forget to floss the innermost side of the last tooth. If you're unsure of your flossing technique, consult your dentist.

In addition to flossing, a professional dental cleaning every six months will keep the gums clear of plaque.

Cleaning alone will not necessarily prevent or arrest gingivitis. The gums are constantly assaulted by an infectious mixture of food particles and bacteria, and need adequate nutrients to resist inflammation and disease. The gums and teeth, however, are the last to receive their share of vitamins and minerals from the nutrition cycle, and the first to lose these nutrients if they are needed elsewhere in the system. If you have gingivitis, you need nutrients to promote healing and get the inflammation under control. For balanced nutrition and to give your gums and teeth the "exercise" and stimulation they need, you should eat a variety of fresh fruit, leafy vegetables, fish, meat and grain breads, and take supplements.

A number of years ago, one of my patients complained that his gums bled when he brushed his teeth, though he flossed every day and went for semiannual professional dental cleanings. I recommended vitamin and mineral supplements, and within two weeks the bleeding stopped. But when he went away on vacation, he didn't take his supplements along; bleeding began within ten days. When he returned, he resumed the supplements, and once again the bleeding stopped. Since adhering to his supplement regime, he has had not further problems with his gums.

Vitamin C is one of the key vitamins needed for healthy gums. While it's not known exactly how vitamin C works, it appears to battle bacteria while promoting the formation of healthy new gum tissue. Numerous experiments in many Western countries have demonstrated that vitamin C as a supplement is extremely effective in reducing the inflammation and infection of periodontal disease, and in promoting the regeneration of gum tissue. To stimulate the gums, eat fresh fruit and vegetables rich in vitamin C, such as oranges, grapefruit, tomatoes, pineapple, broccoli, cantaloupe, cauliflower, asparagus, and strawberries.

Coenzyme Q10, which is essential to healthy tissues, is a significant breakthrough in the fight against periodontal disease. Tests both here and in Japan have shown the remarkable effectiveness of CoQ10 supplements in reversing periodontal disease in both its early and later stages and in growing new tissue. There have been many instances of dramatic improvement in the case histories of patients who were no longer able to eat solid food until given CoQ10. I've had great success with my patients with this supplement.

Folic acid, which appears to make the cells more resistant to infection, is also helpful for periodontal disease. Food rich in folic acid includes spinach, chickpeas, and pinto beans.

Vitamin A, sometimes called the "skin vitamin," is helpful in repairing damaged tissue and fighting infection.

Calcium is also very important to prevent the loss of bone around the gums. This is called the alveolar bone, and it's the most active bone in the body, picking up calcium from the blood and giving it back. Calcium is particularly important for pregnant women and women past menopause, who frequently suffer from calcium deficiencies.

Vitamin E, which promotes a healthy vascular system while enhancing the immune response and fighting toxicity, is also valuable in restoring healthy gums and reducing inflammation. Foods rich in vitamin E that are also good for stimulating the gums include wheat germ, peanut butter, brown rice, walnuts, and almonds.

In addition to eating fresh foods to stimulate your gums, and taking supplements to give your gums the nutrients they need to fight inflammation and infection, you must take a few minutes each day to take care of your teeth and gums.

DAILY CARE

- Floss and brush after each meal. Floss between the teeth and at the gumline.

- Brush at the gumline. Since plaque is trapped at the gumline, hold your toothbrush at a 45-degree angle, so that part of it brushes your gums while the other part cleans your teeth.

- Keep two toothbrushes and alternate them so they can dry between uses.

- Or get an electric toothbrush, which is twice as effective in removing plaque.

- Use one of the rinses intended to loosen plaque.

- Massage your gums to stimulate circulation. Grip the gum between thumb and index finger, with the index finger on the outside, and rub. Better yet, use a rubber gum stimulator.

- If some infection is present, you can use a method recommended by Dr. Paul Keyes, the dentist and researcher who pioneered the nonsurgical approach to periodontal disease: "Dip your toothbrush in a solution of half hydrogen peroxide, half water, then dip it in baking soda, and smear the mixture along the gumline, making sure to get it in all the crevices between the teeth and gums." (See more about Keyes's techniques at the end of this section.)

NATURAL PRESCRIPTION FOR PERIODONTAL DISEASE

- Every six months, visit your dentist for a professional cleaning.

- Follow the recommendations listed above under "Daily Care."

IN ADDITION TO YOUR DAILY SUPPLEMENTS, PAGE xxiv, TAKE

- Vitamin C: 1,000 mg. three times a day.

- Coenzyme Q10: 30 mg. three times a day.

- Folic acid: 800 mcg. a day.

- Vitamin A: 10,000 I.U. a day.

- Calcium: 1,200 mg. a day.

- Vitamin E: 400 mg. a day.

IN ADDITION: Dr. Paul Keyes developed a nonsurgical approach to periodontal disease that involves professional and home care. His approach also includes a particular technique that involves scaling and root planing of the problem area not just above the gumline but within the pocket of the tooth. This technique has been proven to be as effective as surgery for many people. If you're facing periodontal surgery, or if you have gum problems that must be dealt with by a professional, you might first consult with a dentist who is familiar with Keyes's techniques to see if you can remedy the situation without an operation.

•   •   •

PMS

PMS, OR PREMENSTRUAL SYNDROME, first described in the medical literature in 1931, has gotten a great deal of attention in the past decade and has been viewed as everything from an illusion to a defense for murder. PMS is sometimes controversial because it's so complex: Some researchers recognize over 150 different complaints women can suffer from in the week or two before their period. It's difficult to isolate these complaints and to come up with a single medication that will make them all go away. Indeed, the one drug that's been most commonly prescribed for PMS, progesterone, has recently been found to be ineffective.

The natural approach to treating PMS is, I'm convinced, more effective and certainly safer than any drug on the market. In fact, many research articles have pointed to hormone imbalance, prostaglandin imbalance, and vitamin and mineral imbalances as the causes of PMS, and a natural approach seeks to *correct* these imbalances rather than mask the symptoms. I've had success with patients using an approach that combines diet, supplements, and exercise. And one supplement in particular, the amino acid DL-phenylalanine, has been, for some of my patients, little short of a miracle in helping them combat the mood swings of PMS.

Many of my patients who complain of PMS describe symptoms such as tension, mood swings, irritability, anxiety, weight gain, bloating, breast tenderness, and various food cravings, especially for sweets. Only after discussion and evaluation do some women realize that these symptoms are related to their menstrual cycle and occur one to two weeks before their period.

Diet plays a crucial role in the treatment of PMS, and I've found that many women experience exacerbated symptoms of PMS when their blood sugar is not under control. In fact, controlling blood sugar is a crucial step in eliminating PMS. Many of my patients are relieved to learn that their sugar cravings are not the result of a weak character but have an actual physiological cause. After ovulation, which occurs about two weeks before a period, the insulin-binding capacity of the body's cells change, affecting the response to sugar in the diet. Also, certain vitamin and mineral deficiencies, especially a chromium deficiency, can contribute to sugar cravings.

To relieve sweet cravings, you should eliminate sugar from your diet. In addition, to keep insulin levels steady and thus eliminate cravings, it's important to have regular meals at regular times and make sure you have enough protein in your diet—fish, chicken, or turkey—at lunch and dinner.

Chromium is also quite helpful in stabilizing blood sugar and eliminating sweet cravings. Though not many people are seriously deficient in chromium, many have a marginal deficiency. Regular exercisers, people who drink lots of coffee or tea, or people who eat a lot of sugar are more likely to have chromium deficiencies. This means that people who have a sweet tooth are often the least able to metabolize sugar effectively because of insufficient chromium stores. Many of my patients have found chromium to be extremely helpful. For more information see Hypoglycemia, page 202.

Dietary fat is also a factor in contributing to PMS. Studies have linked dietary fat with prostaglandin levels and plasma estrogen levels. If you reduce the fat, the prostaglandin and estrogen levels go down, which helps to relieve symptoms. There are some good fats: olive, safflower, and linseed oil all contribute to the production of certain prostaglandins that can help ameliorate many PMS symptoms.

Salt in the diet will cause fluid retention and thus contribute to weight gain, breast tenderness, swelling, and a generally bloated feeling. There's also recent information that sodium elevates the plasma glucose response. What this means is that excess salt in the diet creates a stronger reaction to the sugar and can contribute to low blood sugar, making you feel weak and irritable.

Most women don't realize the role that fiber plays in PMS. It has recently been recognized that fiber increases the intestinal clearance of estrogen. Too much estrogen is thought to be a contributing factor to the development of certain PMS symptoms. An increase of fiber, particularly in the two weeks preceding the period, can help to cut down on unwanted symptoms as well as contribute to overall good health.

Two interesting studies, one involving women in China and another involving college students in Boston, report the definitive link between the amount of caffeine consumed and the severity of PMS. Women who had the most troublesome symptoms consumed more caffeine-containing drinks per day than those with no PMS.

Caffeine affects PMS in several ways. First, it's known that caffeine affects adenosine receptors in the brain. It's also known that progesterone and other hormones affect these receptors as well. With the double action of both hormones and the caffeine working on the brain, symptoms are exacerbated. Caffeine is also a major contributor to fluctuations in blood sugar. Changes in blood-sugar levels can lead to food cravings as well as fatigue, weakness, headaches, and irritability. Caffeine, which also stimulates the body to produce antistress hormones, creates a stress on the body and thus contributes to PMS.

In addition to dietary changes, taking specific supplements can help. It seems that every day there's increasing evidence that certain vitamins and minerals help to alleviate PMS symptoms. It really isn't news that many women are deficient in so many vitamins and minerals: according to a 1985 USDA study, 87 percent of women were *below* the

RDA in vitamin E, 74 percent in calcium, 56 percent in iron, and 46 percent in folacin. Perhaps PMS is so widespread in part because of these deficiencies.

B_6 has been reported to help relieve fluid retention. In addition, the whole B complex can be helpful in fighting PMS symptoms, by stabilizing hormone levels and fighting stress.

Vitamin A has been shown to be very effective in treating PMS, but unfortunately the studies used it in doses higher than considered safe in an unsupervised atmosphere.

Vitamin E can be very helpful for breast complaints including swelling and tenderness and even fibrocystic disease. In one study, up to 85 percent of patients treated with vitamin E saw improvement. Vitamin E enhances formation of certain prostaglandins, which inhibit prolactin. Elevated levels of prolactin can promote symptoms similar to those of PMS.

There's strong evidence that calcium and magnesium supplements can help reduce PMS symptoms including depression, irritability, headaches, mood swings, abdominal bloating, and back pain, as well as cramps. In one study, patients reported a 50 percent reduction of these symptoms when supplemented with calcium.

Zinc is another helpful mineral. It has been reported that women who suffer from PMS consume *half* the zinc that unaffected women consume. This is further evidence that certain PMS symptoms are the result of deficiencies that supplements correct. Zinc supplementation, by the way, has been shown to be particularly helpful for women who have premenstrual acne.

Evening primrose oil, a nutritional supplement, has been very helpful in lessening certain symptoms including cramping in particular as well as irritability, breast discomfort, anxiety, tiredness, and swollen fingers and ankles. One study found that while sufferers had a significant decrease in symptoms after their first cycle, the best results with the supplement came after the fifth cycle. My patients have found it very helpful for abdominal cramping.

Vitamin C, which helps regulate estrogen clearance from the body, helps combat PMS symptoms.

One of the most exciting PMS treatments I've found is the use of DL-phenylalanine, an amino acid, for moodiness and depression. Many of my patients have found the use of this supplement "something of a miracle" as one woman told me after suffering from years of terrible depression before her period. Phenylalanine is crucial to the body's production of various neurotransmitters that have an effect on moods. In my experience phenylalanine is not effective in fighting mood swings but rather the kind of severe depression and moodiness that can precede a period.

There are certain lifestyle factors that have been proven to contribute to PMS, most notably lack of exercise.

Exercise has long been recommended as a treatment for PMS, but until very recently there was no documented study that validated it. But many women noticed that exercise "seemed to help" and that women athletes and ballerinas, for example, seemed to suffer much less frequently from PMS. A recent study finally confirmed the anecdotal evidence. Women who exercised moderately for a full cycle experienced decreases in fluid retention, breast symptoms, and premenstrual depression. It is believed that the neurotransmitter endorphin is associated with both exercise and mood symptoms and that endorphin withdrawal causes the PMS symptoms. One of my patients who had suffered with troubling PMS told me that she noticed that when she began walking for about a half hour five or six days a week, she had the first cycle she could remember that wasn't heralded by five days of depression, irritability, and tender breasts. Other patients have told me of similar occurrences.

There's so much material available on exercise these days that I won't go into great detail here except to say that exercise, which will be beneficial to every aspect of your health, doesn't have to be strenuous or demanding. A simple program of walking is what I recommend to patients who find it difficult to exercise regularly at a gym.

NATURAL PRESCRIPTION FOR PMS

DIET:

- Follow a low-fat diet.
- Eliminate sweets.
- Eat regular meals at regular times.
- Eat protein at lunch and dinner (fish, chicken, tuna, turkey).
- Limit alcohol.
- Limit salt.

- Limit dairy products.

- Limit caffeine to no more than one caffeinated drink per day.

- Increase complex carbohydrates including green leafy vegetables, legumes, whole grains, and cereals to increase fiber.

- Increase intake of olive or safflower oil.

LIFESTYLE:

- Adopt a regular exercise program.

IN ADDITION TO YOUR DAILY BASIC VITAMIN/MINERAL SUPPLEMENTS (PAGE xxiv), TAKE THE FOLLOWING FOR THREE MONTHS (IF THERE IS NO IMPROVEMENT IN SYMPTOMS, DISCONTINUE):

- Vitamin A: 10,000 I.U. daily.

- Vitamin B_6: 100 mg. three times a day for two weeks prior to period.

- Vitamin C: 1,000 mg. daily.

- Vitamin E: 400 to 600 I.U. daily.

- Calcium: 1,200 mg. daily (best taken at bedtime).

- Magnesium: 400 mg. daily.

- Chromium: 100 mcg. of trivalent chromium three times a day.

- Zinc: 50 mg. daily.

- Evening primrose oil: four 500-mg. capsules in the morning and four 500-mg. capsules in the evening. (Take evening primrose oil for five cycles and if no improvement, discontinue.)

- DL-phenylalanine: one or two 500-mg. capsules three times a day.

•   •   •

POISON IVY

POISON IVY, POISON OAK, and poison sumac come from a family of plants known as Toxidendrons, and the irritating substance is a toxin called urushiol, which is found in the leaves, stems, and roots. They cause the skin to turn red, develop a rash, swell, and blister, all accompanied by an intense and persistent itching that can last for days. The inflammation and itching are an allergic reaction to the toxin, and, while some people are more sensitive than others, almost everybody gets the reaction after exposure. You don't get poison ivy or poison oak just by standing close to the plant: You must touch it. Poison ivy can also be picked up by touching objects that were exposed to the toxic sap, such as unwashed gardening tools or boots. Dogs and cats, while not themselves allergic to poison plants, can brush up against them and get the sap on their fur, exposing people who come in contact with them. (Washing your pet, using rubber gloves, can free him of the toxin.) In addition, if these plants are burned, the toxin is released in the air and can be inhaled with the smoke, causing extreme irritation to the lungs.

The best cure for poison ivy is avoiding it in the first place. Both poison ivy and poison oak have leaves that grow in clusters of three, and both plants, as well as poison sumac, bear white berries in the summertime. Gardeners should wear gloves and boots to protect themselves from poison ivy.

There is a product that creates a barrier between your skin and the poison. It's called Ivy Shield and you can get it at some gardening and outdoor equipment stores. It won't completely protect you, but it's a good beginning if you know you're likely to be exposed.

If you do get some sap on your skin, wash within fifteen minutes, if possible, with plenty of water, being careful not to spread the toxin to other areas of the body. Brown laundry soap is best. A poison ivy and oak cleanser called Tecnu is very effective in removing the toxin. It's an over-the-counter lotion. You just apply the lotion to the affected areas and then wash it off in a shower and towel dry. I've used it myself very successfully.

If you suspect that you've come in contact with the plants, thoroughly wash your clothes with hot water and detergent. Even shoes and garden tools can harbor the poison so that wearing or using them at a later date can cause a reaction. I've had patients who have had cases of poison ivy that just wouldn't seem to go away, and it's usually because they continue to wear contaminated clothes or use contaminated tools.

If you do break out, try not to scratch, because you'll irritate the skin even more and possibly cause infection. However, contrary to myth, scratching will not spread the poison ivy, because the watery blisters don't contain toxin.

Home remedies for poison ivy rashes and itching include calamine lotion, baking soda, or over-the-counter cortisone creams. Calamine lotion helps cool the burning itch and dries up the blisters. Baking soda can be mixed with witch hazel to form a paste and then applied to the rash. Some people find that Tecnu cleanser helps relieve the rash even after it breaks out. And crushed plantain leaves—plantain is a common weed found in lawns—are said to relieve the irritation of poison ivy and to stop the itching. Antihistamines such as Benadryl can bring some relief. Whatever you do, it will take at least one to two weeks for the outbreak to heal (vitamin C seems to help speed the healing).

If home remedies don't help, your doctor may prescribe a stronger cortisone cream or antihistamine. Most people don't need medical attention for poison ivy, but some are so highly allergic that their entire system is affected. They may run a fever, their eyes may swell up, and they may even have difficulty breathing. If you experience any of these reactions, see your doctor immediately, who may give you an injection of cortisone. Intravenous injections of vitamin C have also been found to relieve the symptoms.

One last thing: Sometimes people who are very sensitive to poison ivy will also react to mangoes and cashews while they are suffering from the rash and so they should avoid these foods at that time. In addition, there are some people who have unexplained food allergies and react strongly to poison ivy. If this describes you, you should probably avoid mangoes and cashews at all times.

NATURAL PRESCRIPTION FOR POISON IVY

- Avoid contact with the plants; learn to recognize them. They may grow along the ground or up the trunks of trees or even along fences. The leaves may be dull or glossy but they always grow in triple clusters. In the fall, the leaves may change to a pinkish color, and in the summer the plants have white berries.

- Wash the affected areas as soon as possible after exposure with Tecnu cleanser, brown laundry soap, or any soap available.

- Wash any clothing that might have been exposed to poison ivy. Use hot water and strong detergent.

- For topical relief, use crushed plantain leaves, calamine lotion, baking soda, or cortisone cream. You can mix the baking soda with witch hazel to form a paste and apply it to the rash.

- Take antihistamines such as Benadryl to relieve irritation and itching.

- If you develop severe symptoms such as swollen and reddened eyes, fever, or difficulty breathing, or the rash does not show signs of healing, see your doctor immediately.

IN ADDITION TO YOUR DAILY SUPPLEMENTS, PAGE xxiv, TAKE

- Vitamin C: 2,000 mg. daily to speed healing.

• • •

PROSTATE

THE PROSTATE is the source of most problems with the male genitourinary system. Nearly every man over the age of forty-five will have some enlargement of the prostate, which is a result of hormonal changes and is a normal part of the aging process. Most prostate enlargements don't become really troublesome until a man reaches the age of sixty. Surgery is one route to take with a problem prostate but there are natural means that can be used to control its enlargement and perhaps avoid surgery altogether.

The prostate is a walnut-sized organ situated at the neck of the bladder. It provides the fluid that carries sperm. If the prostate becomes enlarged it can press against the urethral canal and thus interfere with urination. Most men experience this as a more frequent need to urinate, especially at night, as well as pain and burning upon urination and difficulty in starting and stopping.

Most men look upon this enlargement of the prostate and the accompanying symptoms as a nuisance. But any symptoms of difficulty in urination should be investigated by a urologist because, while most enlargements of the prostate *are* mainly a nuisance, there could be a possibility of infection or even cancer. I therefore suggest that if you have burning or difficult urination, you consult a urologist. The urologist will give you a diagnosis and, using a gloved finger, will massage the prostate. In a case of simple prostate enlargement, this often brings temporary relief.

Once you know that your problem is a simple inflammation or enlargement (called benign prostatic hypertrophy, or BPH), you still should not ignore it. The ultimate treatment for severely enlarged prostate is surgery. Whereas most men are able to avoid this, they continue to live with discomfort for years. Although you certainly can live a relatively healthy life with BPH, you can also develop kidney infections or damage as the urine backs up in the kidneys due to the blockage of the enlarged prostate. Bladder infections are also likely to occur.

Natural treatments for prostate problems have been very helpful in relieving the symptoms and reducing the enlargement. One of my patients, who reduced his prostate with supplements, told me that he no longer has to get up three or four times a night to urinate. Perhaps his success with supplements will help him avoid future prostate cancer; in any case, he's far more comfortable right now and sleeping better, too.

The first line of defense is to maintain low cholesterol levels by avoiding a high-fat diet. It seems that the amount of fat, particularly saturated fat, in the diet affects hormone levels, which in turn cause prostate problems. Of course many men are watching their cholesterol levels these days; this is all to the good in controlling an enlarged prostate.

The mineral zinc is the backbone of my treatment for men with prostate problems. Men with BPH have low levels of zinc in prostatic fluids, and supplementation can raise these levels and reduce the enlargement. In one study, fourteen out of nineteen patients treated with zinc supplements had shrinkage of the prostate after two months.

Essential fatty acids are also helpful in relieving an enlarged prostate. Researchers postulate that essential fatty acids work by influencing prostaglandin production; prostaglandin deficiency may be a cause of BPH.

The best common sources of essential fatty acids are flaxseed oil, sunflower oil, and soy oil.

There is a botanical that has given my patients relief and many studies have found it clinically effective for relieving BPH. It's called *Serenoa repens* or, more commonly, saw palmetto. Taken in extract form, it relieves prostate irritation. You can get saw palmetto in health food stores.

It's important to limit the amount of alcohol you consume, particularly beer. One of the hormones that contributes to prostate problems is increased by the consumption of beer and other alcoholic drinks.

Sometimes there is a connection between hidden food sensitivities and prostate problems. If the prostate doesn't seem to be inflamed, frequent urination could be caused by a food. If you find that you have frequent urination on some nights but on other nights you're not having a problem, it could be that something you're eating is the cause (in many causes, spicy foods are the culprits). You have to pay attention to what you eat the day or night before you experience frequent urination. For more information on this see Food Allergy, page 146.

Finally, some men who develop BPH young in life, and even some older men, are suffering in part from years of ineffective voiding technique. Many men rush to relieve themselves, only partly emptying their bladder and never fully relaxing the muscles in the pelvic floor. To help prevent BPH and to relieve its progression, it's important to void whenever you feel the urge; if at all possible, don't hold it. In addition and most important, you should fully relax the muscles in the pelvic floor when voiding and keep them relaxed until the bladder is empty.

NATURAL PRESCRIPTION FOR PROSTATE PROBLEMS

- Follow a low-fat diet and try to keep your cholesterol below 220.
- Avoid margarine, hydrogenated vegetable oils, and fried foods, as they can interfere with prostaglandin metabolism.
- Cut down on alcohol consumption, particularly beer.
- If your frequent urination is irregular, you could be reacting to a particular food. See text for discussion of this and read Food Allergy, page 146, for more information.

- Be sure you void properly: Go when you feel the urge; fully relax the muscles in the pelvic floor; empty your bladder completely.

IN ADDITION TO YOUR DAILY SUPPLEMENTS, PAGE xxiv, TAKE

- Flaxseed oil: one to two tablespoons per day of cold pressed flaxseed oil for several months. In addition, add sunflower oil or soy oil to your diet.

- Vitamin E: 400 mg. daily.

- Zinc: 60 mg. daily.

- The botanical *Serenoa repens* (saw palmetto) in doses of 160 mg. twice daily. You can find it in health food stores.

TAKE ALL SUPPLEMENTS FOR SIX MONTHS. STOP IF YOU SEE NO RESULTS.

• • •

PROTOZOA DISEASE

INTESTINAL PARASITES used to be considered a rare affliction in the United States. Typically, the only people tested for this problem were suffering from unexplained severe gastrointestinal symptoms or had just returned from an exotic trip where they were subjected to tainted water and food or unsanitary conditions that "civilized" people are never exposed to. But today there are enough parasite sources in your own neighborhood, including food and infected food handlers, to give anyone a nasty infection. One doctor has speculated that nearly seven million people in the United States alone are infected: He estimates that in the New York area 25 percent of the population is infected. Of these infected people 15 percent have no symptoms, 25 percent have symptoms that can be ignored, 55 percent have a compromised quality of life, and 5 percent are disabled.

I'm including protoza disease in this book not because it can be successfully treated entirely by natural means but as a cross-reference for people who have unexplained lower intestinal problems. Protozoa disease can cause diarrhea, gas, bloating, weight loss, fatigue, or a range of other intestinal problems. In addition, it can cause a constant feeling of being sick or unwell, confused memory, nightmares, blood-sugar swings, and musculoskeletal pains.

Protozoa disease can be detected by a stool sample test. Usually more than one stool exam is necessary—people have tested negative, but subsequent tests proved positive. I routinely do three tests before arriving at a final diagnosis. Many doctors never think of protozoa disease as being a possible cause of lower gastrointestinal problems. I now test all patients with unexplained lower intestinal problems including people with colitis and with inflammatory bowel disease.

There are three common parasites that usually cause symptoms: *Entamoeba histolytica, Giardia lamblia,* and *Blastocystis hominis.* Your doctor will prescribe medication for you if you test positive for any of these parasites. You should know, however, that treatment sometimes has to be repeated. I've had patients who have felt much better after a single round of treatment and others who have felt relief only after three rounds of treatment.

In addition to the drugs that are used to cure protoza disease, there are natural steps you can take to ease your recovery and to help prevent symptoms.

Many people who have suffered from a parasitic infection will have subsequent difficulty in tolerating milk and grain products. I suggest that after drug treatment has been effective, patients avoid dairy foods including milk and cheese as well as grain products such as oats, rye, barley, and wheat.

A high-fiber diet has been shown to be helpful in fighting parasitic infections. There are speculations that the fiber in the diet promotes mucus production and thereby reduces the opportunity for parasites to form colonies on the intestinal walls.

There are herbal remedies that have been shown to be effective, though I think it is best to use them in conjunction with conventional drug therapy. Look in your health food store for remedies that contain the herbal bitter wormwood *(Artemisia absinthium).* The packages will give precise directions on how much to take and how often.

NATURAL PRESCRIPTION FOR PROTOZOA DISEASE

- If you have unexplained symptoms as described above, you should discuss the possibility of protozoa disease with your doctor. If you test positive for protozoa, you will be given medication that should relieve your symptoms; some people find that they must take as many as three courses.

IN ADDITION TO FOLLOWING YOUR DOCTOR'S MEDICATION RECOMMENDATIONS, FOLLOW THESE SUGGESTIONS FOR THREE MONTHS AFTER ALL SYMPTOMS HAVE CEASED:

- Eat a high-fiber diet, as tolerated.

- Avoid milk and dairy products including cheese if you find they irritate your digestive system.

- There are herbal preparations that have been shown to be helpful in fighting protozoa disease. Available in health food stores, they contain the herbal bitter wormwood *(Artemisia absinthium)*. Follow the directions on the package.

•   •   •

PSORIASIS

PSORIASIS IS A skin disorder characterized by red patches covered by silvery white scales, which can develop almost anywhere on the body, from the scalp down to the soles of the feet. These patches may itch and be quite uncomfortable as well as be a cosmetic embarrassment. The condition is caused by skin cells that divide too rapidly—up to 1,000 times faster than normal skin cells—and accumulate instead of being shed. Psoriasis is not contagious. It sometimes disappears entirely, although once you've had a bout it's always possible that you'll get it again.

Three out of each hundred Americans suffer from some form of psoriasis, which affects some fifty million people around the world. Thousands of years ago, afflicted Egyptians would seek relief by eating an herb that grew along the Nile, and then exposing their skin to the sun. Until quite recently, one medical treatment followed the same approach: Patients were given a derivative of the Nile herb—a medication activated by light—and then were exposed to special ultraviolet (UV) lamps. This treatment, though effective, is now considered risky because of increased incidence of skin cancer.

Another treatment utilizing ultraviolet light consists of applying topical applications of coal tar before exposure to certain light rays. This treatment, though messy, is effective and has the advantage that it can be carried out at home. But it, too, has an increased risk of skin cancer: If you're using this therapy, be sure you have yearly checkups by a dermatologist.

For those with the time and money for an extensive trip, the Dead Sea area in Israel is a famous healing resort for psoriasis. There, the burning rays of the UV spectrum are filtered out by the ever present haze, and patients can spend many hours in the sunlight or the mineral-rich water without becoming sunburned. Although nearly half of the people who try this method will have a recurrence of psoriasis, I'm sure the group that's now psoriasis-free would heartily endorse the Dead Sea cure.

The problem with psoriasis is that there is relief but no permanent cure available as yet. We don't know exactly what causes the condition, though it has been associated with allergies, arthritis, and various dietary and metabolic factors.

In my experience, food allergies, especially to yeast-containing foods, can be a significant factor. For more information on this, see Food Allergy, page 146.

Fish oils (the omega-3's) in supplement form have been helpful in doses of 6 g. daily. Many of my patients have found some relief from the inflammation and itching of psoriasis when they took the fish oil supplements. No matter what other treatment you may be using for psoriasis, I suggest you take this supplement.

Of the topical applications, cortisone works in clearing up psoriasis, but the effect is temporary, and the condition gets worse when the cortisone is discontinued. Sometimes I recommended cortisone—which you can buy over-the-counter in a mild form—for temporary relief, but I don't like to see patients get too dependent on it. Tar, which can be bought in over-the-counter creams, helps keep down the itching and inflammation, and mineral oil keeps the skin from drying out.

Fish oil, or MaxEPA, applied topically has been shown to give relief to psoriasis patients. In one study of eleven patients, eight people found that their lesions treated with MaxEPA had greater improvements than the lesions treated with a placebo. You can use the fish oil in a 10 percent salve.

In addition to fish oil, extralight mineral oil—which you can get at health food stores—can be used as an inexpensive substitute for the moisturizers sold specifically for psoriasis.

Candidiasis can also contribute to psoriasis. There is an increased incidence of candidiasis in the bowels of people with psoriasis, and, if present, the patient must avoid all foods high in yeast, such as baked goods, cheese, mushrooms, vinegar, soy sauce, fermented foods, alcohol, and pickles. For a detailed description of how to deal with this problem see Candidiadis, page 61.

If eliminating yeast from your diet doesn't improve your symptoms, fumaric acid might help. This treatment involves the use of fumaric acid ester, commonly used in the food industry as a food additive in place of citric acid. In healthy individuals, fumaric acid is formed in the skin when it's exposed to sunlight. People with psoriasis appear to have a biochemical defect that requires prolonged exposure to the sun to produce it. Fumaric acid ester capsules have been used in clinical trials in Switzerland and the Netherlands with excellent results. In a recent study, 80 percent of the 285 patients involved reported marked improvement, and 52 percent of those patients were completely cleared of psoriatic lesions.

The fumaric acid will take some time to work—it can take up to three months before any improvement is seen—but it can be highly effective.

The capsules should be taken before meals with plenty of fluids. After taking them, you'll notice a warm feeling and tingling of your skin in the neck and shoulder area. The feeling will last for about fifteen minutes, and it means that the desired metabolic reaction is taking place.

Another side effect of the treatment is that in about fourteen days you may feel a slight worsening of the itching and a slight swelling of the feet and hands. If it occurs, this lasts for only a few days; it is an indication that the treatment is effective.

Last but not least, keep in mind that tension can aggravate psoriasis. Regular exercise and relaxation exercises will help.

NATURAL PRESCRIPTION FOR PSORIASIS

- For immediate relief, topical applications of mineral oils (extralight mineral oil, available at most health food stores) or a 10 percent salve of MaxEPA in mineral oil can be helpful.

- Over-the-counter cortisone creams can be helpful, but their regular use can cause a rebound effect, so try to use them sparingly.

- Investigate the possibility of food allergies. For more information, see Food Allergy, page 146.

- Suspect candidiasis as a cause. See Candidiasis, page 61. If elimination of yeast is not helpful, try fumaric acid treatments as follows.

- Try fumaric acid. Because of possible side effects, I recommend that patients have the treatment under supervision.

  First two weeks: one 500-mg. capsule daily.

  Next two weeks: two 500-mg. capsules daily; one morning, one evening.

  Next two weeks: three 500-mg. capsules daily; one with each meal.

  After the first six weeks you can increase the capsules by one a day for a two-week period until you reach a maximum dose of seven capsules daily.

  After lesions have substantially cleared, a maintenance dose of one or two capsules should be taken daily.

  NOTE: *Patients on this treatment should avoid taking penicillin and pregnant women should not use this treatment, and all people with psoriasis should avoid tetracycline.*

- Relaxation exercises and regular exercise are important to control stress.

IN ADDITION TO YOUR DAILY SUPPLEMENTS, PAGE xxiv, TAKE

- Fish oils in the form of MaxEPA: 1,000 to 2,000 mg. three times daily.
- Evening primrose oil: 500 mg. three times daily.

IN ADDITION: Go for yearly checkups if using ultraviolet treatments.

• • •

RAYNAUD'S SYNDROME

IF YOUR FINGERS and toes tingle and grow numb the minute they're exposed to the cold, it may not be just poor circulation. You may have Raynaud's syndrome, a circulatory disorder that causes the small arteries of the extremities to spasm and constrict. Your fingers, deprived of blood, grow pale and may even acquire a bluish tinge, and then get red when circulation returns and the blood rushes back.

Raynaud's syndrome is thought to be quite common, particularly among women, though there are no actual tallies. Many people who have it probably don't believe it's serious enough to discuss with a doctor, but it can be very painful, particularly in the advanced stages, when poor blood supply can cause lasting damage to the sense of touch. I've had patients who, even suffering from relatively mild cases, felt that their lives were terribly disrupted by the problem.

There are conventional medical approaches to Raynaud's: Calcium channel blockers have been used to dilate the blood vessels in seriously affected patients. This usually won't give complete relief but it can help. Unfortunately, these medications can have side effects and are not always effective. There are some excellent natural therapies I recommend that have proven extremely effective for a number of my patients.

A combination of natural ingredients—magnesium, a mineral, combined with taurine, an amino acid—can be very effective, even in people who have had Raynaud's for a long time.

Vitamin E taken as a supplement helps to decrease the circulatory spasms that cause Raynaud's. It's also extremely helpful as a topical ointment on fingers and toes that become ulcerated due to insufficient blood supply.

Fish oils (the omega-3's) are also recommended because they improve tolerance to cold exposure and delay spasm of the blood vessels.

Be sure that you're getting adequate iron in your diet. Lack of iron can cause anemia, which will increase your sensitivity to cold. Foods that are rich in iron include fish, lean red meat, poultry, lentils, and leafy green vegetables.

There are two particularly effective and simple methods to prevent spasms. One, devised by a dermatologist in Vermont, involves twirling the arms to stimulate circulation. Like a softball pitcher, you swing your arm down behind your body and then upward in front of you, at about eighty twirls a minute. This exercise forces blood to the fingers through both gravitational and centrifugal force, and is effective in warming up chilled hands.

Another method, devised by U.S. Army researchers in Alaska, works by conditioning the hands to counter the cold spasm reflex. You soak your hands in warm water for three to five minutes, in a room where the temperature is comfortable. Next, you go into a freezing room and soak your hands in warm water once again, this time for ten minutes. The cold temperature would normally cause your arteries to constrict, but the warm water keeps them open. Eventually, they will remain open even without warm water. In the army experiments involving 150 people, this procedure was repeated three to six times every other day. After fifty-four treatments, hands were found to be seven degrees warmer in the cold.

In addition to regularly practicing these exercises, avoid anything that hampers your circulation and makes you vulnerable to chill:

- Do not smoke, because nicotine causes vasospasm and encourages plaque to form in your arteries, slowing circulation.

- Do not drink alcohol because though it may seem to make you warm, it actually lowers your body temperature.

- Do not drink coffee or drinks with caffeine, because they constrict blood vessels.

- Drink lots of fluids and eat hot, regular meals to keep off the chill.

- Wear mittens instead of gloves, because mittens trap the heat of your hands. Wear them any time your hands will be exposed to cold: when shopping in the frozen food section, when grasping a cold steering wheel, and so on.

- Dress in loose rather than constricting clothes, layered for warmth. Wear fabrics that will draw away perspiration, keeping you drier and warmer, and use foot powder to keep your feet dry and warm.

NATURAL PRESCRIPTION FOR RAYNAUD'S SYNDROME

- Use the warm water and arm twirling techniques described above to enhance circulation and prevent spasms.

- Avoid smoking, alcohol, and caffeine; all will constrict the blood vessels and promote spasm.

- Dress to ward off cold and perspiration. See the list of tips above.

- Eat hot, regular meals.

- Ingest adequate iron by eating fish, poultry, lean red meat, lentils, and green leafy vegetables. Do not take iron supplements unless indicated by blood testing.

IN ADDITION TO YOUR DAILY SUPPLEMENTS, PAGE xxiv, TAKE

- Magnesium with taurine in the following amounts: magnesium, 200 mg. three times daily, and taurine, 250 mg. three times daily, during the cold season. If no relief after four weeks, discontinue use.

- Vitamin E: 400 I.U. daily

- Fish oils: 1,000 mg. three times daily.

• • •

RHEUMATOID ARTHRITIS

RHEUMATOID ARTHRITIS is really a type of arthritis. Like osteoarthritis it causes inflammation of the joints. Indeed, the word *arthritis* is derived from the Greek word for joint (it actually means inflammation of the joint). Rheumatoid arthritis, unlike osteoarthritis, is a more systemic illness. It begins with an inflammation of the synovial membrane—the source of the fluid that lubricates the bone joints. Rheumatoid arthritis is a chronic inflammatory disease that affects particularly the hands, feet, wrists, ankles, and knees, but it can also affect other organs. It usually begins between the ages of twenty and forty, but it can manifest at any age. It's an unpredictable disease: Up to 20 percent of those affected find that it disappears on its own and never comes back. Others suffer some degree of disability for the rest of their lives. In the past, conventional medicine has concentrated largely on relieving the symptoms with ever larger and stronger antiinflammatory drugs. But many of these drugs cause serious side effects—in some cases worse than the condition itself.

Though the cause of rheumatoid arthritis has yet to be precisely identified, there's evidence that it's related to a failure of the autoimmune system, or, more precisely, a case of an immune system that's fighting the body it's supposed to protect. The immune system breaks down the components of joint tissue, causing joint pain, redness, stiffness, and swelling. What stimulates the immune system to do this? There's increasing evidence that individuals with rheumatoid arthritis have intestines that are more permeable to certain antigens, allowing these antigens to invade the body, stimulating the symptoms.

If you suffer from rheumatoid arthritis, you probably have seen or should see a rheumatologist. Different people will respond to different therapies. It's important to find someone who will not simply rely on relieving your symptoms with drugs but who will be open to finding the *cause* of *your* particular symptoms. I don't mean to imply that I'm against drug therapy for treating RA, but I have seen excellent results in my patients from the use of nutritional therapy combined with physical therapy and/or acupuncture.

While a nutritional approach used to be controversial—the Arthritis Foundation still insists that there is no connection between diet and arthritis—now there's overwhelming evidence pointing to diet as a major factor contributing to the development of symptoms.

Why would diet have an effect on what is essentially an autoimmune disease? Because food makes the greatest demand on the immune system. Foods contain countless allergens that the body is constantly trying to fight or adapt to. Some of these allergens are natural; others come from additives. In any event, finding the foods that stimulate symptoms is one of the first steps that I encourage RA patients to take.

There are many food allergies that can aggravate RA symptoms. Among the most common foods are wheat, corn, milk and other dairy products, and beef. If you had allergies as a child, if there's a history of allergies in your family, if you developed sensitivities in recent years, food allergies could be stimulating your RA symptoms. In order to discover exactly what foods are affecting you, the best approach is an allergy-elimination diet. (I should mention that these reactions may not be true allergies; in some cases they're simply food reactions. For more information on this, see Food Allergy, page 146. However, for this discussion, I'll refer to both as food allergies.)

You may have heard about osteoarthritis and the nightshade family of foods. The connection between rheumatoid arthritis and these foods was originally made by Childers, a horticulturist, who found that eliminating foods of the nightshade family cured his arthritis. While his theory—that long-term consumption of the alkaloids in potatoes, tomatoes, eggplant, peppers, paprika, cayenne, and tobacco inhibit collagen and cartilage repair—has never been proven, it is true that some patients find relief from their symptoms when they eliminate these foods. It is well worth eliminating them entirely from your diet for a month to see if you find any symptomatic relief. Obviously, if you do, discontinue them permanently. If not, reintroduce them gradually.

It's interesting to note that people who eat a more "primitive" diet— one containing fewer refined foods and foods with additives—than ours are generally free from rheumatoid arthritis. This gives even greater weight to the advice that I routinely give all my patients: Modify your diet to reduce sugar, saturated fat, meats, and refined carbohydrates. Increase the amounts of fresh fruits and vegetables, whole grains, and unrefined carbohydrates. Some patients have found that becoming a vegetarian significantly reduced their symptoms. One study tested a one-week fast followed by a year of a lactovegetarian diet in a controlled test group. The group on the vegetarian diet found significant improvement in joint tenderness, swollen joints, pain, duration of morning stiffness, grip strength, and white blood count, among others. The control group found that only their pain improved significantly. The benefits for the vegetarian group were still present after a year.

I've had good results in reducing inflammation with patients when they significantly lower the fat in their diet. This reaction was discovered quite by accident by researchers at Wayne State University in Detroit who were working with obese women, two of whom suffered from rheumatoid arthritis. While on the low-fat diet, both women experienced a complete remission of their symptoms. They stayed on the diet for up to fourteen months without symptoms, but when they ate any fatty foods, their pain and stiffness returned within a day or two. I suggest that you eliminate as many fats as possible (with the exception of fish oil) including animal and vegetable fats. See Blueprint for Health, page xvii, for more information on fats in the diet.

Some of my patients have found relief with an occasional fast of no more than four days. No one knows exactly why fasting helps. Obviously fasting eliminates the source of any food allergies, but also there seems to be some connection with fasting and the suppression of the immune system that fights rheumatoid arthritis symptoms. I tell my patients to go on a vegetable juice fast for three or four days if their symptoms are severe, making sure that the vegetable juices contain no nightshade. Check with your doctor to determine whether fasting would be appropriate for you.

Many studies have shown fish oil to be effective in fighting inflammatory diseases, and my patients have found it helped their symptoms.

You may have heard about the use of evening primrose oil to help RA patients. I haven't seen dramatic results among my patients, but as some doctors swear by it, and there is research evidence that it can alleviate symptoms, I usually recommend it along with the fish oil. Remember, it has been shown that it can take up to three months for the evening primrose oil to have an effect, so be patient.

Selenium has also gotten attention lately as a supplement that can give relief. Many RA patients have lowered levels of selenium, a known antiinflammatory agent. In one study, fifteen women with rheumatoid arthritis of less than five years' duration received either selenium or a placebo daily for three months. The patients treated with selenium found that pain and joint tenderness were improved. The patients receiving the placebo found no change. The improvements in the group treated with selenium disappeared three months after the study ended.

Vitamin C also is frequently below normal in RA patients. There's some speculation that the increased aspirin consumption of RA patients may interfere with the absorption of vitamin C: Average doses of aspirin can triple the amount of vitamin C excreted by the body; therefore, a supplement can help.

Because of its antiinflammatory properties, I also recommend vitamin E supplements.

It seems that the B vitamins, particularly vitamin B_1 and vitamin B_{12}, can enhance the effect of nonsteroidal antiinflammatory drugs, thereby reducing the amount of drugs needed to reduce pain. In one study, the effect was seen in as little as seven days, allowing some patients to reduce the amount of pain medication needed by as much as 90 percent.

If you rely on regular doses of NSAIDs to relieve pain, you should try B_1 and B_{12} supplementation to see if allows you to reduce your drug intake.

There's long been a connection between copper and reduction of arthritic pain. Perhaps you've seen or heard of people wearing copper bracelets for this purpose. Copper is an effective antiinflammatory agent that may be more potent than aspirin. It is known to reduce morning stiffness and help joint mobility, sometimes reducing the need for other drugs. Studies have suggested that rheumatoid arthritis patients are marginally deficient in copper, and supplementation may help relieve symptoms. The best form of copper for this purpose is oral copper salicylate.

Zinc and boron also seem to help reduce swelling in the joints, as well as morning stiffness.

I recently read a very interesting study that tested the use of ginger. Although it was a small sampling—only seven patients—there were dramatic results. It seems that for all the patients who consumed 5 g. of fresh, or 0.5 to 1 g. of powdered, ginger daily, symptoms were greatly reduced. It can take up to three months for results, but I suggest that my patients include ginger in their diet. Ginger capsules are available at health food stores and of course fresh ginger can be had at many supermarkets.

Many of my rheumatoid arthritis patients are dismayed when I suggest that they begin an exercise program. The idea of exercise can seem overwhelming when your joints are painful, but *lack* of exercise can cause the muscles around a joint to begin to deteriorate, causing more pain. Any exercise that you feel comfortable doing is fine. Some people find swimming or pool exercises to be the least traumatic and best tolerated. Others find that yoga is both soothing and energizing.

One of the basics of my treatment of rheumatoid arthritis is acupuncture. There is a long tradition of using acupuncture for inflammatory diseases; it seems not only to reduce pain and swelling but also to contribute to an enhanced sense of well-being. Many of my patients have found it gave them great relief. I suggest that you find a qualified practitioner and begin with two sessions a week for a month to see if it helps.

Finally, all rheumatoid arthritis sufferers must recognize that stress plays an important part in their disease. Of course you cannot eliminate stress from your life, but you can modify your reaction to stress through exercise and stress-reducing techniques. For more information on this, see Stress Control, page 314.

NATURAL PRESCRIPTION FOR RHEUMATOID ARTHRITIS

- Unless noted otherwise, it can take up to three months for this program to have an effect.

- Investigate the possibility of food allergies and/or food sensitivities (see Food Allergy, page 146) and undertake an allergy-elimination diet. Among the most common foods that cause sensitivities in people with rheumatoid arthritis are wheat, corn, milk and other dairy products, and beef.

- Avoid foods from the nightshade family (potatoes, tomatoes, eggplant, peppers, paprika, cayenne, and tobacco) for a month to see if you find any symptomatic relief.

- Modify your diet to reduce sugar and other refined carbohydrates, and saturated fat, including red meats. Increase the amounts of fresh fruits and vegetables and whole grains. In general, a more "primitive" diet seems to be beneficial.

- Eliminate as many fats as possible (with the exception of fish oil, see below) including animal and vegetable fats.

- If your symptoms are very bad, I suggest you try a vegetable juice fast for three or four days, making sure that the vegetable juices contain no nightshade. Check with your doctor about this.

- Adopt a regular exercise program as tolerated. Swimming, pool exercises, or yoga are good choices.

- Develop a program of stress reduction. For more information on this, see Stress Control, page 314.

IN ADDITION TO YOUR DAILY SUPPLEMENTS, PAGE xxiv, TAKE

- Fish oil: Take 1,000 mg. three times a day. In addition, increase your consumption of fish.

- Boron: 2 mg.

- Evening primrose oil: 1,000 mg. three times a day.

- Selenium: 100 mcg. daily.

- Vitamin C: 2,000 mg. daily.

- Vitamin E: 400 I.U. daily.

- Zinc: 22.5 mg.

- If you take NSAIDs for pain relief: vitamin B_1: 100 mg.; vitamin B_{12}, 1,000 mcg. in tablets dissolved under the tongue. (These supplements may allow you to reduce your drug dose.)

- Copper salicylate: 2 mg. one time a day with meals, and zinc: 50 mg. two times a day with meals. Discontinue after six weeks if no improvement.

- Ginger (powdered form is available at health food stores): 500 mg. three times daily.

IN ADDITION: Acupuncture can be extremely helpful. Find a qualified practitioner and begin with two or three sessions per week.

Sea cucumber is another remedy that seems very promising, although the clinical trials are preliminary. No one seems to know precisely why sea cucumber works. Sea cucumbers are actually animals that live on the Great Barrier Reef in Australia. The substance they produce is available at health food stores in pill form. Some patients have had dramatic results taking these pills, and I think it's worth a try. Take one 500-mg. capsule twice a day.

•   •   •

ROSACEA

ROSACEA is a relatively common skin disorder that mainly afflicts adults between the ages of thirty and fifty—women nearly three times as often as men. It usually occurs over the cheeks and nose and looks like a sunburn. Some people will also get pimples that resemble acne. Rosacea can wax and wane; certain foods or alcohol or exposure to the sun can increase the problem.

Unfortunately, no one is certain precisely what causes rosacea. Studies have connected it with everything from menopause to alcoholism, but it seems that the most convincing evidence links it to either food allergies and/or an imbalance of the digestive system.

The traditional treatment is the antibiotic tetracycline. It's unclear precisely how it acts to reduce rosacea, but in many cases it is of some help; in some other cases it seems to have little effect. My own approach is an effort to remedy the two factors most closely connected with the development of rosacea and to make some modifications in the diet. For many patients, these measures will completely clear up their symptoms.

First of all, you should read the section in this book on Food Allergies (page 146). If you know that you have allergies now or have had them as a child, it could be that they are causing your rosacea. Many people find that once they eliminate certain foods, their rosacea disappears. An allergy to yeast is the most common allergenic cause and eliminating yeast from the diet can help such cases (see Candidiasis, page 61).

In addition, you should also avoid foods that cause blood vessels to dilate, including coffee, alcohol, spicy foods, and any other foods that cause a flush.

There is a strong link between a certain digestive imbalance called hypochlorhydria—reduced gastric acid output—and rosacea. Hypochlorhydria sometimes occurs as a the result of stress, worry, or depression, but some people seem to have a natural reduction in gastric juices, particularly as they get older. It's believed that this reduction in digestive juices may somehow allow more toxic substances into the system and thereby contribute to rosacea. Many of these people also suffer from constipation and brittle fingernails and hair.

The solution to hypochlorhydria is hydrochloric acid capsules, but you shouldn't take them before you've had a gastric analysis done by your doctor. If you take the capsules without having been analyzed, you run the risk of developing an ulcer. Be sure not to take the capsules with aspirin or certain other drugs. (See Indigestion, page 212, for more information on this.)

For unknown reasons, taking acidophilus along with hydrochloric acid tablets seems to increase the effectiveness.

One supplement that seems to help is vitamin B_{12}, perhaps because people with a digestive problem also have trouble absorbing vitamins.

NATURAL PRESCRIPTION FOR ROSACEA

- Determine if you suffer from food allergies (see Food Allergy, page 146). If yeast is causing the problem, see Candidiasis, page 61. Eliminate any problematic foods from your diet.

- If a gastric analysis determines that you are suffering from hypochlorhydria, take hydrochloric acid tablets under your doctor's supervision. (If you are taking hydrochloric acid tablets, take one acidophilus tablet three times daily.)

- Avoid foods that cause blood vessels to dilate, including coffee, alcohol, spicy foods, and any other foods that cause a flush.

IN ADDITION TO YOUR DAILY SUPPLEMENTS, PAGE xxiv, TAKE

- B_{12}: 1,000 mcg. dissolved under your tongue.

• • •

SEBORRHEIC DERMATITIS

THIS IS A MORE troublesome version of simple dandruff. It involves scaling of the scalp, eyelids, and eyebrows or of the skin around the nose, behind the ears, under the arms, around the anal and genital areas, and in the body folds of the obese. The rash may involve redness and oozing or hard, dry crusting of the skin. In men, the rash may extend to the beard area and the hairy parts of the chest and back.

I've had numerous patients with seborrheic dermatitis who have seen many physicians in an effort to get it cleared up, to no avail. I think the problem is that it's so commonly misdiagnosed. Many times it's mistaken for a simple rash, another type of eczema, or just a dry skin condition. In fact, seborrheic dermatitis is a specific condition that will not respond to treatments for these other skin problems, and if it's not taken care of it can spread.

Seborrheic dermatitis, we now know, is caused by the yeast called *Pityrosporum ovale,* which also causes dandruff. (See Dandruff, page 104.) In order to fight the yeast and keep the seborrheic dermatitis under control you should eliminate yeast and yeast-promoting foods from your diet. That means giving up many popular foods, but sufferers find the sacrifice worth it. Taking acidophilus capsules also helps.

Don't expect the yeast avoidance diet to work immediately—it may take thirty days or so.

Keeping to a yeast-free diet will keep the condition under control, but I've found that my patients are really helped by using a prescription cream that I describe below.

NATURAL PRESCRIPTION FOR SEBORRHEIC DERMATITIS

- Avoid all sugars and sweets, which promote yeast and make the condition worse.

- Eliminate all foods and beverages that contain yeast such as bread and other baked goods, cheese, mushrooms, vinegar, soy sauce, fermented condiments such as olives and pickles, as well as all wines and alcoholic drinks.

- Acidophilus: one capsule three times a day.

IN ADDITION: Ask your doctor to prescribe nystatin triamcinolone acetonide cream (sold under the name Mycolog cream) for you to help keep the condition under control.

• • •

SHINGLES

SHINGLES ARE CAUSED by herpes zoster, the same virus that causes chicken pox. If you are lucky enough to have forgotten what chicken pox feels like, shingles will remind you. It begins with burning, itching, or pain in one part of the body; after a few days, blisters and a rash appear. *Zoster,* the Greek word for "belt" or "girdle," refers to the tendency of the disease to ring the body on the abdomen or chest area, although it can also affect the neck, lower back, forehead, and eyes. The blisters will usually last for one to two weeks before they crust over and heal. Unfortunately, the pain of shingles can continue long after the initial attack, particularly in older people. Moreover, attacks can recur at any time.

How do you get shingles? Even though your case of chicken pox is long gone, the virus that caused it may have been hibernating in your spinal nerves for years. A trigger such as fatigue, stress, exposure to someone with chicken pox, the use of anticancer drugs, immune system deficiency, Hodgkin's disease, and other cancers causes the virus to travel to the nerve endings near the skin surface, resulting in the pain and blistering rash that is shingles. You cannot catch shingles from someone else *unless you've never had chicken pox*. This is important. If you have shingles, you should take care to avoid pregnant women who have not had chicken pox as you could infect both the woman and her unborn baby.

The pain of shingles can be excruciating. The treatment is twofold: to relieve the pain and to prevent the aftereffects, in particular postherpetic neuralgia, a persistent debilitating pain that is probably caused by the damage the virus has done to the nerves.

If you develop shingles you should first consult your doctor who will probably prescribe acyclovir (Zovirax) to help minimize discomfort and relieve symptoms. In addition, you should adopt natural remedies to help relieve and prevent symptoms.

I advise patients to avoid the routine use of steroids unless they have been prescribed by a doctor and their use is being monitored. There is still controversy about the effectiveness of steroids in relieving shingles; moreover they can negatively affect the immune system and may cause other complications. I also advise against the use of any pain-relieving or itch-relieving cream that contains steroids.

People with singles are looking for immediate relief. Fortunately there are a few natural remedies that have proved helpful for many people. The first and most basic is to apply cool or cold wet dressings to the affected area. Wet a washcloth or towel, wring it out, and then gently press it to the lesions. Some people put the cloth into the freezer for a short while after wetting it to make it colder. Just as coolness is soothing to the lesions, heat is irritating. Avoid heat as well as tight clothes and itchy fabrics like wool.

An excellent topical remedy for shingles is an ointment that you can make at home with aspirin and chloroform. (You can probably get chloroform at your pharmacy, but if you can't, use Vaseline Intensive Care lotion in its place.) Mash up two aspirins (do not use aspirin substitutes) and mix them with two tablespoons of chloroform. Apply this mixture with a clean cotton ball to the shingles lesions. The chloroform dissolves the dead skin and any residue, allowing the aspirin to penetrate and deaden the nerve endings that are causing the pain.

Some people find that calamine lotion can relieve the pain and help dry the lesions.

Something else that can give relief is vitamin E, used both orally and on the lesions themselves. While no one is certain exactly why vitamin E is useful in treating shingles, there's ample evidence that it does work for many people. I suggest you take vitamin E daily. In addition, you can take one or more vitamin E capsules, cut off the tip or stick a pin into one end, and squeeze it onto the lesions.

Vitamin C is another aid in treating shingles. There is speculation that vitamin C increases the body's production of interferon, an infection-fighting protein that promotes healing.

The amino acid lysine inhibits herpes activity and can help shorten an attack. You only need to take lysine supplements during the course of an outbreak. In addition, avoid arginine-rich foods such as chocolate, peanuts, seeds, and cereal grains. Arginine is another amino acid, but its effect on the virus is the opposite of lysine's: It promotes herpes growth.

You can also use lysine cream to hasten healing. It's available in health food stores. I usually advise applying it topically twice a day, but check with the directions on the package label.

Once the shingles lesions have healed, an ointment called Zostrix may reduce any lingering postherpetic pain you may experience. It is available without prescription from a pharmacy. The important ingredient is capsaicin, which is a naturally occurring irritant found in hot peppers. Like hot peppers, it can sting your eyes or irritate a cut. It might well sting when you first apply it to painful areas on your skin, but it's supposed to. It works to deplete a substance manufactured by your skin that transmits messages of pain to the brain; by applying Zostrix regularly, this message can't get through.

NATURAL PRESCRIPTION FOR SHINGLES

- **Cold compresses:** Apply towels or washcloths wrung out in cold water (and stored in the freezer if you want them colder) to the lesions.

- Lysine cream, available in health food stores, can be applied topically twice daily or as directed on package label.

- Make an ointment of two mashed aspirins mixed with two tablespoons of chloroform (or Vaseline Intensive Care). Apply to the lesions and let dry.

- Calamine lotion can be applied to the lesions.

- Vitamin E capsules can be squeezed directly onto lesions.

- Avoid arginine-rich foods such as chocolate, peanuts and nuts, seeds, and cereal grains.

IN ADDITION TO YOUR DAILY SUPPLEMENTS, PAGE xxiv, TAKE

- Lysine supplements: 500 to 1,000 mg. three times daily during an outbreak.

- Vitamin C: 2 to 3 g. daily taken 1 g. (1,000 mg.) every six hours at first sign of pain and continued until the lesions clear.

- Vitamin E: 600 I.U. daily.

FOR POSTHERPETIC PAIN:

- Use Zostrix ointment. After the lesions have healed, apply four to six times a day for several weeks.

IN ADDITION: Acupuncture can be helpful in relieving symptoms of an acute attack as well as postherpetic pain; I recommend it to my patients.

Eighty-eight percent of patients in one study have been freed from pain after receiving intramuscular injections of adenosine monophosphate (AMP), a natural cellular metabolite. Patients remained pain-free from three to eighteen months after the treatment. I have had great success with this treatment.

Vitamin B_{12} injections have also helped my patients with postherpetic neuralgia.

•   •   •

SINUSITIS

THE PAIN AND FRUSTRATION of chronic sinus infections can be truly debilitating. One patient told me that her sinusitis felt like she was hundreds of feet underwater without a diving helmet. That's a good description of the swelling, congestion, pain, headache, and overall misery of a sinus attack. Many people suffer with sinusitis for years because they and their doctors can never identify precisely what's causing the problem and/or they don't take sufficient care to avoid repeated attacks. Unfortunately for some people, sinusitis can be helped only by surgery. But for most people, simple natural measures will help prevent recurrent attacks.

The sinus cavities, which take up about a third of the skull, are believed to be a sort of air-control system for the lungs. Air is brought into the sinus cavities, cleaned of dust and harmful bacteria by the cilia and mucus of the nasal passages, humidified, and then sent to the lungs. Because the single exit from the sinus cavities is tiny—only about as wide as the lead in a pencil—it's relatively easy to clog it. When mucus becomes thick, either in response to a cold or an allergic reaction, the single exit from the sinus cavity becomes blocked and the mucus builds up. The sinus cavity is the perfect place for bacteria to thrive, and thrive they do until you have a full-blown, painful, congested sinus. You can confirm that your problem is your sinus rather than a headache by bending over: If it's a sinus, you'll feel a painful throbbing; if not, you'll feel no change.

Sometimes people will get a sinus infection as the result of a cold, suffer awhile, take some medication, and be better in a few days. But those who are really troubled by sinus infections get them chronically. Patients complain to me that they seem to have a constant "cold" or that they have six or more "colds" a year. This is always a signal to investigate chronic sinusitis.

If you have what you think is a sinus infection with a thick yellowish green discharge, head congestion, and pain, you should see your doctor. You'll probably need to take an antibiotic to get rid of the infection so the sinus can drain. If the infection is so resistant that after a few courses of different antibiotics it still won't clear up, you might be a candidate for surgery to correct a deformity of the nasal cavity.

If there's nothing anatomically wrong with your nose, it's time to take measures to head off the infections before they begin: They're really easier to prevent than cure. Your main goal is going to be to keep the nasal mucus thin and free-flowing so it doesn't breed infection.

The first step—a simple one that really works—is to drink a lot of fluids. You should do this all day long but particularly when you are recovering from a cold, when you're under stress, and when you feel your nose beginning to clog. Force yourself to drink six to eight glasses of water daily. My patients find it helpful to keep a bottle of mineral water or seltzer at hand all day and sip from it constantly. The additional liquid will help keep the mucus flowing. Hot beverages—herbal teas, broths, and soups—are especially good. It might sound odd, but it's helpful to lower your nose to a hot drink and take a deep breath. This humidity will help keep your nasal passages open.

Humidity is very important. The more moist the air, the more efficient the nasal cilia and the more liquid the mucus. Use a cool-mist humidifier, or lean your head over a sink filled with hot water, tent a towel over your head, and breathe deeply.

Moist heat helps, too. Try resting a towel or washcloth that has been wrung out with hot water over your face for a few minutes. It can stimulate blood circulation, loosen mucus, and relieve pain.

Pressure on the sides of your nose can also relieve pain. Press the top of your nose on either side between two fingers for a few minutes and then release. Do this a few times a day to relieve pain and stimulate the flow of mucus.

Many people develop sinusitis as a result of an allergen—typically a food or an inhalant—and in response their mucosal passages swell. The mucus becomes thick, and the result is sinusitis. Many of my patients have found relief when they identified their allergies. In my experience, dairy products are often responsible for sinus problems, but many foods can be a problem. Inhalants that can cause problems include mold and dust; some people are even allergic to cockroaches. For more information on how to identify these problems see Food Allergy, page 146, and Hay Fever, page 167.

Don't forget that a cold can be the first step in developing a sinus infection; take every measure possible to avoid colds. See Colds, page 83.

If you want to take an over-the-counter medication to relieve sinus congestion I recommend a single-action one that's geared only to relieve congestion, like Sudafed. Avoid antihistamines, as they dry nasal secretion and can ultimately make you more congested.

Vitamin A and vitamin C can help with a sinus infection. Vitamin A thins the mucus and promotes the growth of healthy mucus-producing cells. It also strengthens the immune system.

NATURAL PRESCRIPTION FOR SINUSITIS

- Drink plenty of fluids, particularly during a cold or times of high stress. Drink six to eight glasses of water daily. Hot beverages such as herbal tea, broths, and soups can be substituted.

- Humidify your environment. Use a cool-mist humidifier at home (especially in your bedroom) and in your workplace. When you're suffering from symptoms, take hot showers and hot baths. Tent a towel over your head and inhale deeply above a sink filled with hot water a few times a day.

- Use warm compresses on your nose and eyes to relieve pain.

- Use pressure to relieve pain and stimulate circulation: Press the top of your nose on either side between two fingers for a few minutes and then release. Do this several times a day.

- Investigate the possibility of either food or inhalant allergy (see Food Allergy, page 146, and Hay Fever, page 167).

- Colds can trigger sinus infections; do your best to avoid them (see Colds, page 83).

- If you need additional relief from congestion, stick with single-action, over-the-counter decongestants like Sudafed.

IN ADDITION TO YOUR DAILY SUPPLEMENTS, PAGE xxiv, TAKE

- Vitamin C: 1,000 to 2,000 mg. daily.

- Vitamin A: 10,000 I.U. daily.

IN ADDITION: Recent research has shown that there is a natural supplement that can help reduce the incidence of chronic sinusitis. N-acetylcysteine, which is derived from an amino acid, has been shown to help keep mucus fluid, thus helping the sinus drain. It's available at health food stores and can be given in doses of 200 mg. two times a day for children and 200 mg. three times daily for adults.

. . .

SORE THROAT

THE MOST COMMON CAUSE of a sore throat (except that caused by hosting a birthday party for a five-year-old) is a viral infection. But a sore throat can also be a strep throat infected with streptococcal bacteria. This can be a serious condition as it can lead to rheumatic fever and ultimately a damaged heart and kidney. Unfortunately, there has been a resurgence of rheumatic fever in this country. If you have a sore throat, it is very important to determine whether it is also a strep throat.

A strep throat is not easy to recognize. You might have a sudden fever of 102°F or more. A strep throat might make you feel sicker than you would if you just had a sore throat from a cold. In addition, an examination will give evidence: a red, inflamed throat that's covered with white patches. If you have any of these symptoms you should consult your doctor who will probably do a throat culture. If you indeed are suffering from strep, you will be treated with antibiotics.

The average sore throat is the result of a cold or flu virus. For an overall treatment regime for colds and flus, see Colds, page 83. For the pain of a sore throat there are a number of treatments that will give great relief. Gargling with mixtures of water and salt, water and hydrogen peroxide if infection is present, or water and aspirin can all give relief.

Zinc lozenges, which are available in health food stores, can be dissolved on the tongue to relieve pain and fight infection. I think they are the simplest and most effective treatment.

If you suffer from recurring sore throats, it's possible that your toothbrush is the culprit. Many people couldn't tell you how old their toothbrush is; they just use it until it nearly falls apart—a bad policy because a toothbrush can harbor a lot of bacteria. If you get a sore throat often, you should change your toothbrush at least every month, and also after you've had a bout with any cold, flu, sore throat, or other illness that could leave bacteria.

Some people wake up almost every morning with a sore throat that disappears as the day goes on. Then at some point late in the day they develop a runny or stuffy nose. This can happen seasonally or all year long. This kind of sore throat is most commonly due to allergies. Because your nose is stuffed, you breathe through your mouth during the night. When you wake up, your throat is sore from all that dry air. In order to stop this kind of sore throat you have to deal with whatever is causing the allergies. For more information on this, see Hay Fever, page 167.

There can be a connection between a sore throat that's a result of tonsillitis and a milk allergy. If you have a child who is suffering from recurring sore throats especially associated with ear infections that are not related to strep, you might investigate the possibility of a milk allergy (see Food Allergy, page 146; Ear Infections, page 126).

NATURAL PRESCRIPTION FOR SORE THROAT

- Zinc lozenges—each lozenge containing about 23 mg. of zinc—can be taken every four hours. Do not use these lozenges for more than a week.

- Gargle with a mixture of half water and half hydrogen peroxide to help fight infection. Do not swallow this mixture.

- Gargle with crushed aspirin mixed with water to relieve pain.

- Drink warm tea with honey. Use an herbal or decaffeinated tea. Alternatively, you can also sip warm water with honey and lemon.

- If your room is very dry, use a humidifier.

- If you suffer from recurrent sore throats, try changing your toothbrush frequently.

- If you suffer from recurring sore throats, particularly ones associated with ear infections, investigate the possibility of a milk or other food allergy. See Food Allergy, page 146 and Ear Infections, page 126.

- If you suffer from recurring sore throats that are worse in the morning but disappear as the day goes on, you could have some form of hay fever. See Hay Fever, page 167.

• • •

STASIS ULCER

STASIS ULCERS or leg ulcers are open sores that can develop because of poor circulation in the legs that compromises blood flow. Once a cut, an abrasion, or other injury occurs, skin surrounding the site of the wound begins to deteriorate, making it more susceptible to a running sore. Sometimes a statis ulcer will develop on a leg where it was injured in the past. People who suffer from diabetes or varicose veins or who are overweight are especially susceptible. These sores can be difficult to heal and they should be treated by a doctor, but there are steps you can take to speed healing.

Adequate nutrition is essential and I urge patients who suffer from stasis ulcers to make sure their diet is adequate and also to take supplements, particularly those associated with the healing process. For detailed information, see Wound Healing, page 353.

There are natural steps you can take to aid the healing of leg ulcers. Numerous studies have reported that a compress of sugar will inhibit bacterial growth and stimulate healing in an open wound, and I've had success with this compress in my practice. To prepare it, mix common granulated sugar with either Betadine (an antibacterial liquid found in any pharmacy) or hydrogen peroxide until the mixture forms a soft paste. You then apply the paste to the wound and cover it with a gauze bandage. Carefully rinse the wound of the old paste and apply a fresh sugar dressing two to three times daily.

Vitamin E applied topically can help prevent recurrence of the wound once it has healed.

NATURAL PRESCRIPTION FOR STASIS ULCER

- If you have a wound that won't heal, you should be under the care of a doctor. It's possible that you will need to take antibiotics.

- Treating the predisposing condition will help to heal the wound: If you are diabetic, see Diabetes, page 111; if you have varicose veins, see page 344; if you are overweight, make an effort to lose weight as outlined in Blueprint for Health, page xvii.

- A sugar compress can aid healing. Mix common granulated sugar with either Betadine or hydrogen peroxide until it forms a soft paste. Apply this to the wound and cover it with a gauze bandage. Repeat this application two to three times daily after gently rinsing out the old paste with water.

IN ADDITION TO YOUR DAILY SUPPLEMENTS, PAGE xxiv, TAKE

- Vitamin C: 2,000 mg. or 2 g. daily in divided doses at meals and bedtime.

- Vitamin A: 10,000 I.U. daily.

- Zinc: 22.5 to 50 mg. daily.

- Vitamin E: 400 I.U. daily. Also, vitamin E oil squeezed from a capsule directly on the site of the wound can help prevent recurrence.

- Vitamin B$_3$: 100 mg. daily.

- Amino acid glutamine: 500 mg. daily.

• • •

STRESS CONTROL

I BELIEVE THAT STRESS is one of our most serious health problems because it affects every aspect of how the body works. Any illness is made worse by stress. If you have a tendency to headaches, stress will increase their frequency. If you have a predisposition for cardiovascular disease, stress will increase your risk. Even if you're in excellent health, uncontrolled stress will keep you from achieving the sense of calm that can make life far more meaningful and enjoyable.

People talk about stress constantly today, often referring to someone as "stressed-out." But few people really understand the gravity of a highly stressed body.

The body is constantly trying to maintain internal stability and will do what it can to return to stability if that state is altered. This is called homeostasis. If it's a very hot day, your body will cool itself by perspiring. To repair a cut, the body creates a scab, which helps heal the wound and protects the skin from further damage. Homeostatic activities include everything from the replacement of the lining of the digestive tract to the regulation of a woman's menstrual cycle. You depend on homeostasis for your health, and if one of your stabilizing systems breaks down, the result will be disease and perhaps death.

Your body responds to stress with a complex series of biochemical changes that attempt to bring the body back into its prestressed state. This seems like a simple concept, but its ramifications in respect to maintaining health are awesome; indeed, many scientists consider stress theory to be one of the greatest contributions to the understanding of disease made in this century.

In simplest terms stress refers to the everyday wear and tear on the body caused by any physical or emotional demand, from a broken leg to an invading virus to a sexual encounter to a screaming baby. The stress can be physical or emotional. When the body is stressed it reacts with a series of biochemical changes, the most significant being the secretion by the adrenal glands of various hormones, including epinephrine and norepinephrine, which energize the body. This mobilization of energy is commonly known as the "fight-or-flight" response because the body is preparing to react in a decisive, physical fashion to the stress.

When epinephrine and norepinephrine are released, they immediately heighten the nervous system's sensitivity, quicken the heartbeat, and sharpen the reflexes. The muscles tense, the pupils dilate, and the blood vessels of the skin contract so as to retain body heat and force more blood into the major organs. The liver releases stored glucose, for energy to fight the stress. The digestive tract ceases its normal activity, also to conserve energy. The ability of the blood to coagulate is increased so that in case of a severe wound, blood loss will be prevented.

These physical responses are obviously appropriate to someone facing a severe physical trauma, but for someone stuck in a traffic jam or opening a credit card bill, the response is really a primitive reaction to a modern world.

When you experience a stress that's immediate and limited, like a skid on an icy road, your body will quickly recover from its stress response once the event is over. But when the stress is constant anxiety over job performance or an unhappy marriage, then your body has no opportunity to restore its reserves. It goes into what Hans Selye, the father of stress theory, calls the "stage of resistance," or adaptation, where the body tries to adjust to the constant stress. This is useful initially for coping with long-term stress like a severe illness or severe hardships. But for the kind of constant stress most of us endure daily it's overkill. Eventually, in the face of unremitting stress, the body will enter the "exhaustion stage." It can now no longer function properly. At this stage you begin to exhibit minor symptoms of disease. If you have a tendency to develop headaches, you'll have them constantly. If you suffer from digestive problems, they'll worsen. You may begin to develop allergies or constant colds. The weak links in your individual biochemical makeup will begin to break down.

The effects of stress are far more real and visible than most people realize. Animal research has shown in a dramatic way what stress can do. For example, mice flown from Boston to Seattle took three days to recover from dangerous levels of adrenaline, cortisol, and other body chemicals. The stress of the flight had aroused the fight-or-flight response in the mice, yet there was no way for them to discharge the resulting chemicals.

The increased blood pressure caused by constant stress is one of its most dangerous side effects. High blood pressure is one of the major contributing factors to atherosclerosis. If you don't control the stress in your life, you dramatically increase your chances of having a heart attack or a stroke. It has been estimated that deaths traced to high blood pressure account for more than half of the deaths in this country every year. Moreover, varying degrees of hypertension, or high blood pressure, are present in 15 to 33 percent of the adult population. Stress is as important, if not more so, as smoking, high blood pressure, and raised cholesterol levels in determining your chances of heart disease.

You cannot eliminate all the stress in your life. Many people live for years thinking that once they get that new job or once they have their house paid off or once the kids leave home, they'll be free of stress. I have yet to find anyone, in all my years of medical practice, who has finally achieved a stress-free life. In any case, a totally stress-free life is not really a desirable goal.

The challenge is to deal sensibly with stress and to take specific action to defuse it. When I searched for a method of relaxation for myself and for my patients that would be simple to learn, relatively fast, and easy to do anywhere, I eventually selected Dr. Herbert Benson's relaxation response as satisfying every criterion. Dr. Benson is a cardiologist associated with Harvard Medical School, and chief of the Section on Behavioral Medicine at New England Deaconess Hospital. Among the first to do extensive research on meditation, he reported on the connection between meditation and reduced blood pressure and the decreased use of drugs for the treatment of high blood pressure. After researching the literature on meditative practices in yoga, Sufism, Zen, Judaism, and Christianity, Dr. Benson distilled the technique, common to all those practices, that produced a quiet mind and a peaceful heart. He called the technique the "relaxation response." It's really a form of demystified meditation.

The relaxation response (RR) is the physiological opposite of the fight-or-flight response. It decreases the activity of your sympathetic nervous system as it decreases your metabolism, heart rate, and rate of breathing; decreases the blood flow to your muscles; increases the alpha brain waves that are associated with feelings of relaxation and well-being; and decreases your blood lactate levels, which are associated with muscular fatigue. Benson notes that these changes are distinctly different from the physiological changes you experience when you sit quietly or sleep.

Some of my patients initially scoffed at the relaxation response. How could something so simple make a difference in the way you feel? Believe me, it does. Here's what you need to invoke the relaxation response:

A QUIET ENVIRONMENT. This can be anywhere—home or office. Many of my patients sit at their desk and invoke the RR. One man told me that his gym has a "nap room" where people can rest and he uses that. Just be sure to choose a place with no loud noises or distractions.

A MENTAL DEVICE. This is equivalent to using a mantra while meditating. It's a single-syllable sound or word that you repeat silently or in a quiet tone. It helps you to remove yourself from logical thought and distractions. Dr. Benson suggests using the word *one*. A patient told me she uses the word *snow* in the summer and *sun* in the winter.

A PASSIVE ATTITUDE. This sounds simple and it should be, but people sometimes make too much of it, defeating the purpose. A passive attitude means not focusing on how well you're doing in the exercise or whether you're getting the correct response. When either of these thoughts occurs to you, let it go and focus instead on repeating your chosen word.

A COMFORTABLE POSITION. You want to reduce any awareness of your muscles as much as possible. A comfortable chair that supports your head is good. It's even better if you can lie down.

Here's how you invoke the relaxation:

1. Sit in a comfortable position in a quiet environment.

2. Close your eyes.

3. Relax your muscles beginning with your feet, then your calves, thighs, lower torso, chest, shoulders, arms, neck, and head. Pay special attention to the muscles in your neck and face, which get very tense.

4. Breathe through your nose, paying attention to your breathing. As you exhale, say aloud or just think about your chosen word.

5. Do this for at least ten minutes—twenty, if you're able. You can open your eyes to check the time, but Dr. Benson cautions against using an alarm.

I suggest that you practice the relaxation response at least once, better twice, a day. You may come to feel, as many of my patients do, that it's the most important part of your day. Patients who practice the RR regularly are always enthusiastic about its calming and invigorating effects.

I find it is most effective when done in the middle of the day, and again in the evening. Many of my patients do it just before or after lunch at their desks or at home or just after work. It should become part of your daily routine and it will help you cope with daily stresses in your life on both a physiological and psychological level. You'll be amazed to find that such a simple exercise that takes so little time can have such an important effect on your body and mind.

For the nutritional supplements useful in combating stress, see the basic antioxidant vitamin/mineral supplements described in Blueprint for Health, page xvii.

•   •   •

STY

A STY USUALLY BEGINS with irritation in the eye. You find yourself rubbing your eye and after a day or two you notice a tiny lump or pimple on the upper or lower lid. The annoying pimple becomes larger and painful until, within a few days, it bursts, and the pain and irritation ceases. The first thing *not* to do to a sty is to rub or squeeze it.

A sty is in fact an infection in the eyelash follicle or the oil gland. If you're frequently exposed to small particles of any kind, you are more likely to develop sties as tiny particles clog the gland or follicle on the eyelid. One of my patients who complained of frequent sties was a housepainter who developed frequent sties because of exposure to plaster dust caused by sanding. Once he began to wear plastic goggles, his sties disappeared.

Sometimes you can get sties over a period of weeks or you can get a few at the same time. This is because the bacteria that are causing the infection have traveled to another site on the eyelid and infected it.

The best way to cope with a sty is to use frequent warm compresses. Take a clean washcloth and wet it with hot water so that the cloth is comfortably warm to the touch. Press it gently to the affected eye and hold it in place for about ten minutes. This moist warmth helps the sty come to a head and burst, which relieves the pain. If you can see that a white or yellow head has formed on the sty after a few days, you can pull out the eyelash. This will relieve the pain by helping the pus to drain. Again, never squeeze the sty or try to pull the lash or force it to drain before a head has formed.

The sty should disappear in about a week. If it doesn't, or if you have frequent problems with sties, consult a doctor, who will probably prescribe antibiotics.

NATURAL PRESCRIPTION FOR STIES

- Never rub, squeeze, or irritate a sty.

- Use a warm compress three or four times a day, gently pressing a washcloth wet with comfortably hot water over the eye for about ten minutes.

- Once the sty comes to a head with an obvious white or yellow center, you can gently pull the eyelash out, to release pus and relieve pain.

- If the sty does not clear up in about a week, see your doctor.

SWIMMER'S EAR

SWIMMER'S EAR (otitis externa) is a bacterial (or sometimes fungal) infection of the outer ear, which develops when contaminated water gets trapped in the ear canal. At an early stage, the ear itches. If the ear is really painful and the pain intensifies when your earlobe is pulled, it might well be infected. Swimmer's ear got its name because most people contract it after swimming, but it can develop just from showering or washing your hair.

The simplest way to prevent swimmer's ear is to keep your ears dry. That means that you should be sure to dry the outer ear with a soft towel after swimming or showering. Remember not to "put anything smaller than a banana in your ear," including cotton swabs. Just be sure the outer part of the ear is dry.

If you're prone to swimmer's ear you can use ear plugs to help keep water out of the ear canal.

If you swim in lakes frequently, where water is more likely to be harboring infectious bacteria (as opposed to salt water), you might want to use antiseptic ear drops after swimming, especially if you've had swimmer's ear in the past. They will help restore the natural acid balance of the ear, kill bacteria, and help dry it out. If your ears do begin to itch, you can use the drops a few times a day until the itch subsides.

If your ear becomes painful, has a discharge, or hurts when the earlobe is pulled, you might have developed an infection, in which case it's best to see a doctor and begin a course of antibiotics.

NATURAL PRESCRIPTION FOR SWIMMER'S EAR

- Dry your ears thoroughly with a soft towel after swimming, showering, or washing your hair.

- Try using ear plugs when swimming.

- If you're going to swim in a lake and/or if you're prone to swimmer's ear, use drying/antiseptic ear drops after swimming. You can buy them in a pharmacy, or use equal parts of white vinegar and rubbing

alcohol. Put a drop or two in your ears after swimming. If they begin
to itch, use the solution three times a day until the itch stops.

• • •

TENDINITIS AND BURSITIS

TENDINITIS AND BURSITIS are two common disorders of the musculoskeletal system that are usually the result of repetitive activity. Tennis elbow
is one of the most common types of tendinitis. While painful, annoying,
and sometimes immobilizing, with proper care and prevention tendinitis
and bursitis are not ultimately serious. I discuss them together because
their treatment is identical.

Tendinitis is essentially an inflammation of the tendon, a band of
tough, white fibrous tissue that connects the muscle to the bone. Muscle
fibers merge at one end into a tendon while the opposite end is attached
to bone. When the tendon becomes inflamed, usually from a strain—
overexertion, tearing, stretching, and twisting—it swells and causes soreness and impaired motion. This is tendinitis. A tendon can actually tear
away from the bone, resulting in a ruptured tendon. The tendons most
commonly injured include the Achilles (at the back of the ankle), the
biceps (at the front of the shoulder), the pollicis brevis and longus (the
thumb), the upper patella (the knee), the posterior tibial (the inside of
the foot), the elbow, and the rotator cuff (shoulder).

Bursitis is caused when the bursa—a sac or pouch filled with lubricat-
ing fluid that surrounds and protects joints such as the shoulders—
becomes inflamed. Bursitis can be caused by trauma, strain, infection, or
arthritis. The most common sites of bursitis include the shoulder, hip,
elbow, and lower knee.

The most common cause of both tendinitis and bursitis is excessive
tension on the tendon or bursa. Repeated movements, such as are common to sports, can cause both disorders. One way to prevent development of both these problems is to warm up sufficiently before exercising
or engaging in a sport. This allows the tendons and muscles to become
more flexible, thus making strains less likely. If you're just beginning an
exercise routine, it's essential that you work into it at a gentle pace.

I most commonly see bursitis of the shoulder, tendinitis of the elbow, and knee problems. Most of these complaints are sports or exercise related. I tell my patients that they can eliminate chronic problems by modifying or changing their movements, using the RICE technique, and ensuring that their nutritional status is up to par.

Modifying or changing your movements means that you can't keep repeating a movement that's causing pain and disability. If you run and your knees give you trouble, you need to do an alternative exercise until your knees are better and, even then, you'll have to regularly alternate exercises so as not to aggravate your condition. For example, if you are running and the pain is acute, stop running. When the pain lessens, after a period of time, you can begin to run again, but alternate running with another exercise like swimming or cycling. If you have a tennis elbow you'll probably need some expert instruction to help you modify your stroke so that the joint won't be constantly stressed. Whatever you do, if you feel pain—either new pain or a recurrence of a chronic pain— while exercising, don't try to "work through it." You can rupture a tendon, making surgery necessary or putting a permanent halt to your activity.

Many knee problems caused by running are actually due to a condition called pronation of the feet. This means that your weight is not distributed evenly on your feet; running aggravates the problem, causing irritation of the knee. In most cases, this is helped by orthotic supports in your running shoes.

The RICE technique (Rest, Ice, Compress, Elevate), described below, is important if you've just injured yourself in order to minimize inflammation. But it can also be useful if you have a chronic problem. Say your ankle regularly develops tendinitis. To minimize the problem, use the RICE technique after every exercise session or whenever your ankle begins to bother you. This will help to keep your tendinitis or bursitis under control.

THE RICE RECOMMENDATIONS:

- Rest the injured part immediately.
- Ice the injured area to minimize swelling and inflammation.
- Compress the injured area to limit swelling and bleeding.
- Elevate the injured area to a level that's above the heart to increase drainage of fluids from the affected area.

Remember when you put ice on an injury not to apply it directly to the skin—cover the area with a clean cloth or towel. Also, when you "compress" the injured area, be sure not to wrap it so tightly that you limit circulation. The best way to apply ice and compression is to use both on the injured area for a half hour and then remove them both for fifteen minutes to allow full circulation.

The acute, painful stage of tendinitis and bursitis can last from one to five days, sometimes longer. During this period you can use the RICE technique for gradually diminishing amounts of time. You might use it constantly for the first few hours of pain and then five or six times on the second day of pain, three or four times the next day, and so on. In between compression and ice, it's best to keep the area immobilized to minimize pain and inflammation. You can fashion a homemade sling if your arm is affected; if your foot or knee is the problem, stay off it.

Once the inflammation has subsided, which can take from three to five days or sometimes more, you need to gradually begin to exercise the affected area. This is critical. If you keep the area immobilized, it will take far longer to heal and it may heal less completely. As you reach the point where you can begin movement exercise, the inflammation will be gone and the affected area will no longer be warm to the touch. Then, in addition to the exercise, you can apply warm heat, using a heating pad or warm, moist cloths.

The important thing to remember about postinflammation exercise is that when you begin to exercise an injured shoulder, knee, or ankle you're not trying to build muscle strength at first by working it harder and harder: You're merely trying to maintain mobility and enhance your range of motion. This means you need only gently move the injured part in ever-larger circles for just a few minutes, three or four times a day. Only when all pain is gone and the range of movement seems normal should you consider resuming regular exercise.

Adequate nutrition can play a role in preventing and easing the effects of tendinitis and bursitis. The following nutrients, used also for wound healing, are important.

Vitamin C is critical to the repair of injuries. It speeds cellular growth and repair and is important in the production of collagen, which the body uses to create connective tissue. I suggest that patients who suffer regularly from tendinitis and bursitis take regular vitamin C supplementation.

Vitamin A in the form of beta-carotene is also critical to tissue repair.

It's best taken with zinc, which works in conjunction with vitamin A to repair tissue and reduce inflammation.

Vitamin E and selenium work together to limit inflammation and speed healing.

NATURAL PRESCRIPTION FOR TENDINITIS AND BURSITIS

FOR ACUTE PAIN:

- Immediately after injury, for up to five days and sometimes longer, use the RICE technique as described above. Use with decreasing frequency until the pain and inflammation have subsided.

- During acute pain, immobilize the joint either with a sling or keep off the joint if it's a foot or knee.

- When acute pain has subsided, gradually exercise joint with increasingly large movements made very gently and without any kind of bouncing.

- As you begin to exercise, use warm heat either in the form of a heating pad or warm, moist compresses.

FOR CHRONIC PAIN:

- Never exercise without warming up, and begin all new activities gradually. Stretch, without bouncing, before all exercise.

- If you have chronic tendinitis or bursitis, use the RICE techniques immediately after exercise even if you don't feel pain.

- Never "work through the pain." If you feel pain during an activity, stop and use the RICE technique; to continue your activity is to risk rupture and surgery.

- Modify your movements. Try to avoid regular, repetitive movements with any joint that's vulnerable to tendinitis or bursitis. If a particular exercise causes your problem, alternate that exercise with another and/or get professional instruction on how to modify your movements, for instance those that cause tennis elbow, so as to avoid stressing the joint.

IN ADDITION TO YOUR DAILY BASIC VITAMIN/MINERAL SUPPLEMENTS (PAGE ■■■), TAKE THE FOLLOWING UNTIL YOUR INJURY IS HEALED:

- Vitamin C: 1,000 mg. daily.

- Beta-carotene: 10,000 I.U. daily.

- Zinc: 22.5 mg. daily.

- Vitamin E: 400 I.U. daily.

- Selenium: 50 mcg. daily.

IN ADDITION: Acupuncture can be very helpful for people who suffer from acute and chronic tendinitis and bursitis.

• • •

TENSION HEADACHE

ALMOST EVERYONE GETS a tension headache now and again. Your head feels as though it's clamped in a vise, the muscles in the back of your neck feel knotted and sensitive to the touch, and there's pain in your forehead, temples, or through the entire head. A tension headache is caused when the sensitive nerve endings in your head and neck are irritated by tense muscles. (In a migraine headache, the nerve endings are irritated by swollen blood vessels [see Migraine Headaches, page 247; a sinus headache is caused by the inflammation of the sinus tissues [see Sinusitis, page 308.)

For most people, tension headaches last just a few hours and then disappear, with or without the help of a few aspirin. But in some cases, a tension headache can last for days or, rarely, even years.

There are a number of things that can cause tension headaches. We can become tense in response to sensory overload: shrill, persistent noise, harsh lights, feelings of claustrophobia, working against a deadline generates tension, or performing a job where accuracy is essential. (Air traffic controllers are said to suffer frequent tension headaches.) Tension is caused by challenges that cannot be met, such as a pile of bills that exceeds the funds in the bank account. While we cannot avoid all situations that cause tension, we can learn to moderate our response.

A good way to ease work-related tension is to stretch your muscles periodically, before they become rigid and a tension headache sets in. Stand up and stretch, breathe deeply, do a few neck rolls, rolling your head round and round and then side to side. With both your hands, press beneath the bony ridges at the back of your neck until you feel the knotted muscles start to respond.

One of the most effective techniques for relaxing tension is called "progressive relaxation," which has been successfully used to prevent headaches as well as such disorders as hypertension, colitis, and angina. It calls for relaxing the muscles in your body, group by group, starting with the extremities and working toward your neck, face, and head. Many of my patients have mastered this technique and use it frequently. Read Stress Control, page 314, for more details on progressive relaxation. I also recommend a book, *The Relaxation Response,* by Herbert Benson.

Heat helps relax tense muscles. Try soaking in a warm bath with your shoulders and neck submerged. Sometimes a warm shower can relax you. You may find relief with a heating pad.

I've had patients tell me that a nap is the most effective way for them to get rid of a headache. This may be because it relaxes the body so efficiently. Of course a nap isn't always practical.

If you can't take a nap you may be able to take a walk. A brisk walk can often relieve headache symptoms. It reduces tension and increases circulation and oxygen flow, which has been shown to relieve headaches.

In the long run, regular exercise may be the most effective way to prevent tension headaches. Since exercise mitigates the body's response to stress, people given to tension headaches should incorporate exercise into their daily routine.

In addition to actual tension-causing situations, "mechanical" problems such as weakness of the back and neck can also cause headaches, as can a bad bite that sets up tension around the lower jaw. Temporomandibular pressure can be alleviated by correcting the way the teeth come together, and generally requires the attention of an orthodontist. See TMJ Syndrome, page 331.

Some of my patients have complained of tension headaches that are in fact caused by food sensitivities. These are different from migraine headaches in that they don't have the typical migraine symptoms but, like migraines, are caused by particular foods (see Migraine Headaches, page 247, and Food Allergy, page 146).

I've had any number of patients who complain of "weekend" headaches. They're fine all week but by Saturday afternoon they have splitting headaches, many of which are caused by caffeine withdrawal. Used to having up to four cups of coffee by lunchtime on a weekday, they sleep late on Saturday and don't have their first sip of coffee until nearly noon. What they don't realize is that caffeine is addictive and by delaying their "fix" hours past their usual time, they're withdrawing. Blueprint for Health, page xvii, has information on caffeine; suffice it to say, I suggest you drink no more than one cup of coffee per day on a regular basis. And if you still get a withdrawal headache on Saturday or Sunday morning, you'll simply have to have your first cup earlier!

Withdrawal from painkillers can be another cause of headaches. If you regularly take aspirin or acetaminophen you can develop "analgesic rebound headache." Many pain relievers contain caffeine. When you stop the medication, you develop a headache from caffeine withdrawal; as soon as you take it, the headache disappears but the cycle begins again. The medication gives temporary relief but is in fact the cause of the headache. If this describes your headache pattern, try using other nonmedicinal means of dealing with them. I think, in general, it's best to limit your OTC pain medication to no more than three days a week and no more than four tablets a day. Of course this recommendation will depend on your condition and should be discussed with your doctor, but it's what I tell my patients who wonder if they're overusing painkillers.

Many of my patients who complain of afternoon headaches are really suffering from symptoms of low blood sugar. The main treatment for this is to be scrupulous about regular meals at regular times and no skipped meals. For detailed information, See Hypoglycemia, page 202.

NATURAL PRESCRIPTION FOR TENSION HEADACHES

- Learn what triggers your headaches, including sensory overload and stress. When you face any of these triggers, be sure to use relaxation techniques to fight tension. Stretch your muscles periodically, once every half hour, and massage the neck and shoulders. See Stress Control, page 314.

- See Migraine Headaches (page 247) and Food Allergy (page 146) to learn if your headaches are connected to food allergies or sensitivities.

- Use moist heat to relieve pain: take a warm shower or bath or use a moist (or dry) heating pad on your neck.

- Take a nap.

- Take a brisk walk.

- Adopt a program of regular exercise.

- Investigate whether jaw clenching or improper jaw alignment could be causing your headaches (see TMJ Syndrome, page 331).

- Cut down or eliminate your caffeine consumption.

- If the overuse of regular pain relievers that contain caffeine is causing headaches, cut down on use and try natural methods of pain relief.

- Be sure to eat regular meals at regular times and never skip a meal. See Hypoglycemia, page 202.

•   •   •

TINNITUS

TINNITUS, A CONDITION that causes noises in the ear, is a truly perplexing problem. People who suffer from it hear ringing, buzzing, clicking or roaring in their ears even in the dead of a silent night. As you might imagine, it can be distracting and troubling. In most cases, it is difficult to determine precise cause, but the following factors can contribute to the problem. The longer tinnitus is ignored, the more difficult it is to remedy.

Loud noises can cause tinnitus. If you're regularly exposed to construction noise, loud music, or gunshots, you're more likely to develop the condition. Loud noises can actually damage the ear itself; it's important for people who are routinely exposed to protect their ears. This won't cure tinnitus once you've developed it, but it will help prevent it.

High blood pressure and hyperthyroidism can cause tinnitus; if you have or suspect either, you need to get them under control. Discuss hyperthyroidism with your doctor (see Hypertension, page 194). In addition, Meniere's syndrome can cause it (see Meniere's Syndrome, page 239).

A common cause of tinnitus and the most simple to remedy is an accumulation of earwax. Once the wax is removed, the sound will disappear (see Earwax, page 131).

If removing earwax doesn't solve the problem, get a thorough examination by an ear, nose, and throat specialist. Sometimes tinnitus is caused by a tumor affecting a nerve inside the ear. Surgery can remove the tumor—which can be dangerous in any case—and eliminate symptoms.

Some people who suffer from tinnitus are reacting to salicylates, antiinflammatory agents including aspirin, analgesics (pain relievers), and antipyretics (fever-lowering agents). Many over-the-counter as well as prescription medications contain salicylates. If you take any drug that contains salicylates regularly—aspirin being the most common—you should investigate whether this is causing your tinnitus. If possible (after discussion with your doctor), eliminate the drug for a period of time to see if it has any effect. Salicylates also occur naturally in foods such as almonds, apples, apricots, blackberries, boysenberries, cherries, cucumbers and pickles, currants, dewberries, gooseberries, grapes or raisins, nectarines, oranges, peaches, plums or prunes, raspberries, strawberries, and tomatoes.

Other drugs that can cause tinnitus include atropine sulfate, caffeine, chloroquine, Flexeril, ergotamine derivatives, nicotine, Talwin, quinidine, and quinine.

You'll notice that I mentioned both caffeine and nicotine in the list of drugs that can cause tinnitus. Smoking or drinking too much coffee can cause tinnitus. Stop smoking. Eliminate caffeine—from coffee, sodas, medications, and chocolate—for at least a week to see if your symptoms are affected (see Blueprint for Health, page xvii).

Diet can play a role in tinnitus. Both a high-fat and high-cholesterol diet can reduce the flow of oxygen to the inner ear. Studies have shown that many patients with unexplained tinnitus who adopted a low-fat, low-cholesterol diet found a reduction in their symptoms.

Low blood sugar has also been implicated in tinnitus. If you think this might be true for you, read Hypoglycemia (page 202) on how to stabilize your blood sugar through diet and chromium supplementation.

Vitamin A is closely associated with the health of the inner ear. Many studies have shown that people with low levels of vitamin A suffer from auditory problems. If you suffer from tinnitus you should be sure you're getting enough. Zinc could play a role in the development of tinnitus. There's some evidence that patients who have tinnitus may require extra supplementation. Calcium is another supplement that can help relieve tinnitus. Ginko biloba has also been helpful.

Relaxation techniques seem to be very helpful; they don't stop the noise but they make it much easier to live with. I've had patients who, despite every effort at eliminating tinnitus, have been unsuccessful. However, they found that when they adopted specific techniques for controlling stress, the tinnitus was much easier to tolerate (see Stress Control, page 314).

Many people who have tinnitus, especially elderly people, are also hard of hearing. This can exacerbate the condition by making other sounds softer and allowing the sounds of the tinnitus to dominate. It can be very helpful for such people to get a hearing aid. Being able to hear well will relieve the tinnitus to some degree, as well as enhance life in general.

NATURAL PRESCRIPTION FOR TINNITUS

- If you are regularly exposed to loud noises, protect your ears with ear plugs.

- Check for an accumulation of earwax. See Earwax, page 131.

- Have an ear, nose, and throat specialist examine you to rule out the possibility of a tumor affecting a nerve in the ear.

- Eliminate any food that contains salicylates. Foods containing salicylates include almonds, apples, apricots, blackberries, boysenberries, cherries, cucumbers and pickles, currants, gooseberries, grapes or raisins, nectarines, oranges, peaches, plums or prunes, raspberries, strawberries, and tomatoes.

- If you are taking the following drugs, consult your physician to see if they affect your tinnitus: aspirin, atropine sulfate, chloroquine, Flexeril, ergotamine derivatives, nicotine, Talwin, quinidine, and quinine.

- Stop smoking.

- Eliminate caffeine to see if it affects your tinnitus.

- Adopt a low-fat, low-cholesterol diet.

- Check to see if you have a blood-sugar problem. Read Hypoglycemia, page 202, and treat low blood sugar with diet and chromium supplementation.

- Adopt relaxation techniques. See Stress Control, page 314.

- Have your hearing checked, and if necessary get a hearing aid.

IN ADDITION TO YOUR DAILY SUPPLEMENTS, PAGE xxiv, TAKE

- Vitamin A: 10,000 I.U. daily.

- Zinc: 50 mg. daily.

- Calcium: 1,200 mg. daily at bedtime.

- Ginkgo biloba: 40 mg. three times daily.

•   •   •

TMJ SYNDROME

WHEN JOHN, a stock analyst, came to see me about constant headaches, it seemed obvious that they were a result of the recent stock market crash. He'd had occasional headaches in the past but they had become regular and debilitating. He had been to various doctors and tried a variety of pain pills and muscle relaxants, but nothing gave more than temporary relief. As he told me, he was tired of taking pills and tired of getting no results and of course he was more than tired of the headaches.

When I told John he needed to adopt some stress-reduction techniques, he told me that he had tried with no results and was tired of being told that everything was caused by stress. When I told him that I thought his problem was not caused by stress but simply worsened by it, he was surprised. It turned out that John was suffering from symptoms associated with TMJ disorder. I worked with him on reducing stress, particularly the actual stress in his jaw, recommended certain supplements, and referred him to a dentist who worked on the structural problems in his jaw. Within a few months John's headaches had completely disappeared.

Very few patients come to me complaining of TMJ disorder—most have never heard of it. In fact, TMJ disorder is usually defined by its symptoms: headaches; pain in the temples, neck, shoulders, and back; diminished hearing; and "sinus trouble." But the source of the problem is actually constant jaw clenching or teeth grinding. Over a period of time, the muscles that control the temporomandibular joints (where the jaw joins the skull) develop nodules or "trigger points" that produce the symptoms when aggravated.

What causes people to clench their jaws and grind their teeth? Just what you would think: stress. But today there is some question whether stress exacerbates an already existing condition or causes the condition in the first place. Some believe the real cause of clenching and grinding is malocclusion of the jaw. The teeth don't fit together properly and, over a period of time, the muscles must compensate for this poor fit, causing the pain and various symptoms of TMJ disorder. Many people go through life with malocclusion of the jaw and never have any symptoms or even, in fact, know that their teeth don't align properly. But for others stress is the precipitating factor.

If you suffer from persistent headaches, unexplained neck and back pain, stuffiness or swelling or pain in your sinus area that doesn't respond to sinus treatments, you could be suffering from TMJ disorder. A simple self-test is to feel your temples and clench your jaw. You'll feel a muscle tense up under your fingers at the temples. Press on that area with the jaw relaxed: if you feel severe pain and tenderness, it indicates that you're tensing your jaw, the muscles are tender, and TMJ *could* be the cause.

Another easy test is to gently put the ends of your little fingers into your ears and press them forward, toward the front of the ear, while opening and closing your mouth a few times. Most people will feel nothing but if you feel the head of your jawbone pushing against your fingers, you could well have TMJ disorder.

Other clues include:

- clicking sounds when you open or close your mouth
- clenching or teeth grinding during the day or when sleeping
- tenderness in the facial muscles upon awakening.

What's the solution? There are natural approaches that can help but a trip to a dentist is the first step. He will check your bite. It's usually not a major ordeal; often it's just a matter of correcting one or two teeth that are too high or low. For the most severe cases only a dentist who specializes in TMJ problems may be able to give permanent relief.

The next step you should take is to see if dealing with stress will help relieve your symptoms. For more information, see Stress Control, page 314.

You should eliminate caffeine from your diet, as people who drink a great deal of caffeine tend to clench their jaws far more frequently than those who abstain. Low blood sugar can also cause people to clench their teeth (see Hypoglycemia, page 202).

There are two nutrients that are helpful in fighting TMJ syndrome: calcium and pantothenic acid.

Some researchers have made a connection between TMJ disorder and allergies. If you've had food allergies in the past, you should try to eliminate any foods from your diet that might be causing a reaction (see Food Allergy, page 146).

If you suspect that jaw clenching and teeth grinding may be causing symptoms, try using a mouth guard for a few nights. You can buy one inexpensively in a sporting goods store. Put it into hot water so it becomes pliable, then put it into your mouth and bite down on it. If you sleep with it in your mouth for a few nights and notice that your symptoms have diminished, it may be worth discussing with a dentist either correcting your malocclusion or making you a permanent (and more comfortable) mouth guard.

I tell my patients who are jaw clenchers that they must force themselves to become conscious of the problem. I suggest that they make a habit of feeling their jaw during the day to see if it's tense and, if it is, to relax it. Ultimately they get into the habit of keeping their jaw relaxed. Tell yourself throughout the day, "lips together; teeth apart," which is the proper position. One woman told me that she snapped a rubber band that she wore around her wrist every time she felt her jaw clenching, and it helped her unlearn the habit.

If you're one of those people who holds the phone against your shoulder by tilting your head, stop! It's a habit that can encourage TMJ disorder. So can chewing large pieces of food (cut food into small bits) or constantly chewing hard and brittle foods.

One final suggestion: many people who suffer from TMJ disorder sleep on their side. This position puts pressure on the face and seems to encourage teeth grinding. Try sleeping on your back, and you may find your symptoms greatly relieved.

NATURAL PRESCRIPTION FOR TMJ SYNDROME

- Consult a dentist to see if your teeth align properly.

- Learn stress-reducing techniques for dealing with the anxiety in your life (see Stress Control, page 314).

- Eliminate caffeine from your diet.

- Eliminate sugar from your diet if you suffer from low blood sugar (see Hypoglycemia, page 202).

- Buy a mouth guard from a sporting supply store to see if wearing it for a few nights relieves your pain: If it does, ask your dentist to make you a permanent one.

- Try specific techniques to learn to relax your jaw throughout the day.

- Sleep on your back.

- Avoid holding the phone against your shoulder by tilting your head.

- Avoid chewing very large pieces of food and hard brittle foods.

IN ADDITION TO YOUR DAILY SUPPLEMENTS, PAGE xxiv, TAKE

- Calcium: 1,200 mg. at bedtime.

- Panthothenic acid: 200 mg. daily.

IN ADDITION: I've used acupuncture successfully on patients with TMJ syndrome to relieve persistent jaw and neck pain as well as relieve headache. They say it "works like a miracle."

ULCERS

ULCERS, SOMETIMES REFERRED to as peptic ulcers, are ulcerations of the lining of the upper digestive tract. When they occur in the duodenum, which is the upper part of the small intestine that connects to the stomach, they are known as duodenal ulcers. When in the stomach wall itself, they are known as gastric ulcers. Ulcers are caused when the mucous lining of the stomach or duodenum is not sufficient to protect them against the corrosive action of stomach acid and the digestive enzyme called pepsin.

Ulcers are very common, and one in ten men and one in twenty women may expect to have one in their lifetime. Fortunately we've learned a great deal about them in the recent past and there's very good news about their cause and cure.

The common symptom of peptic ulcers is burning and discomfort in the upper gastric area at the base of the sternum before meals, sometimes after meals, or at night. The pain can radiate to the back or the chest. This pain can sometimes be relieved by more food or an antacid. But many people don't have any symptoms at all until they have a bleeding or perforated ulcer. The most common traditional treatments for ulcers are antacids and histamine-2 (H-2) receptor blockers. These medications may help heal the ulcer but do not alter the conditions that caused it in the first place, so the medications have to be taken over long periods— sometimes for life. Since long-term use of H-2 receptor blockers has been associated with increased risk of stomach cancer, the "cure" may be worse than the disease.

At one time, ulcers were thought to be caused solely by stress and a related increase in stomach acid. New research suggests that the majority of both duodenal and gastric ulcers are also related to a bacterium called *Helicobacter pylori*, which can be wiped out by a two-week regimen of antibiotics. This is exciting news for people who have suffered from chronic ulcers without hope of a cure. Patients treated for this bacterial infection had a remarkable rate of recovery, and stayed free of ulcers without additional medication. Over 70 percent of ulcer patients are believed to be infected with the bacterium. In one study, 95 percent of the patients with gastric ulcers who were treated for H. pylori had no recurrence in the next two years while only 12 percent of the patients who had standard treatment had no recurrence. If you have had repeated bouts of peptic ulcers, ask your doctor to test your blood for antibodies to the *Helicobacter* bacterium to determine if you would benefit from the antibiotic treatment. If you do need treatment, you'll need to take acidophilus capsules for the course of your treatment. For more information on *Helicobacter* and details on treatment, see H. Pylori, page 164.

Ulcers are also aggravated by irritants that damage the stomach's protective lining, or by an increase in the production of stomach acid. The key culprits are:

- Spicy and acidic foods.

- Aspirin and other nonsteroidal antiinflammatory drugs, which are gastric irritants when taken regularly, as for arthritis.

- Smoking, which increases the production of bile salts, highly irritating to the stomach. The combination of smoking and aspirin has a particularly damaging effect on peptic ulcers.

- Alcohol, which stimulates acid secretion and aggravates existing ulcers.

- A diet high in sugar, which also stimulates acid secretion.

- Food allergies, which can irritate the stomach. If you have recurring ulcers with no other recognized cause you should investigate the possibility of a food allergy (see Food Allergy, page 146).

While too much sugar in the diet or a simple food allergy might not be the single cause of an ulcer, they are, in my experience, conditions that encourage the development of ulcers. If you do have an ulcer that won't clear up, investigate food allergies. If you have recurring ulcers, be sure that your sugar intake is cut down; this measure has helped many of my ulcer patients.

At one time ulcer patients were told to drink milk and eat a bland diet. We know now this was bad advice. If you have an ulcer, don't depend on milk for relief. While a glass of milk may temporarily soothe your ulcer, it will ultimately make it worse by causing a rebound in stomach acid. (Antacids, made with calcium carbonate [Tums, Alka-2] will make you feel better temporarily, but they might have a rebound effect on the production of stomach acid.) Diets that are high in fiber have been found to be much more effective in healing ulcers and preventing their occurrence than soft diets. Gradually increase your fiber intake.

Linoleic acid, found in unprocessed grains such as maize, also contributes to the healing and prevention of ulcers. It can be supplemented by taking evening primrose oil.

Another natural compound used in ulcer therapy is a derivative of licorice known as deglycyrrhizinated licorice (DGL), which stimulates the production of mucus that coats and protects the digestive tract. One study involving DGL focused on forty patients who had been referred for surgery because of acute and persistent pain, in spite of prolonged treatment with conventional drugs. Half the patients received 3 g. of DGL daily for eight weeks, the other half received 4.5 g. daily for sixteen weeks. Though the higher dosage was more effective, they all showed significant improvement, and none required surgery within the next year. I suggest you take DGL, which you can get in health food stores.

Supplements of vitamins A, E, and C are also helpful in the therapy and prevention of ulcers.

Raw cabbage juice has a remarkable track record in helping people with peptic ulcers. One quart daily of fresh cabbage juice, taken in divided doses, can be enormously effective. In one study, patients taking this amount had total healing of their ulcers in ten days.

Though stress is no longer considered the only cause of peptic ulcers, it's clear that stress, or the way we react to it, does play a role. Regular exercise is a good antidote for stress, as are breathing exercises and various relaxation techniques (see Stress Control, page 314).

NATURAL PRESCRIPTION FOR ULCERS

- If you have recurring ulcers, you should discuss the possibility of *Helicobacter pylori* infection, known as *H. pylori,* with your doctor. Treatment with antibiotics can make a dramatic difference in your cure. For more information on this, see H. Pylori, page 164.

- Eliminate the use of aspirins and other nonsteroidal antiinflammatory drugs.

- Avoid smoking, alcohol, and antacids made with calcium carbonate.

- Eat a high-fiber diet unless your symptoms are acute, in which case you should avoid roughage and raw vegetables.

- Eat regular meals at regular times: Avoid large meals and remember that small, frequent meals are best.

- Eliminate the sugar in your diet.

- Do not rely on milk to soothe your ulcer.

- Adopt an exercise program.

- Practice relaxation techniques. See Stress Control, page 314.

IN ADDITION TO YOUR DAILY SUPPLEMENTS, PAGE xxiv, TAKE

- DGL: 1,000 to 1,500 mg. twenty minutes before meals. You should continue to take it for two to four months depending on the results you get.

- Evening primrose oil: 500 mg. three times daily.

- Vitamin A: 10,000 I.U. daily.

- Vitamin C: 500 mg. two times a day. Be sure to take the buffered form.

- Vitamin E: 400 I.U. daily.

- Raw cabbage juice: 1 quart daily in divided doses. Continue for two weeks. If no results, discontinue.

• • •

URINARY INCONTINENCE

PATIENTS WHO COME to see me with the problem of urinary incontinence are usually near the end of their rope. They've typically been to several other doctors, including a urologist, and have run through a few courses of antibiotics, but nothing seems to help: At the most inopportune times they suffer an involuntary loss of urine. For some people it's only when they laugh, cough, stand up suddenly, or jog. For others, it's any time at all. It's easy to see how this can be an embarrassing problem. In fact, some patients have seriously curtailed their activities because of incontinence. One of the most unfortunate aspects of the problem is that because people are frequently embarrassed by it they fail to seek any help.

Moreover, incontinence is often a reason given for putting a loved one in a nursing home. I think that people would be quite encouraged if they knew the enormous success that one can have in using simple natural treatments to help control or even eliminate incontinence.

Incontinence really refers to the inability to completely control the flow of urine. It's quite common: Up to twenty million Americans suffer from incontinence. Three quarters of these are women and most are elderly. Antibiotics, which are often used to clear up infections that might be causing the incontinence, can also contribute to the problem. (However, if you have burning or irritation with urination, you might also have a bladder infection, which will need to be treated by a doctor.)

If you take any medication routinely, ask your doctor if the drug could be causing incontinence.

Some of the medications that are used to control incontinence can cause side effects including dry mouth, eye problems, and buildup of urine. If you use any medications for incontinence, you must be under a doctor's careful supervision.

The most effective natural remedy is a simple exercise. The Kegel exercises were developed in the 1940s to aid women with incontinence during pregnancy. These exercises strengthen the muscles that surround the opening to the bladder. You can feel them by stopping the flow of urine when you're in the middle of voiding. The exercises simply involve tensing these muscles, counting to four slowly, and then releasing. You do this for at least two minutes three or more times a day.

If you practice these exercises diligently, you will begin to see real results in about three weeks. As I stress with my patients, you *must* do the exercises regularly; you can't expect to do them for a week or two, find relief, and then give them up. Just as a bodybuilder will lose muscle mass if he stops lifting weights, so you'll become incontinent again if you abandon your Kegel exercises.

Though the Kegel exercises are your most important tool in fighting incontinence, there are other factors in your environment that can play a role. For example, a number of substances can irritate the bladder including smoke, caffeine, perfumes in soaps and bubble baths, toilet paper, and feminine hygiene products. Cranberry juice is acidic and is known to be beneficial to the bladder, so add it to your diet.

You should also be reasonable about the amount of fluids you drink. One woman came to see me with incontinence that had confined her to her home for months. She learned the Kegel exercises and found some relief but still was trouble by occasional accidents. Upon further questioning I learned that she was on medication that required her to "force fluids" and she drank nearly twelve glasses of water on some days. In fact, half that amount of water would have been plenty and when she cut down, her incontinence finally came under control. If you suffer from incontinence, you really don't need to drink more than four glasses of liquid a day, unless some other medical reason indicates otherwise.

Finally, you should remember to empty your bladder regularly. A too-full bladder becomes stretched and can become liable to bladder infection. And of course a full bladder is more likely to leak. Try to remember to empty your bladder first thing in the morning, both before and after meals, and before going to bed.

NATURAL PRESCRIPTION FOR URINARY INCONTINENCE

- See if any medications you take could be causing incontinence: Check with your doctor.

- Kegel exercises: Do these every day, tightening and releasing your pelvic muscles for at least two minutes, three times a day or more.

- Avoid caffeine, alcohol, smoking, perfumes in soaps, bubble baths, and toilet papers, and feminine hygiene products.

- Drink cranberry juice.

- Unless there's a medical reason indicating otherwise, drink no more than four glasses of liquid daily.

- Empty your bladder regularly, at least eight times a day.

IN ADDITION: I suggest that all my patients with incontinence subscribe to a newsletter called "HIP: Help for Incontinent People," published by a nonprofit, self-help organization. You can get a free copy by sending a self-addressed, stamped envelope to HIP, Box 544, Union, SC 29379.

•   •   •

VAGINITIS

"VAGINITIS" IS A TERM that refers to an inflammation of the vagina. Most women will experience some disruption of the normal condition of the vagina at least once in their lives; some are plagued by constant and disruptive irritations. One of the problems in dealing with vaginitis is figuring out exactly what's causing it. Often, women are treated for a problem they don't have while the cause of their vaginitis goes undetected.

Many women are mystified because they get frequent vaginal infections. I've had patients who've told me that they are just "learning to live with it." I don't think that's ever really necessary. If you get frequent infections there's a reason. Here are the three main causes of reinfection:

1. You aren't treating the infection correctly in the first place, either because your doctor misdiagnosed the type of infection or because you've been treating it yourself without knowing exactly what type of infection you have.

2. Your infection has become a systemic infection that can't be cleared up with local treatment. This is common with candidiasis.

3. Your boyfriend or husband is infected and keeps reinfecting you. If this is the case, you must be sure that your partner is treated along with you.

Most cases of vaginitis, particularly infectious vaginitis, will need to be treated by a doctor. Because it's so important to identify the cause of the infection and because in most cases the cure requires a prescription medication, you should insist on a precise diagnosis from your doctor. On the other hand, if you've been diagnosed in the past as having a particular type of infection and you are certain that you are experiencing the same thing again, particularly if it's candidiasis, you can begin some treatments yourself. And if your case of vaginitis is not infectious—if it's caused by an irritant—you can probably deal with it yourself. I've outlined the basic types of vaginitis here so you'll be familiar with the possibilities.

The most common type of infectious vaginitis is caused by *Candida albicans,* the fungus that is normally present in the vagina but which grows uncontrolled when something causes an imbalance in its environment. Most women know that they have a *Candida* infection because of the typical itch and cheesy discharge that accompanies it. For a more detailed description of this problem, which is often more than a simple vaginal infection, see Candidiasis (page, 61).

Trichomoniasis or "trich" is the second-most prevalent type of vaginal infection. Its common symptom is a greenish white or yellowish discharge that has a foul odor. Unlike *Candida albicans,* which is normally present in the vagina, trich is a protozoan that is most commonly introduced through sexual contact. A doctor can identify trich infection easily under a microscope and provide a prescription to fight it. A sexual partner should be treated at the same time.

Herpes is a viral infection that's almost always transmitted through sexual contact. Symptoms commonly appear two to eight days after sexual contact with an infected partner. A woman will notice tiny itchy red bumps on her vulva that develop into painful blisters and ultimately burst. (A man will have similar symptoms on his genitals.) A woman who is concerned that she may have genital herpes should see her doctor, as there is now a prescription treatment that is helpful. Also see Herpes (page 182).

Chlamydia is becoming the most common sexually transmitted disease in the United States. Usually there are no symptoms until the disease is fairly well advanced. If you are under the age of twenty-five, if you have had multiple sexual partners, if your cervix bleeds when your doctor swabs it, there is a chance you may be infected. Chlamydia can cause tubal scarring, an important cause of infertility. Women who are pregnant and suspect that they have a vaginal infection should ask their doctor to test them for chlamydia, as it can cause problems for their babies.

Gonorrhea is a sexually transmitted vaginal infection that needs to be identified and treated by a doctor with antibiotics. While a man infected with gonorrhea will have an obvious discharge and painful urination, a woman may have no symptoms and thus has to rely on the honesty of her sexual partner or a lab test. Again, if a woman has any reason to suspect that she has gonorrhea, she should be in touch with her doctor immediately, as untreated cases cause infertility.

In addition to infectious vaginitis, there's also *irritant vaginitis,* which is caused by something that is irritating the vagina. The irritants can include chemicals and/or allergens such as those from laundry detergents, spermicides, feminine hygiene products, latex condoms, or soaps; foreign bodies including tampons or diaphragms left in too long; or traumatic irritants that include sexual activity or physical trauma to the vagina.

Finally, there's *hormonal vaginitis*. The most common hormonal vaginitis is atrophic vaginitis. This is usually a problem for postmenopausal women and women who have had their ovaries removed. Its symptoms include itching, burning, and a watery discharge. It's caused by a thinning of vaginal secretions due to lowered hormonal activity. A woman who suspects this problem should see her doctor.

Another type of hormonal vaginitis is increased vaginal discharge—resulting from monthly changes in hormonal levels. Most women know their bodies well enough to recognize that they will experience different levels of vaginal discharge at different times of the month, but some find that the heavier discharge at the time of ovulation is a disturbance and they ask their doctors about it. Usually it is nothing more than a simple hormonal variation, and there is nothing that can or should be done.

As mentioned above, most vaginal infections will require the help of a gynecologist to treat and cure the condition. As candida and trichomonas can recur in some women, I'm including here a list of precautions that can help maintain a healthy bacterial level in the vagina and prevent recurrence.

NATURAL PRESCRIPTION FOR VAGINITIS

SEE YOUR GYNECOLOGIST TO TREAT AND CURE THE CONDITION. TO PREVENT RECURRENCE FOLLOW THESE SUGGESTIONS:

- Do not wear tight pants or pantyhose. Excessive moisture invites infection. Cotton panties allow air to circulate and are preferable to nylon ones.

- Add the *Lactobacillus acidophilus* culture to your diet by eating a daily portion of yogurt that contains live cultures (it must say so on the label) or by taking acidophilus capsules, available in health food stores. I usually recommend three capsules daily.

- Betadine, an antibacterial agent available at pharmacies, is helpful in fighting vaginal infections including candida and trich. It kills most organisms within thirty seconds. Do not overuse this or any other douche; once a day for one week should be enough.

- Be sure to have your sexual partner treated along with you, especially if you have recurrent infections.

- If possible, discontinue sexual activity for the duration of your infection to reduce irritation to infected tissues and to avoid reinfection.

IN ADDITION TO YOUR DAILY SUPPLEMENTS, PAGE xxiv, TAKE

- Vitamin C: 1,000 mg. daily.

- Vitamin E: 400 I.U. daily.

- Beta-carotene: 10,000 I.U. daily.

• • •

VARICOSE VEINS

I WISH I COULD tell you of a supplement that would help make varicose veins disappear. But, while there are vitamins that can help women with varicosities, once you've developed them there's really no way short of surgery to make them go away. And, despite what you may think (or hope!), even surgery will not completely eradicate them, as they have a tendency to recur. On the other hand, there are natural treatments that can help prevent them as well as inhibit their further development.

Varicose veins are quite common. Nearly one quarter of American women and one tenth of American men have them. They're caused when the veins carrying blood from the legs back to the heart become engorged and dilated. The veins become swollen, bluish, and lumpy in appearance. Fluid leaks into surrounding tissue, and the legs can become swollen and discolored, and feel tired and achy. In addition, in chronic cases, ulcers can form as the skin breaks down (see Stasis Ulcer, page 313). The worst complication from varicose veins is phlebitis, where bloodclots form on the walls of the vein. If they become dislodged and travel to the lungs, they can cause serious—and, very rarely, fatal—damage.

The first warning of varicose veins is a tingling on the surface of the leg, which is caused by the reduced blood flow as the vein weakens. You might also notice small blue veins near the surface of the skin. Some people experience feelings of tightness, congestion, or tenderness in the veins, tired leg muscles, swollen ankles, or muscular leg cramps. Most of my patients are not surprised when the veins develop because their mother or aunt or grandmother had them. Varicose veins are largely an inherited condition: all the more reason, if you have a history of varicose veins in your family, to follow the guidelines that can help prevent and retard their development.

My approach to treating varicose veins relies primarily on treating the factors that cause them to develop. The three crucial treatments include weight control, a high-fiber diet, and regular exercise.

The connection between overweight and varicose veins is fairly obvious: The more weight that is supported by the circulatory system, the more that system is stressed. Excess body weight puts additional pressure on the veins in the leg. If you are overweight, a shift in diet could help relieve your varicose veins. A high-fiber diet and exercise will also help keep weight under control.

Why is a high-fiber diet important? Because a diet low in fiber and high in refined foods encourages the development of chronic constipation, a major contributing factor to varicose veins. The stress of straining to pass a bowel movement puts enormous pressure on the veins by obstructing the flow of blood up the legs. Eventually this stress takes its toll, causing varicose veins as well as hemorrhoids. It's interesting to note that societies where a high-fiber diet is the norm rarely suffer from varicose veins. A high-fiber diet is the single most important factor in relieving constipation (see Constipation, page 92, for further information).

Lack of exercise also encourages the development of varicose veins. I tell my patients that exercise refers to both "major" and "minor" exercise. Major exercise is a regular program of aerobic activity, such as walking, running, or biking, which uses the calf muscles. The contraction of these powerful muscles helps to push blood upward in its journey to the heart and lungs.

Minor exercise refers to regular, nonaerobic movements. People who sit or stand for long periods are more vulnerable to varicose veins than others. They should make an effort to stretch their leg muscles frequently. This may mean simply walking around your desk every half hour or so—any movement that contracts your leg muscles and prevents blood from pooling. Don't forget that airplane flights can have the same effect as sitting at a desk. I suggest that patients with vein troubles try to get an aisle seat so that they can stretch their legs regularly while on a flight.

Elevating your legs whenever possible can help relieve varicose veins because when your feet are higher than your hips, you're taking the pressure off your circulatory system. If you have varicose veins, you should make a conscious effort to raise your legs a few times a day, even if it's only for brief periods.

One supplement that I regularly use to help with varicose veins is vitamin E. I've also been using bioflavonoids, which have been shown to reduce the permeability of capillaries, therefore making it more difficult for fluids to escape. Studies on patients with varicose veins have shown that bioflavonoids can significantly improve the feelings of fatigue and heaviness in the legs. My patients seem to find relief with this supplement. Recent research has shown that a bioflavonoid called quercetin-C, which is derived from blue-green algae, can prevent and relieve varicose veins. I'm just beginning to use it with my patients and it seems promising. If you take quercetin-C, available at health food stores, there's no need to take the bioflavonoids.

Some people find that elastic stockings made for varicose veins give them considerable relief. You can buy support hose in a pharmacy, but the most effective ones are available at medical supply houses. You need to be fitted for a pair. I suggest that the best way to put them on is to lie on your back on the floor with your legs resting perpendicularly against a wall. This position allows the blood to flow toward the heart. Slip the stockings on after you've rested in this position for a few minutes. By the way, if you rest in this position a few times a day, you'll be relieving the pressure and swelling in your legs.

NATURAL PRESCRIPTION FOR VARICOSE VEINS

- Keep weight at appropriate level, avoiding obesity.

- Adopt a high-fiber diet including plenty of fresh fruits, vegetables, and whole grains. Use bulking agents as needed (see Constipation, page 92).

- Exercise: regular "major" exercise to contract the leg muscles, especially running, walking, cycling. Regular "minor" exercise as a relief from sitting or standing for long periods of time such as stretching the legs or briefly walking.

- Elevate your legs—ideally with your ankles higher than your hips—whenever possible.

- Wear support stockings, preferably fitted and from a medical supply house. Lie on your back with hips near a wall and legs perpendicular to the floor to encourage blood flow. Rest In this position for a few minutes before putting on the stockings.

IN ADDITION TO YOUR DAILY SUPPLEMENTS, PAGE xxiv, TAKE

- **Vitamin E: 400 I.U. daily.**

- **Bioflavonoids: 1,000 mg. daily or, alternatively, quercetin-C: 1,000 mg. daily**

IN ADDITION: If varicose veins become a serious problem, either for cosmetic reasons or because of complications such as phlebitis, surgery may be indicated.

• • •

VISION PROBLEMS

THE THREE COMMON vision problems I'm asked about are cataracts, glaucoma, and macular degeneration. These are covered individually on pages 70, 158, 236 respectively. There are also three other conditions—presbyopia, night blindness, and spots or floaters—that are so common that sooner or later most of us have to deal with one or more.

PRESBYOPIA

Presbyopia is the change in the flexibility of the eye that comes with age. When we're young, the lens can readily focus on things that are far away and then quickly assume a more rounded shape to focus on things up close. As we age, the muscles that pull the lens still work fine but the lens itself, like much of the rest of our bodies, is less flexible. To compensate for this, we wind up holding reading materials or close work farther and farther away in order to see clearly. When your arm is no longer long enough to enable you to read, it's time to get some reading glasses.

Are glasses inevitable? There are people who never need to get reading glasses, but they're in the minority. Most people begin to notice the effects of presbyopia in their forties. That's why ophthalmologists recommend that you get a complete eye exam in your early forties if you haven't yet had one.

Most people believe that the degeneration of their eyes is a genetic inheritance. To some degree this is true, but there is also an important nutritional component. Poor nutrition will accelerate the deterioration of your eyes. Once you've developed presbyopia, you can't reverse it with improved nutrition, but it's possible that you can slow down its progress.

The vitamins and minerals that are most closely associated with proper functioning of the eye are vitamins A and zinc. In some parts of the world, vitamin A deficiency is the leading cause of blindness, particularly in children. A deficiency of vitamin A can increase night blindness (see below), a common problem as we age, as well as accelerate the deterioration of the lens.

Vitamin E is also required for proper eye functioning. It works with vitamin A, and a deficiency seems to accelerate the damage if vitamin A is lacking.

Studies have also shown that the B complex vitamins are important for their effect on the health of the optic nerve.

A note on buying reading glasses: The American Academy of Ophthalmology has recently reported that buying the glasses you see in drugstores is acceptable. They are cheap ($10 to $15 versus $100 to $200 for prescription glasses), safe, and effective. There's a chart mounted on the display case that will help you select the right power. Just be sure that you've had a professional eye examination before you buy them to rule out any problem that over-the-counter reading glasses can't correct. For example, if the vision in one eye differs from that of the other, which is common, these glasses won't help you.

NATURAL PRESCRIPTION FOR PRESBYOPIA

TO SLOW, THE PROGRESSION OF PRESBYOPIA, TAKE THE FOLLOWING IN ADDITION TO YOUR DAILY BASIC VITAMIN/MINERAL SUPPLEMENTS (PAGE xxiv):

- **Vitamin A: 10,000 I.U. daily.**
- **Zinc: 50 mg. daily.**
- **Vitamin E: 400 I.U. daily.**

IN ADDITION: In the early 1900s, ophthalmologist William Bates developed a method for improving vision that eschewed the use of glasses. In his book, *Better Eyesight Without Glasses,* he described his techniques, and for a while his methods were extremely popular. They have since fallen into disuse, primarily because there are so few trained technicians to work with people on the techniques. I mention them here, as they have been shown to help many people improve their vision to the point where glasses are unnecessary. Bates believed that nearsightedness, farsightedness, and astigmatism are the result of tension unconsciously placed on the muscles controlling the eye. To be effective, sight, like the other senses, must be used passively: Straining to see distorts the lens and thus creates vision problems. To correct this unconscious strain, you must learn to totally relax your eyes and allow yourself to see without strain. Bates created exercises that included palming the eyes to totally exclude light, then exposing the eyes to bright, comfortable light—body movements that promote relaxation and memory and imagination. For more information on this you can write to Eyesight Training, 123 Lake Street South, Suite #106, Kirkland, WA 98033.

NIGHT BLINDNESS

Night blindness is an inability to see in dim light even though your vision is normal in bright light or daylight. Most commonly, night blindness is a specific symptom of a vitamin A deficiency, which can usually be corrected by supplementation.

If you've experienced night blindness and you're over forty, or even in your late thirties, you should have your eyes examined to be sure that you aren't in the beginning stages of glaucoma. For more information, see Glaucoma, page 158.

NATURAL PRESCRIPTION FOR NIGHT BLINDNESS

- Have your eyes checked by an ophthalmologist to be sure that you aren't developing glaucoma.

IN ADDITION TO YOUR DAILY SUPPLEMENTS, PAGE xxiv, TAKE

- Vitamin A: 10,000 I.U. daily. In addition, eat foods rich in vitamin A, including carrots, sweet potatoes, tomatoes, egg yolk, chicken, fish, and dark vegetables like broccoli.

FLOATERS AND FLASHERS

Floaters and flashers are tiny dark specks or spots that appear before your eyes. Like presbyopia, they usually occur when you're at least forty. Also like presbyopia, they signify the aging of the eye: The spots are caused when the fluid that fills the inside of the eyeball begins to thin out. As the fluid thins, it can trap bits of protein between the thinner and thicker fluid, causing the shadows on the retina that create spots before your eyes.

Spots, floaters, and flashers are not dangerous and they shouldn't concern you unless you suddenly see many of them or they suddenly increase in size. If they persist, you are being warned of a potentially serious problem such as retinal detachment and you should consult with an eye doctor *immediately*.

•   •   •

WARTS

THERE ARE THREE kinds of warts, all requiring different treatment. They include common warts, plantar warts, and genital warts.

COMMON WARTS

The common wart, ranging from a tiny pinhead-sized speck to the size of a dime, can be found on the hands, feet, forearms, and face. A wart is rough, irregular tissue that can be flat or raised, dry or moist, and usually has a rough, pitted surface. If you are uncertain about a wart, be sure to consult a doctor, as in some cases rough growths on the skin can be other types of lesions, including cancerous growths. Warts are caused by a virus and they are highly contagious. If you or someone in your household has warts, it is advisable to use separate hand towels.

The truth about common warts is that if you leave them alone, eventually they are likely to go away. But most people dislike the way they look, are embarrassed by them, and want to remove them. There are folk remedies for ridding yourself of warts that are highly effective. Here are the most popular and successful treatments:

NATURAL PRESCRIPTION FOR COMMON WARTS

- Apply vitamin E directly to the wart, cover it with a bandage, repeat twice daily, and eventually the wart will disappear. It can take from a week to several months to work.

- Put a crushed garlic clove directly on the wart and cover it with a bandage. When blisters have formed after about twenty-four hours, remove the bandage. The wart should fall off within a week.

- Use over-the-counter medications; these contain salicylic acid and are safe and effective.

PLANTAR WARTS

Plantar warts are found on the soles of the feet and, like common warts, are caused by a virus. They're also contagious—and easy to get from walking barefoot at a common shower or health club dressing room. If you have them, it's best not to walk around the house barefoot. Plantar warts can sometimes be painful if their location causes constant pressure from walking and running.

The most effective step to take to rid yourself of plantar warts is over-the-counter medications containing salicylic acid. These preparations are most effective if used when the warts first appear. It's important to soak the foot in warm water to increase the penetration of the medicine, or use it after a bath or shower. I advise patients to put some petroleum jelly on the skin surrounding the wart so the medicine will not affect the surrounding tissue: Sometimes people apply the medicine carelessly and develop damaged tissue that's as painful as the wart itself.

NATURAL PRESCRIPTION FOR PLANTAR WARTS

- Apply the medication containing salicylic acid in the amounts specified on the package and for the recommended duration.

IN ADDITION: If you do not have any luck removing common warts or plantar warts with other methods, you can have them surgically removed by a dermatologist.

GENITAL WARTS

Genital warts, also caused by a virus, are transmitted by sexual contact. It's important if you have genital warts to avoid having sex until the wart is treated. Genital warts appear on the vagina, the tip of the penis, and around the anus. Sometimes they can have a cauliflower shape. If you think you have genital warts, you must see a doctor because they cannot be treated at home. Whereas other warts can be ignored unless they're irritating, genital warts should be treated even if they don't cause any pain or discomfort.

• • •

WOUND HEALING

A WOUND CAN BE anything from a cut finger from slicing potatoes to a deep puncture from a nail to an incision required by a surgical procedure. A minor cut from a clean, sharp object can be treated at home, but a more severe wound should be treated by a doctor or in a hospital emergency room. Controlling blood loss takes precedence over most other emergency procedures. If you are bleeding profusely while waiting for medical help, you should lie down and, if possible, elevate the injured part. Using a clean pad or even your fingers, press hard on the wound, or ask someone else to do this. You should seek medical help when:

- The bleeding can't be stopped or is spurting, which indicates that you may have severed an artery.

- You're unable to clean the wound, particularly if there's gravel or dirt embedded in it.

- The cut or wound is large and gaping so that stitches are needed.

- The wound is on the face or a part of the body where scarring would be particularly undesirable.

If the cut is simple and clean you can treat it at home, taking the steps that will speed healing and minimize scarring.

If a cut is clean, you need to first stop the bleeding. You can do this by simple pressure: Use a clean cloth or gauze pad and press the cut for three to five minutes or until the bleeding stops. Then give the cut a final cleaning by washing it with cool water, using a little soap if necessary.

The next step is to use some kind of ointment to fight infection and speed healing. Many people believe that it's best to leave a cut uncovered, but in fact any cut or wound will heal more rapidly and with less scarring if it is moist since cells regenerate best in a moist environment. A scab actually slows down the healing process, and ointments under a bandage will help prevent a scab from forming. Polysporin and Neosporin are two good antibacterial ointments. You can also use some vitamin E by puncturing a capsule and letting the oil drip onto the cut. Many people claim that vitamin E helps prevent scarring though I don't know of any research that proves this; you can use almost any substance that will keep the area moist and apply a bandage or Band-Aid on top. If the cut is on a finger or in some awkward place where it's difficult to keep a bandage in place and where you don't really care about the possibility of a tiny scar, I wouldn't worry about trying to keep it moist under a bandage.

If the cut gapes or if it's in a place where you're particularly worried about scarring, you can use a butterfly bandage, available at pharmacies, that presses the edges of the cut together. You can fashion your own butterfly bandage by cutting a regular bandage into a butterfly form, placing a sterile pad on the cut itself, and applying the bandage so that the edges of the wound are pressed together.

Often the most difficult aspect of dealing with a minor cut is removing the bandage. One way to make this process easier is to dab the bandage with oil until it's soaked, and give it a few minutes to penetrate. Then when you get up the courage to rip off the bandage, the adhesive will have lost most of its power.

A cut can make you vulnerable to a tetanus infection. You should routinely have a tetanus booster every four years to protect you from tetanus, which can be life-threatening. The tetanus germ is commonly found in the soil, particularly where there are farm animals, and in the dust of city streets. Any cut, particularly a deep one, can allow the tetanus germ to gain a foothold if you are not immunized. If you receive a wound and have not been immunized in the last four years, you should get a shot within forty-eight hours.

If your wound is more than a minor cut, you should know that your nutritional status can have a dramatic effect on your ability to heal. Many studies have shown that vitamin C can be of critical help in healing wounds. In one study, supplements helped wounds heal up to 50 percent faster. In another study, patients with bedsores healed 50 percent faster when supplemented with vitamin C, compared to patients given a placebo. It seems that any kind of injury depletes the body's supply of vitamin C, which is essential to the healing process as it regulates the formation of collagen, the substance necessary to form new connective tissue. Researchers found that the blood levels of vitamin C among one group of surgical patients were down 42 percent three days following surgery.

Vitamin A is also critical for wound healing. It helps strengthen scar tissue and thus promotes healing. Zinc works in conjunction with vitamin A to promote healing. Without zinc, the cells necessary to form new tissue cannot be created. Vitamin E has also been recognized as helpful in speeding the healing process.

Two other nutrients are worth trying. They are vitamin B_3 (or nicotinamide) and glutamine. Vitamin B_3 has been shown to be strongly connected to increased healing rates in wounds, as has the amino acid glutamine. Though the precise reason why glutamine aids healing is unknown, we do know that levels of glutamine are depleted by injury or disease.

NATURAL PRESCRIPTION FOR WOUND HEALING

- For minor cuts, follow the above instructions for cleaning and treatment.

- For more severe wounds, see your doctor or go to your local emergency room for treatment.

TO SPEED HEALING, TAKE THE FOLLOWING IN ADDITION TO YOUR DAILY BASIC VITAMIN/MINERAL SUPPLEMENTS (PAGE xxiv) UNTIL THE WOUND HAS HEALED:

- Vitamin C: 2,000 mg. or 2 g. daily in divided doses at meals and bedtime.

- Vitamin A: 10,000 I.U. daily.

- Zinc: 22.5 to 50 mg. daily.

- Vitamin E: 400 I.U. daily.

- Vitamin B_3: 100 mg. daily.

- Amino acid glutamine: 500 mg. daily.

IN ADDITION: If you have a recent scar, don't forget that it will react to sunlight more quickly than normal skin. I advise patients to apply a hypoallergenic sunscreen liberally to any recent scar if they're going to be in the sun.

• • •

WRINKLE PREVENTION

EVERYONE WANTS TO KNOW how to prevent wrinkles. Despite the popularity of cosmetic surgery, there are still plenty of people who want to live with their own faces forever and want to keep them in as good shape as possible. In fact, with the advent of highly effective sunscreens and more knowledge about maintaining supple skin, we are able to prevent wrinkles more effectively than previous generations were.

Most people aren't aware that one of the primary functions of the skin is to excrete toxins and that some of these toxins cause blemishes, rashes, dryness, and dullness. If you want to help prevent toxins from reaching your skin, the best approach is to drink eight 8-ounce glasses of water daily. This will also help prevent dryness.

You probably already know that tanning is an enemy of the skin. I don't object to moderate *protected* sunning; indeed, a certain amount of sunshine helps vitamin D production and can alleviate depression. But the baking and basting of the old days is just asking for trouble, and not only in terms or wrinkling: The dramatic increase in skin cancer statistics is truly alarming. So, get some sun but never without a sunscreen. When you're in full sun at the beach or playing tennis, I recommend a sunscreen with a sun protection factor (SPF) of 15 or higher. Put it on about half an hour before you get into the sun if possible to give it a chance to work. Reapply it regularly, especially after swimming or sweating heavily.

While sunscreens on the beach are essential, it's a mistake to save them for special occasions; daily use is advisable, especially if you spend any amount of time outdoors. Many of my patients tell me that a sunscreen is the first thing they put on their face in the morning after showering. One woman with beautiful skin told me that she has been using a sunscreen on her face and hands every morning for nearly ten years. I think this is a wise course to take. Fortunately, many makeups are now being formulated with sunscreens included. If you're relying on them, just be sure their SPF is 15 or above.

If you find that after using a sunscreen you break out in a rash or suffer a sunburn, you might be allergic to a common sunscreen ingredient —PABA. Try another formulation with different active ingredients, and before using it in the sun test it on your wrist or arm for a few days to see if you have any reaction.

Smoking is a another major cause of skin wrinkling. I suppose not many people will stop smoking just for vanity's sake; there are so many more compelling reasons to stop. But smoking definitely ages your skin prematurely. In fact, if you smoke a pack and a half a day you'll wrinkle about ten years sooner than a nonsmoker. Smoking affects the skin both because of the physical act of smoking as well as the effect of nicotine in your system. When you smoke you're constantly pursing your lips to inhale and exhale. This action encourages vertical lines to form around your lips. In addition, constantly bathing the skin in smoke dries the face and encourages wrinkles to form. Vitamin C, a nutrient that helps the skin remain supple, and other nutrients are depleted by smoking. In addition, nicotine constricts blood vessels and thus interferes with the flow of nutrients to the cells.

Moisturizing cream will help your skin remain wrinkle-free as long as possible. You'll notice that people with oily skin tend to wrinkle less than people with dry skin; that's because the natural oil keeps their skin lubricated. If you don't have oily skin, you'll want to moisturize it. For more information, see Dry Skin (page 123).

There are two supplements that contribute to the health of the skin and are protective against wrinkling—vitamin C and vitamin A. I suggest you take both supplements daily.

NATURAL PRESCRIPTION FOR WRINKLE PREVENTION

- Drink six to eight 8-ounce glasses of water each day.

- *Always* use a sunscreen with an SPF of 15 or higher, not just when you're at the beach. Apply it each day before you leave the house and reapply it at midday.

- Stop smoking.

- Moisturize your skin (see Dry Skin, page 123).

IN ADDITION TO YOUR DAILY SUPPLEMENTS, PAGE xxiv, TAKE

- Vitamin C: 1,000 mg. daily.

- Vitamin A: 10,000 I.U. daily.

INDEX